D1601498

Children
and
Youth

Issues in Children's and Families' Lives

AN ANNUAL BOOK SERIES

Senior Series Editor

Thomas P. Gullotta, *Child and Family Agency of Southeastern Connecticut*

Editors

Gerald R. Adams, *University of Guelph, Ontario, Canada*

Robert L. Hampton, *University of Maryland, College Park*

Bruce A. Ryan, *University of Guelph, Ontario, Canada*

Roger P. Weissberg, *University of Illinois at Chicago, Illinois*

Drawing upon the resources of Child and Family Agency of Southeastern Connecticut, one of this nation's leading family service agencies, **Issues in Children's and Families' Lives** is designed to focus attention on the pressing social problems facing children and their families today. Each volume in this series will analyze, integrate, and critique the clinical and research literature on children and their families as it relates to a particular theme. Believing that integrated multidisciplinary approaches offer greater opportunities for program success, volume contributors will reflect the research and clinical knowledge base of the many different disciplines that are committed to enhancing the physical, social, and emotional health of children and their families. Intended for graduate and professional audiences, chapters will be written by scholars and practitioners who will encourage readers to apply their practice skills and intellect to reducing the suffering of children and their families in the society in which those families live and work.

University Advisory Committee for The University of Illinois at Chicago Series on Children and Youth

Children and Youth

Interdisciplinary Perspectives

Editors
Herbert J. Walberg
Olga Reyes
Roger P. Weissberg

The University of Illinois at Chicago
Series on Children and Youth

 Vol. 7 *Issues in Children's and Families' Lives*

SAGE Publications
International Educational and Professional Publisher
Thousand Oaks   London   New Delhi

For information:

 SAGE Publications, Inc.
2455 Teller Road
Thousand Oaks, California 91320
E-mail: order@sagepub.com

SAGE Publications Ltd.
6 Bonhill Street
London EC2A 4PU
United Kingdom

SAGE Publications India Pvt. Ltd.
M-32 Market
Greater Kailash I
New Delhi 110 048 India

Printed in the United States of America

Library of Congress Cataloging-in-Publication Data

Main entry under title:

Children and youth: Interdisciplinary perspectives/editors, Herbert
J. Walberg, Olga Reyes, Roger P. Weissberg.
    p. cm.—(Issues in children's families' lives; v. 7)
(University of Illinois at Chicago series on children and youth; v. 1)
    Includes bibliographical references (p. 1) and index.
    ISBN 0-7619-0906-0 (cloth: acid-free paper).—ISBN
0-7619-0907-9 (pbk.: acid-free paper)
    1. City children—United States. 2. Urban youth—United States.
3. Inner cities—United States. 4. Community and school—United
States. I. Walberg, Herbert, J. 1937-   . II. Reyes, Olga.
III. Weissberg, Roger P., 1951- . IV. Series. V. Series:
University of Illinois at Chicago series on children and youth; v. 1.
HT203.C443 1997   96-51276
305.23—dc21

Printed on acid-free paper
97 98 99 00 01 02 03 10 9 8 7 6 5 4 3 2 1

Acquiring Editor:	Marquita Flemming
Editorial Assistant:	Frances Borghi
Production Editor:	Astrid Virding
Production Assistant:	Karen Wiley
Typesetter/Designer:	Danielle Dillahunt
Cover Designer:	Lesa Valdez
Print Buyer:	Anna Chin

Contents

PART V: CONCLUSIONS

Foreword

Several years ago, Olga Reyes, Herb Walberg, and Roger Weissberg of the University of Illinois at Chicago (UIC) proposed a combined annual book and conference series on children and youth, particularly those in Chicago and other urban areas. Originating in a multidisciplinary seminar conducted in the College of Education's Center for Urban Educational Research and Development, the series was in keeping with a new university focus on "great cities" that concentrated university resources and attention on problems and opportunities in Chicago and other cities.

James Stukel, president of the University of Illinois, and I responded favorably to the series idea because we thought it would bring together separate departments and colleges of the university to formulate a more comprehensive understanding, draw on scholars outside the Chicago area, and help concentrate the university's mission of teaching, service, and research on children and youth because their prospects will determine the future of cities and the nation. We saw the series as a way to make an institutional commitment to provide models of scholarship, research, and teaching that might prove useful in our sister institutions in large cities and elsewhere.

Fortunately, others have agreed with our mission: The state of Illinois, the federal government, foundations, and private individuals have provided funds to carry out the Great Cities initiative, and the projects have been well received by Chicagoans. The first volume of this book series offers interdisciplinary perspectives on the "problems and promise" of urban youth; this offering is entirely in keeping with the university's new focus. We look forward to future volumes along the same lines.

—David C. Broski, Chancellor
University of Illinois at Chicago

Series Introduction

This **Series on Children and Youth** (a series within the **Series on Issues in Children's and Families' Lives**) originated in meetings with groups of faculty from several UIC colleges and departments that have one core common interest: the welfare of urban children and youth. From the outset, we recognized that urban children and youth are challenged on several fronts. By the standards of previous eras and other countries, it can be argued that the care and development of large numbers of young people are in a state of crisis. Although many urban children and youth have strengths and resilience and although cities may provide untold opportunities, many young people are growing up in adverse conditions and face numerous obstacles to achieving their potential.

We recognized that the role of universities in helping to solve the urban crisis is to assemble facts, identify trends, and provide information about policies and programs that work. Although universities cannot run government and private agencies, they can design and evaluate experimental and demonstration programs. Although universities cannot solve such pervasive problems as health care or transportation in cities, they can collaborate with others in the planning and evaluation of components of delivery systems. And although universities are not designed to determine policies, they can use their research and evaluation expertise to inform policymakers and those engaged in professional practice.

Like other agencies, however, universities are susceptible to the increasing specialization of lines of inquiry and understanding; this specialization results in the balkanization of knowledge. Indeed, making notable contributions to scientific disciplines often requires knowing more and more about less and less. Such specialization may lead to more fundamental understandings of specific topics but may limit one's grasp of the full scope of problems.

An examination of the history of urban areas reveals that current problems have evolved through time. U.S. cities are composed of immigrants and migrants and their descendants. Demographers, anthropologists, and specialists in ethnic studies have insights to share regarding the cultures and characteristics of such urban people. Similarly, socioeconomic status, wealth, income, and economic development strongly influence the quality of life and the capacity of cities to respond to challenges; economic and sociological perspectives may have much to offer.

Within universities, it is the job of professional schools and disciplines to draw on basic research in the arts and sciences to design policies, practices, and programs. Universities aim not merely to pursue "the truth" but also to do "the good" and to prepare their graduates both to know and to do. Thus, professional schools of education, medicine, nursing, and social work are intermediaries between the sciences and practice. They have important roles to play, and it appears that universities might better help themselves and the groups they serve by encouraging a wider, interdisciplinary view of the problems and potential solutions. We proposed a combined book-conference series called "Children and Youth." In keeping with UIC's Great Cities theme and urban mission, the book-conference series would primarily concern urban children and youth. The series would involve leading scholars from many departments and research units at UIC and other universities who are concerned with the development of urban youngsters. The ensuing discussion, debate, and recommendations would contribute to our overarching goal of a better understanding of the opportunities, problems, and potential uniqueness to growing up in the "great cities."

Although the series would coordinate relevant academic and professional units of UIC in focusing attention on children and youth in cities, particularly inner cities where some problems are most acute, the contributing authors would also identify parallels among urban, suburban, and rural youth, particularly those in poverty or other adverse circumstances. Any given volume in the series might exemplify "big city" problems and programs but predominantly enlist the most distinguished scholars in the nation on one or more of the most critical problems facing children and youth.

Accordingly, we have established two multidisciplinary advisory groups; one with leading UIC scholars, the other comprised of nationally renowned scholars (see the lists of our advisory board members). These advisory groups include representatives from the following disciplines: African American studies, anthropology, business, criminal justice, disability and human development, economics, education, family pediatrics, kinesiology, nursing, occupational therapy, physical therapy, political science, psychiatry, psychology, public health, social work, and sociology. These advisory groups have been enormously helpful in our planning for this volume and the next few volumes. Their constructive suggestions have broadened the perspectives and vision represented here. In addition, we have benefited from their recommendations for contributors. Finally, our understandings of children, youth, families, and communities have been enhanced through meetings with the UIC advisory group, which fosters dialogue and debate among scholars with varied theoretical frameworks and bases of knowledge. The intellectual excitement and stimulation that we have experienced from these interactions influenced the focus of our inaugural volume, described in Chapter 1.

—Herbert J. Walberg
Olga Reyes
Roger P. Weissberg
University of Illinois at Chicago

Acknowledgments

We appreciate the many people who helped make both this inaugural volume and the UIC **Series on Children and Youth** a reality. These individuals have a commitment to understanding and improving the lives of children and youth in cities through scholarship, dialogue, and action.

First, we thank Lascelles Anderson (director of the Center for Urban Educational Research and Development), who helped establish a UIC faculty working group that fostered interdisciplinary dialogue on urban children, families, and community settings from which the present series emerged.

We thank James Stukel (president of the University of Illinois) and David Broski (chancellor of the University of Illinois at Chicago), who provided initial funding for this series. Through their leadership and such initiatives as the Great Cities project, they help make the university an exciting, dynamic, and supportive context for scholars engaged in research with children, families, schools, and communities.

We thank the distinguished members of our University of Illinois at Chicago Advisory Board and our National Advisory Board, who have contributed to the development of the series. They commented on the proposed structure and content of the volume, suggested contributing authors, and coauthored several chapters in this volume.

Thanks go to Thomas P. Gullotta (chief executive officer of the Child and Family Agency of Southeastern Connecticut and senior series editor of "Issues in Children's and Families' Lives"). Among other virtues, Tom is a colleague whose problem solving and encouragement helped forge our working relationship with Sage Publications. We also appreciate the professionalism of C. Deborah Laughton and Eileen Carr from Sage, who simplified the tasks of quickly moving from word-processed manuscripts to published form.

Finally, we thank Carol Bartels Kuster, who collaborated with us on tasks in bringing closure to this first volume. She completed these with efficiency, organizational skill, and a sense of humor—making it possible to meet publication deadlines.

PART I

Introduction and Overview

• CHAPTER 1 •

Introduction and Overview

HERBERT J. WALBERG

OLGA REYES

ROGER P. WEISSBERG

In this chapter, we explain the special purpose and organization of this inaugural volume on interdisciplinary perspectives and identify highlights of each chapter. In the final chapter, we make explicit the transcending themes, particularly those that may have implications for changes in legislation, administrative policies, and professional practices.

Purpose and Organization of the Book

This first volume exemplifies the overall interdisciplinary, multiprofessional view of the problems and potential of urban children and youth. The contributors, who represent a variety of fields, were encouraged to distinguish state-of-the-art programs and policies from standard practice. Identifying current problems as well as better solutions was the primary goal. The gaps between problems and solutions were then to serve as indicators of suggested reforms in policies and practices. In the subsequent chapters, this task was not undertaken in any uniform or mechanical way, but we believe that all the contributors attempted to work such ideas into their writing. The state of the art is of far greater interest than the state of practice and therefore received much more attention.

The advisory committee members and we recognized that if the book is to be read and discussed by the many concerned scholars, policymakers, practitioners, and citizens for whom it is intended, it would have to be less technical than the usual scholarly work. Each chapter, therefore, was to compress the best of a field into a relatively short and appealingly written account. The chapters were to focus more on findings than on methods for arriving at findings; and research-based solutions were to be emphasized more than familiar problems. Because the circumstances of many urban families are favorable, we hoped also that the contributors would describe some positive examples, workable programs, and reasons for hope. Toward these ends, this book is divided into three major parts: Families, Schools, and Health. In the next few sections of this chapter, we identify highlights of chapters in each part. In our concluding chapter, we set forth several chief cross-cutting themes of the chapters.

Families

The family has long been the focus of efforts to understand the difficulties and social ills that plague urban children. An influential context for development, the family deserves such attention, particularly as its character has changed dramatically over the years. Specifically, more households can be found to have an atypical structure, most commonly headed by single parents, and usually mothers, although grandmother-, aunt-, and even sibling-headed households or combinations of these are not uncommon. The authors in this section consider the changing face of the urban American family and the implications of such change. Also, they aim to embed these thoughts in a context of urban family lives.

The point of departure in this section is Chapter 2, Sharon Landesman Ramey and Craig Ramey's "The Role of Universities in Strengthening Families and Enhancing Child Development," which considers the problems of urban children and their families and how academic settings might partner with such families in the generation of workable and cooperative solutions. Case illustrations of two large-scale community-university partnerships complement both a thoughtful history about universities' role as transmitters of knowledge and a conceptual framework for understanding change efforts. The case illustrations elucidate guiding principles for effective partnerships and highlight the importance of university organization, leadership, and incentives in realizing successful community-university partnerships. The Rameys' chapter offers an important and apt vision for our UIC Book Series, given that the series grew out of our university's commitment to collaborating with Chicago communities to improve the quality of urban life.

In Chapter 3, "Youth and Families in the Inner City: Influencing Positive Outcomes," Geraldine Brookins, Anne Petersen, and Lisa Brooks contextualize the urban family. Taking a historical perspective, these authors identify factors that have influenced inner-city life, including migration patterns, middle-class flight from cities and ghettos, and housing and welfare policies. Their perspective takes the reader from the 1920s through today, and the authors focus on how families and communities influence the development of youth in the inner city.

In Chapter 4, "Families and the Development of Urban Children," Patrick Tolan and Deborah Gorman-Smith consider the circumstances of urban families, including the stresses of urban life and the role of coping, resources, and skills in an urban family's successful management of stress. Tolan and Gorman-Smith argue for enhancing, rather than for "blaming," families. Appreciating the demands imposed by the urban context for families, they urge the reader to avoid the problem focus that is inherent in a deficits approach.

In Chapter 5, "Urban Myth: The Family in Hard Times," Sam Redding moves farther within the context of the family, identifying possible solutions to the problems of urban children and families within the family itself. Within this context, however, like Tolan and Gorman-Smith, Redding recognizes the impact of external forces, such as a weak economy, that make jobs unavailable, thereby limiting opportunity to prosper. Focusing on the dynamics of family life, including behaviors, attitudes, beliefs, routines, and interactions, Redding explores how families can change their lot despite the obstacles that threaten them. A personal and fascinating family history spanning 150 years and a peppering of urban anecdotes serve as the backdrop for Redding's ideas.

Schools

The school is the one institution where most children, at least through the middle years of high school, can be reached not only by educators but also by other professionals such as psychologists and social workers. Through schools, educators and other professionals might prevent some problems before they require such drastic measures as hospitalization or incarceration. Because they often lag behind in academic achievement, however, urban schools must also concentrate their energies on helping urban children and youth become better learners. One key to aiding academic achievement is a more complete understanding of impediments to learning faced by urban children. There are only so many hours in the school day, and it is difficult to envision how additional non-educational services may be incorporated. Yet, solutions to health and psychological problems might simultaneously aid learning. As several chapters in this section make clear, one challenge is the coordination of educational and related services within schools.

In Chapter 6, "Fostering Educational Resilience in Inner-City Schools," Margaret Wang, Geneva Haertel, and Herbert Walberg identify features of homes, schools, and communities that promote academic success and healthy psychological development even in adverse circumstances. Within schools, the influence of teachers, instructional strategies, classroom climate, curriculum, and school-wide practices are examined. The authors emphasize the unification of resources of the home, school, and community to yield the best conditions for students. They stress family-school-community partnerships to establish and maintain resilience-promoting educational environments.

In contrast with the previous chapter, which focuses on the psychological character of educative institutions, Chapter 7, "The Problems and Promise of Urban Schools" by William Boyd and Roger Shouse, reviews organizational features of schools. In their view, the barriers to urban schooling include dangerous, turbulent environments; underfunding; dysfunctional bureaucracy; sparse social capital; and teacher overload and role conflict. The most promising avenues of reform are the "effective schools" movement; empowered, debureaucratized schools accountable for value-added and client satisfaction; emphasis on "caring communities"; mentoring and incentive programs; coordinated, community-school linked services; and new organizational models for urban schools. Even in inner cities, small primary schools can be intimate neighborhood institutions. Junior and senior high schools, however, are often farther from children's homes; they are usually larger, more impersonal, and alienating. In Chapter 8, "Normative School Transitions Among Urban Adolescents: When, Where, and How to Intervene," Edward Seidman and Sabine French reveal the difficulties encountered by students in transferring from elementary schools to junior and senior high schools. They critically examine interventions and policies to make such transfer less wrenching and more constructive. They find that small, intimate learning environments in junior high school and restructured high schools are particularly promising.

Although once concentrated in the rural South, many African-American children are now conspicuously concentrated in inner cities from which other ethnic families with children have migrated. In Chapter 9, "Understanding the School Performance of Urban Blacks: Some Essential Background Knowledge," John Ogbu asks why African-American children perform poorly academically. Although some scholars identify school resources, structures, and transactions as causes, Ogbu believes that the ideas and behaviors these children bring to school that arise from their status as an "involuntary minority" may impair their academic performance. He argues that although discrimination and racism remain barriers to achievement, other "community forces," such as adaptation to minority status, are important influences. As in the case of other ethnic groups, Ogbu believes that programs are needed that reduce the psychological burdens on African-American children and allow them to develop both their academic and minority identities.

One estimate is that students spend only 13% of their waking hours in school during the first 18 years of life. In Chapter 10, "Extended Day Programs: From Theory to Practice," Donald Hellison and Nicholas Cutforth consider how the 87% of time outside normal school hours may best be employed to enhance learning and psychological development. Sponsored by YMCAs, churches, parks, and schools, extended day programs offer safe places and supervised activities for urban youth. A core idea of successful programs is responsibility—for oneself, for the rights of others, and for cooperation and group success. Athletics and club programs in Chicago and Denver exemplify the strategies required to bring about such a sense of responsibility.

Health

During the past 30 years, major contributors to morbidity and mortality among young people have shifted from traditional disease-related causes of illness to behavior-related causes such as cigarette and alcohol abuse, high-risk sexual behaviors, motor vehicle accidents, and gun-related homicides and injuries. Creating health-protective environments and instilling young people with skills, values, and knowledge that enhance physical and mental health will require changes in the delivery of health services and education, as well as in the ways that health providers work with families, schools, and community organizations. It will also require the development and implementation of collaborative programs across disciplines. The chapters in this section characterize the health status and care of urban children and youth from the perspectives of public health, nursing, clinical pediatrics, and psychiatry.

In Chapter 11, "A Public Health Perspective on Urban Adolescents," Kelli Komro, Frank Bingchang Hu, and Brian Flay analyze national mortality and behavioral risk data for 12- to 17-year-olds. They find that homicide, suicide, and vehicle crashes are among the five leading causes of death for this age-group. They point out that the high incidence of death from alcohol-involved crashes and interpersonal violence indicate the need for greater emphasis on the problems of substance use and violence among urban youth. The leading causes of death among adults (e.g., cancer, heart attacks) also have many social and behavioral determinants. The authors describe the integrative Theory of Triadic Influence, which offers a model for understanding the cause of health-compromising behaviors and how to intervene to prevent them. Guided by this theoretical framework, they propose strategies for disease prevention and health promotion among urban adolescents.

Using clinical pediatric and psychiatric frameworks in Chapter 12, "Health Perspectives on Urban Children and Youth," Robert Johnson reinforces the viewpoints offered by Komro and colleagues regarding the problems experienced by urban youth in the areas of violence, substance use, high-risk sexual behavior, and nutrition.

He provides a fascinating analysis of urban youth, highlighting the core tasks of urban adolescents, and makes a strong case for middle adolescence (ages 15-17) as a time of heightened risk for engaging in problem behavior. He also sensitizes us to barriers to health care experienced by the urban poor, particularly financial, geographic, language, racial, and ethnic barriers. He concludes that cultural sensitivity and cultural competence training for health care providers, as well as strategies to promote equality in health care access, are critical national priorities.

In Chapter 13, "Families and Health in the Urban Environment: Implications for Programs, Research, and Policy," Suzanne Feetham reviews empirical evidence regarding the impact of families on the health of their members. To support the importance of family-based intervention programs, she highlights the characteristics of effective family intervention programs and the complexity of programs for urban families. She bemoans the isolation among agencies and disciplines in addressing family health issues and argues compellingly for comprehensive, interdisciplinary, family-based strategies to produce more positive health outcomes for urban children and families. Her identification of future directions, which emphasizes collaborative multidisciplinary, systems-oriented programming, provides a fitting final note for the chapters of this volume's contributing authors.

Concluding Remarks

The preceding chapter highlights sections that give an account of how the chapters within sections relate to one another and some major points the reader will encounter. The highlights, moreover, convey the interdisciplinary approach required to achieve a better understanding of children and youth. They also make clear that new solutions and organizational arrangements are likely to be required to improve their environments and solve their problems. Of course, these highlights hardly substitute for the chapters themselves, which yield a far richer understanding of the problems, opportunities, and prospects of children and youth than can be captured in these abbreviated summaries.

As mentioned previously, one purpose of this series is to draw implications for policymakers and practitioners. The contributing authors have been encouraged to make these clear. Active readers may wish to note those that pertain to their scholarship and practice. Reflective readers may wish to draw their own implications from the research findings reported in one or more chapters. In the final chapter of this book, we, the editors, provide an initial list of recommendations that we derived from these chapters and other current research on today's children and youth. They illustrate the kind of concrete recommendations that may serve those responsible for planning and monitoring policies, practices, and programs.

PART II

Families

• CHAPTER 2 •

The Role of Universities
in Child Development

SHARON LANDESMAN RAMEY

CRAIG T. RAMEY

T he challenging life circumstances that families face in urban settings reflect complex historical, political, economic, and psychosocial dynamics. Children arguably are the most vulnerable individuals and the most profoundly affected by these challenges. Can universities assume a significant role in strengthening urban families and enhancing children's development? The answer depends on three critical elements: (a) the degree to which universities have useful knowledge and can initiate practical strategies relevant to solving the most pressing family and child development problems, (b) the willingness of urban communities and universities to work together in sustained and intensive endeavors, and (c) the availability of resources and incentives to ensure that these community-university partnerships advance knowledge. In this chapter, we present evidence that our knowledge base about fundamental principles of child development and family functioning is remarkably strong, although currently fragmented and often only marginally linked to practical problem-solving strategies. University settings typically promote the transmission of this knowledge to highly targeted audiences—primarily students and colleagues in traditional disciplines—and fail to encourage timely and effective communication with key stakeholders in urban communities—namely, community leaders, service providers, and family members, including children. In the past decade, however, diverse new initiatives have fostered community-university partnerships that address major problems such as urban renewal, health care delivery, school reform, the prevention of violence, and teen pregnancy and parenting. At the heart of many of these initiatives is the recognition that universities have good reasons and a societal responsibility to become involved directly in improving the quality of life in urban environments. In this chapter, we propose a conceptual framework to guide change efforts and their evaluation and describe two major initiatives to enhance families and improve child outcomes. These initiatives underscore the importance of university internal organization, leadership, and the reward structure in successfully enacting and sustaining community-university partnerships. The lessons learned from these endeavors encourage new modes of teaching and inquiry and raise provocative questions for society about the future of universities.

Universities as Knowledge Transmitters

Universities historically have served as society's primary transmitters of formal knowledge. Academic institutions have stood apart from society on the basis of a strong belief that the pursuit of knowledge needed to occur in settings free from outside or "real-world" interference. Indeed, the term *academic* is both defined and generally understood as "pertaining to areas of study that are not vocational or applied, as the humanities, pure mathematics, etc." and "theoretical; not practical, realistic, or directly useful," as well as "learned or scholarly but lacking in worldliness, common sense, or practicality" (Flexner, 1987, p. 9).

The formal study of child development and families is relatively young within the academic community and does not reside within a single traditional discipline. Traditionally, psychology, sociology, and anthropology have been the major fields concerned with children and families, generating rich literatures based on both descriptive and experimental studies. Since the 1960s, there has been an exponential increase in the psychosocial research on children and families, accompanied by an expansion of the academic departments engaged in such inquiry, including pediatrics, psychiatry, nursing, family medicine, public health (with its new specialties in maternal and child health, health behavior, and health promotion), education, criminal justice, law, economics, and history. This increase in the knowledge base is evidenced by the many new journals concerning children and families, as well as the creation of new professional societies and groups, often interdisciplinary or transdisciplinary and focused on particular age periods (e.g., infancy, early childhood, adolescence) or key topics related to children or families (e.g., childhood psychopathology, child abuse and neglect, developmental disabilities, marriage).

Traditional Forms of Transmitting Knowledge About Human Development and Behavior

Knowledge Transmission Within the University Setting

Because the study of children and families has not been restricted to a primary discipline or even a few disciplines, knowledge transmission about children and families has been fragmented within the university setting. Professors have understandably focused their teaching on the knowledge base generated by colleagues within their own discipline. Just as important, professors teaching the major undergraduate- and graduate-level survey courses on "child development" often begin their teaching by offering a disclaimer to any students who may be taking the course in the hope of learning how to become good or better parents. This well-known disclaimer affirms the *academic* nature of the knowledge transmitted in the traditional university classroom. Students who raise questions about a particular child or family problem during the course typically are answered in a way that clearly distinguishes the formal knowledge base from its clinical or real-world application. Professors thus usually have refused to answer such practical and specific questions and in so doing have conveyed a message that solving real problems is not necessarily linked to what is known about children from scientific study. *We propose that this distancing between the formal knowledge base about children and families and its application to solving problems warrants major reconsideration.*

Occasionally, groups of faculty members who share a common interest related to children or families form alliances within their universities, sometimes through organized interdisciplinary centers or training programs, at other times through self-initiated or informal groups, colloquia, consortia, or interdisciplinary research and demonstration projects. Information exchange occurring within these nontraditional university groups frequently contributes to a greater appreciation for the contributions of other disciplines, a broadening of the sources used to seek relevant information, a more comprehensive understanding and scholarly citing of the empirical literatures, and sometimes to true paradigm shifts and changes in methodology. Contrary to an academic ideal that advocates for academic inquiry to occur independent of the outside world, the vast majority of recently funded research concerning children and families includes some study of the dynamic interplay that occurs between families and children and their everyday settings, including home, school, health care system, work, and recreation. Increasingly, the research involves assessment of specific intervention efforts designed to enhance child and/or family outcomes. Similarly, scientific inquiry into the change process itself has acquired a legitimate status, critical to understanding the mechanisms responsible for major behavioral, health, educational, and social outcomes. *Significantly, much of this research is now conducted outside universities in nonacademic research organizations.*

Knowledge Transmission
Outside the University Setting

Before proceeding to consider how universities disseminate knowledge about children and families outside the university setting, a cardinal cultural fact warrants stating: Our child-rearing attitudes and practices are shaped primarily by firsthand experience and the advice and approval of individuals (e.g., relatives, friends, pastors, doctors) most immediately connected to a child and family. In today's world, another important fact is that the media have assumed an elevated status of influence, given the pervasiveness of television, radio, and the press in people's lives. Almost all television stations, newspapers, and magazines have their own experts who answer questions about child development and provide helpful strategies to address a broad array of family concerns (e.g., helping children with anger and conflict, preparing children for school, dealing with divorce and step-families, protecting children from abuse). Indeed, there is no shortage of discussion of the urgent problems affecting children and families, most especially the severe and seemingly intractable problems of inner cities. Notably missing from most of these discussions is hard evidence about likely effective solutions and an informed application of the principles of human development to these problems. Rather, the domain of children and families appears to be one with many routes to becoming an expert, with the academician not necessarily being viewed as the leading expert.

Communication by universities to broader outside audiences has long occurred in the form of press releases and press coverage about scientific breakthroughs. In the field of child development, knowledge typically accrues in an incremental fashion, rather than through major discoveries. Similarly, much of what has been learned about marriage and families may be characterized as descriptive and affirming the need for a systems perspective on families; that is, a multilevel system of forces influences a family's well-being and structural integrity (e.g., Hinde & Stevenson-Hinde, 1988; Lewis, 1982). These advances are not generally considered highly newsworthy and in need of immediate media coverage. In contrast, particular child and family specialists have found themselves more sought out by the media over the past decade to provide opinions about broad social issues and to offer advice to parents, policymakers, and the general public (e.g., McCall, 1993). In fact, university professors now serve on the editorial boards of or write columns for popular magazines on parenting and family life.

A key challenge in communicating beyond the university setting to important constituencies has been how to provide information in ways that are both useful and scientifically responsible. Scientists and scholars vary tremendously in their skills, as well as in their willingness to present information. Further, the skills needed for effective classroom teaching or scientific writing are not necessarily the same as those for successfully transmitting knowledge in other settings and formats. A legitimate question is *who* should convey new knowledge about children and families to the general public or to targeted audiences, such as parents, educators, and policymakers. We advocate that most scientists and scholars should be involved, at least to some degree, in an expansion of outreach efforts, to ensure accuracy and comprehensiveness in the presentation of new findings and more thorough incorporation of basic principles of human development (thoughtful application of well-established findings). This responsibility to transmit relevant knowledge beyond the university setting, however, represents a relatively new endeavor for most academicians and one that extends beyond the traditional role of professorial work in almost all disciplines. In times past, spending time transmitting knowledge to general audiences was considered to be not only less valuable than generating new knowledge for peer audiences within academia but often also inappropriate. Clearly, this attitude must change if academicians seek to have a meaningful impact on contemporary society.

Innovative Means of Disseminating Knowledge

Since the social activism of the 1960s and 1970s, some universities have endeavored to become more a part of their local community. These endeavors have included providing innovative programs of coursework for nondegree students, including relevant subjects such as urban revitalization, parenting effectiveness, and strengthening marriages and families, as well as offering lectures, workshops, and special events specifically for the general public. Many universities have sponsored programs to strengthen ties with their local education authorities (e.g., in-service programs for high school science teachers, faculty members teaching minicourses directly in the public schools, collaborative demonstration efforts), and a major expansion has occurred in university-sponsored continuing education programs, largely in response to the increasingly stringent professional standards for individuals to keep up with advances in their fields. Collectively, these innovative educational efforts represent a leading-edge rethinking of the role of universities in transmitting knowledge. The shift has been to a more open environment in which knowledge is more explicitly recognized as a valued commodity to broad segments of society, far beyond traditional students and scholars.

Many benefits have been associated with the increased dissemination of information about children and families. One benefit has been a new influx of information from the outside that is highly relevant to the academic enterprise. This incoming information concerns changing public policies, funding streams, and sociopolitical conditions that might otherwise not be apparent or readily accessible to scientists engaged in studying children and families via standard methods of gathering data. This influx comes from opening lines of communication with a more diverse audience and includes substantive challenges to university-generated knowledge, as well as constructive and supplemental information. Another benefit has been the discovery of exceptional opportunities to develop and implement interventions or programs designed to enhance outcomes for urban families and children. These opportunities are the result of more frequent contact with key individuals and groups and a new level of mutual trust and respect associated with knowledge and its useful application to human problems.

The Need for Knowledge by Communities

The Changing Demography of Families

In the past three decades, the demography of America's children and families has been transformed dramatically (cf. Carnegie Foundation for the Advancement of Teaching, 1991). The structure and stability of the basic family unit has changed, with more single mothers than ever before heading households, more children experiencing both divorce and adjusting to a stepfamily, and more children born into poverty. In two-parent married households, family size has decreased and full-time and part-time maternal employment has escalated. Immigration and fertility patterns each contribute to greater diversification in the ethnic and cultural backgrounds of today's children, with decreasing proportions of children who identify as white/non-Hispanic or Euro-American. The trend has been toward delayed childbearing among higher-income, better educated women, but not a corresponding shift among those who are economically impoverished and poorly educated. In contrast, the prevalence and consequences of very early teen pregnancy—children having children—have escalated in inner cities to become a major societal concern. The rapidity of these demographic changes and, perhaps even more importantly, their incongruence with the dominant portrayal of family life, gender roles, and children's basic needs constitute a de facto social revolution. What is so disturbing is that much of this social revolution has been secondary to shifts in values, economic realities, and altered opportunities, rather than informed by ideals and planning.

Forces Affecting Urban Communities

Urban communities have experienced changes equally as dramatic as those of family life. Indeed, the changes in cities may be inextricably linked to some demographic changes, although not controlled exclusively by them. Cities have shifted to become overwhelmingly a place of residence for low-income and poverty families while continuing to provide supports for industry, business, and cultural entertainment for a large segment of the population. The dismal and now familiar list of problems includes the growth of crime, especially violent crime and gang-related activity; unprecedented drug traffic and associated substance abuse, including by very young children; the decline of urban schools, as documented by all objective indicators; substandard quality of housing, with no affordable alternatives in sight; and the presence of serious pollution, high noise levels, poor transportation systems, inferior supports and services, and unrelenting ethnic/cultural tensions. These problems are predictable when population crowding occurs without adequate community resources. Given the duration and severity of these forces affecting urban communities, money alone is unlikely to solve the problems. More realistically, major new or expanded sources of revenue for urban revitalization are unlikely in the coming decade, given the level of national debt and the increasing general pessimism about changing human behavior. A more likely scenario will involve using existing resources better, establishing alternative coalitions to combine efforts and avoid duplication, developing new styles of leadership for urban communities, and attracting a broader base of people with critical knowledge and skills needed to enhance urban life.

Increased Problems Among
Children and Youth

As this book affirms, the problems among children and youth are staggering. In inner cities, children's basic linguistic, reasoning, and pre-academic skills on entry into school are at a nadir. The magnitude of difference in children's entry-level skills between inner cities and surrounding affluent communities can be as large as tenfold and greater (e.g., Carnegie Foundation for the Advancement of Teaching, 1991; C. T. Ramey, 1995; Schorr & Schorr, 1988) in terms of group percentile performance on standardized achievement tests and placement in special education classes for mental retardation. Translated into practical educational terms, kindergarten teachers in inner-city schools may be teaching 5-year-olds who, on average, may be cognitively similar to 3-year-olds from more advantaged settings. The distance in skill levels between low-income, inner-city children and their affluent, suburban counterparts unfortunately increases rather than decreases over the elementary school years. This fact is not a simple condemnation of inner-city schools. Evidence suggests that inner-city children, when in school, make significant progress in their academic skills (e.g., Alexander & Entwistle, 1988). Although inner-city schools are woefully underfunded to meet the needs of their students, other forces contribute to the poor academic performance of inner-city children. These include limited educational and supportive resources for learning in the children's home and the community at large, as well as lack of summer educational activities that are typically available to middle- and upper-income children from stabler, safer, and more resourceful neighborhoods.

Child abuse and neglect statistics are alarming, and the consensus is that the numbers underrepresent, to a large degree, the severity and prevalence of these problems. Beyond the alarming abuse and neglect rates is the increasingly debilitating symptom of fear among inner-city children. The trip to and from school is fraught with true dangers, often life-threatening ones. Children's recreational activities are increasingly limited to indoors because of threats of random gunfire, violent crime, and illegal drug activities. Further, urban children and youth spend many hours without adequate adult supervision. Especially during these unsupervised times, acts of aggression and violence among children who know one another, as well as crimes against strangers, have increased.

It is important to note that the majority of children living in poverty, inner-city environments remain out of serious trouble. These children often are described as "resilient" or "invulnerable" (e.g., Garmezy, 1983; Rutter, 1985; Werner, Bierman, & French, 1971). Research on low-income, urban children increasingly addresses the "risk" versus "protective" factors present in their lives (e.g., Coie et al., 1993) and seeks to identify the strengths and positive aspects of family life that exist despite challenging life circumstances (e.g., Keltner & Ramey, 1993). Seeking to identify constructive forces operative at the individual child and family level provides a critically needed balance to the alarming descriptive statistics. Yet, undeniably, the alarming reports remain of urgent societal concern.

Uncertainty About How
to Prevent Further Decline

To provide yet another listing of the ills of inner-city life without indicating possible solutions would be unproductive. Similarly, to deny the great uncertainty that surrounds proposals to prevent further decline and to reduce problems at the community and family level would be naive. The sheer complexity of the issues and the multiple levels of influence on a child and family mitigate against quick, inexpensive, or easy solutions. Even people who have deeply held beliefs that underscore a single major theme or solution, such as those who advocate for individual responsibility or those who see more intensive and comprehensive two-generation intervention programs as the solution, recognize that a multipronged endeavor to revitalize urban communities is needed. In this chapter, we offer specific ways in which universities might assume valuable roles in stimulating, advising, assisting, sustaining, and evaluating such multipronged endeavors. An implicit assumption is that the seemingly intractable problems affecting children and youth are *not* beyond solution, even with the limitations of resources and the general pessimism about finding feasible ways to improve the lives of the most vulnerable children.

Universities as Change Agents

In many disciplines, universities have had the distinction of being change agents as a result of scientific discoveries. These efforts have been most notable in medicine, agriculture, physics, and engineering. Similarly, human behavior theories as diverse as economics and history have at times contributed to important societal changes. Concerning the problems of urban children and youth, innovative programs and provocative ideas have emanated from universities, primarily in the areas of education and violence prevention. To the extent that modern universities endorse activism—specifically, the application of relevant knowledge to help solve and better understand human problems—they are increasingly likely to assume a greater role in the change process. That universities in general are cautious and conservative in their willingness to embrace this expanded role is understandable. The future is likely to contain many disappointments and failures and to be fraught with the potential for political and social controversy, as well as abundant misunderstanding about this expanded role of universities. Accordingly, we have identified four strategies that have been successful in facilitating positive change on behalf of children and youth: (a) the development of model programs for families and children, (b) university involvement in public policy and decision making, (c) faculty advising to local, state, and national programs and agencies, and (d) community-university partnerships for societal change. We review each below, indicating some of the lessons learned from each strategy and its limitations. We focus especially on the fourth strategy—the community-university partnership model—because we judge this to afford the greatest promise for sustained change and for generating a more definitive knowledge base for the future.

Development of Model Programs
for Families and Children

At the turn of the century, universities began a variety of model programs in education and family support services. These increased in the 1930s with the establishment of university child study centers, which served as minilaboratories for research and for training child development specialists. In the 1960s and 1970s, universities vigorously established model or demonstration programs. The idea was that a university would develop and thoroughly test the model before exporting it to the real world—a parallel to the model of new product development in industry. Examples include (a) preschool and summer programs for economically disadvantaged children to enhance their intellectual development; (b) programs for special needs children with severe emotional problems or intellectual disabilities, demonstration programs as diverse as early intervention programs, vocational training, and independent living skills programs; (c) model programs to prevent teen pregnancy; (d) social skills programs for children who are disruptive and aggressive in classroom settings; and (e) mother-infant interaction programs to promote more positive parenting behavior.

Many of these model programs formed the basis for programs adopted by schools, clinics, group homes, other service providers, and families themselves. Within a short time, a major limitation inherent in these university-based model programs appeared: The conditions affecting the initiation and operation of these model programs in university settings were not comparable to those in the outside world. Just as importantly, these model programs rarely were designed with awareness of the existing resources (much less the complex legal and regulatory forces, attitudes and values, and the inevitable presence of local politics and territorial concerns) in the local communities where such programs were to be exported. This failing led to a predictable situation in which university model programs came to be viewed with suspicion as to how useful or sensitive these programs would be outside the protected environment of a university. Although such programs undoubtedly served a pioneering role in developing innovative approaches in some areas, a definite shift has occurred away from the creation of university-based demonstration models.

University Involvement in
Public Policy and Decision Making

Another strategy for increasing the utility of the knowledge base about children and families to the problems of urban life is to engage universities more actively in public policy and decision making. This is not an entirely new activity, but rather universities are reevaluating the value of this involvement for both society and their own survival. For decades, individuals such as Ed Zigler at Yale University, Urie Bronfenbrenner at Cornell University, and Bettye Caldwell at the University of Arkansas have been powerful advocates for children and families, sought after by Congress and major policymakers for their expertise in a wide range of areas. What has shifted is the degree to which many more scientists and scholars have become vocal in the formation of key policies affecting children and families. Almost all major scientific and professional associations have established committees or legislative task forces to address public policy issues. These activities often are strengthened considerably by the presence in Washington, DC, of professionals who work for these groups, helping facilitate the involvement of universities in shaping public policy and influencing key decision making affecting children and families. Increasingly, these activities are needed at the state and local levels.

One example of a highly effective university outreach area concerning children began at the University of Minnesota in 1991 when a consortium for children—The Children, Youth, and Family Consortium—was formed (Erickson & Weinberg, in press). This consortium has interdisciplinary representation from within the university and equally broad representation from the community. Within this collaborative framework, barriers to change have been identified, including distrust of the university, the university reward system, turfdom among disciplines, and funding issues. Despite these barriers, the consortium made excellent progress, including sponsoring a first-ever Minnesota Children's Summit to influence future policy making.

Faculty as Advisors to Programs, Agencies, and Organizations

In addition to major policy activities and legislative reform, demand for expert guidance to help in the launching, operation, and ongoing review of local, state, and national programs has been increasing (McCall, 1993). Faculty members often serve on local advisory boards or provide formal consultation or technical assistance to such programs, agencies, or organizations. Within the university setting, these activities historically have been classified as "service" in the tripartite mission of universities: teaching, research, and service. These faculty advisory activities, however, have escalated significantly in the area of children and youth services and often provide exceptional opportunities to engage in research and evaluation. In the course of providing consultation and useful information to community-based groups, opportunities to identify new directions and ways to modify existing programs or strategies arise. When good working relationships are established and when university faculty are viewed as providing relevant, applicable information in a timely and responsive manner, long-term relationships often develop. These frequently result in the identification of needs related to research or formal study of aspects of the service delivery system. Faculty advising thus becomes an important means for faculty members to be in touch with the dynamic service delivery system and to identify opportunities for inquiry (expand the existing knowledge), as well as for application of basic principles and past findings.

Community-University Partnerships for Societal Change

Partnerships have always been a part of the university landscape because they have provided the impetus and resources to engage in major new endeavors. Less acknowledged is that almost all sources of outside funds to universities, both public and private, have involved some degree of partnership. A partnership involves mutual responsibility and the potential for mutual benefit. For example, industry and private philanthropy have invested for years in universities on the basis of the conviction that what will be accomplished by universities will serve their own long-term objectives. Historically, however, universities have been extremely reluctant to relinquish their independence and academic freedom via relationships described as "partnerships." Indeed, many universities have been severely criticized for their joint endeavors with chemical and pharmaceutical companies and their collaborations with the armed forces, to mention a few examples. The area of children and families, however, does not have a comparable history of partnership models.

As often occurs, the connotation of words changes over time. The term *partnership* has recently come to connote a balanced and open relationship, and university leaders readily talk about their "partnerships with the community" as a way to indicate respect for the contributions from the community and to reflect that the university does not have to be the dominant or controlling force. In economically pressed times, the motivation for universities to form partnerships is especially understandable. Far more important, concerning children and families, solutions to long-standing problems probably cannot be found or enacted without the ideas, experience, and support of all key stakeholders. The partnership strategy does not preclude or replace the value of model programs (especially if they are based in the community), faculty participation in major policy making, or the many forms of advising and outreach that can strengthen existing community programs. The unique thing the partnership model affords is a sustained context for identifying mutual goals and objectives, collectively reviewing the merits and limitations of alternative approaches to identified problems, jointly finding and distributing the resources (people, dollars, physical facilities) to launch high-priority programs, and establishing the criteria by which such programs will be evaluated as more or less successful. The partnership model is designed to be efficient, sensitive, and powerful, as well as to avoid destructive competition, misunderstanding, or duplication of efforts when solving the pressing problems of urban children and families.

Needed: A Conceptual Framework for Action and Evaluation of Urban Progress

Importance of a Multilevel, Multidimensional, Time-Distributed Framework

To comprehend the relationship of communities to individual child and family functioning, a conceptual framework is essential to delineate the multiple levels of influence and how negative forces can counter the effects of coexisting positive forces and vice versa. All too often, social scientists have been rewarded for developing narrow and carefully delineated theoretical frameworks for studying a particular social problem. The advantages are that everything within these narrow models can be measured and studied and, presumably, eventually controlled and changed. In fact, the overwhelming limitation is that the complexity of everyday urban life and the interdependencies among the settings and people within an urban setting are too often simplified to a degree that the model becomes merely "academic."

As social scientists and developmentalists, we are aware of the serious challenges faced in endeavoring to understand a set of interconnected human problems and interdependent resources as they are transformed *historically*. An example of the inherent complexity involved in fully mapping a biosocial system (one now used by a number of developmental scientists) is the system to regulate blood pressure. The illustration of this system identifies

more than 100 independent factors, many of which operate within
subsystems. Taken to the level of an entire organism, specifically
the developing child, it is not unimaginable that the conceptual
framework will need to be far more complex. The effort to reduce
what influences human development to only a handful of boxes
with two-way arrows in an illustration clearly is unlikely to yield
major new insights. At the same time, in-depth study of selected
aspects of the complex system are valuable, particularly if they then
can be placed within a broader systems perspective that recognizes
such principles as alternative developmental pathways, compensatory mechanisms, and selective experience within a given setting
(S. L. Ramey & Ramey, 1995).

A Biosocial Ecological Systems
Model of Human Development

Through our own partnership research projects, we have developed a biosocial ecological model of human development. We
present this briefly here to illustrate key elements in such a model,
rather than to propose this as definitive or useful for all community-university research partnerships. This model, shown in Figure 2.1,
has evolved over the past 15 years (e.g., C. T. Ramey, Bryant, Sparling,
& Wasik, 1984; C. T. Ramey, MacPhee, & Yeates, 1982; S. L. Ramey
& Ramey, 1992) and recently has been expanded to identify in
greater detail (a) substantive areas of interventions, (b) potential
developmental mechanisms or processes responsible for improved
outcomes in children, and (c) changes likely to occur in adults and
in the community over the years. For greater detail about the model
itself, refer to C. T. Ramey, Ramey, Gaines, and Blair (1995).

Distinctive features of this model include the following:

1. *An explicit inclusion of the role of biological influences,* beginning with hereditary and prenatal sources of influences and
continuing through the life span (hence the reference to *bio* in the
title of this framework). Even though these influences are often
difficult to study directly or tend to be studied unto themselves, the
codetermination of development by basic biological processes that
co-occur and undergird behavioral and social development warrants clear recognition. Ideally, more detailed longitudinal inquiry
will permit greater refinement in the conceptual framework of key

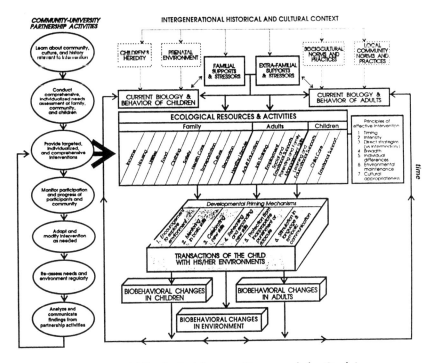

Figure 2.1. A Biosocial Ecological Systems Framework for Studying Comprehensive Community Interventions (modified from C. Ramey, Ramey, Gaines, & Blair, 1995)

biological influences and how these are affected by experience and external forces.

2. *Identification of multiple social influences on a child,* from the most proximal (usually within the family) to the intermediate extra-familial (e.g., teachers, neighbors, extended family) to the more distal (represented in the model by reference to community norms and cultural practices), which theoretically may simultaneously or sequentially influence the course of a child's transactions with his or her environment (e.g., Bronfenbrenner, 1979; Lewis, 1982; Sameroff, 1983) (thus the reference to *social* in the title of the model).

3. *Incorporation of the larger ecology in understanding children's life courses,* which is depicted in Figure 2.1 under the heading "Ecological Resources & Activities" (thus accounting for the term

ecological in the title). Even within the same neighborhood or same family, not all children have the same ecologies. Rather, children spend different amounts of time in different environments and, within these environments, may be exposed to differential settings. For illustration, rather than delineate environments by conventional names per se (e.g., home, school, clinic, playground, place of worship), representative functional resources and activities pertinent to the lives of most inner-city children are shown. This format indicates that environments are rarely limited to only one or a few types of activities (e.g., schools serve far more than an educational purpose in a child's life, and learning occurs in many settings outside the school environment). In many cases, an intervention or program and its accompanying research will focus primarily on a few prespecified ecologies (environments), although the conceptual framework indicates the likely cross-ecology effects that may occur as the result of ecology-specific programs.

4. *Fundamental acknowledgment that children's lives are embedded within a family and community system comprised of many individual elements that generally adhere to the dynamics of systems theory* (cf. Bertalanffy, 1975; Miller, 1978) (hence the inclusion of *system* in the title). A systems theory is based on principles of both homeostasis and change, which can be achieved through particular ways in which organisms adapt to changes in their external environment.

5. *Preliminary delineation of specific developmental processes* (labeled "Developmental Priming Mechanisms" to denote their role in preparing children for developmental advances) hypothesized to be among the effective transactions of children with others in their social environments. The six developmental priming mechanisms identified (see S. L. Ramey & Ramey, 1992, for more details about these) are derived from empirical work with high-risk, low-income children and represent processes proposed as essential for normal intellectual development in all children. We recognize that this list is not likely to be sufficiently comprehensive, and the details of how these mechanisms are effectively realized at different stages in a child's development cannot be shown adequately in a single figure.

The component of a community-university partnership designed to develop, implement, and evaluate (study) system change or a particular program (e.g., a two-generation intervention program to enhance the development of very young children and their parents) appears in Figure 2.1 along the left side as a series of major activities. These activities are intended to maximize the quality and appropriateness of interventions, as well as to meet the needs of a university to be engaged in the generation of new and valid knowledge. These activities closely parallel those identified in the research literature as vital to effective decision making and problem solving (e.g., Landesman, Jaccard, & Gunderson, 1991). To provide more substantive information about how community-university partnerships might proceed and directly build upon a broad biosocial ecological systems framework such as we have proposed, we describe two ongoing endeavors. These new partnerships build directly upon findings from previous research concerning young children and early interventions (e.g., Campbell & Ramey, 1995; C. T. Ramey et al., 1992; C. T. Ramey & Ramey, 1994) yet expand into new domains and seek to enact more comprehensive community-based programs that will become self-sustaining and self-monitoring.

Community-University Partnerships: Case Illustrations

In the past 5 years, we have had two exceptional opportunities to become part of two large-scale community-university partnerships, both addressing the needs of low-income families and children in underresourced environments. These partnerships are quite different in terms of who the key stakeholders are and the scope of what they hope to accomplish, yet they have shared some similar challenges in their early formation and in the establishment of general guidelines for operation. First, we describe the opportunities that become available and how the partnerships were formed, modified, and active in self-defining the parameters for their long-term functioning. After this, we provide more specific details about the goals of each partnership and highlight some key findings.

Establishment of Partnerships

The way in which partnerships are formed varies with the opportunities and individuals involved. One of our ongoing partnerships, known as the UAB-Titusville 2000 Project, was initiated by the president of our university as a major university-wide commitment to enhancing the quality of life for an urban community (Titusville) adjacent to the university. When the idea of a partnership was first discussed with community leaders, a key feature was that the partnership would be sustained over a decade or longer. From the beginning, the idea of equality in the partnership was endorsed, although the means by which this equality could be achieved was less clear. Further, the scope of the partnership was purposefully broad and ambitious, potentially encompassing all aspects of urban life.

Formation of the UAB-Titusville 2000 Partnership with regular meetings *preceded* the identification of any funding for this endeavor, either within or outside the partnership; that is, this partnership was formed in a way that was not linked to any specific outside funding or mandate. Similarly, there were no immediate crises or pressing political concerns. In some ways, establishing community-university partnerships in this manner is ideal, granting maximal control to the local partners and ensuring that the vision for the partnership can be developed and endorsed mutually. At the same time, this is rather atypical: Most community-university partnerships have been prompted by specific opportunities for funding (usually competitive funding) or by urgent conditions necessitating the partnership.

The other partnership we describe here was more typical initially, in that the creation of the partnership was required by a federal request for proposals (RFP) to enact a specific project. The partnership itself is unusual in that it involves two layers of partnerships: (a) local site partnerships at 31 sites throughout the country and (b) a national consortium of all the local partners, plus a national research coordinating team (which we lead), a national research advisory group, and representatives of the funding agency. In 1990, Congress mandated a new program to facilitate the transition of former Head Start children and their families into public schools. This program, titled the Head Start-Public School Early Childhood Transition Demonstration Program, was conceptualized as a multisite randomized trial to extend comprehensive Head Start-like services and supports to children, families, schools, and communities to "maintain the gains" begun during Head Start.

Because Head Start, on average, is provided only part-day, 4 days per week, for 9 months during a child's 4th year of life, its potential to create long-lasting benefits is limited. This new project sought to offer multiple, individualized supports to children and their families from kindergarten through third grade. These included a parental involvement program, health and nutrition services, social services, the use of "developmentally appropriate practices" in the classrooms, transition planning between Head Start and public school personnel, mainstreaming of children with disabilities, and a variety of other efforts to maximize children's school success. To enact such a program of this intensity and breadth clearly would require active involvement from key local groups. Under the auspices of the Administration on Children, Youth, and Families (ACYF)—the federal agency responsible for Head Start—an RFP was issued requiring the formation of a local partnership comprised of (a) the local education authority (LEA), often still referred to as the school district; (b) the local Head Start grantee; and (c) a university or nonprofit research group. This tripartite partnership was to be formed and actively involved in preparing the grant, planning the program and its evaluation over the first year, launching and operating the program, and conducting a prospective evaluation of the impact of the program by studying both the demonstration and comparison groups of children, families, schools, and communities. Just as importantly, the local partnership was charged with the responsibility of planning how to sustain the program after an anticipated 6 years of federal funding ended. This element of sustainability was underscored in the peer review of these competitive applications, with reviewers asked to judge the adequacy of the plans for how the local partnerships proposed to develop adequate resources and local support to continue the beneficial aspects of this innovative demonstration program.

Given the realities of developing grant applications, especially a short time to develop, write, and submit the applications (fewer than 2 months during the summer), the ways in which these local partnerships were formed and actually functioned at the beginning varied tremendously. For a number of local sites, these partnerships already existed, at least at an informal level. In these sites, the Head Start programs already operated within or in close relationship to the local schools; further, a number of these sites had previously engaged in research or evaluation efforts with local universities concerning similar types of low-income children and families and their school adjustment. These partnership teams have been among the strongest and most effective. For most sites, however, the partnerships were new. Accordingly, the early contributions were more likely to be unequal among the partners, with one partner often taking a lead role in almost all the planning and preparation of the grant. Over time, we, as the directors of the National Transition Study for this multisite trial, have had an exceptional opportunity to both observe and participate in the evolution of these local and national partnerships. We describe aspects of these in greater detail below.

Guiding Principles for Partnerships

Each partnership is distinctive in its focus, its players, and the context in which it was formed and will operate. We strongly advocate that explicit principles be developed to guide and inspire the operation of a partnership. For the University of Alabama at Birmingham (UAB)-Titusville 2000 Project, a set of guiding "operating principles" was proposed, modified, and unanimously endorsed by the original planning committee. These guiding principles have been invaluable in furthering the trust and mutual respect within the partnership and in helping the partnership expand to be inclusive of many diverse individuals from the community and university. These guiding principles make explicit that the partnership serves the needs and goals of both the community and the university. They also identify the reason that the partnership was formed: to enhance the quality of life for the citizens in the Titusville community. These principles, which we think are generalizable to a variety of community-university partnerships, are as follows:

Principle 1: A pledge that there will be joint university and community development of all programs

Principle 2: A commitment to research that benefits both the community and the university

Principle 3: A commitment to programs that make a difference in people's everyday lives

Principle 4: A pledge from the consortium members to continue the partnership for an extended period (specifically, at least until the year 2000)

Principle 5: A belief that, over time, both the community and the university will become better places as a direct result of this partnership of excellence

Principle 6: A hope that the university-community partnership will serve as a model for other urban universities and communities

Figure 2.2 provides a project overview that lists the guiding
principles as they apply to this partnership and shows the work
groups that have been established. We have used this figure locally
to convey in a succinct way the breadth and organization of this
partnership. Collectively, the participants in this partnership wanted
to avoid setting up "committees," but rather wanted true work
groups that were empowered to set their own agendas, raise their
own resources, enact innovative programs as well as support or
enhance existing programs, and evaluate their own progress. The
work groups have been co-chaired by community and university
representatives with interest and experience related to a given
topic. The co-chairs serve on the steering committee and have
primary responsibility for coordinating across work groups. They
also are authorized to invite new people to join their work groups
and participate in activities. From the beginning, the partnership
sought to engage as many people as possible from both the community and the university. The local publicity for the partnership was
substantial, and special events were held to involve more people
and to create a receptive environment for future activities. The
university provided a $150,000 grant to further the partnership,
without requiring an advance budget or a written proposal from
the group or without constraints on how or when the funds would
be spent. Decisions about the use of this investment money have
been made by the steering committee.

Two important subsidiary principles were generated once the
partnership had money: One is that funds raised specifically for this
partnership be shared as equitably as possible, ensuring direct
community control over funds and personnel whenever appropriate
and vice versa; and the other is that the partnership have a visible
and daily presence in the community, as well as a home within the
university. Specifically, a full-time community coordinator has a
community-based office and staff, co-located with other valued
neighborhood initiatives and programs, whereas the university
home is currently distributed across three interdisciplinary centers—the Center for Health Promotion in the School of Public
Health, the Center for Urban Affairs in the School of Social and
Behavioral Sciences, and the Civitan International Research Center
devoted to the study of human development. At this stage, more
than 20 identified projects have been launched with a combination
of external funding and volunteer time. In 1996, the Department

A Lifespan, Intergenerational Perspective on Improving Quality of Life for Families in an Urban Community

---

Guiding Principles

- Joint UAB-Titusville development of all programs

- A commitment to research that benefits both the community and the university consortium

- A commitment to programs that make a difference in people's everyday lives

- A pledge from the consortium members to continue the partnership throughout the 1990s

- A belief that by the year 2000 both UAB and Titusville will be better communities as a result of this partnership for excellence

- A hope that the UAB-Titusville 2000 partnership will serve as a model for other urban universities and communities

Organizing Concepts, Working Groups and Technical Assistance Activities

HOUSING	ECONOMIC DEVELOPMENT	NEIGHBORHOOD REVITALIZATION	INFRASTRUCTURE	HEALTH CARE	JOB TRAINING	EDUCATION	CRIME PREVENTION	PLANNING & COMMUNITY ORGANIZING	RECREATION CULTURE & ARTS
Co-chairs*	Co-chairs*	Co-chairs*	Co-chairs*	Co-chairs*	Co-chairs*	Co-chairs*	Co-chairs*	Co-chairs*	Co-chairs*
Members Comm'y UAB	Members Comm'y UAB	Members Comm'y UAB	Members Comm'y UAB	Members Comm'y UAB	Members Comm'y UAB	Members Comm'y UAB	Members Comm'y UAB	Members Comm'y UAB	Members Comm'y UAB
-Technical Assistance - Projects - Research	-Technical Assistance - Projects - Research	-Technical Assistance - Projects - Research	-Technical Assistance - Projects - Research	-Technical Assistance - Projects - Research	-Technical Assistance - Projects - Research	-Technical Assistance - Projects - Research	-Technical Assistance - Projects - Research	-Technical Assistance - Projects - Research	-Technical Assistance - Projects - Research

TIME: 19...	2000

* All Working Groups are co-chaired by a community resident and a faculty member. Co-chairs of the Working Groups serve on the Steering Committee for the UAB/Titusville 2000 Project.

Figure 2.2. The UAB-Titusville 2000 Project: Operating Principles and Organization of a Community-University Partnership

of Housing and Urban Development (HUD) awarded the UAB-Titusville 2000 Project a Community Outreach Partnership Center as part of a national endeavor to strengthen urban renewal via joint university-community projects with explicit research, outreach, and technical assistance activities.

Over the years, changes have occurred in leadership and staffing, including the retirement of two founding leaders—the university president, Charles "Scotty" McCallum; and the director of the

Center for Urban Affairs, Odessa Woolfolk, who was both a faculty member and someone who had grown up in and was still closely linked to the Titusville community. Yet, the guiding principles remain in place. (A noteworthy aside is that the "retired" individuals continue to be part of the partnership endeavor.) We have had the honor of being part of this partnership from early on and of serving as the coordinating leaders within the university since 1993. The partnership itself also has been expanded to include two local colleges, Miles College and Lawson State Community College, both historically black colleges with strong affiliations with the Titusville community. Among the highest priority needs identified by the community have been those related to children and families, including education, provision of basic health care, and jobs.

The Head Start-Public School Early Childhood Transition Demonstration Program has not developed a national set of guiding principles about the partnership per se. Rather, the local partnerships themselves and the National Transition Consortium have evolved over the years and have changed in ways that recognize the need for open and frequent communication, as well as appropriate representation of the various partners in key decision making that affects the members of the National Transition Consortium.

For example, the National Research Advisory Panel for this program was appointed by the Commissioner of ACYF to advise the National Transition Study. In fact, advice from this panel to the National Transition Study has direct implications for the local studies as well, and contributions from both the local evaluators and the local programs (including Head Start and the public schools) are critical to the operation of this advisory panel. The local partnerships sought to have representation at all advisory panel meetings, which has occurred since the second year of the project. This inclusion has contributed to sharing minutes of these meetings widely within the National Transition Consortium and has led to both greater trust and more informed and timely recommendations. Consensus building has been the implicit operating principle, although the funding agency understandably continues to retain its authority regarding all aspects of the program and evaluation. In retrospect, we think each local partnership might have benefited from developing written principles about how it would operate (some have done this). Similarly, a set of operating principles might have been useful for the National Transition Consortium and for the close working relationship that is required between the National Research Coordinating Team and the local evaluators. Explicit operating principles might have helped avert or minimize some local and national struggles; certainly, they would have facilitated greater clarity of roles and responsibilities.

As in all long-term and large-scale partnership endeavors, the individual players in this 31-site program have changed over time; some local sites have had major turnover in key positions, whereas others have remained constant. The local partnerships also work closely with local governing boards comprised of parents (more than 50%), service providers, and interested citizens. Together, they have launched their transition demonstration projects in ways that build upon local strengths and resources and respond to the most pressing needs of their communities. Some are in urban and inner-city settings; others are in rural or mixed environments. Substantial variation is found in the programs, in the degree to which the programs have been implemented, and in the needs of the participants. Within the next 2 years, information will be available to compare the developmental outcomes for children and families in the demonstration and comparison groups to answer critical questions about the effects of supports and services on the transition-to-school process.

Despite their major differences in mission and funding, both of these partnerships highlight that research itself can inform real-world programs rather than be limited to functioning in a detached or solely critical (evaluative) manner. Similarly, the interdisciplinary scientists affiliated with these projects—more than 200 of them—have repeatedly expressed to us their belief in the value of such partnerships; that is, these partnerships have been instrumental in helping scientists better understand the complexity of forces that shape the lives of children and families and have identified new ways to combine and adapt existing methodologies to better document change processes directly.

Human Dynamics of Partnerships

Agreeing on principles for how a partnership should operate is undoubtedly valuable. Explicit principles, however, do not guarantee that the human dynamics will be free of difficulties. The challenges inherent in community-university partnerships are, in many ways, similar to those faced in business partnerships and in marriages. Much can be learned from assessing partnerships in general, and there are extensive literatures about the human dynamics in both marriages and businesses. The most obvious problems are those that reflect fundamental aspects of human development and social dynamics. In our experience, three highly predictable challenges arise in almost all partnerships, at least for some period of time:

1. The first challenge usually is a perception, often backed by more substantial evidence, that there is not true equity in the control of resources within the partnership. Resources here include not only money but also personnel decisions, allocation of space, and prioritization or timing related to expansion of resources. In partnerships that involve many individuals, this is especially exacerbated because it is rarely feasible for everyone to be involved in every decision. More directly, over time, as partners come to know their own strengths and weaknesses better, a division of responsibilities usually occurs, including shifts in who is responsible for or manages specific aspects of resource allocation.

2. A second and closely linked challenge is the feeling that one or more of the partners are not fulfilling their responsibilities and that the other or others are doing more than their fair share of the work. Successful partnerships have an ebb and flow to this perception and an awareness that uneven distribution of work activities often relates to the skills of the individuals involved, to the high-priority tasks at that time, and/or to outside factors influencing the availability or willingness of one or more of the partners to participate fully. This second challenge is particularly problematic when the situation becomes long-standing or static.

3. The third predictable challenge is that complex feelings of frustration, worry, and pessimism will develop around how to solve the above two challenges; that is, individuals within a partnership often are highly motivated to have the partnership succeed. They understandably become concerned that directly addressing the first two problems may threaten the continuation of the partnership itself.

Both the personalities of the individuals involved and the cultural and political context in which each partnership exists have major significance for how to present, review, and solve these partnership challenges. We have learned that no direct prescription will work for all partnerships. Understanding the key individuals, acknowledging and respecting (to the degree possible) the ethos of the settings in which the partnership operates, and being willing to endure the above, highly predictable strains inherent in partnerships are helpful. Seeking ways to emphasize the partnership's achievements, focusing on the positive aspects of the partnership, and proposing specific solutions in a nonthreatening manner also are sound tactics. We humbly acknowledge that the above is all easier to say than do. The successful partnerships we have enjoyed are attributable largely to the dedication, caring, and good nature of highly talented and mature individuals.

Importance of University Internal Organization, Leadership, Reward Structure, and Public Relations

Interdisciplinary approaches are essential to realizing the goals of almost all community-university partnerships formed to enhance the lives of children and families. This means that universities must be prepared to create and encourage such interdisciplinary alliances in ways that will not be eroded by internal politics or the university's incentive and reward system. Ideally, universities would have ways to recognize successful partnerships and their accomplishments and to reward the people who have played important roles in these partnerships. Scholarship and teaching can be closely intertwined with almost all community-university partnerships, which traditionally have been thought of primarily as service. The partnerships are likely to identify the need for developing innovative ways to learn about problems affecting children, families, and communities, as well as new interdisciplinary research collaborations.

We have argued elsewhere (S. L. Ramey & Ramey, 1995) that it is paradoxical that neither contemporary society nor the modern university functions in recognition of the degree to which the development of children will determine our collective future. Rather, interest in children's development has been dispersed across various agencies and institutions in society and multiple programs, departments, schools, and centers within universities. This dispersion has created within society a remarkable fragmentation and duplication of services in a time of limited resources and high need. Similarly, within universities, a highly compartmentalized knowledge base about children and families has evolved with no obvious way to create a unified understanding of child development and effective means of enhancing the development of the most "at-risk" children. At one level, we can easily list many things wrong with the organization of most modern universities. We know it is another thing to propose a solution for reorganization. Some universities where the "walls" between and among departments and schools are "low" or "permeable" may have no major need to reorganize. Yet, an initiative for universities to engage in self-study and to think creatively about ways to create stronger coalitions among faculty members who share interests is likely to stimulate the formation and maintenance of strong community-university partnerships. Reorganization of universities in terms of what is valued and rewarded and how certain methods of inquiry and topics of study are arrayed is increasingly likely in modern universities. The impetus will be twofold: (a) a vision of the modern university as more involved in the everyday world and in patterns of lifelong learning and (b) a practical adjustment related to limited resources in the present and projected future.

Conclusion

In our own experiences, we have found university-community partnerships to be exciting and rewarding. The excitement has come from participation in scholarly and scientific endeavors grounded in the daily lives of individuals and groups as they endeavor to lead their lives as best as they can. The vantage point of ourselves as participant observers has forced us to broaden and deepen our theoretical and empirical orientations. Similarly, both the university and the communities have been affected by their associations. Those alterations contain several salient benefits and risks. The most prominent risks are:

The possibility of a profound misunderstanding of each other's roles, responsibilities, and limitations with accompanying political acrimony.

The possibility that the partnership will be ineffectual with an accompanying disillusionment about such efforts in the future.

Outweighing these risks, we believe, are potential major benefits of university-community partnerships:

Establishing a multidisciplinary, action-oriented focus on current and future social, economic, and political issues that are vexing most communities today. Such a focus should lead to a more refined and effective knowledge base about how best to support the fundamental building block of all societies: the family.

Developing more useful and powerful conceptual models and accompanying analytic methods to assess complex changes and developments in individuals and groups.

Establishing more immediate feedback loops between knowledge generation and knowledge use such that theory and practice become seamless and mutually reinforcing, thus directly reinforcing the viability of university-community partnerships because both sides benefit from mutual activities.

References

Alexander, K. L., & Entwistle, D. R. (1988). *Achievement in the first 2 years of school: Patterns and processes.* University of Chicago: Chicago Press.

Bertalanffy, L. V. (1975). *Perspectives on general system theory.* New York: George Braziller.

Bronfenbrenner, U. (1979). *The ecology of human development.* Cambridge, MA: Harvard University Press.

Campbell, F. A., & Ramey, C. T. (1995). Cognitive and school outcomes for high-risk students at middle adolescence: Positive effects of early intervention. *American Educational Research Journal, 32*(4), 743-772.

Carnegie Foundation for the Advancement of Teaching. (1991). *Ready to learn: A mandate for the nation.* New York: Carnegie Foundation.

Coie, J., Watt, N., West, S., Haskins, D., Asarnow, J., Markman, H., Ramey, S., Shure, M., & Long, B. (1993). The science of prevention: A conceptual framework and some directions for a national research program. *American Psychologist, 48,* 1013-1022.

Erickson, M. F., & Weinberg, R. A. (in press). Creating the new American outreach university: Building university-community collaboration for the 21st century. In R. Leber & L. K. Simm (Eds.), *The Children, Youth and Family Consortium: A University of Minnesota community partnership.*

Flexner, S. B. (Ed.). (1987). *The Random House dictionary of the English language* (2nd ed. unabridged). New York: Random House.

Garmezy, N. (1983). Stressors of childhood. In N. Garmezy & M. Rutter (Eds.), *Stress, coping, and development in children* (pp. 43-84). New York: McGraw-Hill.

Hinde, R. A., & Stevenson-Hinde, J. (Eds.). (1988). *Relationships within families: Mutual influences.* Oxford, UK: Clarendon.

Keltner, B., & Ramey, S. L. (1993). Family issues. *Current Opinion in Psychiatry, 6*(5), 629-634.

Landesman, S., Jaccard, J., & Gunderson, V. (1991). The family environment: The combined influence of family behavior, goals, strategies, resources, and individual experiences. In M. Lewis & S. Feinman (Eds.), *Social influences and socialization in infancy* (pp. 63-96). New York: Plenum.

Lewis, M. (1982). The social network systems model: Toward a theory of social development. In T. Field, A. Huston, H. C. Quay, L. Troll, & G. E. Finley (Eds.), *Review of human development* (pp. 180-214). New York: John Wiley.

McCall, R. B. (1993). A guide to communicating through the media. In K. McCartney (Ed.), *An insider's guide to providing expert testimony before Congress* (pp. 16-24). Ann Arbor, MI: Society for Research in Child Development.

Miller, J. G. (1978). *Living systems.* New York: McGraw-Hill.

Ramey, C. T. (1995). *The scientific framework for a prevention program.* Panel Presentation, 119th Annual Meeting of the American Association on Mental Retardation, San Francisco.

Ramey, C. T., Bryant, D. M., Sparling, J. J., & Wasik, B. H. (1984). A biosocial systems perspective on environmental interventions for low birth weight infants. *Clinical Obstetrics and Gynecology, 27,* 672-692.

Ramey, C. T., Bryant, D. M., Wasik, B. H., Sparling, J. J., Fendt, K. H., & LaVange, L. M. (1992). The Infant Health and Development Program for Low Birthweight, Premature Infants: Program elements, family participation, and child intelligence. *Pediatrics, 89,* 454-465.

Ramey, C. T., MacPhee, D., & Yeates, K. O. (1982). Preventing developmental retardation: A general systems model. In J. M. Joffee & L. A. Bond (Eds.), *Facilitating infant and early childhood development* (pp. 343-401). Hanover, NH: University Press of New England.

Ramey, C. T., & Ramey, S. L. (1992). *At risk does not mean doomed* (National Health/Education Consortium Occasional Paper #4). Washington, DC: Institute for Educational Leadership, National Commission to Prevent Infant Mortality.

Ramey, C. T., & Ramey, S. L. (1994). Which children benefit the most from early intervention? *Pediatrics, 94,* 1064-1066.

Ramey, C. T., Ramey, S. L., Gaines, R., & Blair, C. (1995). Two-generation early interventions: A child development perspective. In S. Smith (Ed.), *Two-generation programs: A new intervention strategy: Vol. 9. Advances in applied developmental psychology* (pp. 199-228). Norwood, NJ: Ablex.

Ramey, S. L., & Ramey, C. T. (1992). Early educational intervention with disadvantaged children: To what effect? *Applied and Preventive Psychology, 1,* 130-140.

Ramey, S. L., & Ramey, C. T. (1995). *Overview of the National Transition Demonstration Study.* Washington, DC: Administration on Children, Youth, and Families.

44   CHILDREN AND YOUTH

Rutter, M. (1985). Resilient in the face of adversity: Protective factors and resistance to psychiatric disorder. *British Journal of Psychiatry, 147,* 598-611.

Sameroff, A. J. (1983). Contexts and development: The systems and their evolution. In W. Keesen (Ed.), *History, theories, and methods: Vol. 1. U.S. handbook of child psychology* (pp. 237-294). New York: John Wiley.

Schorr, L. B., & Schorr, D. (1988). *Within our reach: Breaking the cycle of disadvantage.* New York: Anchor.

Werner, E. E., Bierman, J. M., & French, F. E. (1971). *The children of Kauai: A longitudinal study from the prenatal to age 10.* Honolulu: University Press of Hawaii.

• CHAPTER 3 •

Youth and Families in the Inner City: Influencing Positive Outcomes

GERALDINE K. BROOKINS

ANNE C. PETERSEN

LISA M. BROOKS

In this chapter, we provide a detailed essay of inner-city families in relation to development of children and youth. We focus primarily on African American families because they comprise a disproportionate percentage of inner-city dwellers and are the subjects of most studies of inner-city life. We pay particular attention to the social structure in which the urban family is embedded today as compared with 20 to 30 years ago. We then examine how the composition of social relations gives rise to family structure, contexts, strategies, and legacies. We propose that it could be more productive to frame a discussion of inner-city families from the perspective of strengths to be drawn on than from only the problems encountered. We conclude with recommendations regarding theory, policy, and practice.

Current State of Knowledge

Dramatic demographic change in the United States has reduced the traditional two-biological-parent family households to only 25.5% demanding more information on other types as effective socializing units and systems for the healthy development of their children and youth. Although this concern covers a broad base of socioeconomic strata, ethnic and racial groups, and regions of the United States, there is little doubt that the group evoking the most concern and attention is that of families and especially children residing in the inner cities of large metropolitan areas. Although most cities served as critical contexts for the industrialization of the United States during the late 19th and early 20th centuries, the economy became less dependent on national industry during the latter half of the 20th century. The economy is increasingly dependent on market forces around the globe and is based less on physical, often unskilled labor than on information technology and service-related skills. Some have argued that this deindustrialization left inner cities devoid of a social and cultural capital infrastructure from which remaining families could draw. Consequently, these once vital centers of activity for all aspects of life are now characterized as cauldrons for a plethora of ills including crime, violence, illegitimacy, educational deficit, and disease, both mental and physical. Thus, the residents in these centers are viewed often as the carriers of these ills. Importantly, families continue to have the responsibility of raising children and youth who are expected to become, over time, competent, contributing, well-rounded adults. Is this charge still possible, given the untold contextual obstacles thrust before them?

At the dawning of the 21st century, inner-city families are viewed, at best, as problematic. In many cities, the unemployment rate soars above the national average; households are typically headed by females with few skills corresponding with labor force demands; many mothers not only lack skills for the labor force but also are characterized as deficient in their abilities to nurture and protect their children in order to promote healthy developmental outcomes. Often, the mothers have not reached adulthood themselves and are identified as "children raising children." Males present an equally pessimistic profile. Residents in many inner-city neighborhoods do not include employed males. According to sociologist William Julius Wilson (1987), adult males are nearly absent in some neighborhoods. As the developmental literature suggests, fathers serve a critical role in the development of their children. The extant literature on inner-city families points to the ongoing physical and emotional absence of fathers as a typical experience in the lives of children and youth and offers depressing and distressing predictions for those children's developmental trajectories across the life course, including lives replete with crime and incarceration, welfare dependency, disease, and truncated life spans.

In general, today's inner-city youth are seen as being at high risk for a host of negative developmental outcomes. In some school districts, a mere 50% of youth graduate from high school. School dropout presents its own set of downwardly spiraling consequences. High school dropouts earn considerably less than do their high school graduate peers and less than half of what college graduates are likely to earn in their lifetimes (Annie E. Casey Foundation, 1996). High school dropouts are also more likely to experience poverty than are those who complete high school. While in school, many inner-city elementary and middle school children fall far below the national means on standardized tests for reading and mathematics achievement. Violence among youth is approaching epidemic proportions. Although no part of the nation appears immune to this phenomenon, it seems more heightened in the inner cities, with gang violence, rising homicide rates, and drug-related crimes. Nationally, the juvenile violent arrest rate has increased, with a significant proportion of those arrests occurring in inner cities.

Although the birthrate among African-American adolescent girls in the inner city has declined while increasing among European American girls, the numbers and consequences are still significant in both cases. Today, motherhood among single adolescents portends a life of poverty with associated negative outcomes for mothers and children. Young mothers are less likely to complete high school, to be employed, and to have requisite skills for competent parenting. Research studies indicate that children of single teenage mothers are more likely to drop out of school, to give birth out of wedlock, and to be welfare dependent than are those children with two parents. Decades ago, many of these outcomes were moderated by marriage or extended family relations. For example, earlier studies (Kellam, Ensminger, & Turner, 1977), in which 84 forms of family structures were identified, noted that alternative family structures, such as mother-grandmother, tended to be as effective as mother-father family structures in minimizing risk for social maladaptation among school-age children. More recent studies (Hatchett, Cochran, & Jackson, 1991) suggest that alternative family structures are not likely to substantially increase family income in today's economy, a stressor that ultimately affects social and psychological well-being and life chances among all family members, but especially among children and youth.

The condition of African-American males tends to be somewhat more problematic. Young African-American males have been disproportionate victims of drug-related crimes both as perpetrators and as victims. Males between the ages of 15 and 24 are more likely to die from homicide than from any other means. In their lifetimes, one in three African-American males are likely to be involved in the criminal justice system whether by arrest, incarceration, or probation. They are also victims in the educational process. A decade ago, African-American males between the ages of 10 and 15 were 2 or more years behind their grade level (Mincy, 1994), and evidence suggests that the trend has continued into the 1990s. This phenomenon serves as a precursor to dropping out of school and subsequent poor labor market opportunities.

The problems we have highlighted have been studied from several perspectives examining root causes as residing in individuals, specific kinds of families, and community composition. Some suggest that young inner-city females get pregnant purposely to feel loved or wanted (Musick, 1993); others propose that because of family dysfunction, youth in the inner city are without moral values, lack discipline, and do not know how to delay gratification and therefore get into trouble attempting to satisfy either material desires or ego needs; and still others focus on the social structure of communities (Orfield & Ashkinaze, 1991) as a significant influence on the negative outcomes for many inner-city youth. Importantly, each perspective takes a problem-focused approach in its discussion of inner-city youth and families. Is this approach warranted? Is it historically consistent? What data are missed by employing this approach solely? In the next section, we explore the nature of the inner-city family within a historical context.

Contextualizing the Urban Family

Historically, urban environments have been viewed as places of opportunity for foreign-born and rural migrants (see Katz, 1995, for extensive review). In the 1920s, waves of immigrants and former rural residents migrated to the industrial cities to make a better life through employment in low-skilled jobs. As each successive group became more assimilated into the mainstream economy and institutions, it moved up the socioeconomic ladder and often out into housing that was less racially and ethnically segregated. This process became an established pattern of spatial and temporal assimilation and mobility for urban dwellers (cf. Brookins, 1991). During the 1940s, as a result of a significant need for semiskilled and unskilled labor in burgeoning industries, a notable wave of African Americans from the rural South moved to Northern cities to fill those positions and to pursue a more humane quality of life as compared with that experienced in the deep South. Arguably, the established pattern of spatial and temporal assimilation and mobility was foreclosed for the majority of these urban immigrants.

A confluence of factors occurred around the same broadly defined time period that seems to have influenced the nature of inner-city life in the latter half of the 20th century. These factors shaped the social structure of the present inner city and provided a template for the evolution of the social relations currently observed in inner cities across the United States. Beginning in the 1960s, subsequent to civil rights legislation, some African Americans who managed to move up the rungs toward middle-class status also moved out of the ghettos into more desirable residential housing. This migration of skilled human capital, both African American and European American, however, transpired concurrently with structural changes occurring in a postindustrial economy. This concurrence required different and more differentiated technical skills, which in effect precluded numbers of individual residents lacking the requisite educational background from entry into higher-paying jobs (Brookins, 1991). Concomitantly, some employers moved their companies out of the central city, where other than public transportation was required to get to work. This shift in job location is associated with a subsequent labor-force detachment among young African-American men. Also, according to some (e.g., Wilson, 1987), the out-migration of skilled laborers and the professional class left the inner city lacking in the social capital necessary to maintain viable communities.

Another important factor influencing the state of today's inner city came in the form of housing policies. Rules regarding mortgage eligibility effectively prevented African Americans from receiving mortgages insured by the Federal Housing Administration (Weir,

1995). Additionally, public housing policies served to ensure that public housing would be located in the inner city, rather than be distributed more broadly in areas outside the city. Many low-income African Americans had no other choice than to remain in already crowded areas of the inner city.

Other policies also affected the day-to-day lives of inner-city families. When Aid to Families With Dependent Children (AFDC) was initially put forth, it was intended for widows with young children because conventional wisdom at the time dictated that mothers needed to stay at home with their children. Over time, women who had never married became recipients of AFDC benefits. Although other factors, such as large numbers of women entering the workforce, increases in welfare benefits, and reduced employment opportunities for males, are credited for the prevalence and growth of mother-only families, conventional wisdom suggests that the nature of AFDC itself contributed to this phenomenon. Importantly, during the 1960s, among several reforms in welfare policy and public concern for "deserving" recipients, the eligibility requirements for AFDC mandating single status for women were more stringently enforced. Thus, coupled with the male detachment from the labor force, it would seem that women had been provided incentives for remaining single.

Within the past 40 years, the context of family development has changed markedly in the United States among many segments of the population. Included in this context are dramatic increases in divorce rates, the number of dual-working families, and increased numbers of mothers with young children in the labor force. Structural transformations of the cities posed consequences for family formation and development as evidenced by increasing proportions of mother-only households, teenage childbearing, high rates of unemployment, rising delinquency, and poor educational outcomes. Important to this discussion of families is that change in family functioning relative to social structural parameters is not new. What is different in many inner cities is the number and density of impoverished families who seem to be (a) increasing rapidly, (b) steeped in persistent poverty, and (c) restricted in mobility, in part, because of low educational attainment and lack of job opportunities. The inner city had been perceived as a transitional setting for many groups during the 19th and early 20th centuries. Unfortunately, a confluence of factors has made it a permanent and isolated setting for many children, youth, and families of color.

Amid these ecological niches, however, are variations among families. Some families scarcely eke out an existence materially, spiritually, and psychologically, whereas others manage somehow to elevate themselves, surmount risk factors associated with living in the inner city, and navigate these realities from a reservoir of resilience. In the next section, we examine varying family processes and developmental outcomes for urban adolescents.

Families, Neighborhoods, and Differential Developmental Pathways

Research on youth has begun to integrate social and psychological perspectives to understand how youth behavior is influenced by their families, schools, and neighborhoods (e.g., Petersen, 1988). The integration of context effects with human development is especially important for examining inner-city youth. In the past, research on these populations, and especially minority populations, has been primarily the province of sociology, with a problem-oriented focus. Conversely, human developmental research has used largely white, middle-class populations of subjects and has focused on positive development, rather than on problems (Spencer & Dornbusch, 1990). The resulting combination of knowledge tells us relatively little about the populations and issues of focus here (see especially Spencer & Dornbusch, 1990). Research now emerging using a contextual developmental perspective will dramatically improve this situation. To date, however, we have learned where models and theories do not work and relatively little about how context influences development in the inner city. But we shall attempt to discuss the extant literature nonetheless.

Both the family and the community, construed as the neighborhood for urban youth, may be important for adolescent development. Although the family has traditionally been considered the most important context, recent research suggests that the neighborhood becomes increasingly important with age for poor youth, especially males. Both families and neighborhoods are discussed in turn. Given the importance of urban schools in the lives of inner-city youth, an entire section of this volume is devoted to that topic. Thus, while recognizing the potential intersecting influences of school, neighborhood, and family contexts on adolescent development, we leave that discussion to our colleagues.

Families

Both poverty and growing up in a family headed by a single mother are risk factors for negative adolescent outcomes. African-American adolescents are more likely to be poor than are adolescents in any other ethnic group, and the rate of poverty is increasing among African-American families. Indeed, poor African Americans constitute 45% of all African-Americans under 18 years of age, and 57% of poor African-American adolescents and 54% of nonpoor African-American adolescents live in inner-city neighborhoods (Dryfoos, 1990). Studies have also focused on family factors that protect youth. Clark (1983) studied influences on school achievement of African-American adolescents growing up in poor neighborhoods and found that parents of high-achieving youth were nurturing and supportive, established clear role boundaries, monitored their children's activity in the home and in the community, consistently enforced rules, engaged their children in various learning activities, and supported social and academic learning. This description sounds similar to the description of authoritative parenting, but Steinberg and colleagues (Steinberg, Lamborn, Dornbusch, & Darling, 1992) found that parental authoritativeness was unrelated to school performance of both Asian-American and African-American students, although this factor was predictive for Hispanic and Caucasian students. This study also found, however, that low peer support for achievement among African-American youth undermined parental authoritativeness.

Recent theorizing (Scott-Jones, 1996) suggests that urban families hold five basic goals for their children:

1. *Achievement*—placing high value on education and schooling
2. *Social relations and socioemotional health*—wanting their children to have good social skills with appropriate emotional regulation
3. *Physical health*—desiring their children to be healthy and safe from harm

4. *Moral behavior*—wanting their children to develop a sense of right and wrong
5. *Identity*—wanting their children to develop a sense of positive identity and self-worth, including positive outlooks on ethnic identity

Scott-Jones notes that these goals are not appreciably different from those of white, middle-class parents living in the suburbs. What is different are the external circumstances that may limit urban families in developing effective strategies for achieving those goals.

Neighborhoods

The body of research on community effects demonstrates that minority or poor neighborhoods are more likely to have higher crime rates (with residents both more frequently perpetrators and victims), higher rates of out-of-wedlock births, more racial discrimination, higher rates of drug abuse, and lower educational attainment. Interestingly, both African-American and European-American males appear to have better outcomes when they live in neighborhoods with the other racial group. The recent generation of developmental neighborhood studies has produced some confusing and mixed results (see Coulton, 1996). Identification of the best methods may be needed before replication yields clarity in the results. It is interesting to note that neighborhoods appear to have only weak effects with middle-class youth, with the evidence suggesting that, for them, a higher level of community aggregation has influence on, for example, job opportunities.

Differential Pathways

Recent research demonstrates that concepts of adolescent development may not hold for these populations. As demonstrated dramatically in such books as *There Are No Children Here* (Kotlowitz, 1991) and *Amazing Grace* (Kozol, 1995), growing up in very adverse circumstances requires children to work hard and respond effectively to challenges and does not permit them to develop "normally" in more protected circumstances. The resulting adult may not necessarily be less well off but will be different from one who had the luxury of a protected childhood. For example, Burton (Burton, Obeidallah, & Allison, in press) documents from her research the ways in which the poor African-American child is likely to traverse a different developmental path from those children described in the current "normative" developmental literature. The families of these children have different expectations for them than do other social institutions such as schools. According to Burton, the developmental pathways of poor African-American children differ not only in nature but also in timing and pace of events in the life course.

It is likely that the major societal impediment to successful development, in conventional terms, is that adult work roles are severely constrained for these youth, especially for males. Whereas in the past, lower-income youth could become successful breadwinners through employment as unskilled workers, these jobs have now largely disappeared from the United States, and especially from the inner city. The people- or technology-intensive jobs that are available require education, and education is limited for these youth because of the inadequate state of many inner-city schools and because of the negative effects that structural factors inflict on students (Fine, 1991). Therefore, some young people look to the illegal job markets (e.g., drug trade) or to federal aid. Even the traditional role of the military in helping lower-income youth acquire needed skills has dramatically diminished as an opportunity for all youth, and especially for those who have not completed high school with the basic skills of literacy and numeracy.

Restricted opportunity for inner-city families has also led to an increased focus on the present rather than the future among these young people. Simply surviving in the inner city is viewed by these families as evidence of successful developmental outcome (Burton et al., in press). In addition, high value is placed on youth developing the skills to contribute in positive ways to family and community well-being even if these do not bring the usual resources of money. For example, Burton et al. (in press) found that some youth were considered by their families and communities to have successfully achieved adulthood if they were able to facilitate family cohesion, negotiate with social institutions for elderly family or community members, or serve as peacemakers for the community.

These important family and community roles may conflict with other social institutions, especially those that represent the majority culture. For example, schools frequently assume that children are cared for by their parents and that being schooled is the children's full-time responsibility. But inner-city children may have significant responsibilities for the care of younger children or older family members. Tremendous responsibility may be placed on even young children, compromising their time and energy available for school. If school personnel do not understand and appreciate this conflict, they may evaluate absence, distractedness, or fatigue as laziness or disinterest.

Some researchers (e.g., Jarrett, 1995) have identified, also within the inner city, "community-bridging" families with characteristics that promote social mobility among poor African-American adolescents. The activities of these community-bridging families serve as a conduit to opportunities in the larger society. Jarrett has identified five characteristics of youth social mobility outcomes:

1. Parents provide their youth a broad opportunity base through kinship networks. This network supplies the youth greater coverage in terms of care and resources, as well as economic assets. Regarding adolescent girls and pregnancy, the kinship network emphasizes completing school, obtaining economic independence, and foregoing the advent of more children. Another strategy is restricted family-community relations; family life is confined to community members who have the same lifestyle ideals as the community-bridging family.

2. Symbolic and physical barriers are constructed around the family to exclude community members whose lifestyle is not in keeping with the community-bridging family's mainstream emphasis. Stringent parental monitoring strategies are critical for the community-bridging family.

3. Parents are watchful over their youth's time, space, and relationships. There is constant monitoring of the adolescent's friends in an attempt to encourage friendship with youth who are "worthwhile."

4. These parents seek to involve children in school and church activities that may enhance mobility opportunities and skills.

5. Similar to findings in Burton's work, youth assume adult-level responsibility in the household. They are expected to contribute through household chores such as cooking and cleaning and financially through part-time work. The expectations and responsibilities have the effect of bolstering self-esteem and bringing the family together as a unit.

As noted earlier, the life course of inner-city youth is likely to be quite different from that of their more affluent age-mates. For example, African Americans have a shorter life expectancy than do European Americans by 7 years for men and 6 years for women. Poor African Americans have especially high mortality rates in childhood and adolescence. Burton et al. (in press) report that poor African Americans anticipate that males especially are likely to die before age 21. This perception is based on experience; among the families in their research, every one had had at least one male die or be incarcerated before the age of 21. Evidence also suggests that the development of poor African Americans is accelerated both biologically and socially with earlier parental or family responsibilities. Therefore, some poor African-American youth may skip major developmental adolescent tasks entirely even though adult work roles are constrained for many.

Wilson (1987) has argued that social isolation in many poor African-American communities has resulted from the departure of middle- and working-class families from these neighborhoods. Further, traditional social institutions such as the church have weakened in these communities, removing what had been a buffer for the inhabitants. Thus, urban, poor youth have few positive role models. Current research testing these and other hypotheses should illuminate the processes by which some young people reach successful adulthood whereas many others experience significant difficulties or fail to reach that age at all. Spencer, Cole, Dupree, Glymph, and Pierre (1993) have suggested, appropriately, that as there are multiple pathways to negative outcomes, "there are multiple pathways to resilient outcomes and competence irrespective of exacerbating environmental constraints" (p. 737).

Reframing the Realities

The inner city has come to be understood as a conglomerate of hopelessly dysfunctional families condemned to spawn a new generation of dysfunctional youth who, in turn, will reproduce dysfunctional families. Viewing the inner city in this way—as a monolithic dysfunctional community—has certain policy repercussions for its inhabitants. In this section, we explore this inner-city family stereotype and the consequences that its perpetuation has had for families and youth. We also examine the larger ideology of the

American family and how this ideology both constricts and limits mobility and opportunity for families residing in the inner city.

The characterization of the inner-city family as dysfunctional is largely limited, but not completely so, to African-American people and is a by-product of how norms are promulgated that often redirect and bias fields of inquiry. The lens through which the researcher approaches social phenomena dictates what might be seen, understood, and addressed. Politics notwithstanding, arguably the inability to reduce the seeming intractable problems of inner-city life may be exacerbated by research paradigms generally employed in this arena.

Some researchers working to understand the urban or inner-city family note that a problem with previous research has been reliance on a standardized family model. A researcher who explored this issue (Smith, 1993) labeled this research model the "standard North American family," or "SNAF"—a conceptual tool that establishes a widely used definition of family. According to Smith, the model from which research typically begins represents the typical household as a married heterosexual couple: The male is the primary wage earner; the female, if employed, is the supplemental wage earner. In other words, the model family in research is the two-parent, middle-class, nuclear family. Using this model as the normative point of departure for family research casts a discriminatory lens on those families who do not fit or measure up to this "traditional" picture.

This standardization also encompasses adolescent research. Several authors note that white, middle-class youth are the likely comparison group in this field of inquiry (Ford, 1992; Jarrett, 1995; Phelan, Yu, & Davidson-Locke, 1994). Having white, middle-class, two-parent families and youth as comparison groups of family and adolescent research may initiate a biased approach to understanding how families function in the context of cultural and ecological imperatives. It is likely that research taking the two-parent, nuclear family or the white, middle-class adolescent as its normative point of departure will find other family structures or youth anomalous rather than different. For example, this socially constructed universal measure, by definition, suggests that a single-parent, African American or any other minority-status family is held to a standard not always plausible, often because of experiences within the larger social structure beyond these families' control (e.g., discrimination).

Smith's (1993) SNAF theory also notes the gender-specific discriminatory practice of family research, particularly as it relates to single-parent families. According to Smith, because of a dearth in research regarding male-only-headed families, women are specifically and negatively implicated in the SNAF model. These models persist even after many researchers have noted glaring discrepancies of this characterization of family and youth. Mornell (1979) suggests that the attempt by social scientists to maintain an ahistorical and apolitical posture in their research endeavors accounts for some of this persistence. Mornell suggests that social science is married to dominant cultural and political values and is a tool to support those values. Understanding that social science is a historically and politically grounded endeavor that "may also reflect a [researcher's] specific cultural reality with a circumscribed epistemology" (p. 307) is a way to begin to get at the persistent reliance on the model family and adolescent stereotype.

Recognizing the lack of understanding of how different family structures function in specific ecocultural niches and under adverse conditions elicits the use of different methodological tools. Ethnographers have been especially helpful in identifying what meaning inner-city families draw from their subjective experiences and how those meanings give rise to certain forms of behaviors, coping mechanisms, and strategies. According to Jarrett (1995), whose work focuses on low-income African-American youth, the use of qualitative data enables design of more effective, long-term programs targeted at low-income African-American youth. She finds that quantitative studies that are typically used to inform program design do not provide a full assessment of family life behaviors. Phelan et al. (1994) asserted that many studies start with the assumption that certain ethnicity or family socioeconomic status places youth "at risk." Their own work takes the perspective of youth as the point of departure and includes youth from all walks of life in an attempt to cultivate a more holistic understanding of adolescent life. Furthermore, their methodology relies on a generic rather than race-, class-, or gender-specific framework that they propose allows for illumination of diversity within groups.

Ramondo (1991) explores white, middle-class, Western family bias in family therapy and how that bias tends to neglect the cultural standpoint of the nonwhite client. The work is illustrative in that it assesses the role that culture plays in epistemology and subsequently in practice. Although Ramondo's work centers on family therapy, his assertions regarding how cultural oppression can have negative consequences for diagnosis and treatment are useful because they can apply to research and social policy when addressing issues among diverse populations.

The culture of an ethnic group—the code that enables people in a community to live and work together and provides the rules that allow people to make sense of the world—informs its epistemology. Culture determines normalcy; it influences and dictates what will be understood as, for example, family organization. It also determines what is considered a problem or a deviation from the norm and what procedures will be used to solve that problem. Ramondo suggests that, to optimize family practice therapy, therapists acknowledge their cultural location and prejudices and also recognize the biases in therapy theory and practice. These suggestions also can be applied to family and youth research.

It is difficult for people who have not experienced long-term poverty, racism, social contempt, police brutality, and political neglect to fathom the kind of deprivation that structures people's struggle for psychic survival and self-esteem in U.S. inner cities. Research efforts typically present a bleak picture of the inner city, its families, and the consequences of both of these factors for adolescent development. Little mention is given to the larger socioeconomic factors that give rise to the many problems of the inner city. The problems that inner-city families manage are seldom viewed as systemic barriers and obstacles to a mainstream notion of success. Nor are they typically viewed as the ubiquitous limits for poor or lower-class people, minorities, and women present in the form of racism, classism, or sexism.

Inner-city families and adolescents must manage a reality that falls outside the traditionally defined normative reality. As pointed out earlier in this chapter, these families do navigate this reality, many times with positive outcomes, using such tactics as extended kinship networks and community bridging. Conventional strategies for success (e.g., encouraging education as a path to mobility) that are fruitful for some in the dominant European-American middle-class world are not always evident in the inner city. How some African-American youth perceive and respond to the mainstream U.S. educational system helps illuminate how reliance on a conventional idea of success and path to mobility is problematic in research focusing on "nonstandard" families and youth.

Ford (1992) suggests that social injustice is widely believed to be conquerable through success in the educational system. Theories regarding achievement motivation propose that motivation to achieve increases when expectations are attainable. Through the use of one-on-one interviews with young, African-American, urban students, Ford discovered that the "American achievement ideology" holds lackluster appeal in the early-adolescent African-American community. Although these students acknowledge and agree that hard work is necessary to become socially and economically mobile, they admit that they often do not work as hard as they could or should. As Ford proposes, the more aligned one is with this ideology, the more likely one is to "succeed" in the dominant system. Support of the achievement ideology is difficult for African-American youth who experience a social, cultural, and psychological world that often does not promote an acceptance of this ideological construct. In the African-American adolescent community, many forces are at odds with the achievement ideology, including psychological factors (e.g., lowered self-esteem and increased fear of success, self-contempt, and isolation that comes with the onset of adolescence), societal constraints (e.g., racism, discrimination), and cultural factors. Many of the tenets of urban African-American culture conflict with dominant (European-American) culture. This conflict can leave some African-American students with the dilemma of living in and managing two worlds at once as they navigate the dominant educational system. Pursuing education is often viewed as part of "white" culture; to reject it is to reject subscribing to that culture, thereby avoiding being viewed as abandoning "African American." Further, some African-American students forego achievement in order to maintain cultural ties and not be characterized by peers and community as rejecting African-American culture. An interesting finding of this work was that gifted children are especially troubled by and reactive to the achievement ideology. The work of Spencer and colleagues (Spencer, Cunningham, & Swanson, 1995; Spencer & Swanson, 1991, 1996; Spencer, Swanson, & Cunningham, 1991) on identity processes and their interactions with mastery and achievement for adolescent African Americans provides a broader conceptual framework for findings such as those in Ford's work.

Prescribing education as a way to success is not always tenable, given that minorities in urban/inner-city areas start out with poorer educational chances (e.g., smaller tax base of poor school districts, which influences lowered educational quality) and obtain fewer opportunities to have their educational pursuits rewarded because of the institutionalized discriminatory practices within the larger system. The lack of regard for educational achievement may result from interpretations these youth have made with respect to discrimination and life chances, rather than from laziness or inability. Resentment, defiance, and resistance toward the status quo exhibited by these youth can be construed as contextually appropriate.

Perception of the inner-city family is filtered through a standardized definition. This normative model of family—two-parent, white, middle-class—often is antagonistic to other family structures, minorities, and classes. Just like research efforts that find "nonstandard" families and youth problematic from the outset, research that begins with a standardized setting in mind can only find the inner-city community to be aberrant and the tactics used to navigate the circumstances of the inner city lacking. The inner-city family is less likely to fit the parameters of standardized models that are consistently employed in family and adolescent research. As we have emphasized, the inner city today bears little resemblance to that of even 40 years ago. Assessing family relations and adolescent development without addressing the context in which the behavior occurs will place the science at a disadvantage and perhaps put families and youth at further risk from misguided policies and programs.

As noted earlier, ethnographers (e.g., Burton, Jarrett, Ogbu) and others (e.g., Spencer) have facilitated new understanding about the nuances of living in inner-city environments, how structural factors are experienced by residents, and how families and their youth perceive their worlds and subsequently act on those perceptions. Using the lenses of the residents allows the researcher to explore different hypotheses and conceptualizations about urban life and its influence on developmental trajectories for youth. Ethnographic and other qualitative methods promote paradigmatic shifts and facilitate new quantitative measures. Ethnographic work complements aggregate data. Research now emerging (Spencer & Dupree, in press) tends to reframe, with ecological and developmental conceptualizations, the realities of urban adolescent and family life toward a balance of resilience versus risk, rising expectations versus despair, and competence and success versus failure. Such work allows a more honest appraisal of urban life and facilitates a more targeted approach to prevention and intervention programmatic efforts.

We turn in the last section to identifying a few features of "best practices" from programs designed to address youth, family, and community issues and problems of the inner city. By examining components of exemplars of practice, we illustrate possible approaches toward problem solution. We also make suggestions regarding social science and policy in this section.

Conclusions and Recommendations: Forging New Realities

Many programs across the country try to address the problems of youth and families who reside in U.S. inner cities. Some place emphasis on change within the individual, some focus on family function, and still others address factors affecting social and cultural capital of specific communities. Many programs that have been effective emerged as responses to policy initiated at state, local, and national levels; others emerged from a perceived need within communities. In all cases, components are replicable.

McLaughlin, Irby, and Langman (1994) identified effective nurturing programs in which the program developers demonstrated commitment, respect for youth, and confidence in the untapped capacity of these youth to achieve. These program operatives are often called "wizards" for their perspicacity, ability to capitalize on opportunity, and wondrous outcomes with at-risk youth. An example of someone we identified as a wizard is Joseph Marshall of the Omega Boys' Club in California. Among several programmatic approaches, his understanding of inner-city youth and his use of the radio call-in program, "Street Soldiers," as a means of connecting with inner-city youth, have proved very successful in addressing pressing problems, alerting youth to educational opportunities, and even averting gang warfare (Marshall & Wheeler, 1996). In keeping with our earlier discussion regarding the context of inner-city life, we found that the more effective programs and social services for youth and families were those that drew on the resources identified as being part of youths' social worlds. Importantly, effective programs were focused on youth and their goals, rather than on externally derived goals put forward by policy makers or program developers far removed from the realities of the youths' lives. Programs and activities organized around school, after-school facilities such as Boys' and Girls' Clubs, or YMCAs and YWCAs can reinforce existing interests and enhance particular skills.

Similarly, efforts to provide services to families or parents require acknowledgment of their interests allowing for opportunities to enhance parenting skills. Some citywide programs (e.g., Way To Grow, Minneapolis) build upon the existing strengths and articulated goals of parents to increase human capital and cultural capital within specific neighborhoods. This effort, although designed for parents of young children, sets in place opportunities to minimize and ameliorate the effects of risk across stages of development, including adolescence.

Although we have highlighted those aspects of programs that appear to be more grassroots in nature and form, the role of governmental and business support cannot be overemphasized. For example, the Way to Grow program in Minneapolis, bolstered by catalytic nonprofit organizations such as United Way, is supported by city and county funding and is also partially financed by major corporation and business partners in the surrounding area. These major corporations perceive their participation as an investment in future human capital. As changes in how welfare will be administered in the United States emerge, there will be increasing need for state and local governing entities to ensure that new and promising realities for inner-city youth and their families will be forthcoming even within the context of diminished fiscal resources. Identifying, developing, and sustaining human capital within inner cities may well be one of the more challenging but necessary tasks during the next several decades. Synergistic partnering may be one approach toward that goal. With block grants being the probable primary tool for funding programs, the opportunity should arise to take advantage of best practice knowledge and to creatively meet the needs of families and their youth at risk for unhealthy and nonproductive outcomes. Forging new realities requires individual agency, parental efficacy, community support, and national will. Youth and fami-

lies in the inner cities of the United States can navigate and negotiate negative realities if they perceive purpose in positive pursuits
and receive assistance along the path.

As researchers, we see the need for more research that examines
the diversity of family processes and individual efficacy in inner-city
enclaves. As noted earlier, scant research focuses on normative
development among ethnic minorities. Accordingly, we have often
formulated policy or initiated programs that have not achieved the
desired goals. It is our belief that, too often, both government and
philanthropic organizations move toward addressing problems when
underpinning issues have not been fully understood. Well-designed
research focused on particular issues of the inner city can provide
information toward the development and implementation of successful preventive and interventive strategies designed to address
the realities of inner-city life.

References

Annie E. Casey Foundation. (1996). *Kids count data book*. Baltimore, MD: Author.

Brookins, G. K. (1991). Families in urban environment: Psychosocial, structural,
and policy implications. In M. Lang (Ed.), *Contemporary urban America: Problems, issues, and alternatives*. Lanham, MD: University Press of America.

Burton, L. M., Obeidallah, D. A., & Allison, K. (in press). Ethnographic insights on
social context and adolescent development among inner-city African American
teens. In R. Jessor, A. Colby, & R. Schweder (Eds.), *Essays on ethnography and
human development*. Chicago: University of Chicago Press.

Clark, R. (1983). *Family life and school achievement: Why poor black children
succeed or fail*. Chicago: University of Chicago Press.

Coulton, C. (1996). Effects of neighborhoods on families and children: Implications
for services. In A. Kahn & S. Kammerman (Eds.), *Children and their families in
big cities: Strategies for service reform*. New York: Columbia University, Cross-
National Studies Research Program.

Dryfoos, J. (1990). *Adolescents at risk: Prevalence and prevention*. New York:
Oxford University Press.

Fine, M. (1991). *Framing dropouts: Notes on the politics of an urban public high
school*. Albany: State University of New York Press.

Ford, D. (1992). Self-perceptions of underachievement and support for the achievement ideology among early adolescent African Americans. *Journal of Early
Adolescence, 12*(3), 228-252.

Hatchett, S. J., Cochran, D. L., & Jackson, J. S. (1991). Family life. In J. S. Jackson
(Ed.), *Life in black America* (pp. 46-83). Newbury Park, CA: Sage.

Jarrett, R. L. (1995). Growing up poor: The family experiences of socially mobile youth in low-income African American neighborhoods. *Journal of Adolescent Research, 10*(1), 111-135.

Katz, M. B. (1995). *Improving poor people.* Princeton, NJ: Princeton University Press.

Kellam, S. G., Ensminger, M. A., & Turner, R. J. (1977). Family structure and the mental health of children. *Archives of Psychology, 34,* 1012-1022.

Kotlowitz, A. (1991). *There are no children here: The story of two boys growing up in the other America.* Garden City, NY: Doubleday.

Kozol, J. (1995). *Amazing Grace.* New York: Crown.

Marshall, J., Jr., & Wheeler, L. (1996). *Street soldier.* New York: Delacorte.

McLaughlin, M. W., Irby, M. A., & Langman, J. (1994). *Urban sanctuaries: Neighborhood organizations in the lives and futures of inner-city youth.* San Francisco: Jossey-Bass.

Mincy, R. (Ed.). (1994). *Nurturing young black males.* Washington, DC: Urban Institute Press.

Mornell, E. S. (1979). Social science and social policy: Epistemology and values in contemporary research. *School Review, 87*(3), 295-313.

Musick, J. S. (1993). *Young, poor, and pregnant: The psychology of teenage motherhood.* New Haven, CT: Yale University Press.

Orfield, G., & Ashkinaze, C. (1991). *The closing door: Conservative policy and black opportunity.* Chicago: University of Chicago Press.

Petersen, A. C. (1988). Adolescent development. *Annual Review of Psychology, 39,* 583-607.

Phelan, P., Yu, U., & Davidson-Locke, A. (1994). Navigating the psychosocial pressures of adolescence: The voices and experiences of high school youth. *American Educational Research Journal, 31*(2), 415-447.

Ramondo, N. (1991). Cultural issues in therapy: On the fringe. *Australian and New Zealand Journal of Family Therapy, 12*(2), 69-78.

Scott-Jones, D. (1996). *Urban children in family context: Ethnic variations.* Paper presented at the 104th Convention of the American Psychological Association, Toronto, Canada.

Smith, D. E. (1993). The standard North American family: SNAF as an ideological code. *Journal of Family Issues, 14*(1), 50-65.

Spencer, M. B., Cole, S. P., Dupree, D., Glymph, A., & Pierre, P. (1993). Self-efficacy among urban African American early adolescents: Exploring issues of risk, vulnerability, and resilience. *Development and Psychopathology, 5,* 719-739.

Spencer, M. B., Cunningham, M., & Swanson, D. P. (1995). Identity as coping: Adolescent African American males' adaptive responses to high-risk environments. In H. W. Harris, H. C. Blue, & E. H. Griffith (Eds.), *Racial and ethnic identity* (pp. 31-52). New York: Routledge.

Spencer, M. B., & Dornbusch, S. (1990). Minority youth in America. In S. Feldman & G. Elliott (Eds.), *Early adolescents at the threshold.* Cambridge, MA: Harvard University Press.

Spencer, M. B., & Dupree, D. (in press). African American youths' ecocultural challenges and psychosocial opportunities: An alternative analysis of problem behavior outcomes. In D. Cicchetti & S. Toth (Eds.), *Development and psychopathology.*

Spencer, M. B., & Swanson, D. P. (1991). Youth policy, poverty, and African American youths' identity and competency. *Education and Urban Society, 24*(1), 148-161.

Spencer, M. B., & Swanson, D. P. (1996). Developmental considerations of gender-linked attributes during adolescence. In R. Taylor & M. C. Wang (Eds.), *Social and emotional adjustment and family relations in ethnic minority families* (chap. 11). Hillsdale, NJ: Lawrence Erlbaum.

Spencer, M. B., Swanson, D. P., & Cunningham, M. (1991). Ethnicity, identity, and competence formation: Adolescent transition and identity transformations. *Journal of Negro Education, 60*(3), 366-387.

Steinberg, L., Lamborn, S. D., Dornbusch, S. M., & Darling, N. (1992). Impact of parenting practices on adolescent achievement: Authoritative parenting, school involvement, and encouragement to succeed. *Child Development, 63*(5), 1266-1281.

Weir, M. (1995). Poverty, social rights, and the politics of place in the United States. In S. Leibfried & P. Pierson (Eds.), *European social policy* (pp. 329-354). Washington, DC: Brookings Institution.

Wilson, W. J. (1987). *The truly disadvantaged: The inner city, the underclass, and public policy.* Chicago: University of Chicago Press.

CHAPTER 4

Families and the Development of Urban Children

PATRICK H. TOLAN

DEBORAH GORMAN-SMITH

During a series of meetings with a group of inner-city families helping us develop a family intervention, one set of parents explained their delay in arriving by telling the group about the troubles they faced in trying to get their monthly supply of groceries earlier in the day. A friend of a cousin offered to drive them to and from the store for $15, which was less expensive than a cab and much more reasonable than the extra 2 hours of travel that was necessary if they took public transportation to reach a supermarket that did not have inflated prices. When they got out of the car and took the children to a safe place to stand while they got the groceries, however, this person took off with their groceries! Not only were they without food, but they also had to spend the rest of the day tracking down this person and attempting to get their groceries back. Their simple domestic task was suddenly encumbered by a dilemma of seeking out and exacting their justice or foregoing the accompanying danger of such a confrontation and suffering the devastating economic loss. Their weary voices as they

AUTHORS' NOTE: Preparation of this chapter was supported in part by NIMH grants R18MH48034 and RO1MH45936 and by the UIC Great Cities Faculty Scholar Program. Correspondence should be directed to the authors at the Institute for Juvenile Research, The University of Illinois at Chicago, 907 South Wolcott Avenue, Chicago, IL 60612.

told the story, betrayed the difficulties they faced in attempting to cope with the most current of common economic, emotional, and safety threats. Their matter-of-fact presentation and the nodding heads of the other group members revealed how common such stresses and events were for all of them.

This story is one of many that vividly and disturbingly portrays a life dictated by frequent but unpredictable threats and dire consequences for any failing. These intrusions overlay a level of ongoing demands that would strain the capabilities of the most able families. It is a life of struggling to fulfill desires common to most families, to try for the best for their children and to maintain family well-being. It is doing so within a perilous environment, however, with fewer resources and more extreme consequences than faced elsewhere. The coincidence of a stressful daily life exacerbated by frequent crises and faced with limited resources distinguishes family functioning within the inner city from those living elsewhere (Bane & Ellwood, 1989). This chapter is an attempt to provide a synthesizing description of functions and demands that organize inner-city family life and to suggest a conceptual approach that has utility for research and policy.

There is little doubt about the increased risk to children residing in the inner city. Children and youth from these neighborhoods have lower average academic performance, lower rates of high school completion (Kozol, 1992), higher rates of psychopathology and co-occurring multiple types of psychopathology (Tolan, Guerra, VanAcker, Huesmann, & Eron, 1995; Tolan & Henry, 1996), greater probability of serious criminal behavior (National Institute of Justice, 1992), and death from intentional injury (Centers for Disease Control and Prevention, 1992). They have a greater chance of becoming teenage parents (National Commission on Children, 1991) and have greater difficulty obtaining and maintaining regular employment (Jencks, 1992). Similarly, families residing in the inner city are more likely to be single-parent households (Sampson & Lauritsen, 1992) and to face underemployment (Stephens, Foote, Hendershot, & Schoenborn, 1994), irregular employment (Gorman-Smith, Tolan, & Henry, in press), and economic stress (McLoyd, 1990). It is more likely that children have adolescent parents (Crane, 1991), family members incarcerated (Chicago Department of Public Health, 1995), and a parent with alcohol and drug problems (Aday, 1994). In addition, families are more likely to live

in substandard housing, and their children are more likely to attend
inadequate schools (Hernandez, 1993). They are more likely to be
burdened by chronic and serious health problems (Banc & Ellwood,
1989; Hernandez, 1993), with less access to and familiarity with
health care services (Aday, 1994).

We approach understanding this elevated risk by focusing on the
coping demands and functions of families (see Figure 4.1). The
family is conceived as a multidimensional unit that acts on and
reacts to external and internal demands, stresses, and goals (Tolan,
1990). Our prospective approach is based in a systems view that
assumes each family member's beliefs, motivations, and behaviors
are best understood as part of the whole family (Tolan, Gorman-
Smith, Huesmann, & Zelli, in press; Zaretsky, 1976). This approach contrasts with other theoretical perspectives that view the
family as a collection of individuals (Rowe, 1994), as a mere
reflection of parenting practices (Blechman, Tryon, Ruff, & McEnroe,
1989), or as a passive context for individual development (Lytton,
1990). In our opinion, these other approaches, if applied to inner-
city families, will be misleading and oversimplify the problems
faced by families. We focus on the major types of internal and
external demands and potentially stressful forces encountered by
these families and how coping responses can mitigate such stress.
A coping perspective permits recognition of how community context and differences among families transactionally influence development (Sameroff & Feise, 1989; Tolan, Guerra, & Kendall, 1995).
We illustrate these processes as a conceptual model in Figure 4.1.
As illustrated in the figure, understanding coping for an inner-city
family requires consideration of the stressors acting on the family,
the access to resources and skills of the family, the internal limitations of the family, and the goals and desires of the family.

This perspective provides an alternative to two more extreme
perspectives: one being that we cannot use information gained from
studying families living elsewhere to understand families living in
the inner city, and the other being that we do not need to consider
these families as any different from other families. The first perspective assumes that because of the unique nexus of historical,
social, and economic forces, families living in the inner city cannot
be understood by applying information and paradigms developed
with families living elsewhere or at another time (Hardy, 1989).
That inner-city neighborhoods seem to have a unique nexus of

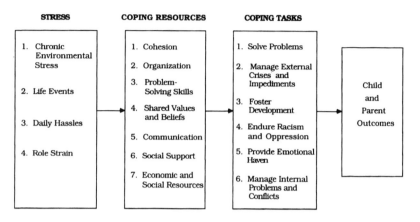

Figure 4.1. Conceptual Model of Family Coping in the Inner City

social problems, economic distress, and low opportunity plus are mostly comprised of ethnic groups facing greater than average prejudice may seem to, by definition, require a unique understanding of families residing there. One reason why this perspective is given credibility is if one attempts, as we have, to review the research literature on families living in the inner city and other urban, poor neighborhoods,[1] one is struck by how few studies can be found that (a) do not focus on pathology, (b) do not apply standards without considering the ecological validity,[2] and (c) do not confound ethnicity and cultural characteristics with poverty and social organization characteristics of these neighborhoods (Parke, 1994). The sparse information available makes any generalization or inferences tentative and prohibits adequate evaluation of the overlap of family functioning and problems in this context to others. Thus, it is unclear to what extent concepts, relations, and developmental pathways focused elsewhere apply to families occupying inner cities. The emerging research however, suggests, considerable overlap in basic processes and functions but variation in challenges and effects (Gorman-Smith, Tolan, & Henry, in press; Gorman-Smith, Tolan, Zelli, & Huesmann, 1996; McLoyd, 1990).

The second extreme perspective is that there is no substantial difference between the problems, needs, and goals of families living in the inner city, compared with families living elsewhere, particularly other impoverished families (Lykken, 1994). Differences are seen as the contrivances constructed by social scientists and misled social reformers (Murray, 1984). Any differences in problems related to the family are considered simply attributable to debilitating social welfare policies, the prevalence of single parents, and/or parental and familial pathology (Lykken, 1994). Those people holding this position suggest that others have faced relative poverty and social inequities equal to or beyond those currently facing inner-city families and have overcome these demands or have not succumbed to the levels of social pathology one sees in today's inner city. The belief is that opportunity structures are adequate and are undermined by disincentives offered to poor families. For example, providing basic economic support (welfare) relates to a disincentive to work and to feel responsibility to provide for one's own family. The disincentives are thought to explain alleged moral and social decay. This view has an appeal of reducing extremely complex and troubling information to a matter of personal resolve and adherence to platitudinal moral bromides. Evidence to support this perspective is drawn from studies that make comparisons of large groups but focus on one or two members of a complex social ecology (e.g., percentage of single parents). Too literal interpretation of marker correlations can seem to support reductionistic explanations (McLanahan & Garfinkel, 1988). More importantly, as with the other extreme view, the lack of sound empirical information on normative and effective functioning of inner-city families prohibits sound, empirically-based refutation or support.

In contrast with either polemic, we believe that the existing empirical evidence and much of the descriptive information on families living in today's inner cities suggest that a single standard approach is unrealistic because all settings do not make the same demands and because some impose more constraints on families than others. Specifically, the inner city seems to be an unusual and recent social setting with particularly deleterious risk impact (Gorman-Smith, Tolan, & Henry, in press; Tolan, Montaini, & Gorman-Smith, 1995; Wilson, 1987). At the same time, it is misleading to underestimate the similarity in day-to-day tasks and goals of families in this society even if the neighborhoods and communities in which they reside vary substantially. In any community, much of family life is about completing mundane tasks and maintaining safety, economic viability, and health (Coontz, 1992). Thus, for example, the perspective taken here recognizes the harmful impact high rates of single parenthood can have on community functioning, as well as the greater economic and parenting challenges that often accompany being a single parent (Florsheim, Tolan, & Gorman-Smith, in press; Sampson & Lauritsen, 1992). The recognition of and focus on the family effects of prevalent single-parent households, however, does not mean that single-parent families are the only cause of problems for those living in the inner city or are pathogenic. Other aspects of family functioning are at work here (Laosa, 1990; McLoyd, 1990; Tolan, Montaini, & Gorman-Smith, 1995). A multidimensional coping perspective is a more sufficient understanding that permits consideration of complex multiple forces affecting behavior. Also, within any setting there is considerable heterogeneity in demands on and skills and resources of residing families even if they share a common characteristic such as single-parent families.

The Concept of Family Coping

Families can vary in the internal and external resources available, the extent to which they provide or accomplish basic family functions, and the extent and specific form of stressors and adaptive tasks they face. Inner-city families face the common and normative demands that other families struggle with but also are encumbered with additional stresses and a more precipitous existence. Thus, their concerns are remarkably similar in many ways to those faced by all families in society, yet they face additional unique problems and concerns.

Although recognized as important, scant research has been done on family coping processes or on the impact of family coping on children's development. Existing theory has most commonly differentiated two major functions of coping: (a) problem solving, which is intended to diminish or remove the cause of stress; and (b) emotion focus, which are attempts to obtain or provide emotional soothing, expression, or adjustment to lessen the distress caused by a stressor (Band & Weisz, 1988; Compas, Worsham, & Ey, 1992; Lazarus & Folkman, 1984; Tolan, Montaini, & Gorman-Smith, 1995). Most studies have found that use of the two dimensions is not independent. The tendency is to use multiple coping responses and to use emotion-focused coping to correlate with use of problem-solving coping (Compas et al., 1992).

The applicability of any of these typologies to residents of the inner city has not been tested until recently. Tolan, Gorman-Smith, Hunt, and Chung (1996) applied confirmatory factor analyses to the coping responses of inner-city adolescents and found responses represented by seven types of coping (seeking support, seeking guidance, seeking distraction, venting emotions, positive thinking, avoidance, and humor). These seven types could be collapsed into two basic dimensions that correspond conceptually to the problem-solving and emotion-focused differentiation found elsewhere. Whether these categories and dimensions can generalize classifying family coping remains to be determined (Compas et al., 1992). However, differentiation of types of family coping into efforts to solve or overcome problems versus efforts to manage the emotional harm and demoralization resulting from stress seems relevant to the tasks facing inner-city families. In addition, the context of the inner city brings to the foreground a distinction between coping responses that are adaptive, meaning they provide momentary relief or short-term problem solving, and those that are competent, defined as those that have longer term beneficial impact. For example, avoiding gang threats by keeping a child home from school is an adaptive response, but the long-term cost of lack of education makes it a less competent response (Tolan et al., in press). Competent responses may be impractical or untenable in an immediate crisis or in considering the constraints of the inner city, whereas immediately adaptive responses may carry long-term costs that eventually overshadow the immediate benefits (Garbarino, Kostelny, & Dubrow, 1991).

We present here the major coping tasks of families in the inner city, distinguishing problem-solving from emotion-focused types.

Problem-Solving Coping

Family as Resource to Members

In facing the contextual and developmental demands of the inner city, children's adaptation and outcome can depend on the extent to which the family can provide access to needed resources and vital sustenance (Elder, Caspi, & Nguyen, 1986; McAdoo, 1982). For example, in our study of inner-city adolescents, we found that seeking help and support from family members was the most common method of coping reported and correlated significantly with levels of depressive and aggressive symptoms (Tolan et al., 1996). This aid can be in the form of problem solving, guidance, or provision of economic and other resources. Similarly, the adaptation and well-being of the family unit depend on its ability to act cooperatively to efficiently problem solve (Reiss, Oliveri, & Curd, 1983). Resourcefulness and adaptability are two characteristics that seem to aid problem solving of inner-city families (Laosa, 1990; McAdoo, 1982). As with other aspects of family functioning, the relative capability of families to coordinate to solve problems may have greater impact in high-risk environments (McLoyd, 1990). For example, in evaluating the impact of parenting style and practices on cognitive functioning of children from low-socioeconomic-status neighborhoods compared with those living in middle-class neighborhoods, Baldwin, Baldwin, and Cole (1990) found that parenting variables accounted for 34% of the variance in child cognitive functioning in the middle-class neighborhoods, but for 75% in the poorer neighborhoods.

Parenting and Coping

The rules and practices used in rearing children comprise the second major aspect of family problem-solving coping. These include discipline methods and values inculcation. The experience of stress and economic distress has been related to parenting practices (Conger et al., 1992; Gorman-Smith, Tolan, & Henry, in press; McLoyd, 1990). The most robustly demonstrated link has been the extent to which parent practices can mediate the impact of economic stress on child functioning (McLoyd, 1988). Although the use of consistent and warm parenting methods seems to lessen children's risk for psychopathology and school failure in the face of economic distress, economic distress consistently relates to poorer parenting (Coll, Meyer, & Brillon, 1995; Conger et al., 1992). Most studies, however, have been conducted with other than inner-city samples. It may be that the parenting style that mediates economic and other risk factors in other settings is not the style that is protective in the inner city. For example, Baldwin et al. (1990) reported restrictive parenting to be more common among the inner-city families in their study, but that this style of parenting was adaptive. The lower-socioeconomic-status children who fared best came from families whose restrictiveness was accompanied by warm and loving indications about why the vigilant and authoritarian parenting views were necessary. Similarly, we found such complex parent-child messages related to risk for adolescent males (Flor-sheim et al., in press). This combination of strong directives and underlying warmth illustrates a differential parenting task for in-ner-city parents; they must remain vigilant and insistent with their children about behavior but do so as an outgrowth of concern (Coll et al., 1995; Mason, Cauce, Gonzales, & Hiraga, in press).

Teaching Coping

Another coping function of families is to teach and model coping methods (Laosa, 1990; Littlejohn-Blake & Darling, 1993; Sameroff & Feise, 1989). In addition to the buffering and refuge from harm that families can provide, inner-city families may enhance the coping of children by teaching them strategies for survival and methods of mutual support and by fighting myths of society (Massey, Scott, & Dornbusch, 1975; Spencer & Markstrom-Adams, 1990). For example, Peters (1976) found that most parents of African-American children expect their child to encounter racism by age 6. Although it was clear that parents saw this as an inevitable stressor to try to prepare their children for, they also reported fears about influencing the children to be overly self-conscious about race and racism. The direct modeling and strategizing about these problems are taught. For inner-city families, critical social and historical understanding of injustices faced can aid children and parents (Lyles & Carter, 1982).

Emotion-Focused Coping

Family as Buffer

Families cope not only by acting as problem-solving units and resources but also by buffering members from external stressors.

For inner-city families, buffering may take the form of protective parenting styles (Clark, 1983; Ogbu, 1985), creating extended family networks (Boyd-Franklin, 1989; Massey et al., 1975), including fictive kin and situational mentors (Taylor, Casten, & Flickinger, 1993), and altering family roles to minimize internal strain due to external stress (Mason et al., in press). In addition, family relation characteristics such as support and cohesion in the face of stress have been related to child functioning (Gorman-Smith, Tolan, & Henry, in press; Hardy, Power, & Jaedicke, 1993; Peters, 1976; Tolan, 1988). Two characteristics noted as particularly important for families struggling with the demands of the inner city are (a) a strong structure with vigilant and restrictive parenting (Baldwin et al., 1990; McAdoo, 1982; McLoyd, 1990) and (b) the development of reliable and effective social ties (Coll et al., 1995; Taylor et al., 1993; Zayas & Solari, 1994). Staples (1978) noted that, historically, African-American families have provided their members with a sanctuary that buttresses against pervasive oppression and racism.

Family as Stressor

The other side of families providing an emotional haven to buffer stress is that the family can be the source of considerable stress for a variety of reasons, including members' psychopathology (Goldstein, 1984), internal conflict (Hetherington, 1984), and chronic health problems (Compas et al., 1992). Families must manage stressors and apply resources strategically to keep such problems from overwhelming other family members and prohibiting any functional behavior. For example, parental psychopathology can seriously impair children's development apart from and in addition to the impact of environmental restraints (Goldstein, 1984; Hetherington, 1984). Importantly, individual coping of children usually occurs within the constraints of family functioning and as part of family functioning. Similarly, marital discord can drain systemic resources and morale so that coping effectiveness is diminished (Hetherington, 1984). It is likely that these problems are more problematic for inner-city families because marital distress and social isolation of parents relate to greater negative influence of economic risk factors (Ray & McLoyd, 1986).

Inner-city families may also face diminished functioning of members as a result of the stressful nature of daily life. Parental distress can limit a parent's ability to aid children with their coping. Parents may need additional support to help shield their children from risk (Coll et al., 1995). For example, Pearlin (1983) reported a correlation between level of life stress events and parental role strain. Acquiring social support, mobilizing the family to seek help, and passive appraisal showed a moderating effect on maternal distress. Acquiring social support, however, was the only response that related to fewer problems in boys, and this same response related to increased problems for girls. Similar results were reported by Myers, Taylor, Alvy, Arrington, and Richardson (1992). They found that high family stress related to maternal psychological distress and that both predicted behavioral problems in inner-city children. Family involvement in shared recreational activities seemed to moderate stress effects for boys but exacerbated problems for girls. These constraints illustrate that the coping of each member must be understood as reflective of and connected with the coping methods and goals of the family (Reiss & Oliveri, 1980). Coping for both families and children becomes oriented toward minimizing actual and potential harm.

These aspects of coping represent major foci of energy and organization for inner-city families. They must cope with internal as well as external sources of distress. They must effectively and efficiently solve problems, negotiate transitions, and maintain the health and well-being of members. They must also manage conditions and events they cannot prevent or control. They face all the concerns, frustrations, and demands that other families in this society face. However, the inner city seems to be a particularly risky setting for children and families: They face not only high levels of common stressors but also some that are limited to this setting.

The Inner City as a Developmental Setting

The elevated risks to children and families living in the inner city are attributed to the coincidence of a deteriorating economic base, the loss of a middle class in these neighborhoods, a rising concentration of social problems, and the ensuing estrangement of the inner-city community from the larger society (Guerra, in press;

Wilson, 1987). Wilson and others have termed the residents of these neighborhoods an "underclass," set apart from the rest of society in terms of access to resources, social interests, and day-to-day concerns, creating a distinct developmental ecology. This ecology can be traced to a poor economic base resulting from the loss of manufacturing jobs in these neighborhoods. The manufacturing industry provided the most common jobs to those living in poorer urban areas prior to the shift in the national economy to service and technical industries. Many residents of the inner city lacked the education and training needed to enter these latter types of positions. The lack of access to jobs, combined with lack of skills, has contributed to spiraling rates of unemployment for urban families (Jencks, 1992). With the middle class leaving these communities, the opportunities for children and youth to interact with economically successful persons of their own ethnicity and backgrounds are lessened. As a result, neighborhood networks were undercut by the lack of this core social group. The accompanying exit of the middle class brought loss of economic support for schools and other community institutions and a rapid deterioration in housing. Inner-city families must not only live in substandard housing but also send their children to schools that have inadequate supplies and demoralized teachers. For example, in the Chicago Public Schools, approximately 5,700 children come to school each day and find they have no teacher (Kozol, 1992).

When such devastating economic and social losses occurred, the level and number of types of social problems increased and concentrated in inner-city neighborhoods. One finds particularly elevated rates of teenage pregnancy, single parents, substance use, violence, and gang activity (Crane, 1991). Children are exposed to unprecedented levels of violence and other stressors (Attar, Guerra, & Tolan, 1994; Garbarino et al., 1991; Gorman-Smith & Tolan, 1995; Schwab-Stone et al., 1995). Families must not only focus limited resources on keeping their children safe from such harm but also helping children cope with the traumatic influence of such exposure (Tolan et al., in press). The co-occurrence of these problems creates a pervasive experience that engenders an ecology of isolation, despair, and danger (Wilson, 1987) and a psychological focus on safety and fear (Fagan, 1994).

Among the social problems imposing on inner-city families, the problem of violence may be particularly pernicious. With crime rates twice that of other urban areas and four times that of rural areas, crime and violence become ubiquitous psychological concerns (Federal Bureau of Investigation [FBI], 1992). The possibility of injury is great; violence is the most likely cause of death of children and youth in these neighborhoods (FBI, 1992). Also, the occurrence of violence is unpredictable (Guerra, in press). Failure to heed this threat or a momentary lapse of vigilance or forgetting can lead to injury or death. Keeping safe can become an organizing principle of managing such mundane concerns as getting to and from school or work and deciding whether or not the children will play outside (Attar et al., 1994; Garbarino et al., 1991). The commonality and unpredictability of violence can lead to a preoccupying vigilance accompanied by blunted emotional reactivity (Garbarino et al., 1991). Thus, rather than assume that children are safe and can have carefree moments, inner-city families need to train children to be on their guard and see such playful moments as dangerously foolish.

Another important effect of this concentration of social problems is isolation from persons in other social and economic positions. In particular, these forces have acted to create a distancing from persons of different economic levels but of similar ethnicity and origin. There are fewer stories about how people from the neighborhood "made it." There are few if any regular encounters with those one "rung up" on the economic ladder. These lost interactions combine with the limited economic opportunity to lessen the belief that conventional accomplishments and avenues to success are possible. The attraction to such adult roles is further diminished because the likelihood of reaching adulthood is questionable (Tolan et al., in press), and the probability of gaining access to the larger society seems minute. Further, unlike much of the rest of society, obtaining these conventional markers of success and following conventional pathways is likely to require moving away from one's family and friends and possible alienation from them (Coontz, 1992; Kotlowitz, 1991).

These conditions create challenges that would strain any family and may suggest that the challenges are overwhelming. At least, these characteristics indicate the need to recognize that setting characteristics carry much risk for inner-city residents and must be included as foci of interventions. In addition, the risk associated with the social ecology of the inner city is direct, as well as through straining family functioning (Gorman-Smith, Tolan, & Henry, in press). Thus, a third implication is that coping may be a more useful and user-friendly organizer of family interventions than problem solving or parent education (Tolan & McKay, 1996).

Understanding the nature of the stress facing inner-city families can facilitate the usefulness of interventions and policies. In previous writings, we have suggested a typology for stress types that is meant to capture the nature of the greater stress faced in the inner city (Tolan et al., in press). We believe that this typology aids a coping conception of the family.

A Typology of Stress in the Inner City

Building on stress typologies offered by others (e.g., Anderson, 1991; Peters & Massey, 1983; Pierce, 1975), we suggest that the nature and impact of stress for inner-city families are characterized by four types of stress: (a) *chronic environmental stress,* (b) *life events,* (c) *daily hassles,* and (d) *role strain.* This organization differentiates each stress type by the specific impact and by the needed coping responses (Tolan, Miller, & Thomas, 1988). It also permits examination of how conditions of chronic environmental stress relate to increased levels of the other types of stressors in this setting (Garbarino & Crouter, 1978).

Chronic environmental stress is defined as a baseline or background level of stress because of specific characteristics of the environment. As previously described, large-scale unemployment, violence, and widespread social problems are examples of chronic environmental stressors that contribute to a pervasive and persistently stressful life experienced by all inner-city residents. Because these social conditions are largely uncontrollable, they cause harm by their demoralizing presence and in how they impede normal development and accomplishments. Because such stress becomes part of the background noise of the community, it has been referred to as "mundane extreme environmental stress" (Peters & Massey, 1983; Pierce, 1975). These stresses are particularly detrimental to ethnic minority groups living in central cities because these mark and add to the effects of racism and oppression (Anderson, 1991). Also, these pervasive conditions may seriously constrain the effects that coping can have. Not only do they limit the efficacy of direct action and problem solving, but they also may promote development of short-term coping skills that result in detrimental long-term outcomes (Garbarino et al., 1991). For example, if one lives in a neighborhood where legitimate, dependable, and economically viable employment is rare, how does one socialize children about work and employment? If one also experiences subtle and obvious prejudice when one seeks work, how does this experience get explained to children without conveying bitterness and cynicism? Perhaps one becomes less planful and optimistic about one's control over these forces. Perhaps one teaches children to work when and if they can, rather than to train and plan for a lifetime of working in a career area.

Life events are defined as events and life transitions that, by their occurrence, impute direct distress to the person experiencing them. Most studies include tallies of a variety of stressful life events, including temporary economic disruptions, death of a family member, and property loss (Tolan et al., 1988). These events are distinguished from the ongoing conditions associated with chronic environmental stress and the minor irritations that result from daily hassles. Although all families experience stressful life events, inner-city families are likely to experience more of these events simultaneously and to have fewer resources for responding than other families. For example, our data on a general sample of urban poor children found that close to 50% of children surveyed reported a loss of a friend or family member, significant health problems in the family, or witnessing violence in the preceding year (Attar et al., 1994). When we divided the sample on the basis of neighborhood distress, children from the most distressed neighborhoods experienced rates of life event stress twice as high as those of children from the moderately distressed neighborhoods, although all children experienced rates four to six times higher than those reported in other studies of suburban children (Dubow, Tisak, Causey, Hryshko, & Reid, 1991).

Inner-city families are also likely to be more vulnerable to the impact of stressful events. Indeed, studies have shown that both the greater frequency of events and the greater impact of these events increase the harmful consequences for inner-city residents (Kessler, 1979; Neff, 1985). In some cases, this increased impact is compounded by the status of being both poor and minority (Kessler & Cleary, 1980; Ulbrich, Warheit, & Zimmerman, 1989). This greater impact seems to reflect not only the stress experienced but also the rapidity and elevated number of stressful events, having fewer resources to facilitate coping, and the lesser impact of common coping responses on outcome (Anderson, 1991).

Daily hassles are minor stressors that are part of day-to-day life. In some studies, daily hassles have been found to be the most significant predictors of distress (Felner, Farber, & Primavera, 1983; Tolan et al., 1988). The impact of daily hassles is thought to be harmful because the hassles detract from well-being and lower productive activity. In addition, it has been argued that chronic environmental stress, high levels of stressful life events, and limited resources and support make it more difficult for families to manage daily hassles.

Two common complications for inner-city families are (a) the exacerbation of daily hassles because of racism and (b) the difficulty managing normal minor disruptions. Racism can take the form of enduring an insult or personal humiliation, the sudden interruption of normal interaction or completion of daily tasks, or the frustration related to coping with normal stress. For example, approaching a teacher about schoolwork or a dispute with a grade can be overwhelming if children must also tolerate prejudice as part of the interaction. Similarly, a common minor hassle such as needing milk late at night becomes a substantial problem if no store is nearby or if it is simply too dangerous to go out at night. In either case, normal coping responses may be irrelevant or actually increase risk for harm or humiliation.

Role strain is defined as stress because of one's inability to fulfill socially ascribed roles (Pearlin, 1983). Originally, role strain was seen as a result of personal inadequacies, such as severe psychopathology, that kept one from fulfilling the ascribed responsibilities of one's social position. For example, a man's alcoholism could cause role strain if it prevented fulfillment of his role as the family breadwinner. It is also clear, however, that role strain can result from contextual factors that limit access to legitimate social roles or undermine effectiveness. Because of diminished resources, many inner-city residents experience limited access and blocked opportunities for meeting social role demands.

Furthermore, members of ethnic minority groups can experience role strain because of conflict between the values of their culture and those of mainstream society (Anderson, 1991; Ogbu, 1985).

This conflict creates stress because attempts to fulfill mainstream role demands may require individuals to compromise, disregard, or fail to achieve the role demands of their own culture. For example, an inner-city child who focuses on achievement at school as a means of attaining higher economic and social status may be forsaking cultural values requiring duty and loyalty to the extended family (Laosa, 1979). The lack of occasion to capitalize on this achievement because of low employment opportunity or the implausibility of attending college may result in further role strain. Not only are the child and family facing cultural conflict, but also external constraints are preventing the ability to fulfill role demands (Anderson, 1991).

Role strain for inner-city families may be expressed as social class differences. For example, group identity may be considered more salient than individual achievement (Boykin, 1979; Spencer, Dobbs, & Swanson, 1988). Any individualism may lead to criticism and create role strain. This role strain not only is a situational or event stress but also can influence outcome by affecting developmental processes. The meaning of developmental tasks, such as achieving autonomy, and parental support (or lack of it) for the inner-city child's management of cultural conflict can lower esteem and security (Spencer et al., 1988). Role strain can thus insidiously lead families to impose onerous restrictions on children's aspirations.

Conclusions

We have provided a detailed explanation of the types of stress facing inner-city families, the social forces within such neighborhoods that seem to constitute a unique social ecology, and the resulting coping issues that are central in the day-to-day and long-term functioning of these families. This approach is offered as a pragmatic model that can serve as an alternative to more polemic and simplistic approaches. The model incorporates most of the extant research and integrates concerns about differences among families with recognition of the power of setting influences. By placing the family and its concerns within the social and economic forces that define the inner city, this perspective should direct programming and policy to target aspects of the setting and the family that can best enable families to cope adequately and fulfill their intended functions and goals.

Rather than suggest specific programs or policies, we focus here on how this perspective should influence understanding of what programs and policies should do—their orientation. Most fundamentally, we suggest a need to orient programs and policies to recognize the persistent struggle that characterizes day-to-day life in these neighborhoods. Rather than an assumption that difficulties must reflect some failure of a given family or indicate some underlying pathology, we are suggesting that inner-city families are in need of the supports, aids, resources, and opportunities that are available to most families in most other communities in society at this time. The purpose of interventions and programs is to help families who are facing extraordinary difficulties to carry out normal functions.

The needed shift in orientation can be operationalized by moving from an emphasis on remediation to an emphasis on enhancement. Many of the existing programs and policies are oriented toward remediating assumed deficits in values and skills of specific families. Often, such an emphasis means that programs target only the most incapable or needy families. Even if offered as early intervention or other preventive efforts, such programs tend to accomplish little structural change or to lessen prevalence. They may aid a few families, but the benefits do not accrue for the community overall, and the proportion of families in need does not change. The purpose of programs with an emphasis on remediation is to provide time-limited aid to bring those showing impairments up to a level of functioning presumed to be self-generated by others. Such an emphasis seems to ignore the contextual forces constraining family options and the community structures perpetuating the overwhelming stress (Seidman, 1983).

In contrast, an enhancement emphasis focuses on improving functioning from baseline, whatever that may be. The goal is to increase the potential and achievement of those facing difficulty, limited resources, or blocked opportunity. The presumed focus is on populations, rather than on subgroups or specific families (Tolan, in press). Interventions and policies with this emphasis tend to focus on harnessing family capabilities and access to needed resources, rather than remediation of presumed deficits. Program design and resource allocations are evaluated in terms of how they improve the well-being of the community as a whole. The planning and organization of resources and services are focused on setting up flexible systems that draw on strengths and motivations of the involved families. There is an explicit recognition that programs must affect social structures and must be fit to the local social ecology (Mitroff, 1983).

As one can see, the difference in the remediation and enhancement approaches are not only about specific programming or preference for prevention over treatment. Rather, an enhancement approach emphasizes overcoming constraints, managing limitations, and increasing ability to affect the environment (Tolan & McKay, 1996). An important assumption is that most families residing in the inner city are in need of help because of the higher levels of stress experienced, the unique types of stressors, the environmental constraints on families, and the limited resources available. Others have substantial personal and situational limitations that need more aid than typical, but for the most part the focus is on aiding the functional skills of the majority of families.

In addition to the general difference in program emphasis, the coping approach also suggests some key aspects of family functioning and development for program focus. Traditionally, coping interventions have targeted increasing access to social support (Heller & Swindle, 1983). In regard to inner-city neighborhoods, examples of these targets include building networks among parents for watching over children (Tolan & McKay, 1996), increasing neighborhood safety and political efficacy (Garbarino et al., 1991), and advocating for educational and economic resources and opportunities (Seidman, 1983). Additionally, coping interventions often focus on accurate identification of the source of the stressor, determination of what is under the control of the person (family), and then actions designed to minimize harmful impact or to stop the stressor (Compas et al., 1992). Examples of such efforts for families living in the inner city include programs that enhance understanding of historical and political issues underlying many of the social problems facing inner-city families (Coll et al., 1995). Parenting skills training and other family interventions that aid family cohesion and support of members can also help by reducing stress and discord and by improving problem solving and organization (Laosa, 1990; McAdoo, 1982; Tolan & McKay, 1996).

All of these program ideas will have limited effect, however, unless the major issues of economic viability, safety, and opportunity are addressed. This stark fact is important to emphasize in this time when fairness is connoted as not aiding anyone and policies are formulated as though there are no substantial differences in probability of having adequate housing, having opportunities for sustainable employment, having children achieve to their potential, and feeling confident that they will be safe through the end of the day. As we argue here, the need is to attempt to enhance families' abilities to cope with the adverse circumstances they face, not to begrudge them this basic support.

Notes

1. We distinguish inner-city from other urban-poor neighborhoods following Wilson's (1987) critique and analyses that suggested multiple distinctions other than average-economic-level differentiated inner city from other urban neighborhoods with high poverty rates.

2. *Ecological validity* refers to applicability of concepts, measures, or findings to a specific population or segment of the population.

References

Aday, L. A. (1994). Health status of vulnerable populations. *Annual Review of Public Health, 15*, 487-509.

Anderson, L. P. (1991). Acculturative stress: A theory of relevance to black Americans. *Clinical Psychology Review, 11*, 685-702.

Attar, B. K., Guerra, N. G., & Tolan, P. H. (1994). Neighborhood disadvantage, stressful life events, and adjustment in urban elementary school children. *Journal of Consulting and Clinical Psychology, 23*, 391-400.

Baldwin, A. L., Baldwin, C., & Cole, R. E. (1990). Stress-resistant families and stress-resistant children. In J. Rolf, A. S. Masten, D. Cicchetti, K. H. Nuechterlein, & S. Weintraub (Eds.), *Risk and protective factors in the development of psychopathology* (pp. 257-280). Cambridge, UK: Cambridge University Press.

Band, E. B., & Weisz, J. R. (1988). How to feel better when it feels bad: Children's perspectives on coping with everyday stress. *Developmental Psychology, 24*, 247-253.

Bane, M. J., & Ellwood, D. T. (1989). One fifth of the nation's children: Why are they poor? *Science, 245*, 1047-1053.

Blechman, E. A., Tryon, A. S., Ruff, M. H., & McEnroe, M. J. (1989). Family skills training and childhood depression. In C. E. Schaefer & J. M. Briesmeister (Eds.), *Handbook of parent training: Parents as co-therapists for children's behavior problems* (pp. 203-222). New York: John Wiley.

Boyd-Franklin, N. (1989). *Black families in therapy: A multisystems approach.* New York: Guilford.

Boykin, A. W. (1979). Black psychology and the research process: Keeping the baby but throwing out the bath water. In A. W. Boykin, A. J. Franklin, & J. F. Yates (Eds.), *Research directions of black psychologists.* New York: Russell Sage.

Centers for Disease Control and Prevention. (1992). Behaviors related to unintentional and intentional injuries among high school students: United States, 1991. *Morbidity and Mortality Weekly Report, 41,* 760-765.

Chicago Department of Public Health. (1995). *Big cities health inventory.* Chicago: Author.

Clark, R. (1983). *Family life and school achievement: Why poor black children succeed or fail.* Chicago: University of Chicago Press.

Coll, C. T. G., Meyer, E. C., & Brillon, L. (1995). Ethnic and minority parenting. In M. H. Bornstein (Ed.), *Handbook of parenting.* Hillsdale, NJ: Lawrence Erlbaum.

Compas, B. E., Worsham, N. L., & Ey, S. (1992). Conceptual and developmental issues in children's coping with stress. In A. M. LaGreca, L. J. Siegel, J. L. Wallander, & C. E. Walker (Eds.), *Stress and coping in child health* (pp. 7-24). New York: Guilford.

Conger, R. E., Conger, K. J., Elder, G. H., Jr., Lorenz, F. O., Simons, R. L., & Whitbeck, L. B. (1992). A family process model of economic hardship and adjustment of early adolescent boys. *Child Development, 63,* 526-541.

Coontz, S. (1992). *The way we never were: American families and the nostalgia trap.* New York: Basic Books.

Crane, J. (1991). The epidemic theory of ghettos and neighborhood effects on dropping out and teenage childbearing. *American Journal of Sociology, 96,* 1226-1259.

Dubow, E. F., Tisak, J., Causey, D., Hryshko, A., & Reid, G. (1991). A two-year longitudinal study of stressful life events, social support, and social problem-solving skills: Contributions to children's behavioral and academic adjustment. *Child Development, 62,* 583-599.

Elder, G. H., Caspi, A., & Nguyen, T. (1986). Resourceful and vulnerable children: Family influence in hard times. In R. K. Silbereisen, K. Eyferth, & G. Rudinger (Eds.), *Development as action in context* (pp. 167-186). New York: Springer-Verlag.

Fagan, J. (1994). *Legal and illegal work: Crime, work, and unemployment.* Report prepared for the Metropolitan Assembly, Center for Urban Affairs and Policy Research, Northwestern University.

Federal Bureau of Investigation (FBI). (1992). *Uniform crime reports.* Washington, DC: Author.

Felner, R. D., Farber, S. S., & Primavera, J. (1983). Transitions and stressful life events: A model for primary prevention. In R. D. Felner, L. A. Jason, J. N. Moritsugu, & S. S. Farber (Eds.), *Preventive psychology: Theory, research, and practice* (pp. 199-215). Elmsford, NY: Pergamon.

Florsheim, P., Tolan, P. H., & Gorman-Smith, D. (in press). Family processes and risk for externalizing behavior problems among African American and Hispanic boys. *Journal of Consulting and Clinical Psychology.*

Garbarino, J., & Crouter, A. (1978). Defining the community context for parent-child relations: The correlates of child maltreatment. *Child Development, 49,* 604-616.

Garbarino, J., Kostelny, K., & Dubrow, N. (1991). What children can tell us about living in danger. *American Psychologist, 46,* 376-383.

Goldstein, M. J. (1984). Family affect and communication related to schizophrenia. In A-B. Doyle, D. Gold, & D. S. Moskowitz (Eds.), *Children in families under stress* (pp. 47-62). San Francisco: Jossey-Bass.

Gorman-Smith, D., & Tolan, P. H. (1995). *The role of exposure to community violence and developmental problems among inner-city youth.* Manuscript submitted for publication.

Gorman-Smith, D., Tolan, P. H., & Henry, D. (in press). The relation of community and family to risk among urban poor adolescents. In P. Cohen, L. Robins, & C. Slomkowski (Eds.), *Where and when: Influence of historical time and place on aspects of psychopathology.* Hillsdale, NJ: Lawrence Erlbaum.

Gorman-Smith, D., Tolan, P. H., Zelli, A., & Huesmann, L. R. (1996). The relation of family functioning to violence among inner-city minority youth. *Journal of Family Psychology, 10,* 115-129.

Guerra, N. G. (in press). Intervening to prevent childhood aggression in the inner city. In J. McCord (Ed.), *Growing up violent: Contributions of inner-city life.* Cambridge, UK: Cambridge University Press.

Hardy, D. F., Power, T. G., & Jaedicke, S. (1993). Examining the relation of parenting to children's coping with everyday stress. *Child Development, 64,* 1829-1841.

Hardy, K. V. (1989). The theoretical myth of sameness: A critical issue in family therapy training and treatment. In G. W. Saba, B. M. Karrer, & K. V. Hardy (Eds.), *Minorities and family therapy* (pp. 17-33). New York: Haworth.

Heller, K., & Swindle, R. W. (1983). Social networks, perceived social support, and coping with stress. In R. D. Felner, L. A. Jason, J. N. Moritsugu, & S. S. Farber (Eds.), *Preventive psychology: Theory, research, and practice* (pp. 87-103). Elmsford, NY: Pergamon.

Hernandez, D. J. (1993). *America's children: Resources from family, government, and the economy.* New York: Russell Sage.

Hetherington, E. M. (1984). Stress and coping in children and families. In A-B. Doyle, D. Gold, & D. S. Moskowitz (Eds.), *Children in families under stress* (pp. 7-33). San Francisco: Jossey-Bass.

Jencks, C. (1992). *Rethinking social policy.* Cambridge, MA: Harvard University Press.

Kessler, R. (1979). Stress, social status, and psychological distress. *Journal of Health and Social Behavior, 20,* 259-272.

Kessler, R., & Cleary, P. (1980). Social class and psychological distress. *American Sociological Review, 45,* 463-478.

Kotlowitz, A. (1991). *There are no children here.* Garden City, NY: Doubleday.

Kozol, J. (1992). *Savage inequalities.* New York: Harper Perennial.

Laosa, L. (1979). Social competence in childhood: Toward a developmental, socioculturally relativistic paradigm. In M. Kent & J. Rolf (Eds.), *Primary prevention of psychopathology: Social competence in children.* Hanover, NH: University Press of New England.

Laosa, L. M. (1990). Psychosocial stress, coping, and development of Hispanic immigrant children. In F. C. Serafica, A. I. Schwebel, R. K. Russell, et al. (Eds.), *Mental health of ethnic minorities.* New York: Praeger.

Lazarus, R. S., & Folkman, S. (1984). *Stress, appraisal, and coping.* New York: Springer.

Littlejohn Blake, S. M., & Darling, C. A. (1993). Understanding the strengths of African American families. *Journal of Black Studies, 23,* 460-471.

Lykken, D. T. (1994). On the causes of crime and violence: A reply to Aber and Rappaport. *Applied and Preventive Psychology, 3,* 55-58.

Lyles, M. R., & Carter, J. H. (1982). Myths and strengths of the black family: A historical and sociological contribution to family therapy. *Journal of the National Medical Association, 74,* 1119-1123.

Lytton, H. (1990). Child and parent effects in boys' conduct disorder: A reinterpretation. *Developmental Psychology, 26,* 683-697.

Mason, C., Cauce, A., Gonzales, N., & Hiraga, Y. (in press). Neither too sweet nor too sour: Antisocial peers, maternal control, and problem behavior in African American adolescents. *Child Development.*

Massey, G. C., Scott, M., & Dornbusch, S. M. (1975). Racism without racists: Institutional racism in urban schools. *Black Scholar, 7,* 3.

McAdoo, H. P. (1982). Stress-absorbing systems in black families. *Family Relations, 31,* 479-488.

McLanahan, S., & Garfinkel, I. (1988). *Single mothers, the underclass, and social policy.* Madison: University of Wisconsin, Institute for Research on Poverty.

McLoyd, V. (1988). Socialization and development in a changing economy: The effects of paternal job and income loss on children. *American Psychologist, 44,* 293-302.

McLoyd, V. C. (1990). The impact of economic hardship on black families and children: Psychological distress, parenting, and socioemotional development. *Child Development, 61,* 311-346.

Mitroff, I. I. (1983). Beyond experimentation: New methods for a new age. In E. Seidman (Ed.), *Handbook of social intervention* (pp. 163-177). Beverly Hills, CA: Sage.

Murray, C. (1984). *Losing ground: American social policy, 1950-1980.* New York: Basic Books.

Myers, H. F., Taylor, S., Alvy, K. T., Arrington, A., & Richardson, M. A. (1992). Parental and family predictors of behavior problems in inner-city black children. *American Journal of Community Psychology, 20,* 557-576.

National Commission on Children. (1991). *Beyond rhetoric: A new American agenda for children and families.* Washington, DC: Author.

National Institute of Justice. (1992). *Community policing in Seattle: A model partnership between citizens and police.* Washington, DC: Author.

Neff, J. A. (1985). Race and vulnerability to stress: An examination of differential vulnerability. *Journal of Personality and Social Psychology, 49,* 481-491.

Ogbu, J. (1985). A cultural ecology of competence among inner-city blacks. In M. B. Spencer, G. K. Brookins, & W. R. Allen (Eds.), *Beginnings: The social and affective development of black children* (pp. 45-66). Hillsdale, NJ: Lawrence Erlbaum.

Parke, R. D. (1994). Epilogue: Unresolved issues and future trends in family relationships with other contexts. In R. D. Parke & S. G. Kellam (Eds.), *Exploring family relationships with other social contexts* (pp. 215-229). Hillsdale, NJ: Lawrence Erlbaum.

Pearlin, L. I. (1983). Role strain and personal stress. In H. Kaplan (Ed.), *Psychosocial stress*. San Diego: Academic Press.

Peters, M. F. (1976). *Nine black families: A study of household management and child rearing in black families with working mothers.* Ann Arbor, MI: University Microfilms.

Peters, M. F., & Massey, G. (1983). Mundane extreme environmental stress in family stress theories: The case of black families in white America. *Marriage and Family Review, 6,* 193-218.

Pierce, C. (1975). The mundane extreme environment and its effect on learning. In S. G. Brainard (Ed.), *Learning disabilities: Issues and recommendations for research.* Washington, DC: National Institute of Education.

Ray, S. A., & McLoyd, V. (1986). Fathers in hard times: The impact of unemployment and poverty on paternal and marital relations. In M. Lamb (Ed.), *The father's role* (pp. 339-383). New York: John Wiley.

Reiss, D., & Oliveri, M. E. (1980). Family paradigm and family coping: A proposal for linking the family's intrinsic adaptive capacities to its responses to stress. *Family Relations, 29,* 443.

Reiss, D., Oliveri, M. E., & Curd, K. (1983). Family paradigm and adolescent social behavior. *New Directions for Child Development, 22,* 77-92.

Rowe, D. C. (1994). *The limits of family influence: Genes, experience, and behavior.* New York: Guilford.

Sameroff, A. J., & Feise, B. H. (1989). Conceptual issues in prevention. In D. Shaffer, I. Philips, & N. B. Enzer (Eds.), *OSAP Prevention Monograph 2: Prevention of mental disorders, alcohol, and other drug use in children and adolescents* (pp. 23-53). Rockville, MD: Office for Substance Abuse Prevention.

Sampson, R. J., & Lauritsen, J. (1992). Violent victimization and offending: Individual, situational, and community-level risk factors. In A. J. Reiss & J. Roth (Eds.), *The understanding and control of violent behavior.* Washington, DC: National Academy Press.

Schwab-Stone, M. E., Ayers, T. S., Kasprow, W., Voyce, C. K., Brone, C., Shriver, T., & Weissberg, R. P. (1995). No safe haven: A study of violence exposure in an urban community. *American Academy of Child and Adolescent Psychiatry, 34,* 1343-1352.

Seidman, E. (1983). Unexamined premises of social problem solving. In E. Seidman (Ed.), *Handbook of social intervention* (pp. 48-67). Beverly Hills, CA: Sage.

Spencer, M. B., Dobbs, B., & Swanson, D. P. (1988). African American adolescents: Adaptional processes and socioeconomic diversity in behavioral outcomes. *Journal of Adolescence, 11,* 117-137.

Spencer, M. B., & Markstrom-Adams, C. (1990). Identity processes among racial and ethnic minority children in America. *Child Development, 61,* 290-310.

Staples, R. (1978). *The black family: Essays and studies.* Belmont, CA: Wadsworth.

Stephens, E. H., Foote, K., Hendershot, G. E., & Schoenborn, C. A. (1994). *Health of the foreign-born population: United States, 1989-90* [Advance data from Vital

and Health Statistics of the Centers for Disease Control and Prevention].
Hyattsville, MD: National Center for Health Statistics.

Taylor, R. D., Casten, R., & Flickinger, S. M. (1993). Influence of kinship social support on the parenting experiences and psychosocial adjustment of African American adolescents. *Developmental Psychology, 29,* 382-388.

Tolan, P. H. (1988). Socioeconomic, family, and social stress correlates of adolescents' antisocial and delinquent behavior. *Journal of Abnormal Child Psychology, 16,* 317-332.

Tolan, P. H. (1990). Family therapy, substance abuse, and adolescents: Moving from isolated cultures to related components. Invited essay review. *Journal of Family Psychology, 3,* 454-465.

Tolan, P. H. (in press). Prevention research with families. In H. Liddle, D. Santisteban, R. Levant, & J. Bray (Eds.), *Family psychology intervention science.* Washington, DC: American Psychological Association Press.

Tolan, P. H., Gorman-Smith, D., Huesmann, L. R., & Zelli, A. (in press). Assessment of family relationship characteristics: A measure to explain risk for antisocial behavior and depression among urban youth. *Psychological Assessment.*

Tolan, P. H., Gorman-Smith, D., Hunt, M., & Chung, S. (1996). *Types of coping of inner-city youth.* Manuscript submitted for publication.

Tolan, P. H., Guerra, N. G., & Kendall, P. C. (1995). A development-ecological perspective on antisocial behavior in children and adolescents: Toward a unified risk and intervention framework. *Journal of Consulting and Clinical Psychology, 63*(4), 579-584.

Tolan, P. H., Guerra, N. G., VanAcker, R., Huesmann, L. R., & Eron, L. (1995). *Patterns of psychopathology in inner-city children: Vol. I. Gender, ethnicity, age, and location trends.* Manuscript submitted for publication.

Tolan, P. H., & Henry, D. (1996). Patterns of psychopathology among urban-poor children: Co-morbidity and aggression effects. *Journal of Consulting and Clinical Psychology, 64,* 1094-1099.

Tolan, P. H., & McKay, M. M. (1996). Preventing serious antisocial behavior in inner-city children: An empirical-based family intervention program. *Family Relations, 45,* 148-155.

Tolan, P. H., Miller, L., & Thomas, P. (1988). Perception and experience of types of social stress and self-image among adolescents. *Journal of Youth and Adolescence, 17,* 147-163.

Tolan, P. H., Montaini, L., & Gorman-Smith, D. (1995). *Dimensions of coping in a high-risk urban adolescent sample.* Manuscript submitted for publication.

Ulbrich, P. M., Warheit, G. J., & Zimmerman, R. S. (1989). Race, socioeconomic status, and psychological distress: An examination of differential vulnerability. *Journal of Health and Social Behavior, 30,* 131-146.

Wilson, W. J. (1987). *The truly disadvantaged: The inner city, the underclass, and public policy.* Chicago: University of Chicago Press.

Zaretsky, E. (1976). *Capitalism, the family, and personal life.* New York: Harper & Row.

Zayas, L. H., & Solari, F. (1994). Early childhood socialization in Hispanic families: Context, culture, and practice implications. *Professional Psychology: Research and Practice, 25*(3), 200-206.

CHAPTER 5

Urban Myth:
The Family in Hard Times

SAM REDDING

Here is a thing my heart wishes the world had more of:
I heard it in the air of one night when I listened
To a mother singing softly to a child restless and angry
in the darkness.

—Carl Sandburg (1970)[1]

The Family in Perspective

Always children have cried in the night. These times are no worse than other times for families; a hard look at history tells us that. But a clear image of the ideal family life is hard to find, public policy discourages family choice and action, the connection between personal behavior and family well-being is too casually acknowledged, and the potential power of transcendent faith is met with embarrassment by the professional class. In effect, the incentives and motives that once propelled family progress, especially for poor families, have diminished.

Estimating the condition of the American family depends largely on perspective—the length of the time line and the vantage point of the observer. In the waning hours of the 20th century, the time line typically begins or places its fulcrum in the 1950s. Impressions of the family's current condition are filtered through the economic/political biases of observers whose referential time frame spans a mere half century. For the eldest observers of the modern family, the 1950s were the years of deliverance, the first sighting of the land of milk and honey after two generations of world war and depression. For the youngest observers, the 1950s were the good old days that their big brothers and sisters never let them forget. For the bulk of observers, in the prime of their professional lives, the 1950s were the cherished rooted years of childhood or the time of coming of age. Our understanding of the contemporary family is colored a great deal by the decade we place so prominently as our chief referent.

Writing of the family in the postmodern world, David Elkind (1993) carefully delineates the modern from the postmodern world, and his descriptions of each of them sound like our stereotypical impressions of the 1950s and the 1990s. The 1950s may have been the culmination of modernity, the denouement of a long era. Elkind's modern family conformed to a constricted model: nuclear with two parents, one working and one at home with the children. The postmodern family knows no model, no ideal type; today, we care more about the quality of relationships than the configuration of kinship.

David Halberstam (1993), in his popular study of the 1950s, asserts that our retrospective image of the decade is not completely consistent with the reality of the time, even though it is consistent with the view most Americans held of themselves during the 1950s. In the 1950s, Halberstam says,

> the American dream was . . . located in the suburbs, and for millions of Americans, still living in urban apartments, where families were crunched up against each other and where, more often than not, two or more siblings shared the same bedroom, these shows [television family sitcoms] often seemed to be beamed from a foreign country, but one that the viewers longed to be part of. One young urban viewer, hearing that Beaver Cleaver was being threatened yet again with the punishment of being sent upstairs to his room, could only think to wish for a home of his own with an upstairs room to go to. (p. 511)

Arlene Skolnick (1991) proclaims that the "view of 'the fifties'—shorthand for the period from the late 1940s through the early 1960s—as a golden age tells us more about the discontents of our own era than about the experience of people living through those years" (p. 50). But whatever the reality of the 1950s, "the 1950s family remains the baseline from which current changes in family life are frequently measured" (p. 51). The problem with the 1950s, Skolnick charges, was that the image of normality shone so bright that it made invisible the many American families who failed to achieve prosperity, did not live in suburbs, were not white, and did not conform to the standard of a working father and a domestic mother. The decade was an anachronism, a temporary deviation from the Zeitgeist. Yes, says Skolnick, the vast majority of American families achieved unprecedented prosperity, but constraints on individual expression and frantic devotion to conformity only held inevitable change at bay for a brief moment in history. With the 1960s came an explosive change in family norms.

If the American dream was not a universal reality in the 1950s, it was nevertheless a compelling dream. And while millions of American families did, in fact, live the dream, millions of other American families pursued its clear signal without reservation. If we do not recall exactly the facts of life in the 1950s, we remember unerringly the motivating vision that inspired families to strive. In this respect, the 1950s were different from the 1990s. The 1990s are not a time without hope, but the dream is far more particular to the dreamer, less a nationally understood vision of what a family should be and where it should be headed.

The American dream of the 1950s centered around the family home. This, however, was not peculiar to the 1950s. For two centuries, Americans had sought evidence of their social advancement in the style of the family dwelling. "The nineteenth-century gentry and people with newly acquired wealth were as determined to present themselves as refined members of polite society as their eighteenth-century predecessors, and as before, the great house was the most forthright statement of a person's cultural condition" (Bushman, 1992, p. 239). A benchmark of social advancement for many poor American families in the 18th and 19th centuries was the move from the rough-hewn log cabin to a frame house. For urban families, the step up came in the move from the tenement to the row house.

The history of the American family is a history of movement. One by one, families immigrated to this country, and one by one they moved West to improve their lot. Although Halberstam (1993) points to family sitcoms and game shows as the quintessential television fare of the 1950s, he overlooks the salience of the TV Western. When American families huddled on Friday evenings to catch the latest episode of *Gunsmoke*, they saw the great story of American migration played out on the screen. Sheriff Matt, Doc, Kitty, and Chester maintained order, represented a natural decency, and laid the foundation stones of community. Around them swirled people in motion: settlers newly arrived from the East, fortune seekers headed West to California, cowboys driving cattle to the railheads, freed slaves searching for their place in the sun, Civil War veterans displaced from their homes. In the TV Western, America's morality play was presented as clear, unadorned, dramatic, and filled with action. Families were in motion; they were starting anew; they clung to themselves and to small communities of intimates; and their enemies were external, palpable, and part of a cold, natural world. Images of America's great Western movement were far more vivid and impelling in the minds of the television-viewing family of the 1950s than the facile family sitcoms. In the 1950s, American families were, like the families in the Westerns, on the move.

According to Nicholas Lemann (1991), the largest movement of families from one place to another in U.S. history was the migration of black families from the rural South to the urban North, an odyssey that began in the second decade of the 20th century but accelerated sharply during the 1940s and 1950s. As middle-class whites left the cities for the suburbs, poor blacks left the farms of the South for the factories of the North.

> Between 1910 and 1970, six and a half million black Americans moved from the South to the North; five million of them moved after 1940, during the time of the mechanization of cotton farming. In 1970, when the migration ended, black America was only half Southern, and less than a quarter rural; "urban" had become a euphemism for "black." The black migration was one of the largest and most rapid mass internal movements of people in history. (Lemann, 1991, p. 6)

Not unlike the European migration to the United States, many black families sent their men ahead of the women and children to secure employment before the family joined them. The action of movement relieved men's frustration with their lot in the South and gave them a mission as heads of their families.

Mass movement of families and the uncontested expectation that movement would bring prosperity were the realities of the 1950s. Although family migration has been a pattern of social advancement from the beginning of U.S. history, it was greatly accelerated after World War II. Family migration was fueled by many factors: the return of the GIs, the spawning of Levittowns, the construction of interstate highways, and the flight of black families from the agricultural South. But more than anything, family migration was propelled by the universal vision, the national hope, indeed the national expectation that a better life waited just around the bend. With this impression of the 1950s in mind, we must take a longer view of history to put the 1990s in truer perspective. Otherwise, we are influenced too greatly by one extraordinary decade.

The politics of the 1990s lean heavily on family themes: Family values, family tax credits, the relationship between welfare and family structure, and family choice in education are hot issues. In an age characterized by scrutiny of institutions, the family has been thoroughly scrutinized. The media's penchant for economic charts, graphs, and statistics is matched by a steady marshaling of facts and figures about marriage rates, divorce rates, and "illegitimate" births. The issues of the day are ineluctably tied to the fate of the family.

Examination of the family typically focuses on two areas: (a) socioeconomic status (income, place of residence, parental education) and (b) family structure (number of parents, family size, sibling gender and spacing, birth position). Because many observers intend to make a political point, wishing to affect public policy with their observations, the family's socioeconomic status or its structural configuration is linked to a desired or deplored social outcome such as success in school, criminal behavior, or talent. Liberal observers favor the socioeconomic angle, whereas conservatives tend to focus on family structure; so a liberal observer might trace the roots of crime to poverty, whereas the conservative would point to the absence of a father in the home.

In this chapter, we depart from the standard perspectives and foci as we look again at the American family. Our referential time line stretches from 50 years to 150 years. We focus on the dynamics of family life—behaviors, attitudes, beliefs, routines, and interactions—rather than socioeconomics or structure. We pay special attention to the family's influence on children's success in school.

I beg the reader's indulgence as I retrace 150 years of my own family's history. I hope this diversion is instructive. If not, I hope the reader will at least enjoy this peek into my ancestors' odyssey half as much as I have enjoyed uncovering it. At any rate, please trust that I eventually bring our discussion to the streets of 1990s Chicago and matters close to home.

One Family's Story

I begin my tale in early Victorian England, described in retrospect by my great-great-grandfather, Christopher Allen, in an 1874 letter written from his Ohio home to his nephew:

> I feel a little inclined to tell thee how I had to pick up the little learning I have. My going to day school terminated when I was about ten years of age. I could hardly read and write when I was put to work in a factory in Manchester and then for the first time I began to "think of myself." I saw if I obtained no more learning I must eventually become a carter, laborer or common factory hand, but if I aimed at any higher position I must contend with many obstacles and pursue learning under no small difficulties. This I resolved to do, carrying my book in my bosom, looking occasionally at my task and working my examples on the carding machine. For a short time I attended a night school but found after 13 hours I was in a poor condition of mind or body to study so as to make much advancement. Having access to a large library I read many useful books such as History, Biography, Science and poetry. After being apprenticed to a trade about 15 years of age, a number of poor boys like myself who were struggling to improve ourselves met with a friend named Ralph Nicholson, who benevolently offered to teach a grammar class without charge to as many as would conform to his rules. This was a great lift to many of us and I never knew any person so conversant with Lindley Murray rules and notes as he was. I had to go 2 miles to this class every week for near to two years and altho I was far from being perfect yet I shall ever gratefully remember the benefit received. At another time W. S. Buckingham M.P. gave me a course of lectures on Palestine. We all wanted to have this privilege but poverty said "NO." Two shillings and six pence for each lecture equaled half a week's

wages and was a barrier to our going. After consideration we agreed that one of twelve was to attend and write to the rest. I need not say this was a great means of improvement. There was an eminent writing master visited Manchester of whose lessons we all wished to profit, poverty again set our wits to work. We selected one to take the lessons and teach the remainder of the class.

Christopher Allen brought his family—including his 7-year-old son, Richard (my great-grandfather)—to Ohio in 1842. Attracted first to Cleveland, he managed to apply his skills in the burgeoning industries of this New World city, save a little money, and move south into the interior of Ohio to buy a farm and a grist mill. In 1866, he returned for a visit to England and kept a diary of the journey. From the diary, we learn more of life in 1820s Manchester, the cradle of the Industrial Age:

I went to meeting and was pleased to meet with James and E. Leed. James when I first knew him was a poor drunkard yet the son of respectable parents. I often in a friendly way used to talk to him and tell him how it was with my poor father till he was near 60 years of age. How I used to have to pilot him home in a state of intoxication. How we were reduced to poverty and how my noble mother, when he was almost in despair, encouraged him by telling him poverty was nothing if he would but keep sober. She and the children could make a living. He took her advice. Knowing himself to be weak he sought divine assistance which I think was in Mercy granted. He commenced taking his family to a place of worship and finally was enabled nearly to overcome his habit of drinking which I might say he had indulged from very childhood.

We were all employed in the cotton Factory and what learning we got was afterwards through the first-day school, and we were all thankful to the giver of all good that we were brought so low as to be sold up. Yet then the Lord helped us. James Leed when he saw me after meeting almost embraced me telling me how much indebted he was to me for interesting myself in his welfare and following him with my effort and advice when he broke his pledge again and again. This reformation had taken place after I left England; he said he had been a total abstainer for over 20 years and has been re-instated in meeting and was at that time a keeper of the meeting house and large grave yard. I took time with him and his wife. She had many questions to ask concerning my dear departed Amelia. I felt glad to see them so comfortably fixed. Hope they may be preserved but felt "Not unto me, not unto us but to thy name be all glory." After dinner walked over the beautiful burying ground. Saw among others Robert Leinley's grave with inscription on stone. All graves that are occupied have flat stones laid on them. A few without inscriptions such was my beloved friend Geo. Danson. As I stood beside his grave, his unaffected humility, his disinterested benevolence was remembered.

This excerpt from Christopher Allen's diary ends with the mention of two decidedly Victorian virtues: unaffected humility and disinterested benevolence. To say that the virtues are Victorian is not to deny that they are also close to Grandfather Allen's Quaker faith.

Gertrude Himmelfarb (1995) explains that Victorians spoke of *virtues,* meaning perennially desirable human qualities, whereas the modern world speaks of *values,* presuming that individuals may pick and choose among a menu of attributes, deciding for themselves their relative worth. *Virtue,* she says, is now a word disparagingly assigned to matters of sex. Those who now call for a revival of values in society do not necessarily argue from this relativistic perspective; for the most part, they are searching for universal touchstones of acceptable behavior. Our culture, however, discounts the universal; we simply hold too high the value of individual choice in matters moral. The roots of our caution are deep because we fear that declaring certain behaviors universally desirable inevitably leads to legal codification and enforcement by government sanction. The Victorians, Himmelfarb asserts, did not expect such formal, governmental enforcement of individual behaviors because they knew that behavior yielded its own just consequences. They relied on social persuasion of the individual actor and natural consequences of behavior.

Thus, the Victorians were convinced of the inherent value of thrift, hard work, and moderation of appetite; they believed that practicing these virtues would result in a better life for the individual (and his or her family). Inattention to these virtues would bring poverty, ignorance, and disease. In other words, people reaped what first they sowed. This is not to say that the Victorians disregarded the cumulative effects of virtuous (or nonvirtuous) behavior on the broader society; but the vehicles of social improvement were nongovernmental, and the ultimate choice rested with the individual.

Between the state and the individual, in Victorian England, grew a wide array of private, charitable societies and institutions devoted to improving the morals, manners, and living standards of the English, especially those in greatest need of uplift—the lower classes. Charitable endeavors provided the English upper and middle classes ways to voluntarily ameliorate suffering while firmly connecting relief with standards of behavior. To a great extent, religion was the impetus for altruism. Private charities permitted people of faith and means to, at once, practice their beneficence and further their views. "Disinterested benevolence" was a mark of virtue. Never doubting the utility of virtue, the people did not need pragmatic evidence of the "rightness" of virtuous behavior because these behaviors were commanded of them through revelations of their deity.

Chris Allen profited from the benevolence of library patrons, the generosity of a teacher—Ralph Nicholson—and the lectures of a Member of Parliament—W. S. Buckingham. Only the M.P.'s benevolence turned eventually to lecture fees. But Allen's climb up the ladder of learning was not propelled by benevolence alone; his own motivation to take up books after long days of labor in the mills is remarkable, and the collaboration among a dozen of his fellows— alternately attending lectures and sharing their notes—attests to the powers and practicalities of cooperative learning, more than a century before "cooperative learning" was discovered by educators.

In the Allen family, we discover virtue's primal battleground. The family was placed at peril, not by industrialism or disease, not by crime or misfortune, but by the father's behavior. Because he was a drunk, his wife and children worked 13 hours each day in the cotton factory to sustain themselves. Chris Allen viewed indenture as a blessing; having been "brought so low as to be sold up," he learned to work and to pursue learning as the only path from poverty. The noble mother wanted only sobriety from her husband, and he was able to meet her expectations only with help from above.

Thus, the essence of Victorian morality: Man reaps what he sows; man is weak without the strength of God; the family cleaves unto itself; work and learning pave the way to advancement; support is found in the circle of one's friends; disinterested benevolence is the mark of virtue and the vehicle for the improvement of society. These are the lessons and beliefs that followed Christopher Allen to the United States, where he found kindred souls among the Quakers of eastern Ohio in the 1840s and 1850s. But soon there would be trouble in paradise: In the 1850s, Quaker pacifism confronted the stirring rage of Quaker abolitionism.

Captured by Robert E. Lee with John Brown at Harper's Ferry was Edwin Coppoc, a native of Winona, Ohio. Coppoc was hanged in December 1859, and his body was transported to Ohio for burial. More than 2,000 people, mostly Quakers, came to the burial in Winona. Eastern Ohio had also been the rearing grounds of John Brown, who grew to manhood there and preached in Ohio churches before moving west to contest the Kansas-Nebraska Act of 1854, which made the plains a battleground over slavery. At Coppoc's burial, Rachel Whinnery (related to the Allens by marriage) read an address charging the Virginians with murdering their Quaker brother "who was only acting in freedom's Cause." The event inspired many young Quaker men to defy the pacifism of their fathers and take up arms on behalf of the Union and emancipation. Christopher Allen's son Richard set out for Kansas, and the other Allen boys left Winona, Ohio, for parts unknown. In 1860, Richard married Melinda Reynolds, daughter of an antislavery doctor who had moved from Kentucky to Illinois and then to Kansas. They were married at Pardee, Kansas, a town named for Pardee Butler, a Christian Church minister who had been tarred, feathered, and floated on a log down a Kansas river by a band of proslavery Missourians. Richard Allen later served in the Army of the Republic during the Civil War.

In 1891, Richard Allen sent a letter to his son Eugene. He spoke of his daughters, Irene and Maud, and his sons, Chris and Sam. A passage from the letter follows:

> Times are hard here, but if we have good crops everything will be all right. Sam is still at Rock Creek and doing a little better. Chris is at home but he is going to work soon at $18 per month. Irene is in Topeka working. I miss her more than ever since dear Maud's death. Irene is a Noble Girl. Her whole life is wrapped up in trying to do good for us.
>
> We have just got a life size crayon picture of Maud. It looks very much like her. It cost me $8.00 but is a good picture.
>
> Now Eugene I have one request to make. Last winter when Maud was sick and after her death I had to have money and we have a very fine cow that I mortgaged for $20.00. Now my note comes due June 17, and from the way things look now I am afraid I will lose my cow. Irene says she will raise the money but it is not right for me to take

her money. She has to work too hard for it. Now if I find that I can't
raise it, will you send part of it?

Well I must close.

Your father—

R. Allen

Two years later, Sam Allen, my grandfather, wrote to his family
from Oklahoma Territory:

Dear Father and all.

Well I received your letter some time ago, but I have been so busy
that I have not had time to answer. That is, I have been busy doing
nothing. As I told you in my last letter, I have rented a blacksmith shop
here in Edmond. I am right in the center of town, next door to the
post office. There is five shops in this place, and they all have been
here longer than I have, but I get more work than any one shop in
town.

You folks coming down at the opening of the new country? If you
do, Edmond is the best place to come to. And you could come and stay
with me too.

Okay I have quit chewing tobacco and smoking too, and I don't
drink a drop now. I have quit that also. Now I am not lying about this.
It is true.

Well I must close. Write soon.

With love to all,

Sam Allen

Perhaps his great-grandfather's curse of alcohol had crept into
young Sam Allen's life, and he had joined the Oklahoma land rush
to start life anew. But the new country was opening at a propitious
time for many "second sons" of Kansas farmers beset by a long
slump in the agricultural economy. Times were hard.

Later in 1893, Sam Allen returned to Kansas and took up the
blacksmith trade near his parents' home in the small town where
he had lived as a boy. In 1906, his young wife died shortly after
giving birth to their second child. He later married a widow whose
husband had died while she was pregnant; the child died in its
second year. Sam and Myrtle Allen had four children, and three
lived to adulthood. One was my mother, for whom the kitchen stove
served as an incubator after a difficult birth.

At age 57, established in his trade with four children at home, Sam Allen was forced to move again. Boycotted by the Ku Klux Klan for refusing to join their cause, he set out for western Kansas, where he scratched a bare living for his family as a blacksmith during the Dust Bowl and the Depression. My mother tells of her childhood on the plains. Each day, her older sister took a quarter to the store to buy food for the family. In the winter, their father broke boards from the horse stall to burn for heat. These are Depression stories familiar to many baby boomers; our parents told them with a mixture of sadness and longing. Their Depression years merged with the war years, when sons and brothers finally found employment in the service of their country. In the late 1940s, the fortunate ones returned to their hometowns, and the saga of the 1950s began.

My father was one of the returning servicemen. From small-town Kansas, he had joined the Navy and served as a gunnery officer aboard an LST. After duty in North Africa and Italy, his tour culminated with multiple crossings of the English Channel, delivering troops to their death at Omaha beachhead on D-Day. Ten years after returning home to Kansas, he moved his wife and three children (a fourth arrived soon after) to Illinois, where, in 1955, construction of the Eisenhower highway system promised jobs and prosperity. At last, we return to the 1950s, that pivotal decade of my youth.

If I remember the 1950s fondly, it is because my parents made me believe that these postwar years were the beginning of light after generations of wandering in darkness. Retracing the family history, I cannot conclude that they were wrong. We never moved to the suburbs; we stayed in small towns. We did not gain wealth, but we escaped want. Our family suffered its setbacks, including my brother's terrible crippling from multiple sclerosis, but compared to 13-hour days in the cotton mills, skirmishes with Missouri ruffians, mortgaged cows, crayon pictures of dead daughters, fights with the Ku Klux Klan, hunger in the Dust Bowl, and world war, we had it pretty good.

The real question for my family and all American families is not whether the 1950s were as good as we remember them, but what has happened since. Answering that question requires a perspective that does not begin in the 1950s but does include both the 1950s and the 1990s in a longer view. In the long view, poor families have improved themselves, or at least have enjoyed the expectation that progress is possible, by picking up stakes and moving. Sometime since the 1950s, the movement for many urban families stopped, and with it ended the hope, the anticipation of progress.

The Urban Family in the 1990s

As Nicholas Lemann (1991) makes clear, urban America is, to a large extent, comprised of African Americans whose families recently migrated from rural areas in the South. Hispanic Americans are another sizable, and in many cities the fastest growing, segment of the urban population, and most of them have family roots in rural areas in their countries of origin or rural areas elsewhere in the United States. Family migration brought the mass of urban populations, black and Latino, to the cities, a migration both in miles and in culture—from rural to urban. For literally millions of these families, the migration did not stop in the inner cities but continued to the better neighborhoods and the suburbs, following the postwar pattern of U.S. social advancement. We must ask, however, whether the city remains a viable way station between rural regions and suburbs. Or is the city increasingly a trap, an obstacle to a family's social progress? In asking this question, we need not imply that the suburbs are the ultimate promised land. They are not. But Americans are accustomed to the vision of a promised land, a better life just over the horizon, even if that horizon falls between the tenements and the row houses. A better life is strongly associated with a different place in the American psyche. The transitions are generational, each newly formed family finding greater opportunity in a new place. Americans born to privilege may find continued opportunity in the place of their birth, but Americans born to poverty have traditionally moved to a new location, where land, jobs, or freedom were more likely to be found.

Family migration holds with it the spirit, the promise, the vision of progress, but it also contains elements of loss, especially loss of community and extended family. To some extent, these losses were ameliorated by the typical mode of family migration: Families moved in clusters of acquaintance and quickly established new communities. Indeed, the excitement of community formation may produce a stronger *sense* of community than is generated by community maintenance or re-generation in a settled neighborhood.

Let's come to the point of this long discourse. A family's social and economic advancement is propelled by (a) the family's dissatisfaction with its current situation, (b) the vision of a better life and the expectation that it can be attained, (c) the ability and inclination to act, and (d) virtuous personal behavior. I use the term *virtuous* both advisedly and intentionally, knowing that it grates on the sensitivities of many readers. But returning to the Himmelfarb analysis of Victorian virtues, there can be little doubt that thrift, hard work, and moderation of appetite serve, perennially, to improve the odds for a family's progress.

Public subsidies—housing and welfare—make life in pathetic urban environments possible if not desirable. Public schools create the illusion that parents are providing for their children's education even when parents are given no choice of schools and children receive sub-par instruction in facilities that would not be tolerated outside the city. Public policies militate against the efficacy of family action by removing choices and disconnecting actions from consequences. There is no acknowledged vision of the good family life. In the 1950s, the ideal family looked like the Nelsons, the Andersons, or the Cleavers. Even for families of different circumstances, different colors, and different configurations, the ideal of comfortable home life, domestic civility, and constant attention to children's development was accepted and aspired to. What are today's ideals? To what do poor, urban families aspire?

From a structuralist's perspective, the greatest flaw in the American family of the 1990s—particularly the poor, urban family—is the scarcity of fathers. David Blankenhorn, in his book *Fatherless America* (1995), underscores the deprivation that children suffer from the retreat of fathers from family life. His statistics are, indeed, alarming: On any given night, 40% of American children go to sleep in homes where their fathers do not live; before they reach age 18, half of American children will spend at least a portion of their childhood living apart from their fathers (p. 1). These are national statistics; in many inner-city neighborhoods, two thirds of children are fatherless. Our national house is divided into two equal parts—families with fathers and families without fathers. The quality of a particular father's presence aside, two parents have more time to attend to children than one, and men are capable of supplying a type of influence different from that of women. In the aggregate, children suffer from the loss of fathers in their lives. In particular families, however, the effect is less certain. Virtuous behavior is the compensating factor.

Shawndra is 12 and attends public school in Chicago. Arriving home from school, she instinctively grabs the telephone and calls her mother at work. If she connects only with voice mail, she leaves a long message, relating the day's events. When her mother answers, Shawndra giggles and asks how things are going. Her mother begins to tell her and then says she will continue the story later. The conversation is a daily ritual, a touchstone event in the lives of an urban family of two. Evening conversations about the day's events and discussions of Shawndra's homework occur with such regularity that they, too, can be described as family rituals. Shawndra is an honor student, her mother's pride and joy. With no father in the home, Shawndra's mother endures an added hardship; there is little doubt that her noble efforts would be less arduous if a capable and willing partner shared them. But this mother is rising to the challenge; she is ably filling the void. Shawndra's future is endangered by factors other than the absence of a father.

Mixed with her delight in Shawndra's achievements is a fear never far from her mother's consciousness: Will Shawndra stay on this successful path, be admitted to a good high school, and eventually escape the neighborhood? Or will she fall prey to the gangs, become pregnant too soon, and lose her motivation to excel in school? The unexpressed, subdued anger that complicates the mother's fear stems from her realization that she must hover over her daughter, keep her nearly captive in her home, and protect her from the very neighborhood she herself cannot escape. Shawndra's mother feels stuck in a place she fears; her hope rises from the chance that her daughter will be able to move on. The mother's source of hope is not unlike that of generations of American mothers, and her dissatisfaction with her current situation makes her dreams for her daughter all the sweeter.

Shawndra is very likely to buck the odds, to finish school without becoming pregnant, to leave the neighborhood and go to college, and to form a family of her own that is close to the ideal her mother has in mind for her. Shawndra will buck the odds, in large part, because of her mother's virtuous behavior. The fact that Shawndra's mother does not pursue the dream for herself is evidence of the weight of immobility that her urban environment places on her. Without a father in the home, Shawndra's mother must work or receive public aid. She chooses to work but earns too little to break away from subsidized housing. She feels sufficiently entrenched to stay where she is and concentrate on her daughter's future. She is also trapped in a school system that allows her little choice; her daughter must attend the neighborhood elementary school, a school of dubious quality in a neighborhood shell-shocked by gang and domestic violence. Perhaps Shawndra's mother should be encouraged to move on. Uprooting a family and moving away from familiar surroundings is an act of courage, one that reinforces in the actor a sense of control, an affirmation of personal choice.

If Shawndra and her mother do not move, if they stay where they are and attempt to barricade themselves from the negative environment that surrounds them, where might they find a community of support for their values? Traditionally, that community of support was found in the church. But although the school is a dominant institution in the neighborhood, the church is a struggling institution dependent on the slim resources of its few congregates. There is a lesson here about disinterested benevolence, a Victorian virtue, and the role of U.S. churches. I echo the sentiments of Gertrude Himmelfarb (1995) in her description of Mrs. Jellyby, a Dickens character in *Bleak House,*

> who was too engrossed in the affairs of a tribe on the banks of the Niger to attend to her own brood of hungry, dirty, neglected children. For Dickens she was the exemplar of "telescopic philanthropy," her eyes having the "curious habit of seeming to look a long way off, as if . . . they could see nothing nearer than Africa!" (pp. 260-261)

Let U.S. churches take note. Shawndra's mother deserves more from them.

Another concern lies with the uneasy relationship between public institutions, especially the school, and religious expression. Of course, parochial education is a remedy chosen by many urban families, even at a huge cost in scarce family resources. But the public schools (and the professional class of public school employees, foundation managers, and government officials) can also be made more hospitable to the invigorating effects of personal religious expression on communities. Let me illustrate the problem with an anecdote:

"Kids repeat what they hear at home," Dora asserted. "In the past, my husband and I used bad language, and our boys picked it up. But now we are with the Lord again, we are *in* the world but not *of* the world, and we don't swear anymore. We are still trying to break our children's bad habits; we are no longer contributing to them." Dora was sharing her observation with a small group of mothers gathered in a Chicago public school for a parent education program. Her division of life's options into two paths—"of the world" and "with the Lord"—made perfect sense to her peers but not to the program facilitators who nervously pulled the conversation back from a taboo topic and channeled it toward a discussion of "modeling," "expectations," and "peer pressures." Although Dora found the rock of her existence in religion, she also found the most prominent institution in her neighborhood—the public school—an inhospitable place for her convictions. School personnel and other education professionals are so apprehensive about the separation of church and state that they shy from discussions of a motivating force, religion, that has the power to improve the lives of children.

In a similar incident, I watched foundation executives shrink in horror when a group of inner-city mothers shared the following story:

"We decided it was time to take our park back from the drug dealers," a mother from the inner city told the group of program officers and project directors gathered for a foundation-sponsored retreat. "First, we met at the school, in the parents' room. We closed the door so no one would see, and we prayed for strength from the Lord. Then we marched to the park and confronted the drug dealers one by one. We told them to leave and never return. They left. We went back to the school and prayed again, thanking God for His goodness."

Unfazed by the mothers' courage in driving drug dealers from their park, the professionals at the retreat were shocked that the mothers had prayed in a public school. Their faces showed their chagrin, and they smugly initiated a discussion of the Bill of Rights. Despite the fact that many of the professionals at this meeting send their own children to church-affiliated schools, they were adamant in protecting poor, public school children from expressions of their mothers' spiritual strength. They would argue that they only want to keep religion away from the schools, not from the lives of children, but in neighborhoods where the school is the strongest institution, that is asking a great deal.

Some gentler relationship between the schools and their clients' religious expression can certainly be achieved without forfeiting constitutional guarantees and without pressuring children of different faiths. The details of these relationships can be negotiated, but only when more school officials respond with less alarm, less embarrassment, to the spiritual energies of their students' families.

These tales of inner-city families are typical in their paucity of male characters, not because no males are in the cities, but because too many men are detached from families. In schools, half of the students are male, and schools can improve their efforts in preparing boys for manhood. Another example from a Chicago family will make the point:

Tracey worries about her nephew, Poco, who spends endless hours listening to music in his room but refuses to do his homework. A volunteer at Poco's school, Tracey tries to solve the riddle of Poco, talking with his teachers and with Poco's mother. Tracey's own son is 18 now and has not been in school for 2 years. At one time, he was a fairly good student; Tracey hopes Poco will not drop out of school like his cousin. The boys are an enigma to Tracey. "What goes on in their heads?" she asks. "I can mark the day when their problems begin. It is the first day they come home and announce that they are 'men.' It happens when they are only 10 or 12 years old. But that's when the attitude begins. To them, being a man means bucking the system. Being a man means turning away from your family. It's like some crazy code of honor. Where do they learn what being a man is all about?"

One can assume the answer to Tracey's question: Boys learn what manhood is about from other boys in a world without men. As schools scurry about, implementing "character education" programs, they might take a second look at an organization that has taught boys to be men for more than a century—Boy Scouts. Boy Scouts provides role models and programs to help boys know what it means to be a man. If an "Every Boy A Boy Scout" campaign seems a naive response to the calamity of the fatherless inner city, it is nonetheless a potent arrow in the quiver. Schools, government agencies, and community organizations are spending millions of dollars wrestling with the problems of boyhood; focusing on a tried and proven program like Boy Scouts may make more sense. Populating Scout troops with adult role models is the biggest part of the challenge, but the United States is filled with successful adults who were once Boy Scouts; perhaps, through their disinterested benevolence, they could become a liberating army for inner-city youth.

Positive programs like Boy Scouts for preadolescent boys will not, of course, keep all of them on the straight and narrow. But for boys who choose the right path, we must provide schools and neighborhoods less hostile to them. Quite simply, this means removing from the schools and neighborhoods the young men and women who have chosen the wrong path. Chicago is enlarging its system of alternative high schools, an act that will greatly improve the other high schools and the lives of the students who attend them. Expansion of reform schools for the most incorrigible youth would likewise improve the neighborhoods. If this dichotomy between Boy Scouts for the good guys and reform schools for the bad guys seems harsh and overstated, it at least offers sharply contrasting consequences for sharply contrasting behavior. We must reward young people for making good choices, and no reward is greater than removing from their schools and neighborhoods the thugs who prey on them and the slackers who disrupt their classes.

In summary, the urban families of most concern to us—the urban poor—live in a time that is not particularly hard by historical standards. But the family itself is weak in its ability to respond to the challenges of the time. Like poor families for many generations, urban families have plenty of reason to desire change; their current situation is sufficiently distasteful. But unlike past generations in U.S. history, they are disinclined to move to another place. Public policy should provide incentives for them to move, rather than to stay put. Regional housing policies that encourage movement to areas outside the city, perhaps to small towns, is one possibility. But to prosper, families must move to places with economic promise, and tracking these places is beyond the capability of government. Instead, each family must have a reason to find its own niche in the complex and changing economic environment. The reason may come when the cost of staying is greater than the cost of leaving. That means reducing the public subsidies that hold families in places with little economic opportunity.

Dreams are better incentives than government policies; visions of a better life attract like a powerful magnet. If life in the inner city is next to intolerable, life elsewhere must be better. But who recruits inner-city families to come where life is good? Who tells them they are welcome? Who aids their passage? Who paints with vivid colors the ideal of what a family could be in a different place? Perhaps that is another role for disinterested benevolence. And where is this promised land? It is almost anywhere that a single family or cluster of families with confidence in one another can start anew. Young men, especially, need a place to go. Their violence and their apathy stem, in part, from a sense of being stuck. Movement provides a constructive release for frustration. Movement lifts the spirit. New communities command strong allegiances. Action impels the actor to act again.

Moving is not a solution for those who stay behind, and it provides only a chance at a solution for those who leave. For poor families who remain in the inner city, each, like Shawndra's mother, must first look out for its own. Institutions capable of invigorating the spirit and disciplining habits, the church in particular, must elevate their commitment to the inner city. The public school, already prominent in every neighborhood, must be more congenial to the spiritual lives of their students and their students' families. School systems must also give parents greater choice in selecting their children's schools and the programs within schools. Choice impels the chooser to choose again.

Restoration of manhood in the inner city is a critical need, not merely to repair the structural deficiency of many families, but to define patterns of male behavior commensurate with civility and social responsibility. If "Every Boy A Boy Scout" rings trivial and naive, elevating the slogan to a serious goal for every school community, matched with a commitment by the national Boy Scout organization to mobilize thousands of former Scouts for service in the inner cities, begins to reveal the promise of the idea. The solution to the malformation of masculinity in the inner city is more complicated and more difficult to effect than giving hundreds of thousands of boys access to thousands of male role models within the structure of programs as sound as Boy Scouts and under the roofs of the neighborhood schools now standing idle at the end of each school day. But that is a good place to start.

Families that make choices and take bold actions (including the act of moving to unfamiliar places); churches that marshal with missionary zeal their resources in inner cities; and schools that offer choices for families, are hospitable to the power of belief, and open their doors to solid programs that teach discipline and responsibil- ity—this picture of new hope for urban families looks a lot like the 1950s. Maybe so. It worked for millions of poor families then, and it can work for millions more today.

Virtuous Family Behavior
and School Learning

Sweeping changes in public policy, dramatic reformation of school systems, massive economic development, and a religious Great Awakening may reverse the fortunes of poor, urban families, but my advice would be: Don't count on it. The fate of children in any one family is more likely to hinge on the actions of the adults in that family. In today's world, and even more so in the world of tomorrow, access to the good life is gained through the door of education. In the worst of schools, some children succeed. The goal of every parent must be that his or her children are among those who succeed. By success I mean that, at a minimum, they graduate from high school with solid skills in reading, writing, and arithme- tic, good study habits, and a desire to learn. That set of attributes will stand them well in the job market or in higher education. Arriving on graduation day without having parented a child and with some job experience will add icing to the cake. Of course, many inner-city students achieve far beyond these minimal levels. But many do not, and they are the focus of our concern.

A massive meta-analysis of research on school learning, con- ducted by the National Center on Education in the Inner Cities for the U.S. Department of Education, explored 28 variables (Wang, Haertel, & Walberg, 1994). Whereas such *distal* variables as "school policy and organization," "school demographics," and "state and district policies" were weak predictors of school learning, "home environment and parental support" stood proudly in the fourth position among the 28 variables. This finding comes as no surprise. For the past three decades, researchers have consistently affirmed the connection between the "curriculum of the home" and school learning. In fact, measures of parent-child behaviors in the home are twice as predictive of school achievement as the family's socio-economic status (Walberg, 1984, p. 400).

Dissection of family life has produced various laundry lists of characteristics of an optimal home environment. Most common among these factors are the following:

Informed parent-child conversations about everyday events
Encouragement and discussion of leisure reading
The monitoring and joint analysis of televiewing
Deferral of immediate gratification to accomplish long-term goals
Expressions of affection
Interest in children's academic and personal growth
The monitoring of the child's peer group outside the school
Parental knowledge of the child's progress in school and personal growth
Family visits to libraries, museums, zoos, historical sites, cultural activities
Encouragement to try new words, expand vocabulary
Formal study time at home
A daily routine that includes time to eat, sleep, play, work, study, and read
A quiet place to study and read
Family interest in hobbies, games, and activities of educational value
Priority given to schoolwork and reading over television and recreation
Expectation of punctuality
Parental expectation that children do their best
Concern for correct and effective use of language

The most hopeful aspect of this list of family behaviors is that the behaviors do not depend on the parents' economic position, education, or social standing. These family behaviors, which correlate with children's success in school, are within the reach of nearly every family. They are "virtuous" behaviors that can be practiced by single-parent families (with greater demand on the single parent, to be sure), merged families, and immigrant families. These family behaviors may be a poor child's ticket out of poverty, and it behooves every school to help families employ them.

With increased fragmentation of responsibility for child rearing, the family, which views the child as a whole person rather than as the recipient of a specific service, remains central to the preparation of children for academic learning. But the family is also fragmented and separated from other families and other sources of support for child rearing. Modern society, especially for poor children, is deficient in "social capital," James Coleman's (1990) term for an asset found in the connections and supports of human relationships. Children can count as an asset their parents' concern for them. Parents create social capital when they band together in a parent-teacher organization and bolster each other's child-rearing capacity. In their many relationships, people enter into informal and unspoken transactions in which they help or support one another. The social capital available to a child is diminished when fewer parents reside in the home, when parents and children spend less time interacting, when groups of parents whose children attend the same school are not in association with one another, and when parents and teachers do not know each other. Modern society tends to move in directions that reduce social capital.

The motivation to attend and persist in school, the desire to achieve, the discipline to do homework, the interest in reading, and the feeling of fitting comfortably into the school environment are all functions, in part, of a child's support system of parents, other interested adults, and peers. The child can redeem this social capital when necessary. As social capital declines, so does its asset value for the child.

A group of children particularly lacking in social capital are those in the new underclass. As they do not have a stable and supportive network at home, they lack an adequate learning environment and can rely only on a very small or non-existent amount of social capital. Many children of the new educational underclass, lacking sufficient support from a network of caring adults, become truants at an early age, and some eventually drop out completely from school. All too often, this dropping out sets the stage for a lifelong cycle of accumulated disadvantage.

Restoring the role of the family in taking care of the "whole child" may reverse the decline in social capital that is harmful to children. Closer cooperation among families in the neighborhood and between home and school will generate new social capital. The curriculum of the home, that set of virtuous family behaviors that enhances a child's success in school, can serve as a rallying point around which adults in school communities organize themselves and augment children's social capital.

Perhaps the child, "restless and angry in the darkness," is struggling with homework, and his mother is soothing him, praising his perseverance. Wouldn't that make a lovely Victorian scene, or a great episode from a 1950s sitcom, or a glimpse at the brave new world of virtuous family behavior in the city of tomorrow? The vision may even cause families and communities to act. This is "a thing my heart wishes the world had more of."

Note

1. Excerpt from "Poems Done On a Late Night Car" in *Chicago Poems* by Carl Sandburg, copyright 1916 by Holt, Rinehart and Winston, Inc. and renewed 1944 by Carl Sandburg, reprinted by permission of Harcourt Brace & Company.

References

Blankenhorn, D. (1995). *Fatherless America: Confronting our most urgent social problem*. New York: Basic Books.

Bushman, R. L. (1992). *The refinement of America*. New York: Knopf.

Coleman, J. S. (1990). *Foundations of social theory*. Cambridge, MA: Belknap.

Elkind, D. (1995). School and family in the postmodern world. *Phi Delta Kappan, 77*, 8-14.

Halberstam, D. (1993). *The fifties*. New York: Villard.

Himmelfarb, G. (1995). *The demoralization of society: From Victorian virtues to modern values*. New York: Knopf.

Lemann, N. (1991). *The promised land*. New York: Knopf.

Sandburg, C. (1970). Home. In *The complete poems of Carl Sandburg* (p. 62). Orlando, FL: Harcourt Brace.

Skolnick, A. (1991). *Embattled paradise: The American family in an age of uncertainty*. New York: Basic Books.

Walberg, H. J. (1984). Families as partners in educational productivity. *Phi Delta Kappan, 65*, 397-400.

Wang, M. C., Haertel, G. D., & Walberg, H. J. (1994). *Toward a knowledge base for school learning* (Office of Education Research and Improvement report). Washington, DC: U.S. Department of Education.

PART III

Schools

• CHAPTER 6 •

Fostering Educational
Resilience in Inner-City Schools

MARGARET C. WANG

GENEVA D. HAERTEL

HERBERT J. WALBERG

As the 1990s unfold, the nation's attention has been captured by the plight of increasing numbers of children and youth in circumstances that place them at risk of educational failure, particularly in inner-city communities. The quality of life in these communities is jeopardized by poverty, lack of employment opportunities, poor health care, crime, fragmented services, and despair. But this is only one side of the story; inner cities are also rich in culture, institutions, and other resources that can mitigate against adversity and promote healthy development and learning. Perhaps more importantly, these resources can further the capacity of individuals to overcome adversity and to develop educational resilience. Identifying conditions that promote resilience and pathways that lead to learning success is an area of investigation that has gained increasing attention in efforts to improve educational

AUTHORS' NOTE: The research reported herein was supported in part by the Temple University Center for Research in Human Development and Education (CRHDE) and in part by the Office of Educational Research and Improvement (OERI) of the U.S. Department of Education through a grant to the Mid-Atlantic Laboratory for Student Success at CRHDE. The opinions expressed do not necessarily reflect the position of the supporting agencies, and no official endorsement should be inferred.

success of children and youth in U.S. inner cities. The purpose of this chapter is twofold: (a) to provide an overview of the research base on fostering educational resilience among children whose circumstances place them at risk of educational failure; and (b) to describe educational practices that are resilience-promoting and their implications for student development and learning success.

Contexts That Foster
Educational Resilience

Educational resilience in the context of our discussion is defined as the heightened likelihood of educational success despite personal vulnerabilities and adversities brought about by environmental conditions and experiences (Wang, Haertel, & Walberg, 1994). Furthermore, educational resilience is conceptualized not as the product of a single precipitating event, but of continuous interaction between an individual and characteristic features of the environment. A key underlying premise is that educational resilience can be fostered through interventions that enhance children's learning, develop their talents and competencies, and protect or buffer them against environmental adversities.

Research on factors that influence learning can be culled to identify protective mechanisms that mitigate against adversity and support healthy development and educational success. Findings from a research synthesis (Wang, Haertel, & Walberg, 1993) demonstrate the range of contextual influences that can be maximized to serve as protective mechanisms that mitigate against negative life circumstances while facilitating development and educational resilience. Based on results of 91 meta-analyses, 179 authoritative review articles, and a survey of 61 educational researchers, 7 characteristics of the learner and 22 features of the home, classroom, and community contexts that influence student learning were identified. Figure 6.1 shows the relative influences of the 22 influence categories. The rankings are based on the calculated scores of the 22 influences, which were transformed into T-scores. (*T-scores* are standard scores with a mean of 50 and a standard deviation of 10.) As shown in Figure 6.1, the influences are depicted along a continuum of proximity to the learner, with those influ-

TABLE 6.1 Average Influence Scores for Five Sources/Contexts

Source/Context	Average Influence-on-Learning Score
Classroom Practices	53.3
Home and Community	51.4
Curriculum Design and Delivery	47.2
Schoolwide Practices and Policies	45.1
State and District Policies	34.5

ences and contexts that are more proximal exerting more influence than those that are more distal.

Table 6.1 presents the average influence scores for the five contexts presented in Figure 6.1. Classroom, home and community, and school contexts, which are more proximal to learners and directly affect their day-to-day activities, have larger influence scores on average than the state and district policy context, which is more distal and indirect in its influence.

The synthesis findings suggest that classroom, home and community, and school contexts can play a key role in fostering development and educational achievement. The research base on how each of these contexts affects the development of educational resilience is discussed below.

The Family

Of the 22 contextual influences on learning, "home environment/ parent support" is the second most influential category (see Figure 6.1). The home environment provides an abundance of resources even among families that are of limited economic means and/or facing severe hardships such as chronic illness, divorce, or early parental death. Parents (as well as other adults and older siblings) serve as children's first teachers, filling both nurturing and educative roles. Families foster not only children's physical growth but also their motivation to master the environment, their competence development, and their self-esteem. They provide knowledge about the world, opportunities to learn, models of behavior, and social and functional connections to the larger community.

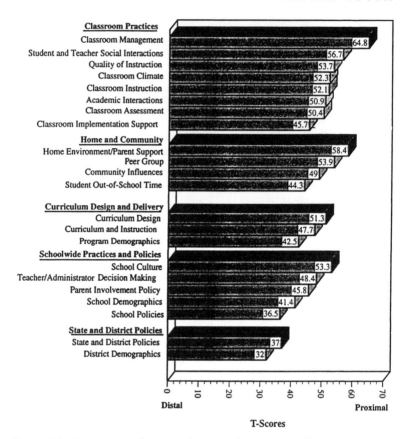

Figure 6.1. Continuum of Proximal to Distal Learning Influences and the Magnitude of Their Influence on Learning

Short-term prospective studies demonstrate that factors protecting against adversity include a positive parent-child relationship, family cohesion, warmth, assigned chores, responsibilities for the family's well-being, an absence of discord, and other secure childhood attachments. Other family attributes associated with school attendance and achievement among at-risk students include monitoring television viewing, reading to young children on a daily basis, expressing high expectations for academic success, and helping with homework. Family dysfunction, including marital instability and frequent relocations, predicts school disruptiveness and low achievement (Masten, Best, & Garmezy, 1991; Wang & Gordon, 1994).

Active engagement of family members (e.g., participating in school management teams, being involved in parent-developed workshops, providing tutoring, assisting teachers in classroom or after-school activities) is associated with improved student achievement; increased school attendance; and decreased student dropout, delinquency, and pregnancy rates. Furthermore, educational intervention programs designed to involve family members are significantly more effective than those targeted exclusively at students (Epstein, Salinas, & Simon, 1996; Walberg, 1984). Parents who participate in these programs are more often pleased with themselves, are more likely to enroll in educational courses, and tend to provide better support to their children. The love, interest, and support of a single family member can mitigate against adversities and promote children's educational resilience (Taylor, 1994).

The School

Influences such as teacher actions and expectations, effective instructional methods and curriculum, schoolwide policies, and school climate play key roles in raising student learning, motivation, and attitudes toward school. These influences are briefly discussed below.

Teachers

A teacher's concern, high expectations, and role modeling are key protective factors that mitigate against the likelihood of academic failure, particularly for students in difficult life circumstances. Sustained, close relationships between teacher and student can reduce stress and provide positive supports. Teachers not only provide institutional support for academic content and skills, but also serve as confidants and positive role models for children. They help students to develop the values and attitudes needed to persevere in their schoolwork and to achieve a high level of academic performance, and they also promote educational resilience by encouraging students to master new experiences, believe in their own efficacy, and take responsibility for their own learning. As shown in Figure 6.1, the relationship between teacher and student is highly important. "Student and teacher social interactions," for example, is the third most potent of the 22 influences on student learning.

Classroom Instruction and Climate

Instruction and classroom climate affect student learning in significant ways, as Figure 6.1 indicates. Contextual influences such as classroom management, quality of instruction, classroom climate, classroom instruction, and academic interactions are proximal to the learners, affect their day-to-day activities, and have a larger influence on school learning than more distal influences. Furthermore, the research base on classroom instruction indicates selected practices that have consistently produced achievement advantages, including maximizing learning time, setting high expectations for all students, providing ample opportunities for student-teacher interaction, maintaining a high degree of classroom engagement, tailoring instruction to meet the needs of individual students, engaging students in setting goals and making learning decisions, and participating in group learning activities. Selected dimensions of classroom climate are also consistently associated with enhanced student cognitive and affective outcomes, including cooperation among teachers and students; shared interests, values, and goals; an academic orientation; well-organized lessons with clear learning objectives; and student satisfaction.

Curriculum

On the basis of the research synthesis results depicted in Figure 6.1, the influence of curriculum on student learning is moderate. Of the 22 contextual influences, the three representing curricular influences were the 9th, 14th, and 18th most powerful. Although curriculum influences are less powerful than classroom practices and the home environment, they play a pivotal role in the provision of quality education to children who are placed at risk of school failure. In fact, providing all students with the opportunity to learn advanced subject matter content is a tenet of current educational reform efforts and a key resilience-promoting strategy. This is particularly important to children enrolled in compensatory or remedial programs such as Title I, bilingual, and special education.

Although schools attempt to provide for the greater-than-usual educational and related services needs of students who are not achieving well for a variety of reasons, many continue to experience serious difficulties in attaining learning success. Research suggests that the curriculum of the prototypical remedial or compensatory education program often contributes to children's learning problems. Students in pull-out categorical programs often receive watered-down curricula, including less instruction on higher-order skills, comprehension, and problem solving than their advantaged counterparts receive (Allington & McGill-Franzen, 1989; Pugach, 1995).

We know now that all children, including those with special needs, can achieve high academic standards when provided with challenging curriculum content and instruction tailored to their individual strengths and learning needs. Superior curricula contain learning activities and materials that promote higher-order thought processes and are responsive to student diversity and needs. Such curricula enhance students' motivation and serve as protective factors that promote educational resilience and learning success. By contrast, curricula that are disconnected from students' experiences, culture, and needs can contribute to their learning problems (Wang & Reynolds, 1995).

Schoolwide Practices

Changes in school life, organization, and culture can improve student learning and motivation (Newmann & Associates, in press; Newmann & Wehlage, 1995). Schoolwide practices associated with student achievement and psychosocial benefits include a schoolwide culture that reinforces students' academic accomplishments; public recognition, awards, and incentives associated with school-level achievement; smaller organizational units (minischools, charter schools, houses); an emphasis on student involvement and belonging that reduces feelings of alienation and disengagement; attachment to teachers, classmates, and the school; effective and responsive instructional programs that shield against adverse circumstances; student engagement in school life; and positive social interactions among peers and with adults.

These positive schoolwide practices appear to enhance life satisfaction and general well-being of students, particularly adolescents in schools with a high concentration of students whose circumstances place them at risk of educational failure. As shown in Figure 6.1, school culture was the sixth largest influence on student learning, with a greater impact on students' day-to-day lives than school policies or school demographics. Resilience-promoting school-wide practices include those that contribute to a positive school culture, foster academic achievement, and promote a sense of belonging in the school context.

The Community

Figure 6.1 reveals that community was the 12th most powerful contextual influence on student learning. Communities with well-developed and integrated networks of social organizations demonstrate how community-based actions can help children and youth who live in high-risk circumstances overcome adversity and facilitate resilience development and schooling success. These communities promote social and cultural norms that consistently express high expectations for good citizenship and educational success of children and youth. This expectation and the key role the community plays in providing protective mechanisms are seen most clearly in efforts to establish cultural norms on alcohol and drug abuse (Bell, 1987). The effectiveness of substance abuse programs is greatly enhanced by integrating community resources.

Local communities can positively affect the social well-being, health, safety, and intellectual life of their residents. Social support by caring adults in the community helps sustain support for task accomplishments and increases community-based opportunities for students to develop new interests and skills (Rigsby, Reynolds, & Wang, 1995). Community-based programs that engage children and youth in such activities as protecting the local environment, conducting food drives for the hungry, and participating in library-based reading programs provide youngsters with firsthand experience cooperating with their neighbors. These activities not only develop participants' knowledge and skills, but also provide powerful evidence that communities support their residents. Through their participation, youngsters learn that they are valued community members, can contribute to the community's well-being, and can help overcome a sense of alienation and disenfranchisement.

Fostering Educational Resilience
in Inner-City Schools

Findings from a long-term program of research on resilience development at the National Center on Education in the Inner Cities (CEIC) at the Temple University Center for Research in Human Development and Education are discussed in this section. The program, designed to address the question "What conditions are required to bring about massive improvements in the development and learning of children and youth in this nation's inner cities?" encompasses a range of studies, including synthesis studies of the knowledge base on resilience; comparative field-based studies of low- and high-achieving inner-city schools; correlational studies linking characteristics of resilient students to attributes of their families, classrooms, schools, and communities; survey studies that identify effective practices and policies to promote student learning and other educational outcomes; and intervention studies that demonstrate the impact of resilience-promoting strategies on students' learning, affect, and behaviors (Wang, in press).

Characteristics of Educationally Resilient
Students in Inner-City Schools

Using the National Educational Longitudinal Study database, Peng, Wang, and Walberg (1992) found that resilient students had higher self-concepts and educational aspirations, felt more internally controlled, interacted more with parents, and had parents who encouraged them to do their best. Similarly, a consistent pattern of proactive participation and a high level of academic and social interaction with teachers and peers were salient in the findings comparing educationally resilient and nonresilient students in inner-city schools in Houston and Philadelphia (Wang, Waxman, & Freiberg, 1996). Resilient students in the study generally perceived their school and classroom environments to be conducive to learning and deemed as appropriate the standards established by teachers and parents for their academic performance and conduct. Although both groups of students—"resilient" and "at-risk"—reported that a good or bad day depended on the occurrence of classroom fights or disruptions requiring teacher intervention, resilient students tended to perceive the problem from a nonparticipatory perspective, whereas at-risk students often were directly involved.

A consistent characterization of resilient students in inner-city schools has also surfaced from the interview protocols of teachers participating in the study. Teachers described resilient students as having someone who cares for them, doing well academically despite exposure to a variety of adverse situations, being responsible and more mature socially, completing school assignments, being focused and not distractable, valuing education, and having the ability to draw on personal strengths. These characterizations are also consistent with those described in the early resilience literature (Masten et al., 1991).

The resilience construct has also provided the conceptual base for a series of studies on the capacity of adolescents from minority backgrounds to maintain a positive self-concept and constructive attitudes toward school and education despite exposure to adverse social circumstances (Taylor, 1994). For example, Taylor found that, despite perceived discrimination, many African-American adolescents maintain a positive self-concept. This finding contradicts the argument that African-American adolescents' perceptions of discrimination result in low academic achievement, a devaluing of the importance of school performance, and a social and racial identity at odds with academic achievement. Taylor's research suggests that African-American adolescents do not necessarily internalize negative messages—rather, that awareness of racial discrimination may cause them to attach greater importance to educational accomplishment. Even in the face of threats to self-concept, such as discrimination, individuals may be able to maintain positive views of themselves—an attribute of resilient adolescents that allows them to react in constructive ways that advance their development and learning success.

Characteristics of Inner-City Classrooms and Schools That Promote Educational Resilience

Research on effective inner-city schools (Wang, Freiberg, & Waxman, 1996; Zetlin, Reynolds, & Wang, 1995) has found consistent patterns of organizational and behavioral characteristics that are reflective of findings from the general literature on effective schools. Among the effective organizational features are strong leadership by the principal, shared decision making, and esprit de corps among staff. Instructional features linked to positive educational outcomes include well-managed classrooms, challenging instruction, and student choice in selecting instructional activities. The schools had strong parental involvement programs and were described as having a pleasant school climate and attractive physical facilities.

Inner-city schools with these features also are linked to more positive classroom processes and higher academic performance, compared with other schools that have high concentrations of students living in adverse circumstances (Wang, Waxman, & Freiberg, 1996). Students in the effective schools spent more time working independently, teachers spent more time interacting with students, and students expressed more positive perceptions about their schools overall. Students were more satisfied with their schoolwork and peer relationships, thought classroom rules were made clear to them, felt more involved in school, perceived their parents as more involved in their schoolwork, and believed that their teachers were supportive and held high expectations of students. Further, students had higher aspirations, more achievement motivation, and better social and academic self-concepts than students at risk of school failure enrolled in ineffective schools.

These findings are consistent with recent studies of effective schools that identified organizational and instructional practices that enhance student achievement, motivation, and positive attitudes and promote educational resilience among socially and economically disadvantaged children (Teddlie & Stringfield, 1993). Greater achievement than one would predict from socioeconomic status was obtained at schools that devoted a high percentage of time to academically focused tasks. The atmosphere in these schools was generally described as friendly; principals and teachers protected the time spent on academic tasks and ensured that students' academic programs were well coordinated; and principals were engaged in school events, led the selection and retention of their faculties, valued high academic achievement, and supported library activities in the life of the school. Teachers whose students achieved higher levels of academic attainment employed planning, clearly specified management and disciplinary rules, set high academic standards for all students, actively taught higher-order thinking skills, and used direct instruction when appropriate.

Similarly, high-achieving inner-city schools show evidence of enabling conditions that result in high levels of student engagement (Freiberg, Stein, & Huang, 1995; Wang, Freiberg, & Waxman, 1996). These include, for example, an orderly and safe school campus; student-centered and highly responsive classroom learning environments with well-structured classroom management systems; a site-specific and ongoing professional development program for the school staff, based on implementation needs identified by teachers and administrators; and parents with high educational aspirations for their children. These enabling conditions, coupled with an organizational capacity for continuous learning and renewal, produced high levels of student engagement and achievement.

Research and practical wisdom suggest that when competently implemented, effective schoolwide strategies serve as protective factors that mitigate against the adversity that abounds in inner-city environments. As noted by Rutter, Maugham, Mortimore, Ouston, and Smith (1979), children living under conditions that are not supportive of psychosocial well-being may experience their school as a force for good or for bad, depending on the programs and internal conditions.

Effective School Responses
to Student Diversity

Schools today, particularly urban schools, are challenged to serve an increasingly diverse student population. In the past, schools responded to the diverse needs of students through specially designed categorical programs. Albeit well intentioned, these narrowly framed approaches to serving the often multiply co-occurring needs of students frequently place children at even greater risk. Recent research on effective school responses to student diversity suggests the need for major—in some cases, revolutionary—institutional changes (Wang & Reynolds, 1995; Wong & Wang, 1994). These changes require a broad-based approach that considers all organizational and operational features of the school context: classroom practice, curriculum, school organization, restructuring of service delivery, and school and district policies. These essential components of schools can be coherently joined to create nurturing learning environments that are responsive and effective in fostering educational resilience and learning success of every student.

Meta-Analysis of Inclusive Approaches
to Provide for Student Diversity

Historically, categorical or so-called second systems programs have been used to provide services to special education, Title I, limited-English-proficient, and other students with diverse needs, including gifted and talented children. The benefits of the categorical approach to addressing the needs of diverse student populations have been challenged, particularly the use of extra-class placement. In 1982, a National Academy of Science report (Heller, Holtzman, & Messick, 1982) specified that children should be placed in separate classes only if they could be accurately classified and if the noninclusive practices demonstrated superior benefits. Disturbingly, Heller et al. reported that not only does placement of large numbers of children in special programs not lead to improved learning, but it also adds further risk through demeaning labels and increased educational segregation.

The educational segregation of students who require greater than usual educational and related services support is particularly troubling in urban schools where more than 50% of students are in pull-out programs (Wong & Wang, 1994). Rules and regulations put these programs largely out of local control, and procedural requirements often overshadow attention to educational substance and learning progress. Furthermore, the requirements do not ensure the kind of accountability intended for achieving better educational outcomes of children and youth from ethnically and language-diverse backgrounds or for those considered at risk of educational failure.

The inclusion of children with special needs in regular classrooms and schools has received increasing support as a systemic educational improvement strategy (Commission on Chapter 1, 1992; Wang & Reynolds, 1995). Implementing inclusion requires changes in educational philosophy, curriculum, instructional practices, and school organization. Further, such approaches respond to the increasing demands for schools to address the scientific and legal basis for noninclusive practices and to explain why so many students are set aside in categorical programs in which they continue to fall behind their peers. Findings from a recent meta-analysis (Baker,

Wang, & Walberg, 1994) indicate that inclusive practices confer small-to-moderate benefits on the standardized achievement test scores of special needs students and on their social outcomes as measured by self, peer, teacher, and observer ratings of classroom behaviors and interactions. Outcomes for nonspecial needs children indicate that many benefit socially from their relationships with students with disabilities and from participating in a caring school community (Staub & Peck, 1995).

School Restructuring of
Curriculum and Service Delivery

Researchers using an action research design conducted a series of intervention studies on how schools can be more responsive to student diversity by changing their organization and by using innovative approaches to service delivery. A series of studies in an inner-city comprehensive high school and a middle school examined the feasibility and effects of implementing small unit organization to improve student engagement, curriculum articulation across disciplines, and cross-disciplinary collaboration and collegiality among school staff (Oxley, 1994). Findings suggest the following requirements: (a) a consistent pattern of changes that modify the school culture (e.g., changing the mind-set of administrators and the teaching staff on how learning takes place); (b) implementation of coordinated approaches to organizing school resources; and (c) staff development that focuses on developing strategies and expertise for meeting the diverse needs of students. These changes produced significant improvements in teacher attitudes toward school and in the ability of teachers to institute radical changes in the service of students, as well as enhanced student motivation and improved student achievement.

Collaborative studies have focused on improving the learning of individual students by providing a systematic process of learning needs assessment and coordinated service delivery in five inner-city elementary schools (Zetlin & MacLeod, 1995). These studies involved planning and implementation activities to adapt school programs and related services to meet the unique needs of many students from ethnic and language-diverse backgrounds. The findings suggest five common features that facilitated program implementation at the study sites:

1. The school staffs believed that students of diverse backgrounds and educational histories could succeed, and they tailored their teaching methods to meet the needs of those students who did not adapt well to traditional schooling. No students were intentionally screened out, nor were any programs permitted that would attract only certain groups of students.

2. The schools using either small unit organization or the restructuring of school curriculum, resources, and service delivery had a stable, intimate, and collegial context for teaching and learning that helped meet the needs of students at the margins.

3. A decentralized system of school management was employed in which school staff had greater authority and flexibility and engaged in collaborative group processes; parents accessed teachers more readily; students' academic programs were more coherent; and all teachers shared a sense of responsibility for student success.

4. The school staffs had access to the knowledge base on effective classroom and schoolwide practices and systemic reform strategies.

5. The schools employed systematic, site-based, professional development.

Findings from the research syntheses and intervention studies discussed indicate the feasibility and effectiveness of improving a school's capacity for achieving educational resilience and learning success of students by using an inclusive approach to service delivery. The restructuring of schools' curriculum and service delivery, when combined with the creation of inclusive, stable, supportive learning environments and increased access to family, school, and community resources, can promote the healthy development and learning success of students at risk of school failure.

Forging Family-School-Community Connections

It is widely acknowledged that working alone, neither schools, nor social and health agencies, nor the fundamental unit of our society—the family—can meet the needs of children and youth in circumstances with co-occurring risks. Thus, an organizational, professional, and institutional movement has emerged from the current wave of school reform efforts to address the multiple and interconnected needs of inner-city children and their families. Referred to variously as the "integrated," "collaborative," "coordinated," or "school-linked" services movement, its goal is to harness the resources of family, school, and community to create contexts that support students' learning success by meeting the physical and social wellness needs of students and their families (Dryfoos, 1995; Flaxman & Passow, 1995; Rigsby et al., 1995).

Although a variety of innovative programs have emerged across the United States, all of them emphasize coherent and seamless child and family services that promote educational resilience and improved life circumstances of children and youth placed at risk. Ranging from local grassroots community efforts to state- and federal-level initiatives, these programs seek to transform fragmented, inefficient systems of service delivery into a network of coordinated partnerships that cross programmatic and agency lines. Despite unprecedented national attention and a myriad of programmatic initiatives at all levels, solid information on the features, scope, and effectiveness of these programs is just becoming available.

A practical savvy about what does and does not work is emerging. Although many of the coordinated service programs are still in the formative stage, the extant database suggests some insights and practical guidelines. Crowson and Boyd (1993) concluded that cost savings from service coordination should not be expected. Further, implementation of service coordination can be an extremely difficult undertaking—in terms of organizations (with legal complications, bureaucratic immobility, turf battles, and communication breakdown) and the deep structures of schooling (the fundamental ways schools work and professional role interpretation).

Future Directions and Conclusions

Advances in resilience research have led to more detailed descriptions of educationally resilient inner-city children and the identification of protective features of their families, schools, and communities. These protective factors mitigate against risks, vulnerabilities, and adversities while promoting academic and later life success. Evidence from these research studies has informed the design of resilience-promoting interventions for inner-city environments. On the basis of the research studies described in this chapter, we suggest two potentially fruitful areas for further development: (a) implementing an inclusive approach to respond to student diversity; and (b) implementing family-school-community partnerships.

Implementing an Inclusive Approach to Respond to Student Diversity

Educational environments that are responsive to human diversity treat differences among students as strengths that can be built upon or as needs that must be accommodated. Unresponsive and ineffective systems of delivery ignore individual differences or, even worse, treat student differences in a stigmatizing manner that reduces learning opportunities. Research on educational resilience stresses the importance of responding to children's differences, not as deficiencies, but as starting points for uniting the resources, talents, and efforts of families, teachers, schools, and communities in order to overcome adversity and promote learning success. A major premise of implementing inclusive practices is the restructuring of curriculum and service delivery to promote academic and social benefits for children at risk of school failure and to enhance the sense of community among all participating students.

Taking stock of what is known from research and practical knowledge of educational reform, specific recommendations were made by participants in one of CEIC's invitational conferences on making a difference for students at risk (Wang & Reynolds, 1995). The recommendations serve as a provocative list of strategies for improving schools' capacity for addressing the diverse needs of individual students:

- Make public schools inclusive and integrated.
- Organize schools into smaller educational units—minischools, charter schools, or houses—in which groups of students and teachers remain together for several years of study.
- Augment research on "marginal" students to provide a growing knowledge base and credible evaluation system.
- Implement new approaches based on what is known about teaching in schools that have a high concentration of students with special needs.
- Expand programs for the ablest students.
- Integrate the most current findings in general and special education and special language learning areas into teacher education.

- Apply concepts of inclusion and integration to the bureaucratic structure of educational governance, professional organizations, and advocacy groups.
- Challenge federal and state authorities to create broad, cross-departmental "empowerment zones" for delivering coordinated, comprehensive child and family services.
- Encourage public dialogue about education.

Implementing Family-School-Community Partnerships

The multiple risks and adversities faced by many children and youth cannot be addressed by the family, school, or community alone. Rather, the resources within these three contexts must be harnessed if we are to advance toward solving the educational, health, psychological, and social problems that confront families and their children. Strategies for successful partnerships have been culled from the research base on implementing family-school-community partnerships (Grey, 1995; Kirst, Koppich, & Kelley, 1994; Rigsby et al., 1995; U.S. Department of Education & American Educational Research Association, 1995). These strategies can be used to build the capacity of inner cities and their institutions to promote healthy development and educational resilience among children and youth. Research-based knowledge and a philosophy of cultural diversity serve as the foundation of successful partnerships. The research community provides school practitioners, parents, and community service providers with easy access to the knowledge base on the contexts, processes, and outcomes for successful family-school-community partnerships.

Prior to establishing successful partnerships, participants must realistically assess the money, time, and tangible resources needed for sustained successful operation. Effective partnerships are site-specific and designed to meet the local needs and co-occurring risks that are prevalent in the lives of the children and families being served. Their program design takes into account stakeholder interests, staff expertise, resource availability, and policy guidelines. Administrative mechanisms are created that manage the partnership's processes and that authorize actions to implement agreements. Participants in the partnership should be provided with ample opportunities to learn about the cultures of participating clients, agencies, and organizations. Although high engagement of all participating groups is encouraged, long-standing difficulties among participating groups need to be addressed and differences among clients' levels of active participation should be acknowledged. Successful implementation of partnerships depends on a shared responsibility among all local stakeholder groups.

Research also indicates that long-term resources, support, and follow-through for the partnership depend on the establishment of a constituency that supports its efforts. In particular, partnership stability can be enhanced through changes in funding that would reduce the currently fragmented grant structure and new noncategorical ways to support services. A final strategy for successful implementation is to conduct formative evaluations of the partnership program and redirect program efforts based on results. Summative evaluations can be conducted when the program has been in place long enough to allow a fair evaluation of effects.

Educational resilience is a potentially powerful construct for fostering resilience and educational success of children and youth who are enduring stressful life circumstances. Research has identified a compelling set of protective factors within the child, family, classroom, school, and community that mitigate against failure and promote healthy development. The family, school, and community environments are overlapping contexts in which the events and conditions that influence one context also influence the others. Resilience is promoted when the resources in these contexts are united and dedicated to the healthy development and academic success of children. The likelihood of successful educational outcomes further increases when the values and norms expressed in these three contexts are congruent.

Using resilience-promoting strategies, schools can enlist the tangible and intangible resources of families and communities to better meet students' needs. Research results suggest a portrait of a resilience-promoting inner-city school that includes the following characteristics:

Inclusive practices

Small school size

Heightened engagement of students and teachers in the life of the school

Effective instructional practices empirically linked to achievement advantages

Orderly and structured academic school climate

Sustained, caring, supportive interactions among teachers and students

Challenging curricula tailored to meet the needs and talents of individual students

Active parent-school-community partnerships that make health, social, and educational resources more accessible to students and families

Ample opportunities for students to participate in valued activities

Site-specific professional development program

Organizational capacity for change and renewal

A decade ago, research on resilience reflected the influence of developmental psychologists, psychiatrists, and psychopathologists. Today, the research of educational psychologists and sociologists and the practical knowledge and wisdom of teachers, school administrators, and educational policymakers have introduced new data, hypotheses, and methods that further illuminate the phenomenon of resilience. Increasingly, evidence from school implementation, intervention, and evaluation studies is used to design resilience-promoting interventions that protect inner-city children and youth against stressful life circumstances.

The picture of U.S. cities that emerges out of the resilience research should encourage hope, not despair. The research findings are contrary to the picture of inner-city life that stresses deficiency, negativity, and hopelessness. As the research on educational resilience expands, inner-city educators will have more information on how to construct positive, healthy environments that advance the psychological and social abilities of their most vulnerable students. In this way, the research community contributes to revitalizing our nation's inner cities.

References

Allington, R. L., & McGill-Franzen, A. (1989). School response to reading failure: Instruction for Chapter 1 and special education students in grades two, four, and eight. *Elementary School Journal, 89*(5), 529-542.

Baker, E. T., Wang, M. C., & Walberg, H. J. (1994). The effects of inclusion on learning. *Educational Leadership, 52*(4), 33-35.

Bell, P. (1987). Community-based prevention. *Proceedings of the National Conference on Alcohol and Drug Abuse Prevention: Sharing knowledge for action.* Washington, DC: NICA.

Commission on Chapter 1. (1992). *Making schools work for children in poverty.* Washington, DC: Author.

Crowson, R. L., & Boyd, W. L. (1993). Coordinated services for children: Designing arks for storms and seas unknown. *American Journal of Education, 101*(2), 140-179.

Dryfoos, J. G. (1995). *Full-service schools: A revolution in health and social services for children, youth, and families.* San Francisco: Jossey-Bass.

Epstein, J. I., Salinas, K. C., & Simon, B. (1996, April). *Effects of Teachers Involving Parents in Schoolwork (TIPS)—Interactive homework in the middle grades.* Paper presented at the annual meeting of the American Educational Research Association, New York.

Flaxman, E., & Passow, A. H. (Eds.). (1995). *Changing populations/changing schools: The 94th yearbook of the National Society for the Study of Education.* Chicago: University of Chicago Press.

Freiberg, H. J., Stein, T. A., & Huang, S. L. (1995). The effects of classroom management intervention on student achievement in inner-city elementary schools. *Educational Research and Evaluation, 1*(1), 33-66.

Grey, B. (1995). Obstacles to success in educational collaborations. In L. C. Rigsby, M. C. Reynolds, & M. C. Wang (Eds.), *School-community connections: Exploring issues for research and practice* (pp. 71-99). San Francisco: Jossey-Bass.

Heller, K. A., Holtzman, W. H., & Messick, S. (Eds.). (1982). *Placing children in special education: A strategy for equity.* Washington, DC: National Academy of Science Press.

Kirst, M. W., Koppich, J. E., & Kelley, C. (1994). School-linked services and Chapter 1: A new approach to improving outcomes for children. In K. Wong & M. C. Wang (Eds.), *Rethinking policy for at-risk students* (pp. 197-220). Berkeley, CA: McCutchan.

Masten, A. S., Best, K. M., & Garmezy, N. (1991). Resilience and development: Contributions from the study of children who overcome adversity. *Development and Psychopathology, 2,* 425-444.

Newmann, F. M., & Associates. (in press). *Authentic achievement: Restructuring schools for intellectual quality.* San Francisco: Jossey-Bass.

Newmann, F. M., & Wehlage, G. (1995). *Successful school restructuring.* Madison: University of Wisconsin, Center for Organization and Restructuring of Schools.

Oxley, D. (1994). Organizing schools into small units: Alternatives to homogeneous grouping. *Phi Delta Kappan, 75*(7), 521-526.

Peng, S. S., Wang, M. C., & Walberg, H. J. (1992). Demographic disparities of inner-city eighth graders. *Urban Education, 26*(4), 441-459.

Pugach, M. C. (1995). Twice victims: The struggle to educate children in urban schools and the reform of special education and Chapter 1. In M. C. Wang & M. C. Reynolds (Eds.), *Making a difference for students at risk: Trends and alternatives* (pp. 27-52). Thousand Oaks, CA: Corwin.

Rigsby, L. C., Reynolds, M. C., & Wang, M. C. (Eds.). (1995). *School-community connections: Exploring issues for research and practice.* San Francisco: Jossey-Bass.

Rutter, M., Maugham, B., Mortimore, P., Ouston, J., & Smith, G. A. (1979). *Fifteen thousand hours: Secondary schools and their effects on children.* Cambridge, MA: Harvard University Press.

Staub, D., & Peck, C. A. (1995). What are the outcomes for disabled students? *Educational Leadership, 52*(4), 36-40.

Taylor, R. D. (1994). Risk and resilience: Contextual influences on the development of African American adolescents. In M. C. Wang & E. W. Gordon (Eds.), *Educational resilience in inner cities: Challenges and prospects* (pp. 119-130). Hillsdale, NJ: Lawrence Erlbaum.

Teddlie, C., & Stringfield, S. (1993). *Schools make a difference: Lessons learned from a 10-year study of school effects.* New York: Teachers College Press.

U.S. Department of Education & American Educational Research Association. (1995). *School-linked comprehensive services for children and families: What we know and what we need to know.* Washington, DC: U.S. Department of Education.

Walberg, H. J. (1984). Families as partners in educational productivity. *Phi Delta Kappan, 65,* 397-400.

Wang, M. C. (in press). Next steps in inner-city education: Focusing on resilience development and learning success [Special issue]. *Education and Urban Society.*

Wang, M. C., Freiberg, H. J., & Waxman, H. J. (1996, April). *Case studies of inner-city schools.* Paper presented at the annual meeting of the American Educational Research Association, New York.

Wang, M. C., & Gordon, E. W. (Eds.). (1994). *Educational resilience in inner-city America: Challenges and prospects.* Hillsdale, NJ: Lawrence Erlbaum.

Wang, M. C., Haertel, G. D., & Walberg, H. J. (1993, Fall). Toward a knowledge base for school learning. *Review of Educational Research, 63*(3), 249-294.

Wang, M. C., Haertel, G. D., & Walberg, H. J. (1994). Educational resilience in inner cities. In M. C. Wang & E. W. Gordon (Eds.), *Educational resilience in inner-city America: Challenges and prospects* (pp. 45-72). Hillsdale, NJ: Lawrence Erlbaum.

Wang, M. C., & Reynolds, M. C. (Eds.). (1995). *Making a difference for students at risk: Trends and alternatives.* Thousand Oaks, CA: Corwin.

Wang, M. C., Waxman, H. C., & Freiberg, H. J. (1996, April). *Classroom and shadowing observations: An integrative analysis.* Paper presented at the annual meeting of the American Educational Research Association, New York.

Wong, K. K., & Wang, M. C. (Eds.). (1994). *Rethinking policy for at-risk students.* Berkeley, CA: McCutchan.

Zetlin, A. G., & MacLeod, E. (1995). A school-university partnership working toward the restructure of an urban school and community. *Education and Urban Society, 27*(4), 411-420.

Zetlin, A. G., Reynolds, M. C., & Wang, M. C. (Eds.). (1995). Special and remedial education: Future directions [Special issue]. *Education and Urban Society, 27*(2).

CHAPTER 7

The Problems and Promise of Urban Schools

WILLIAM LOWE BOYD
ROGER C. SHOUSE

For many Americans, the words *urban schooling* conjure up bleak images: old buildings; glass-strewn concrete playfields; hallways and classrooms decorated more by graffiti than by the signs and symbols of learning; and teachers and students struggling against, but often succumbing to, defeatism and apathy. For those closer to the daily life of city schools, however, the image is more likely one of contrast: caring teachers and principals striving to create countercurrents of hope; students and parents working to overcome endemic social obstacles to educational attainment; and the daily exchange of enormous efforts for "small victories" (Freedman, 1990). In fact, both sets of images are real, for indeed, urban schools in the United States epitomize both its greatest problems and its greatest promise for addressing some of its most perplexing social issues.

The greatest challenge of "urban schooling," of course, relates to the fact that the term connotes concerns about the educational experiences of minority and socioeconomically disadvantaged youth. Improving urban schools thus conveys the notion of overcoming inequalities in educational, occupational, and social opportunity across racial and economic categories. The great promise relates to the evidence that urban schools can become more effective and thereby truly contribute to the attainment of these goals (Boyd, 1991).

Although school "effectiveness" is typically, and with justification, understood in terms of achievement test scores, equally important is the school's ability to attract, engage, and establish social bonds with students at all ability levels. It is also clear that researchers have generally understood the task of improving school effectiveness as relating mainly to the needs of "disadvantaged" students. Numerous barriers to this task confront urban schools, including gangs, violence, and dangerous neighborhoods; dysfunctional, top-heavy bureaucratic governance; highly politicized and unionized environments constraining leadership and management; funding problems; inadequate employment opportunities for inner-city youth and adults; weak morale, academic climate, and motivation; insufficient social capital and support in the surrounding community; and role conflict, overload, and "burnout" for teachers. In short, urban schools seem bogged down in a mire of social, economic, and structural constraints.

Despite all of this, however, it is strange that so little progress has been made in improving the academic effectiveness of urban schools. Beginning with the so-called Coleman Report of the mid-1960s (Coleman et al., 1966), the past 30 years have witnessed a burgeoning of research studies aimed at reducing the gap in quality between the school experiences of disadvantaged and more affluent youth. Many of these studies, moreover, have actually identified samples of "effective urban schools," and considerable agreement exists among researchers about the characteristics contributing to their effectiveness. Still unattained, however, is the most crucial research goal—that of establishing a reliable set of techniques for transforming ineffective schools into effective ones. This challenge still confronts and perplexes today's school "restructuring" movement. As we discuss below, however, progress is being made in learning how to reconstitute the sense of professional and academic community within schools.

To a real extent, then, the issue of how to change urban schools takes on an importance equal or even paramount to that of school effectiveness. Improvement requires fundamental change in urban schools, but the forces arrayed against change in schools (and especially in urban schools) are truly formidable. So, if change and improvement are vital, then the barriers impeding this in urban schools demand special attention. In this chapter, we look at both the impediments to change and improvement and the characteristics of effective urban schools, tracing the path followed since the Coleman Report and describing what appear to be promising further avenues for improving urban schools. In doing so, we note how school effectiveness research has shifted in emphasis over the years, from economic to structural and on to social models of urban school effectiveness—for example, from highlighting school funding and physical resources to teachers' instructional behaviors and on toward a school's sense of community and academic culture. What is important about this shift is not that older perspectives have been left behind, but rather that new perspectives have allowed the old ones to become better refined and applied.

Unfortunately, although a more sophisticated understanding of the factors determining school effectiveness now exists, our inability to quickly and effectively implement this knowledge in schools has contributed, along with adverse social and economic trends, to declining public confidence in public schools (and, needless to say, in educational research as well). Urban school systems, in particular, now face nothing less than a crisis of public confidence and legitimacy. Demands are mounting for radical reforms to alter the governance structure or to break up, privatize, or "voucherize" urban systems (replace them with more or less privatized systems of school choice for parents and students; Education Commission of the States, 1995). Indeed, this crisis is now so acute that calls for the reform of their governance and institutional structures increasingly eclipse demands for programmatic and pedagogical reforms within these systems (Cibulka, 1995, 1996). Critics assert that fundamental flaws in the governance and institutional structures of urban school systems (including especially their tendency to have dysfunctional incentive systems) impede the basic changes that are essential for real reform (Boyd, 1991). Consequently, a question we address in the conclusion of this chapter is whether real improvement is possible in urban schools in the absence of fundamental reform of their governance and institutional structures.

Early Waves of
School Effects Research

As suggested above, the quest for more effective forms of schooling has traditionally been synonymous with the quest for greater educational equity across racial and socioeconomic levels. The basis for this understanding was established more than 30 years ago by James Coleman et al. (1966) in *Equality of Educational Opportunity*. In trying to explain the significant achievement gap between racial and socioeconomic groups through an analysis of survey data on a large national sample of schools, these researchers examined how differences in various types of physical, human, and social resources across schools related to average school achievement levels. The Coleman Report reached four major conclusions. First, the strongest predictors of achievement across all racial groups were social characteristics of the student's home environment (e.g., parents' education, income). For minority students, the next strongest predictor of achievement related to social characteristics of the school (its percentage of white students and the average economic background of all students). Third, but exclusively for Southern black children, teacher characteristics (education and years of experience) had a modest impact on achievement. Fourth, after controlling for all of the above characteristics, factors related to school fiscal resources (per-pupil spending and curricular and instructional facilities) appeared to have little or no effect on school achievement.

The Coleman Report posed a tremendous challenge to educational researchers and policymakers, no doubt troubled by the surprising finding that inequities in fiscal resources had little or no influence on student learning across schools. And although it received a good deal of methodological criticism (e.g., see Murnane, 1975), later investigations have tended to support its general pattern of findings. A main weakness of the study, however, was its "production function" framework. In other words, schools were implicitly conceived of as "black boxes" through which resource inputs were somehow converted into educational outputs. Although a reasonable first step in understanding school effectiveness, it did not accurately portray the way schools actually work. Students within the same school, for instance, do not typically receive equal doses of school resources. They tend not to share equal access to the library, to the computer lab, or to the most experienced teachers and often are exposed to different types and levels of instruction via tracking or ability grouping. In reality, then, schools are better understood as "switching yards" than as units of instruction (Barr & Dreeben, 1983). Left to be explored, then, were the internal processes of schools, their relationship to student learning, and the possibility that their quality might vary within and across schools as a function of students' race, urbanicity, or economic background.

The Coleman Report thus triggered a new wave of "process-product" research, epitomized by the so-called effective schools studies of the 1970s and 1980s (e.g., see Rosenholtz, 1985). Peeling the lid off the black box, these studies took primary aim at the workings of urban (usually elementary) schools. The typical methodological approach was to identify samples of significantly effective (and sometimes of significantly ineffective) schools, with "instructional effectiveness" typically defined by student test score results higher than one would predict on the basis of the socioeconomic status (SES) of students' families. Next, an attempt was made to identify school processes and characteristics that actually seemed to make a difference in student learning. Collectively, these studies produced lengthy lists of "effective practices" or "best practices" for classroom instruction and school management and organization.

Summarizing these findings, Odden and Odden (1995) note that effective teachers maximize instruction time, are well prepared, maintain a smooth and steady instructional pace (especially during the first few weeks of school), focus on academic learning, and emphasize student mastery of material. With regard to organizational characteristics, effective schools evidence strong instructional leadership, usually provided by the principal; a consensus on academically focused school goals; realistic but high expectations for student learning; regularized monitoring of progress toward academic goals; ongoing staff development; and an orderly and secure environment with a strong, consistently enforced student discipline program (Odden & Odden, 1995, p. 67).

The effective schools "movement" was extremely influential among researchers and educators, as well as among policymakers at all levels of U.S. government. Equally important, it signified a major shift in the understanding about how schools work, moving from explanations involving fiscal capital to those centered around human and social capital. Questions persist regarding its various recommendations, however, particularly the direction of causal effect. In other words, although certain characteristics might produce higher-achieving students, the reverse might also be the case; that is, schools may maintain these characteristics because they are fortunate enough to have greater numbers of high-achieving students. That some schools identified as effective at one point in time were found not to be so a few years later might, for example, suggest the latter possibility. Thus, although "effective schools" clearly share important practices, it was never consistently established that *ineffective* schools could become more effective by adopting these features.

Schools as Social Systems: Some Problematic Implications for Inner-City Schools

It has become increasingly clear that changing urban schools amounts to something deeper than simply adjusting key processes. More than switching yards, schools are, in fact, small societies in which beliefs, values, and informal norms and sanctions help shape and redirect those processes. As some classic sociological studies indicate (Bidwell, 1965; Coleman, 1961; Gordon, 1957; Waller, 1932/1967), the day-to-day realities of classroom life draw teachers away from objective, "universalistic" interactions with students toward those more subjective and "particularistic." A strong student culture (or particular characteristics of student culture) can thus have tremendous power to either reinforce or erode teachers' academic standards and success with students.

The problem is particularly acute for urban schools in two distinct but complementary ways. First, behavioral norms among urban students often run in opposition to academic goals. As described by one inner-city high school teacher, "To be intelligent around here is considered a crime. They don't bring in their books or supplies because of peer pressure. If you're making real good grades and everybody else is not, . . . you're just not going to be part of the group" (Shouse & Schneider, 1993, p. 80). Moreover, in the case of African Americans, Ogbu (1978) contends that their background as an involuntary minority group in the United States led them to develop a subculture in opposition to their oppressors.

Ogbu believes that this subculture promotes an especially strong resistance to schooling that is perceived to be controlled by the dominant culture—an analysis that supports calls for Afro-centric schooling.

A second problem associated with the stark realities of urban life is that teachers are naturally drawn away from *academic* concerns and toward *social* concerns. An art teacher at the same school mentioned above asked, "How can I ask this kid to be concerned with principles of color composition when there are people outside who want to *kill* him?" A less extreme but more insidious example of this is reported in *The Shopping Mall High School* (Powell, Farrar, & Cohen, 1985): A Spanish teacher remarks that a particular student, though "not very good at all in the language . . . tries very, very hard, and she always attends, and it makes you feel very sorry for her. So she'll probably get a B or a B minus" (p. 59).

Under such conditions, changes in curricular and instructional processes and practices are likely to be co-opted or redirected to suit the perceived needs and limitations of students. In other words, even as best practices become implemented in urban schools, their students may still be more likely to experience educational treatment more socially therapeutic than academically challenging. This likelihood helps in explaining the lack of success of the effective schools movement in establishing a "portable" model: The movement underestimates the "DNA" of educational organizations, those deep social structures that work to either constrain or promote academic teaching and learning.

Shifting to Social Models of Urban School Effectiveness: Schools as Communities

Numerous scholars have used the concept of "sense of community" to explain or highlight social differences between schools. Coleman and Hoffer (1987), for example, argue that, in contrast with modern-day public schools, Catholic schools tend to be based around "functional" communities in which school members share the same place of worship and interact with each other both in and out of the classroom and in and out of the school. They also make the point that urban Catholic schools are able to attract large numbers of non-Catholic families by offering a "value" community supportive of their beliefs and expectations about schooling and child rearing. For the school and its members, the result is a network of mutually reinforcing social relationships—a well of "social capital" to be tapped for the purpose of attaining meaningful educational goals.

Bryk and Driscoll (1988) expand this understanding of school communality, clarifying its organizational foundations and showing how they apply to public as well as Catholic schools. In a key study combining elements of theoretical and empirical analysis, Bryk and Driscoll argue that whether public or private, "communally organized" schools evidence (a) a consensus over beliefs and values; (b) a "common agenda" of course work, activities, ceremonies, and traditions; and (c) an ethic of caring that pervades the relationships of student and adult school members. On the basis of analyses of a national sample of schools and students, Bryk and Driscoll found that schools with higher levels of communality (as measured by an array of survey items representing each of the three core components) also evidenced higher attendance rates, better morale (among both students and teachers), and higher levels of student achievement.

The fact that there is nothing explicitly "academic" about any of the three core components described above or, in fact, any of the survey items representing them is perplexing. Would it not be possible for schools to become "dysfunctional communities" (Monk, 1992), where common values, activities, and styles of caring run counter to academic goals? Would this most likely occur in urban schools where teachers, daunted by daily realities, came to view positive social relations and student self-esteem as reasonable substitutes for meaningful academic demand and student effort?

These questions were recently explored as part of a broader investigation into improving math and science performance among U.S. high school students (Shouse, 1996). Based on data from a national sample of schools, the study separately examined the achievement effects of communality (measured along lines similar to those of Bryk and Driscoll's study) and "academic press" (measured in terms of an assortment of survey items reflecting school academic climate, disciplinary climate, and teachers' instructional behavior and emphasis).

The findings with respect to low-SES schools were quite striking. Academic effectiveness among these schools was significantly tied to academic press and to *combined* levels of academic press and communality. Average achievement in low-SES schools having high levels of both academic press and communality, in fact, rivaled that of schools serving more affluent students. But, the least academically effective low-SES schools were those that combined strong communality and *weak* academic press. Although these findings reveal the tensions between meeting students' social and academic needs, they also reveal the tremendous potential of school social networks that are supportive, cohesive, and academically oriented to spark a quantum leap in the quality of urban students' educational experiences (Shouse, 1996).

These findings indicate that school leaders must strive for a management style and school culture that successfully balance a *concern for performance* with a *concern for people and community*. This indication underscores the significance of the classic tension for managers between the task or performance dimension and the caring or consideration dimension of leadership. In the case of schools, research suggests four types of "school cultures" based on combinations of high or low emphasis on academic performance and on a caring community.[1] Schools with high levels of concern for both academic performance and communality can be said to have an *integrative culture*. The phrase that characterizes this culture is "No one fails here who works hard." Schools that emphasize performance but are low on communality have an *exacting culture,* characterized by the phrase "Some will fail here no matter what they do." Schools that emphasize community but de-emphasize performance have a *caring culture,* which is captured by the phrase "No one fails here who shows up." Finally, schools low on both performance and community have an *apathetic culture*. The phrase that best characterizes these schools is "No one fails whether they show up or not." As we have discussed above, the challenging context of urban schools makes it especially important that educators resist the pressures pushing schools toward the deceptive *caring culture* (or possibly the defeatist *apathetic culture*).

Still, the Issue of Change

Despite the encouraging findings about urban schools that combine a strong emphasis on both academic performance and communality, is it possible that the dilemma we now face is similar to that of the effective schools movement? That is, we can suggest where urban schools should be, but we still cannot offer a reliable map for getting there. If student background and school composition factors remain the strongest predictors of school achievement, could effective urban schooling be merely related to attracting the most able and motivated students? Or, might catalytic factors or incentives exist to help schools evolve into strong, academically oriented communities? Several possible avenues warrant discussion and further research.

Increasing School Funding

Despite the lack of consistent empirical evidence during the past 30 years in its support, the idea that having more money would allow urban schools to overcome their most serious barriers remains an intuitively attractive one. More money leads to newer facilities, more talented and motivated teachers, and a higher quality and quantity of teaching equipment and supplies, things all seemingly connected to increasing students' social attraction to school. Nowhere, perhaps, is this point (and its converse) illustrated so pointedly as in Jonathan Kozol's *Savage Inequalities* (1991).

Although Kozol's work commands attention—and money certainly makes a difference (Ferguson & Ladd, 1995)—it is probably unfair to characterize the fiscal resource deficiencies of most urban schools as "savage" or to point to them as the primary source of urban school ineffectiveness. A great deal more is involved, as Hanushek (1995, p. 22) notes, in reflecting on Kozol's analysis:

> The dichotomy between the good intentions of school finance and the reality of schools is pervasive. For example, it is instructive to contrast the school spending version of Jonathan Kozol with the school policy version of Jonathan Kozol. His recent book [*Savage Inequalities*], which identified truly outrageous situations in some of our nation's schools, pointed to fixing everything simply by bringing the unsafe and unsanitary schools up to the spending levels of the most opulent public schools that could be found (Kozol, 1991). On the other hand, the main theme of the equally as compelling *Death at an Early Age* (Kozol, 1967) is that the current organization of schools with few

incentives to improve student performance squanders the good resources that are available. Nothing in Kozol (1991) indicates how the problems of Kozol (1967) will be overcome.

That greater funding is not, by itself, the solution to the problems of urban schools comes through rather clearly from an experience in Kansas City (Armor, 1995; CBS News, 1994). Under a 1986 federal court order aimed at redressing decades of de facto school segregation, the Kansas City School District spent more than $1 billion to improve the quality of its schools in order to attract suburban students. New schools were built with up-to-date materials and state-of-the art computer labs. Teachers received significant raises, and class size was limited to 25 students. Despite these material improvements, white enrollment continued to decrease and student test scores continued to lag behind those of other comparable big-city school districts. In sharp contrast, however, were the significant achievement gains made at one of the district's middle schools, which, although making modest physical improvements, required its students to wear uniforms and their parents to sign contracts promising to oversee their children's attendance and homework.

The Kansas City case illustrates a major problem with using money as a catalyst for school improvement. It tends to be "broadcast" at districts, schools, or broad programs, and those most responsible for eventual student outcomes (teachers) have little power to direct it toward their own specific needs and problems. If money is to work as a catalyst for school change, it may need to be "narrowcast" to create new incentives and relationships at the bottom of the organizational pyramid—that is, for teachers, students, and parents.

As an example of this, consider a recent school business partnership program designed to improve graduation and college attendance rates among students at two "at risk" inner-city high schools. During a 4-year period, the sponsoring company offered students college tuition vouchers of up to $4,000 for maintaining reasonable attendance and at least a C average. During the same period, teachers could earn up to $4,000 for serving as regular mentors for small groups of students. Although a systematic evaluation of the program's impact revealed contrasts between two schools, it reported several significant improvements in such areas as attendance, educational aspirations, and achievement among "borderline" students (Shouse, 1991; Shouse & Schneider, 1993).

One story from this particular program reveals not only the stifling effects of insensitive bureaucracy but also the contrast between the power of narrowcast money and the impotency of broadcast money. Having taken on the task of mentoring, an English teacher at one of the schools directed her stipend toward engaging her group of 15 students in a series of school fix-ups, cleaning and painting areas of the school, inside and out. For one of these fix-ups, students painted bright colors and original designs over dismal lavatory walls. Not long afterward, when it became time for the school to receive some general maintenance, a team of district painters obliterated the students' work with their own standard issue battleship gray. Stunned and disappointed, the teacher and her students complained about the action. Word was eventually passed down to them that they really had no business painting anything anyway.

In short, modest amounts of money could be redistributed to provide resources, incentives, and a sense of empowerment and ownership to those on the "front lines" of urban schooling. This theme, of course, parallels that of the area to which we now turn, that of school restructuring.

School Restructuring

Like the effective schools movement, the school restructuring movement has come to denote a fairly specific array of prescriptions for improving organizational effectiveness and student achievement. At its foundation, the restructuring idea is a response to concern that school systems have become too large and bureaucratic to permit the types of effective site-level management and professional and instructional practices necessary to meet the teaching and learning needs of teachers and students. Teachers work in isolation from each other, as well as from critical decision-making processes. School principals are too often handcuffed by bureaucratic rules and central office edicts. For the sake of efficiency, students are often sorted by ability and are exposed to instruction driven primarily by short-answer standardized tests. Finally, because of bureaucratic and professional barriers to lay involvement, schools tend to be poorly linked with the parental and community networks that can support and facilitate the successful education of children. The prescriptions offered by the restructuring movement thus center around three basic areas:

1. Shifting the thrust of school governance to a more "bottom up" direction through decentralization, site-based management, staff professional development, teacher empowerment, and greater parent involvement
2. Refocusing curriculum and instruction toward cooperatively organized, mixed-ability classrooms; greater emphasis on higher-order learning; and the use of performance-based student assessment
3. Reducing school size, typically through the creation of "schools within schools"

Several more specific changes have been recommended across these three areas by reformers, and some recent evidence links their collective adoption with significant gains in high school achievement. A study by Lee and Smith (1994), for example, contrasted achievement gains in three types of school: (a) those with no reform or restructuring, (b) those that had sought to improve on their traditional, more bureaucratic practices, and (c) those that had engaged in some level of organizational restructuring. Although students in traditionally oriented schools that were seeking improvement outgained those in nonreform schools, students in restructured schools (those having adopted at least 3 out of 12 restructuring practices) significantly outgained those in both other types of schools. More important, the greatest achievement differences occurred among students at the low end of the socioeconomic scale. In other words, the achievement gap between more and less economically advantaged students was narrowest within restructured schools.

And yet, before educators bestow panacea status on school restructuring plans, they need to look closely at some key questions. For instance, were we to imagine school restructuring as represented by a "check off" of reforms, we should expect the items on the list to vary greatly in terms of their actual contribution to student achievement. In fact, for some items on the list (e.g., cooperative learning, heterogeneous grouping), the evidence is either inconclusive or extremely complex. Moreover, there is considerable potential for friction among these restructuring reforms. At a recent national conference, for instance, a well-known researcher be-moaned the fact that resistance to de-tracking plans increased as teachers and parents gained a greater share of decision-making power. Apparently, their intuitive sense of the practicality and logic of grouping students according to their interests and learning pace conflicted with the commitment to "de-tracking" of educator elites.

Sooner or later, decentralizing decision-making power—to school-site administrators, teachers, and parents—raises questions about standards and consistency across a "system" of schools. The central office of school districts is naturally inclined to resist decentraliza-tion or to try to "recentralize" power when it can (Crowson & Boyd, 1992), in large part for reasons of consistency and account-ability. Further, with its advocacy of national standards and associ-ated testing schemes, the recent "systemic" school reform movement tends to conflict with the desire to decentralize and empower site-level educators.

Effective school reform thus requires us to look at the separate components of the restructuring agenda—and they may or may not fit together—rather than to accept them all as a package deal. As an example, consider the restructuring practice of students keeping the same homeroom throughout their high school careers (one practice included in the Lee & Smith [1994] study cited above). Although urban students might benefit from sharing the first 15 minutes of each day with the same people, evidence from Asian secondary schools indicates that a stronger sense of belonging and cooperation would result if they shared the entire day in the same classroom, with their teachers being the ones moving around the school. With regard to ability grouping, evidence from U.S. Catho-lic schools suggests that narrowing the range and coordinating the content of ability groups makes more sense than the complete abandonment of curricular differentiation (Bryk, Lee, & Holland, 1993).

Further, a strange irony surrounds the school restructuring move-ment. Although it aims to debureaucratize and decentralize school organization, it also tends to carry its own specific agenda of reform. Not so many years ago, as a teacher at an urban high school, one of the authors observed a beautiful illustration of this. The faculty were considering and discussing their concerns about the district's new plan for local school control. On the basis of a majority vote, a school could become "empowered"—that is, be

governed by a small local school council consisting of the principal
and parent and teacher representatives. Confronting a list of teacher
concerns over the proposal, the principal exclaimed, "People, understand this! We *will* become an empowered school!" What the
teachers feared (and perhaps what the principal understood) was
that empowerment could actually lead to disempowerment; that is,
in this case, because teachers might end up in a minority on the
council, overruled by the parents and the school principal, it might
de-legitimate teachers' experiential knowledge about what does
and does not work in schools and about what they are and are not
professionally capable of accomplishing in the classroom.

In short, for urban school restructuring to be effective—for it to
be *honest*—requires that teachers' understandings not be viewed as
obstructions to change. Put another way, new educational structures must result as much, if not more, from bottom-up than from
top-down efforts. Thus, to be effective and honest, restructuring
must provide teachers formal and informal opportunities to develop appropriate professional norms; to examine, question, but in
the end *select* effective instructional methods based on what they
know and can learn about their craft.

Indeed, significant, collective involvement of teachers appears to
be a key to effective school restructuring, based on the extensive
program of research on restructuring conducted by the federally
supported Center on Organization and Restructuring of Schools at
the University of Wisconsin-Madison (Newmann & Wehlage, 1995).
The center's researchers found that school effectiveness and student learning were enhanced when schools took on the qualities of
"professional communities" (Louis & Kruse, 1995; Newmann &
Wehlage, 1995). Such communities had three basic features: "Teachers
pursue a clear shared purpose for all students' learning. Teachers engage
in collaborative activity to achieve the purpose. Teachers take
collective responsibility for student learning" (Newmann & Wehlage,
1995, p. 30). Summarizing the center's findings, Newmann and
Wehlage (1995) stated:

> The recent education reform movement gives too much attention to
> changes in school organization that do not directly address the quality
> of student learning. New administrative arrangements and teaching
> techniques contribute to improved learning only if they are carried
> out within a framework that focuses on learning of high intellectual

quality. . . . Student learning can meet these high standards if educators and the public give students three kinds of support: Teachers who
practice authentic pedagogy. Schools that build organizational capacity by strengthening professional community. External agencies and
parents that support schools to achieve the high quality student
learning we have described. (p. 51)

Significantly, the center's researchers found that professional community in schools "not only boosted student achievement gains,
[but] also helped to make the gains more equitable among socioeconomic groups" (Newmann & Wehlage, 1995, p. 37).

The quest for more effective community and professional involvement in the education of urban children is central to two of
the most promising approaches to the reform and restructuring of
urban education, the programs led by James Comer and by Henry
Levin. Comer's work began with an intervention project in New
Haven, Connecticut. His analysis of his two project schools "suggested that the key to academic achievement is to promote psychological development in students which encourages bonding to the
school. Doing so requires fostering positive interactions between
parents and school staff, a task for which most staff people are not
trained" (Comer, 1988, p. 46). This interaction requires that school
staff and parents overcome a natural resistance to cooperation,
which seems to pervade the schools. The intervention required the
reduction of "destructive interactions" and the establishment of
"cohesiveness and direction to the school's management and teaching" (p. 46).

To accomplish these purposes, a team was formed to "govern and
manage" the school (Comer, 1988, p. 46). This team included the
principal, a mental health professional, representatives from the
nonprofessional staff, and elected representatives from among parents and teachers. Guidelines were established to mediate between
the needs of the principal for authority and those of the team to
represent concerns and needs of the students, as well as their
respective constituencies. To ensure cooperation, consensus decision making was required (p. 47).

In addition to policy development, parents are also encouraged
to participate in the life of the school and to assist in the growth of
bonds between the community and the school. Concerted efforts
among social workers, school psychologists, and special education

teachers combine to establish "school policies and practices so that students' developmental needs would be served better and behavior problems prevented" (p. 47). In addition to minimizing psychic distress and behavior problems to facilitate the student-school relationship, Comer's efforts also include a social skills curriculum to redress "the problem of social misalignment" (p. 48).

The totality of Comer's program is intended to develop the child socially as well as academically. Whereas the social skills curriculum moves to align economically disadvantaged and minority students with mainstream society, the "team approach" to school management and governance represents an effort to modify school-community relationships. By involving parents and the community in the formation of social capital, the program also alleviates some of the cultural discontinuity problem emphasized by Ogbu (1978).

Henry Levin's (1987) "accelerated school" program represents another effort to achieve both academic and social success by combining effective pedagogical techniques with efforts to build social capital and reduce cultural discontinuity. Thus, Levin tries to build on the strengths of culturally different children, rather than focus on their "deficits." His emphasis on the strengths and abilities of disadvantaged students contradicts conventional wisdom that assumes a need for slower, remedial treatment of such students:

> The accelerated school is a transitional elementary school designed to bring disadvantaged students up to grade level by the end of sixth grade so they [can] take advantage of mainstream secondary school instruction. . . . The goal . . . is to bring all children up to grade level, rather than limit interventions for the disadvantaged to "pull out" sessions. This approach requires an assessment of each child's performance at school entry and sets a series of objectives.
>
> Parents are deeply involved in two ways. First . . . [by] a written agreement that clarifies the obligations of parents, school staff, and students. Second . . . [by] opportunities for parents to interact with the school program and actively assist their children.
>
> Another aspect of the program is an extended day. . . . During this period, college students and senior citizen volunteers work with individual students. . . . These broad features make the accelerated school a total institution rather than a graft of compensatory or remedial classes onto conventional elementary schools. (Levin, 1987, pp. 20-21)

Much of the promise for more effective schooling for disadvantaged children seems to lie with such programs as Levin's and Comer's. It is encouraging that many serious efforts are being made to implement these models across the United States today (e.g., see Finnan, St. John, McCarthy, & Slovacek, 1996).

One further important idea for restructuring urban education involves the widespread movement to achieve coordinated, school-linked services for at-risk children. The traditional fragmentation of responsibility among a variety of agencies for the large array of social and health services needed by poor children and their families is increasingly viewed as dysfunctional and unacceptable. Consequently, with substantial support from foundations and reform-minded state officials, the coordinated services movement has blossomed. Numerous projects and experiments with coordinated services are in progress across the United States. Usually linked with or centered on schools, these ventures have the potential not only to deliver much more coherent and satisfactory services but also to link the school far more effectively with its supporting community. This effort has come to be seen as part of the restructuring movement, and some advocates have even expected substantial changes in the internal operations of schools to flow from involvement with coordinated services approaches. However, for a variety of reasons related to such matters as "turf issues" and differences in professional cultures and languages among service agencies, research indicates that coordinated service ventures have been difficult to achieve and have rarely had much impact on the actual culture and operation of schools, although they are beneficial for at-risk children and their families (Crowson & Boyd, 1993, 1996). Significantly, sense of community emerges as a key factor in this domain too. Research by White and Wehlage (1995) indicates that the more bureaucratic and less communitarian the coordinated services projects, the less likely they are to succeed.

In closing this section, we want to emphasize again that a major challenge for educators as they strive to meet the social, as well as educational, needs of disadvantaged children is to not allow concern for their students' disadvantaged backgrounds to pull them away from high academic standards and expectations. As a report by the Committee for Economic Development (1994) stresses, the primary mission of schools is learning and academic achievement; social services "may be *placed* in the schools, they may be *delivered* through the schools, but they should not be made the *responsibility* of the schools" (p. 5).

Redesigning School Social Environments: Standards and Incentives

In the years just prior to his untimely death in the spring of 1995, James S. Coleman considered the problem of how external incentives might be structured to produce more academically effective schools. His notion of the "output-driven school" (Coleman et al., in press) conveys the idea that schools could become more effective in response to academic standards established beyond the institution by employers, colleges, or even standardized exams. For Coleman, the ability to raise or lower academic standards amounts to a burden from which, once freed, teachers could act more as coaches or supportive adults than as authoritative distributors of academic reward. For schools, the result would be the development of more academically oriented, informal work groups. In a real sense, then, Coleman's idea uses a relatively small amount of organizational change to produce a much larger change in the social understandings and relationships of school members. Fully realized, the result is a broad set of social incentives for high student achievement.

In addition to externally imposed standards, output-driven schools would include five other key elements:

1. Evaluations (not just for students, but for teachers and schools as well) based on level of performance and performance gain (or "value added")
2. Yearly rewards to teachers, students, and parents, based on both types of criteria
3. The final output criteria at a given stage of schooling serves as the starting point for designing evaluations at each subsequent stage of schooling, thus creating a system of "short feedback loops"
4. Allocation of rights and responsibilities not only to individuals but also to groups of teachers, groups of students, and groups of parents to encourage the development of informal norms that support educational goals
5. Academic performance and performance in other specialized areas (possibly nonacademic) as the basis for student evaluation

Coleman's vision of the output-driven school challenges several traditional elements of U.S. public education. For example, the reallocation of "rights" to which he refers would literally grant to teachers the right to decide which students to accept from an earlier stage of schooling and which students to send on to a later stage of schooling. Although on first glance this seems rather cold and at odds with popular notions of inclusiveness, it is countered by the fact that teachers, students, and parents would receive rewards (e.g., salaries, bonuses) based, in part, on student achievement *gain*. This "value added" incentive encourages teachers not only to raise their students to the level necessary for entry into the next schooling stage but also to accept lower-ability students (for it is here where more value can be added). Notice, too, that the reallocation of rights would allow parents to opt out of or into schools on the basis of whether they met their child's particular needs, thus requiring some sort of school choice mechanism.

As an analogy for how a system of output-driven schools might function, Coleman offers the example of the "string of rights" motivating workers on a Japanese automotive assembly line. Workers along the line have the right to "reject" outputs from earlier stages of production (thus affecting the pay of workers at those earlier stages) or to hold back and improve the quality of their own outputs (thus affecting their own pay). Shippers, dealers, and customers outside the organization hold the "ultimate" right to reject unsatisfactory finished products and to accept those they consider satisfactory. In other words, the quality of a product at one stage drives the performance at the preceding stage all the way back through the production process of the organization.

This short-loop feedback process contrasts sharply with the long-loop feedback processes found in most bureaucratic organizations, including schools. Driven more by external demands than by internal characteristics, trading control over standards for control over how best to achieve them, teachers would become naturally engaged in common academic activity, and schools could become transformed into meaningful learning communities.

Coleman's idea reminds us that, like its larger real-life counterparts, the small society of the school owes much of its power to shape young people to forces beyond its immediate control. Like other key social institutions, schools must therefore often grapple with the tension between setting a course and following one. For

example, although the attainment of equal educational opportunities and outcomes has been a primary research and policy interest
during the past 30 years, the public is clearly quite willing to
tolerate and even demand a fair amount of educational inequality.
This is evident in current policy battles over school funding, school
choice, outcome-based education, de-tracking, and so on. The
implication would appear to be that those examining or promoting
school change need to consider and be more open about their own
ideological preferences and how these jibe with popular notions of
school effectiveness.

Conclusion

James Coleman's visionary conception of an output-driven school
stands in stark contrast with the reality of the schools we have.
Public schools in general, and especially urban schools because of
their greater propensity to be highly bureaucratized, are input-
driven and inclined toward dysfunctional incentive systems. With
a near monopoly relationship with their clients and with few
rewards (or penalties) linked with the achievement gains of their
students, public schools too often lack any meaningful accountability for their performance (Boyd & Hartman, 1988). As a result,
the burden of success (or failure) falls mainly on the shoulders of
the poor children and families that the schools serve. Although
learning clearly is co-produced, requiring a vital contribution of
effort on the part of students (and families) as well as teachers, the
incentive structure of schools needs to be modified to provide more
rewards and accountability for educators to engage in the hard
work of improving their effectiveness. As explained in this chapter,
that will involve transforming their schools and pedagogical approaches in accord with the promising findings we have discussed
concerning the power of academic press combined with a caring
and "professional" community.

One final issue that needs to be addressed is the overall strategy
for urban school reform: Must the governance and/or institutional
structure of urban school systems be changed to enable real reform,
or can school improvement be pursued effectively from the "bottom
up," one school at a time? Ideally, of course, the system should be
transformed so that schools can succeed because of it, rather than

in spite of it. As we noted at the outset of this chapter, there is a growing sense that the crisis of urban school systems has so undermined their legitimacy that nothing short of a complete overhaul of their governance and institutional structure can enable them to regain the public's confidence (Cibulka, 1995, 1996). Although reform still can be undertaken one school at a time, the scale and severity of urban education's problems cry out for a more comprehensive solution. Moreover, schools that are reforming are quite vulnerable if they are at the mercy of unreformed school systems. Ultimately, the real test (and requirement for regaining legitimacy) is whether reformed schools or school systems can actually succeed in giving students the kind of education needed for a postindustrial society. On this point, Kerchner, Koppich, and Weeres (1995) argue incisively that today's students must be prepared as "mind workers" for the complex demands of an information society. This means, these researchers believe, that to develop the higher-order thinking skills required by a knowledge society, classroom instruction must be based on cognitivism rather than on behaviorism:

> A century ago, education underwent its modern reformation. The challenge now is to design an institutional arrangement that once again aligns public education to the emerging knowledge society. Like the transition from an agrarian to an industrial economy, the passage to a knowledge society will necessitate a fundamental alteration of the instructional core of public education, and then the construction of a new institutional shell of governance, funding, and organizational structures around that core. (p. 81)

On balance, then, the ultimate challenge for the improvement of urban education—and, more broadly, public education in general—will be to achieve and sustain the social and political consensus required to facilitate and support the work of "reinventing" U.S. public education around a core of high academic expectations, "authentic pedagogy" (Newmann & Wehlage, 1995), and caring and "professional" community. Although building the needed consensus will demand extraordinary professional and political leadership and, most likely, new political arrangements in many settings, the stakes involved and the returns to be gained make the effort imperative.

Note

1. This discussion is based on a typology adapted from Sethia and Glinow (1985) and on characterizations of school cultures drawn from Bryk, Lee, and Holland (1993).

References

Armor, D. J. (1995, August 2). Can desegregation alone close the achievement gap? *Education Week, 14,* p. 41.

Barr, R., & Dreeben, R. (1983). *How schools work.* Chicago: University of Chicago Press.

Bidwell, C. E. (1965). The school as a formal organization. In J. G. March (Ed.), *Handbook of organizations* (pp. 972-1022). Chicago: Rand McNally.

Boyd, W. L. (1991). What makes ghetto schools work or not work? In P. W. Thurston & P. Zodhiates (Eds.), *Advances in educational administration: Vol. 2. School leadership* (pp. 83-129). Greenwich, CT: JAI.

Boyd, W. L., & Hartman, W. (1988). The politics of educational productivity. In D. H. Monk & J. Underwood (Eds.), *Microlevel school finance: Issues and implications for policy* (pp. 271-308). Cambridge, MA: Ballinger.

Bryk, A. S., & Driscoll, M. E. (1988). *The school as community: Theoretical foundations, contextual influences, and consequences for students and teachers.* Chicago: University of Chicago, Benton Center for Curriculum and Instruction.

Bryk, A. S., Lee, V., & Holland, P. (1993). *Catholic schools and the common good.* Cambridge, MA: Harvard University Press.

CBS News. (1994). On the money. *60 minutes,* XXVI, 24 [Transcript]. Livingston, NJ: Burrelle's Information Services.

Cibulka, J. G. (1995, October). *Two eras of urban schooling: The decline of the old order and the emergence of new organizational forms.* Paper presented at Wingspread Conference on Next Steps for Education in the Inner Cities, Racine, WI.

Cibulka, J. G. (1996). The reform and survival of American public schools: An institutional perspective. In R. L. Crowson, W. L. Boyd, & H. B. Mawhinney (Eds.), *The politics of education and the new institutionalism: Reinventing the American school.* London: Falmer.

Coleman, J. S. (1961). *The adolescent society.* New York: Free Press.

Coleman, J. S., Campbell, E. Q., Hobson, C. J., McPartland, J., Mood, A. M., Weinfeld, F. D., & York, R. L. (1966). *Equality of educational opportunity.* Washington, DC: Government Printing Office.

Coleman, J. S., & Hoffer, T. (1987). *Public and private high schools: The impact of communities.* New York: Basic Books.

Coleman, J. S., Schneider, B., Plank, S., Schiller, K., Shouse, R., & Wang, H-Y. (in press). *Redesigning American education.* Boulder, CO: Westview.

Comer, J. P. (1988, November). Educating poor minority children. *Scientific American, 259*(5), 42-48.

Committee for Economic Development. (1994). *Putting learning first: Governing and managing the schools for high achievement.* New York: Author.

Crowson, R. L., & Boyd, W. L. (1992). Urban schools as organizations: Political perspectives. In J. Cibulka, R. Reed, & K. Wong (Eds.), *The politics of urban education in the United States.* London: Falmer.

Crowson, R. L., & Boyd, W. L. (1993, February). Coordinated services for children: Designing arks for storms and seas unknown. *American Journal of Education, 101*(2), 140-179.

Crowson, R. L., & Boyd, W. L. (1996). Structures and strategies: Toward an understanding of alternative models for coordinated children's services. In J. Cibulka & W. Kritek (Eds.), *Coordination among schools, families, and communities: Prospects for educational reform.* Albany: State University of New York Press.

Education Commission of the States. (1995, July). *The new American urban school district.* Denver, CO: Author.

Ferguson, R. F., & Ladd, H. F. (1995, April). *Additional evidence on how and why money matters: A production function analysis of Alabama schools.* Paper presented at the Conference on Performance-Based Approaches to School Reform, Brookings Institution, Washington, DC.

Finnan, C., St. John, E., McCarthy, J., & Slovacek, S. P. (Eds.). (1996). *Accelerated schools in action: Lessons from the field.* Thousand Oaks, CA: Corwin.

Freedman, S. G. (1990). *Small victories: The real world of a teacher, her students, and their high school.* New York: Harper & Row.

Gordon, C. W. (1957). *The social system of the high school.* New York: Free Press.

Hanushek, E. A. (1995, October). *Incentives and the schooling of disadvantaged populations.* Paper presented at the Wingspread Conference on Next Steps in Inner-City Education, Racine, WI.

Kerchner, C. T., Koppich, J. E., & Weeres, J. G. (1995). *United mind workers: Representing teaching in the knowledge society.* Unpublished manuscript.

Kozol, J. (1967). *Death at an early age: The destruction of the hearts and minds of Negro children in the Boston public schools.* New York: Houghton Mifflin.

Kozol, J. (1991). *Savage inequalities: Children in America's schools.* New York: Crown.

Lee, V. E., & Smith, J. B. (1994). *Effects of high school restructuring and size on gains in achievement and engagement for early secondary school students.* Madison: University of Wisconsin, Wisconsin Center for School Research, National Center on Effective Secondary Schools.

Levin, H. M. (1987, March). Accelerated schools for disadvantaged students. *Educational Leadership, 44,* 19-21.

Louis, K. S., & Kruse, S. (1995). *Professionalism and community: Perspectives on reforming urban schools.* Thousand Oaks, CA: Corwin.

Monk, D. H. (1992). Educational productivity research: An update and assessment of its role in education finance reform. *Educational Evaluation and Policy Analysis, 14*(4), 307-332.

Murnane, R. J. (1975). *The impact of school resources on the learning of inner-city children.* Cambridge, MA: Ballinger.

Newmann, F. M., & Wehlage, G. G. (1995). *Successful school restructuring*. Madison: University of Wisconsin, Wisconsin Center for Educational Research, Center on Organization and Restructuring of Schools.

Odden, A. R., with the assistance of Odden, E. (1995). *Educational leadership for America's schools*. New York: McGraw-Hill.

Ogbu, J. U. (1978). *Minority education and caste: The American system in cross-cultural perspective*. San Diego: Academic Press.

Powell, A. G., Farrar, E., & Cohen, D. K. (1985). *The shopping mall high school: Winners and losers in the educational marketplace*. Boston: Houghton Mifflin.

Rosenholtz, S. J. (1985). Effective schools: Interpreting the evidence. *American Journal of Education, 93*(3), 352-388.

Sethia, N. K., & Glinow, M-A. (1985). Arriving at four cultures by managing the reward systems. In R. Kilmann et al. (Eds.), *Gaining control of the corporate culture*. San Francisco: Jossey-Bass.

Shouse, R. C. (1991). Teachers as mentors: Building communality in an urban school. *Administrator's Notebook, 35*, 7.

Shouse, R. C. (1996). Academic press and sense of community: Conflict, congruence, and implications for student achievement. *Social Psychology of Education, 1*(1), 47-68.

Shouse, R. C., & Schneider, B. (1993). *Pepsi School Challenge final report*. Chicago: Ogburn-Stouffer Center and the University of Chicago.

Waller, W. (1967). *The sociology of teaching*. New York: John Wiley. (Original work published 1932)

White, J. A., & Wehlage, G. (1995, Spring). Community collaboration: If it is such a good idea, why is it so hard to do? *Educational Evaluation and Policy Analysis, 17*(1), 23-38.

• CHAPTER 8 •

Normative School Transitions Among Urban Adolescents: When, Where, and How to Intervene

EDWARD SEIDMAN

SABINE E. FRENCH

It is well known that the high rates of educational failure and concomitant problem behaviors among adolescents diminish their opportunities for achieving productive and satisfactory lives. These outcomes are a consequence of the progressive disengagement of youth from the educational enterprise. The costs in lost human capital and increased need for social services are astounding. Moreover, the rates of educational failure are disproportionately higher among adolescents growing up in economically impoverished urban communities, and in particular among Latino and African American youth.

Even under adverse economic conditions, many poor and racial/ethnic minority adolescents thrive, entering adulthood with equivalent opportunities to become productive citizens similar to youth growing up under less adverse conditions (Seidman, 1991). Very little is known, however, about which psychological factors and environmental circumstances set such positive (or negative)

AUTHORS' NOTE: The authors are indebted to Tracey A. Revenson and Peggy Clements for their constructive comments on a prior draft of this chapter. This chapter was written with support from a grant from the National Institute of Mental Health (MH43084).

developmental trajectories into motion. As Rutter (1987) noted, "Particular attention needs to be paid to the mechanisms operating at key turning points in people's lives when a risk trajectory may be redirected onto a more adaptive path" (p. 329). The transition to junior high school may represent just such a key turning point or risky transition and, as such, can serve as a critical locus for preventive interventions.

In developing our argument, we begin by examining the social ecology of urban public schools that adolescents confront as they move from elementary to junior to senior high school; the biological, cognitive, and interpersonal development of urban adolescents; and the intersection of these changing school ecologies and developmental processes. The reader will see that the developmental needs of the young adolescent and the social and organizational structure of the junior high school that they experience are quite incompatible. Next, we critically examine the nature and timing of educational interventions and policies that have been addressed to the needs of adolescents in urban public schools, including recent efforts aimed at restructuring high schools. We close with a discussion of the salience of the transition to junior high school as an ideal time and place at which to create small intimate learning environments that engage young adolescents in the educational enterprise at a critical juncture in their lives.

The Ecology of Urban Public Schools

The ecology of urban schools presents students with a complex set of challenges—some positive, others negative. One of the most positive aspects of many urban public schools is that children often are surrounded by more children from different backgrounds than is found in most schools outside the city. This cultural diversity can teach tolerance and promote harmony among its young students. Unfortunately, race can also be used as a divisive tool, resulting in violent territorial battles. Some urban schools, however, are entirely made up of one racial or ethnic minority group, especially at the elementary and junior high school levels.

Youth in the city have to grow up a bit faster than suburban school students. Often, they are expected to assume greater responsibilities in their families. Young students are often privy to drug deals, gang violence, and victimization, as the violence of the surrounding neighborhoods often infringes on the school's boundaries. Urban schools are often large in size, with overcrowded classrooms, and entrenched in bureaucratic red tape. The poverty level tends to be much higher and more concentrated, and an overwhelming majority of students receive free or reduced-cost lunch. Because of their urban location, where real estate is quite costly, schools often lack the space allotted to suburban schools, including large playgrounds and sports' fields.

As students make the transition from elementary to junior high school and from junior to senior high school, they are confronted with dramatically different social contexts, each with its own norms, expectations, and behavioral and social regularities that, in large part, define the role of student. Norms, expectations, and regularities take many forms, including expectations and unwritten rules for the behavior of all members, students, teachers, and principals; the physical and social organization of the learning environment, such as task versus ability grouping, daily routine and scheduling of activities, and school size; teacher supportiveness, demands, and expectations for academic performance; and peer supportiveness and pressure. In addition, each school differs in its geographic proximity to students' homes and in the connectedness of their families. Thus, in the following subsections, we examine the social ecology of urban elementary, junior, and senior high schools, with particular emphasis on the role these contextual changes play in adjustment across normative school transitions.

Elementary School

The elementary school is known to be a community school, in that it is generally located close to students' homes and is a tightly knit, intimate, and safe setting. Families are more likely to feel a sense of ownership than with junior or senior high schools. Children spend the day with one teacher, in one classroom. They leave the teacher only for special classes such as art, music, or physical education; thus, teachers know each of their students well. When changing classrooms for a special class or going to lunch, teachers line up students and guide them to their destination. Children are not permitted to wander around the school alone, except to use the rest rooms. The different school grades do not mix except at lunchtime and perhaps during recess. Teachers believe that it is important to protect the younger children from the older children of the higher grades.

The most common social regularity of school is that the teachers must spend much of their time lecturing to the class, although children often participate in small-group instruction and projects. Elementary school teachers are supportive of their students' creativity and innovations. Sixth-grade teachers often have great expectations for their students who go off to junior high school, and they are generally surprised when they hear negative comments about their students' performance or behavior in junior high school.

Transition From Elementary School Into Junior High School

When students make the transition into junior high school, they enter a larger and much more chaotic school environment. Students are drawn from several elementary schools; thus, the community feeling of the school is lost. Teachers are now departmentalized, teaching the same subject to several groups of students all day long. As a result, they are often more committed to their subject matter and department than to the school as a community. Students generally have six to eight teachers. Although in some schools students in one homeroom class move together from one class to the next, in many schools, students switch rooms, teachers, and classmates multiple times a day.

Academic ability tracking begins or becomes more stratified in junior high school. If an elementary school has tracking, students can find themselves in different tracks, depending on the subject (e.g., the highest-level reading group and the middle-level math group); in junior high school, students remain in one track. Students are well aware of their track placement, and lower-track students suffer in terms of their self-esteem and academic achievement. Often, the best teachers are assigned to the higher-tracked students; this assignment results in lower-tracked students receiving lower-quality instruction.

In his book *The Culture of Schools and the Problem of Change,* Seymour Sarason (1971) eloquently described an alien from another planet who, from a different *weltanschauung,* observed and questioned the meaning and purpose of the behavioral and social regularities of a typical elementary school. Invoking the same metaphor, the alien returns to an urban metropolis and observes junior high schools as well as elementary schools and notes the following social regularities that we as humans take for granted: Little critters spending most of the day with the same big critter and all of their day with the same little critters. When little critters move from one room to another, which they do infrequently, the big critter walks in front of the little critters, making sure they are all there and holding the hands of another little critter. As in the elementary school, in the junior high school, the alien sees the little critters sitting in a room with a big critter at the front. In the junior high school, however, the alien hears a noise go off approximately every 45 minutes, at which time all the little critters jump out of their seats and run for the door. Even prior to the noise, the anxiousness of the little critters is quite visible. Often, they start putting their objects into their sacks and fidgeting in their seats. Then, the big critter at the front of the room raises her voice at the little critters, but as soon as the noise goes off, the little critters run. The orderliness of the elementary school hallways is nowhere to be found in the junior high school. The little critters run off in all directions. For 2 minutes, the halls are filled with running, yelling, and laughing little critters. Occasionally, a big critter steps out of a classroom and yells at a little critter, and then the little critter stops running until she is out of sight of the big critter.

Beyond the differences noted by our alien, contemporary research underscores several other differences between the regularities that contrast elementary and junior high schools. Teachers teaching the final year of elementary school and teachers teaching the first year of junior high school perceive their students very differently and approach teaching very differently. Elementary school teachers generally get to know their students well. They have a great deal of faith in their students, try to bring out their potential, and to an extent, encourage autonomy. Junior high school teachers expect the worst from their students. These teachers generally believe that the incoming students are ill-prepared for junior high school work and that students are out of control. Junior high school teachers keep a firm grasp on their classes and do not encourage small-group work. Detention and suspension are used far more often than in the elementary school. Discipline must rule the classroom.

Following the transition to junior high school, both grades and self-esteem have been found to drop (Simmons & Blyth, 1987). Students in junior high school report a lower quality of life than those in elementary school. Daily hassles with school-based academic demands tend to rise, and social support from teachers and participation in school activities decrease. Peer values tend to become more nonconforming than in elementary school (Seidman, Allen, Aber, Mitchell, & Feinman, 1994). Often during these years, students begin to pull away from school.

Parenthetically, it is important to note that some students make a transition to middle school in sixth grade, rather than to junior high school in seventh grade. True middle schools are more similar to elementary schools than to junior high schools. The teaching philosophy of middle schools calls for a more nurturing environment that maintains the close-knit structure of the elementary school. Nonetheless, many schools that call themselves middle schools do not embrace this pedagogy and operate much like junior high schools.

Transition From Junior High School Into Senior High School

The next transition the majority of students make is from junior to senior high school. In most school systems, students generally enter high school in the ninth grade, although some will enter during the 10th grade. In some cities, such as Chicago, the school system has a K to 8 and 9 to 12 grade structure, so the transition to high school is the first normative school transition that students make.

In terms of visible daily routines, this second normative school transition is not as dramatically different an experience from the first transition from elementary to junior high school. Students still follow the pattern of changing teachers and classmates every 45 minutes. Again, they find themselves to be the youngest in the school.

There are, however, notable differences in school size and related dimensions. Senior high schools are commonly twice the size of junior high schools and draw students from several junior high schools. Students find themselves surrounded by many more unfamiliar faces. Many schools are overcrowded, and teachers are overwhelmed by the sheer size of their classes. Teachers have no time to get to know their students. Different groups of students go in and out of their classrooms all day; to be noticed, a student must be highly bright and vocal or quite disruptive. Most students fall into the cracks. Guidance counselors are the primary source of social support for senior high school students, but they are often overwhelmed with the number of advisees and generally do not see students until a problem arises. At this point, it is often too late. Students are not encouraged, nor do not feel empowered enough, to actively seek out guidance counselors for more routine academic or personal concerns.

With the transition from junior to senior high school, the problem of school dropout becomes prevalent. The academic achievement of students generally declines. The pressures to succeed academically intensify in high school; students are well aware that high school grades determine their future. The pressure to work hard and get good grades so they can get into college or to get a job at which they can make a decent living comes from parents and teachers. Failure in high school is known to be related to difficulties in subsequent years, especially in terms of employment opportunities.

The rigid academic tracking in senior high school is even more detrimental than in junior high school. Students virtually never change tracks, and students in the lower tracks are seldom enrolled in college preparatory classes. Disengagement from the educational enterprise increases. As a result, their chances for college and scholarships are often predetermined. Urban students, in large high schools and dealing with many other problems in their environment, may not feel as pressured to do well at school, yet they, too, are eventually faced with the reality that at least a high school degree is necessary for reasonable employment.

During high school, social support from school staff continues to decrease from the already low levels of junior high school (Seidman, Aber, Allen, & French, 1996), and students turn toward their peers for advice and support. The pressures on students to participate in antisocial behavior and substance abuse intensifies in senior high school. Students who have been "turned off" by school lead others to follow them in antisocial behavior.

For students who are not academically driven, yet not anti-school, sports teams are a popular school activity. Participation in sports can prevent students from getting into trouble but often keeps students from focusing on their academics. Coaches can fill the void of mentor for a select group of students. For the most part, however, urban senior high schools do not have enough opportunities to engage students. The disengagement with the educational enterprise that began developing in junior high school expands in scope and intensity.

Development During Adolescence

Developmental research has illustrated that many biological, cognitive, and interpersonal changes occur during the early adolescent years, whereas many negative outcomes such as school dropout and delinquency are manifested during the middle adolescent years. (For comprehensive reviews of these and other areas of adolescent development, see Feldman & Elliott, 1990.)

Biological Development

Although all youth go through puberty during early adolescence, the timing of this development is related to some negative outcomes. It is well known that girls mature earlier than boys. With improving nutritional practices, girls are reaching puberty earlier than their counterparts less than a century ago. During the late elementary school years, girls begin breast development, and many also begin to menstruate. Early-maturing girls are pressured to begin dating early by older boys because their bodies appear mature, but their psychological maturity does not match their physical maturity. Boys generally do not begin puberty before the junior high school years, and those who develop early benefit, in contrast with girls, because they are bullied less by older students.

Cognitive Development:
Strivings for Autonomy and Identity

During early adolescence, children begin to strive for independence, struggling between wanting the security of the family and wanting to be completely independent. Adolescents begin testing the waters of independence by testing the family rules that had once gone unquestioned; they request a voice in family matters and insist on making their own decisions. In poor, urban, African

American families, however, recent evidence suggests that children are forced to grow up faster than middle-class, suburban adolescents (Burton, Allison, & Obeidallah, 1995). Families begin to place more responsibility on adolescents; this responsibility can include financial support for the family, caregiving for younger siblings or an elderly family member, and emotional support for a parent under duress, especially in age-condensed generational families (families with only 13 to 17 years between generations). These adolescents do not always have the luxury of a period in life when they are not a child but not an adult. The striving for independence reaches into the school. Students want more control in what goes on in the classroom and in the school. They would like to be able to have choices in class assignments and class structure, from working in small groups to choosing their own seating assignments. In addition, the growing cognitive abilities of early adolescents that give them the ability of higher-order thinking and learning are generally accompanied by a desire to learn and use these skills. Despite these evolving needs and skills and the fact that some of these youth function in adult roles outside the school environment, many secondary school teachers treat adolescents as if they were children.

The salience and self-consciousness about identity issues can be paralyzing to the academic development of students during early and middle adolescence. While adolescents wrestle with who they are, what they are, and why they are what they are, all realms of experience have an impact on their search for identity. Every event that occurs makes them more self-conscious, and thus the norm among adolescents of engaging in constant social comparisons can be quite destructive.

Interpersonal Development

The most common change during early and middle adolescence is an increasing peer orientation. No longer are parents and teachers the most important persons in a child's life. The focus on peer values and approval often frightens teachers into believing that they will lose control of their class if they allow students to interact freely. To discourage any further communication, teachers have been known to read aloud, to the entire class, any confiscated notes passed between students.

This peer orientation grows stronger as the adolescent grows older, and it often leads to antisocial behaviors during the high school years. Adolescents are most likely to engage in substance or alcohol abuse in the company of peers. The desire to be similar to others and "cool" makes it difficult for adolescents to avoid at least minimal involvement in "partying" with their friends. These pressures also can lead to premature and unprotected sexual activity. The push for such actions increases steadily as adolescents pull away from their parents and family rules and move toward peers and the new rules, freedoms, and acceptance of what their parents consider inappropriate behavior. The opportunities to engage in such behaviors increase as parents reduce their monitoring and adolescents spend less time at home.

The pull toward peers, antisocial behavior, and substance abuse contributes to adolescents' disengagement from school activities and academic achievement. The pressures for academic success in high school are in direct opposition to the desire to be with and please friends. This opposition can lead to progressive academic failure and eventual school dropout. The path to dropping out begins long before the student actually drops out of school, often as early as middle or junior high school (Roderick, 1995).

The Intersection of Changing School Ecologies and Human Development

The intersection of the biological, social, and cognitive changes of adolescence collides with the impersonal school atmosphere after a normative school transition; the collision leads to numerous developmental difficulties. The research of Eccles and Midgley (1989) suggests that the developmental mismatch between the junior high school and the maturing adolescent causes negative outcomes, especially in terms of self-esteem and academic achievement. Research on the effects of the school transition on self-esteem, however, has been mixed. When such contextual variables as school location and nature of teaching practices are taken into consideration, it is evident that the studies that failed to find negative results occurred in smaller, suburban schools or in schools organized pedagogically as middle schools (Ruble & Seidman, 1996).

The greatest mismatch between the adolescent and the school structure is visible on the transition to junior high school. As illustrated most poignantly in *Turning Points* (Carnegie Council on Adolescent Development, 1989, p. 37),

> Such settings virtually guarantee that the intellectual and emotional needs of youth go unmet. Consider what is asked of these students: Every 50 minutes, perhaps, 6 or 7 times each day, assemble with 30 or so of your peers, each time in a different group, sit silently in a chair in neat, frozen rows, and try to catch hold of knowledge as it whizzes by you in the words of an adult you met only at the beginning of this school year. The subject of one class has nothing to do with the subject of the next class. If a concept is confusing, don't ask for help, there isn't time to explain. If something interests you deeply, don't stop to think about it, there's too much to cover. If your feelings of awkwardness about your rapid growth make it difficult to concentrate, keep your concerns to yourself. And don't dare help or even talk to your fellow students in class; that may be considered cheating.

Thus, the evolving needs of early adolescents for greater choice and control of the activities, structure, and atmosphere in their classrooms is thwarted. Elementary schools often provide their students with more choice and more independent or small-group work than middle and junior high schools. In fact, as we have seen, junior high school teachers withdraw many of the privileges given to students in elementary school, focus more on discipline, and trust their students less than elementary school teachers do. This behavior occurs when the need for increased trust and independence is becoming foremost on the adolescent's mind.

Urban minority adolescents are at a greater disadvantage than their more sheltered and privileged middle-class counterparts. Poor urban teens often have greater responsibility in their homes and are often treated as adults by their families. Many females are biologically mature. This role of adulthood in the family often conflicts with the role of student in the school. As Candyce, a 13-year-old mother, stated about school: "I am a grown woman. Why these people keep treating me like a kid. I don't even know what being a kid is like" (Burton et al., 1995, p. 129). Teachers have a great deal of difficulty dealing with adolescents such as Candyce because they challenge the teacher's role as the only adult in the room. This rift contributes to the urban adolescent's disengagement from school.

The growing cognitive abilities of the adolescent are generally accompanied by a desire to use his or her burgeoning skills; however, this desire to learn is often stifled by the rote memorization tasks and dull repetition exercises of junior high school classrooms. Research has demonstrated that the final year of elementary school is often more challenging intellectually than the first year of junior high school. In taking away some of the independence and in trusting students less, teachers also restrict the way they teach and interact with their students. While the students are craving more challenging work, they are being given more tedious work that teaches them very little. This mismatch between the students' needs and the teacher's practices plays a significant role in undermining students' interest in and motivation for learning.

For minority adolescents, the transition to both junior and senior high school may serve as an "encounter" experience by initiating a search for one's ethnic identity and bringing to bear many racial issues. With each transition, there are generally fewer and fewer minority teachers to serve as positive role models for students and, hence, the increased likelihood of disengagement from the educational enterprise with each successive transition.

Junior high school teachers, more so than elementary school teachers, encourage competition among students. High grades are often displayed and low grades ridiculed. Both these practices can lead to a break in the trust between a teacher and a student, academic self-doubt, and disengagement with the school system.

The disruption of friendship patterns in the transition to junior high school can also be detrimental. Although the majority of elementary school students move together to a local junior high school, it is likely that several other elementary schools feed into the junior high. This makes the chances of maintaining friendships from elementary school and being in class together less likely than in the change from one grade to the next in elementary school. Making new friends is also more difficult; the constant flux of peers from one class period to the next makes it difficult to connect with any one student.

Upon entrance to senior high school, these issues become even more salient. High schools draw students from more feeder junior high schools and do not attempt to keep students together in any systematic way (with the exception of a few special programs). During high school, friends can become the be all and end all of existence, whereas teachers remain distant. In many high schools, all the teachers in a school do not even know each other, let alone their students. It is easy to see how adolescents become more and more disengaged with the school, when there are fewer and fewer opportunities to become involved or to create meaningful relationships with teachers. Barker and Gump (1964) showed that smaller schools create greater opportunities for meaningful involvement. The growing disengagement often leads to disruptive and antisocial behavior, substance abuse, and school dropout.

Educational Interventions and Policies

The transition to a new school and a new school structure, whether into junior or senior high school (or, for that matter, into elementary school or college), is fraught with increased demands, pressures, and environmental changes, as well as an accelerated likelihood of maladaptive academic (e.g., school dropout) and socioemotional (e.g., alienation, delinquency) outcomes. As a result, numerous educational responses have been made to adolescents' changing developmental needs as they make the journey from elementary to junior to senior high school.

Early Intervention and
Inoculation Approaches

The most common responses of educators and interventionists to academic, socioemotional, and behavioral difficulties experienced by school-age children and youth has been to develop either early intervention programs for the most vulnerable children or programs to inoculate or strengthen the resources and competencies of all children. In the *early intervention approach* (commonly known as *secondary prevention*), the objective is to identify children (potential "casualties") on the basis of early signs of poor performance, problem behavior, or disorder even though the difficulty has not yet fully manifested itself. Here, vulnerable children are offered individual tutoring, counseling, and so on. For example, early indications of learning difficulties raise the likelihood that these children will manifest socially deviant behavior in the future. Consequently, upon identification, these children receive intervention, perhaps in the form of remedial academic training. Most often, the early intervention approach tends to focus exclusively on a single problem.

Contemporary *inoculation approaches,* however, have the virtue of providing intervention to all youth who may be placed at risk, and not simply those identified as manifesting early signs of difficulty. The expectation is that children are capable of responding in different and more adaptive ways to the pressures, demands, and expectations they encounter. Increasingly in recent years, inoculation methods have been used to target basic psychological processes and skills related to a variety of problem outcomes, in contrast with a single outcome. Thus, in some instances, all youth in a grade or classroom may be provided with a series of lectures and exercises in decision making and problem solving, particularly in the context of difficult social situations (Weissberg, Caplan, & Sivo, 1989). The goal has been to enable youth to become more resourceful in resolving future dilemmas and conflicts—for example, when they are confronted with peer pressure to use drugs or feel lonely and lack social relationships.

The underlying premise of both the early intervention and inoculation approaches, is that the person is the ultimate agent or locus of change (Seidman, 1987). On the other hand, these approaches differ in who the target of intervention is: vulnerable individuals in the early intervention approaches and a group or population of individuals in the inoculation approaches. Although early intervention is a more promising and less costly approach than treatment and rehabilitation, the act of intervening with individuals runs the risk of creating unwanted stigmatizing and iatrogenic effects. On the other hand, a major advantage of the inoculation method is the ease with which it can be incorporated into the curriculum as another set of "lessons" delivered to a class of students by an instructor. As such, it tends not to stigmatize individuals. More recently, inoculation approaches have been used to target a population of individuals shortly before or after they make a risky transition. Thus, the implementation of inoculation approaches in the first year of high school, as well as before and after the transition into junior high school, has become more commonplace.

Neither the early intervention nor the inoculation approach targets change in the social regularities of a group or organization as the primary objective and locus of change. For instance, the social regularity common to most junior high schools in which students move from class to class with minimal opportunities for getting to know each other well is not the target of intervention in the early intervention and inoculation approaches. The early intervention and inoculation approaches still characterize the intervention policies in most high schools, but we are beginning to see the implementation of policies aimed at a different target/level of change: restructuring the organization of the high school.

School Restructuring

For educators, policymakers, and the public at large, academic failure and school dropout are dramatic and poignant events. Thus, because the rates of these negative outcomes peak shortly after entry into high school, particularly among poor ethnic minorities in urban public school systems, the high school years have received the greatest attention from educators, the media, corporate America, governments, foundations, and the public. Similarly, resources for experimental innovations have been directed to this place and time. Witness the recent largesse from the Annenberg Foundation, aimed at creating smaller urban high schools.

In recent years, the social and physical organization of large, urban, public high schools has become recognized as, at least, part of the problem of dramatic surges in rates of academic failure and social deviance. This recognition has led to efforts to restructure the organization of high schools, with a primary emphasis on creating smaller educational units or "schools." Such school reform efforts have been referred to by several different but related designations, including "schools-within-schools," "house systems," "academies," and "charters."

Implicit, if not explicit, in the efforts aimed at school restructuring is the engagement, empowerment, and sense of ownership of students and staff within the educational enterprise. The lack of commitment to the educational enterprise seen in schools undergoing or ripe for restructuring efforts stems jointly from a lack of academic involvement and of social bonding or integration. The alarmingly high national rate of school dropout signifies one end-point of disengagement with the educational enterprise for students (Whelage, Rutter, Smith, Lesko, & Fernandez, 1989). The joint and ongoing processes of disengagement and alienation from the educational enterprise often eventuate not only in the departure from school but also in attendance at "the school of the streets," with its concomitant exposure to and involvement with antisocial peers, delinquency, and substance abuse.

Beyond the reduction in school size, other obvious changes are associated with these efforts to restructure schools (e.g., see Oxley, in press). Smaller units are created in terms of the number of students and teachers (or ancillary personnel), and these integral units are housed in a particular wing or floor or adjacent spaces of a building. These smaller units permit fewer teachers to know more children intensively and to teach fewer children multiple subjects in a more holistic and integrated fashion. School restructuring allows for and encourages both innovations in pedagogy and teacher awareness of students' lives that go beyond the perimeter of the classroom. At the same time, students "live and learn" with a common set of classmates throughout most of the day and week, except for elective subjects. For the most part, these integral cohorts of students and teachers stay together throughout the high school years. Not only do these programs alter the physical and social context of secondary education, but they also change fundamentally the day-to-day social regularities among all the school's inhabitants.

In a concrete example, Fine (1994) described the Philadelphia School Collaborative as follows:

> Anywhere from 200 to 400 students constitute a charter, with 10 to 12 core teachers who work together from ninth or tenth grade through to graduation. The charter faculty enjoy a common preparation period daily, share responsibility for a cohort of students, and invent curriculum, pedagogies, and assessment strategies that reflect a common intellectual project. Students travel together to classes and across their four years in high school. With teachers, counselors, and parents, they constitute a semiautonomous community within a building of charters. Charters result in diplomas and prepare all students for college and/or employment; the student body must be, by definition, heterogeneous. (p. 5)

She cogently underscores the point that restructuring represents nothing less than full school transformation, where all teachers, staff, and students, as well as parents, feel attached to and engaged with the community of school.

Some of these schools-within-schools innovations have been implemented *exclusively* at the critical juncture of entry into high school, where they have been tailored to the transition year and the specific elements of the risky transition that place all youth at increased risk. Here, the goals are to reduce the flux or disruption in social regularities that youth experience when they make the transition to high school (Felner & Adan, 1988). Movement into high school disrupts the pattern of peer relationships; upon entry to high school, students are confronted with new peers, and many prior classmates are left behind. In addition, the new classmates change as students move from class to class during the school day. Having been among the oldest students in junior high school, ninth graders once again find that they have lost their "top dog" status as they become the youngest students in the school. For students who previously attended a junior high school, entry to high school and movement from class to class and teacher to teacher every 45 minutes is not new or as likely to be as disruptive as it was during the earlier transition to junior high school. Though of course, the pedagogical value of these movement patterns, as well as the ability of teachers to really understand individual students' strengths and limitations in the context of the fabric of their lives, remains quite limited.

The strength of these restructuring strategies lies in their ability to affect directly the processes of engagement with the educational enterprise at an important ecological and developmental transition for adolescents. As such, these strategies can promote positive well-being, as well as reduce negative sequelae. Restructuring strategies do not target or stigmatize individual students. Moreover, if successful, the creation of a more stable and constructive environment enables educators and students to collaboratively use the most creative, engaging, and effective educational techniques available, of which there are many.

Conceptually, strategies aimed at restructuring high schools along the lines of the schools-within-schools model are appealing. A few research investigations provide support for the idea in terms of educational indexes (Fine, 1994; Oxley, in press).

More comprehensive research investigations that included so-cioemotional as well as educational outcomes focused on reducing the flux in the transition year alone. As an example, the School Transitional Environment Project (STEP; Felner & Adan, 1988) endeavored to reduce the flux for youth making the transition to an inner-city high school in New Haven. A small, intimate learning environment was created to which STEP youth were randomly assigned. Students and teachers were placed in one section of the school. Students moved through all their primary classes (e.g., English, math) as a single unit, and one adult was assigned to each child as an ombudsperson/advocate/counselor. The long-term findings were impressive: Youth randomly assigned to STEP in ninth grade, in contrast with the control condition, were more likely to remain in high school; 76% of STEP youth versus only 57% of control youth remained in school by the 12th grade. In Chicago, however, a similar teacher-designed school restructuring intervention for the first year of high school (eighth grade) failed to yield positive effects (Reyes & Jason, 1991).

Summary

As we have seen in the past few years, the importance of efforts to restructure schools along the lines of charters or schools-within-schools has become increasingly prevalent. Reducing the flux and turbulence inherent in making a normative school transition, particularly in urban public schools, is vital to the continued engagement of youth in the educational enterprise and their ultimate life chances. Even the probable efficacy of such innovative preventive programs as inoculation programs are likely to be enhanced in potency and scope if they are implemented following a fundamental restructuring of the social regularities of secondary schools.

School Transitions and Preventive Interventions: When and Where?

Is entry into high school the optimal time and place at which to implement a policy of restructuring the physical, social, and academic organization of secondary schools? Because the rates of educational failure, school dropout, substance use, and antisocial behavior peak shortly after the transition into high school, the early years of high school have often been viewed as representing a critical turning point and, consequently, have become the locus of many recent educational interventions. The preceding question should not be answered without posing (and answering) two salient questions in tandem, however: (a) When and where is the mismatch between the developmental needs of the adolescent and the social ecology of the school greatest? and (b) when and where is the process of educational disengagement set into motion?

With regard to the first question, and as our prior analysis suggests, it is at the transition to junior high school, not at the transition to high school, where the developmental needs of adolescents are most discrepant with the changing school ecologies. Moreover, this is clearest in the case of urban, economically at-risk adolescents. In some cities, such as Chicago, the first normative school transition during adolescence occurs between eighth and ninth grades. For these youth, this early transition into high school creates similar turbulence as it does for younger adolescents making the transition into an intermediate or junior high school in sixth or seventh grade, respectively, perhaps because it is the *first* school transition during adolescence.

With regard to the second question, recent evidence suggests that the transition to junior high school may set into motion this dynamic and accelerating process of disengagement from the educational enterprise. In a cohort of urban Massachusetts youth, Roderick (1995) demonstrated that the drop in grades after the transition to middle school increased the probability of school dropout independent of students' later school performance. In another recent study of poor urban public school children (Seidman et al., 1994), disengagement from school upon entry to junior high school corresponded with a decline in academic performance: Youth reported decreased preparation for classwork, decreased involvement in extracurricular activities, less social support from teachers and school personnel, and increased daily hassles over academic performance. In a parallel study of the transition to high school (Seidman et al., 1996), the process of disengagement from school continued, although in a somewhat attenuated fashion.

The school transition and accompanying changes represent a disruption in the adolescents' social relationships with both school-affiliated adults and peers (Ruble & Seidman, 1996). Early adoles-

cents' evolving need and motivation for autonomy and challenge
are disrupted by the organization of school after the transition to
junior high school. Students have moved from a setting in which
they deal primarily with one teacher who knows them well and a
familiar peer group to a setting in which they change teachers and
classmates every 45 minutes. The "developmental mismatch" hy-
pothesis of Eccles and her colleagues is the most parsimonious
explanation of the declines in performance, affect, and engagement
after the transition to junior high school.

Intervention Recommendations

The developmental mismatch between the nature of the young
adolescent's psychological needs and the first dramatic disruption
in the social and physical organization of schools that occurs with
the transition into middle or junior high school is greater than the
mismatch that occurs when the middle school adolescent makes the
transition into high school. "Most American junior high and middle
schools do not meet the developmental needs of young adolescents.
These institutions have the potential to make a tremendous impact
on the development of students—for better or worse—yet they have
been largely ignored in the recent surge of educational reform"
(Carnegie Council of Adolescent Development, 1989, pp. 12-13).
This statement remains true 8 years after the publication of this
seminal report.

We have endeavored to demonstrate that, on the one hand,
disengagement from the educational enterprise, and the concomitant jeopardy this places on future life opportunities, is more likely
to be set in motion with the developmental mismatch that occurs
with the transition into junior high school than with the transition
into high school. On the other hand, this does not mitigate the need
for innovative policies and programs, as well as for additional
resources, to continue efforts to restructure high schools in ways
that enable urban, public school youth to more effectively remain
engaged with the educational enterprise and to increase their life
opportunities.

The reform of urban, public middle and junior high schools is
more likely to yield greater benefits by maintaining students' engagement with the educational enterprise and forestalling a disen-

gagement trajectory. The optimal timing and locus of such an intervention policy may not only promote positive educational and socioemotional well-being but also prevent many negative and costly outcomes, such as school dropout, alienation, delinquency, depression, and unemployment. A policy aimed at the reform of high schools may occur too late to be cost-effective.

What should the reform efforts look like? Earlier, we described interesting reform efforts undertaken in high schools to restructure the social regularities of schooling. The efforts, though far from being proved, offer considerable promise. We, too, subscribe to the core recommendations of the Carnegie Council on Adolescent Development (1989):

> *Create small communities for learning* where stable, close, mutually respectful relationships with adults and peers are considered fundamental for intellectual development and personal growth. The key elements of these communities are schools-within-schools or houses, students and teachers grouped together as teams, and small group advisories that ensure that every student is known well by at least one adult. (p. 9)

The "creation of small communities for learning" upon the transition into junior high school is a critical first step in thwarting or forestalling a trajectory of disengagement from the educational enterprise. By smoothing or minimizing the disruption inherent in such a drastic social and organizational shift at a pivotal time in the biopsychosocial development of early adolescents, the "face" of junior high schools is likely to genuinely change the culture of the school. In this way, the knowledge and creativity of teachers, staff, students, and others now have room for expression. Teachers and staff may begin to see young urban adolescents as struggling to develop, learn, have their voices heard, and find a niche where they can be guided, valued, and supported, in contrast to being viewed as unruly monsters driven by hormones and controlled by antisocial peers. If successful, such reform efforts can provide places where an adolescent and an adult, and an adolescent and an adolescent, can "connect" on a one-to-one basis.

To initiate such small communities of learning, intervention researchers must collaborate with teachers, administrators, other school personnel, and, we hope, students and parents in the design and implementation of these innovations. These central stakeholders must "own" these new organizational structures. They must be genuinely engaged in the process at the outset. Only with such ownership can the culture of junior high schools truly be transformed.

With the creation of such small communities for learning comes the increased likelihood that all inhabitants of these settings can be fully engaged in the educational enterprise. Notable corollaries of this engagement include greater success in implementing innovative educational curricula and inoculation programs. One illustration of a curricular innovation for early adolescents is HumBio, an educational package that teaches concepts of biology and behavior in ways that make science exciting (conducting scientific experiments) and relevant to the lives of early adolescents. For example, HumBio begins with a focus on the biological bases and social responses to puberty as they are related to high-risk behaviors and health hazards encountered by early adolescents. (See the full report of the Carnegie Council on Adolescent Development, 1989, for further details.) Inoculation programs that, for example, teach and train students how to deal with others in a socially competent manner are likely to be more efficacious in these small communities of learning.

With teachers and administrators cooperating with each other and communicating with students, the possibilities of reaching out to parents and community-based organizations are greater. New opportunities for shared decision making and governance among key stakeholders are likely to develop, as deemed vital by proponents of the charters and other successful secondary school reform efforts.

These new organizational structures should not cease at the end of the transition year into junior high school, but instead should continue throughout junior and senior high school, albeit in modified forms. The implementation of these new organizational structures at a critical juncture in adolescent development and their maintenance during the secondary school years should facilitate engagement of adolescents in the educational enterprise and enhance their life opportunities.

References

Barker, R. G., & Gump, P. V. (1964). *Big school, small school: High school size and student behavior.* Stanford, CA: Stanford University Press.

Burton, L. M., Allison, K. A., & Obeidallah, D. (1995). Social context and adolescence: Perspectives and development among inner-city African American teens. In L. J. Crockett & A. C. Crouter (Eds.), *Pathways through adolescence: Individual development in social context* (pp. 119-138). Mahwah NJ: Lawrence Erlbaum.

Carnegie Council on Adolescent Development. (1989). *Turning points: Preparing American youth for the 21st century.* New York: Carnegie Corporation.

Eccles, J., & Midgley, C. (1989). Stage/environment fit: Developmentally appropriate classrooms for early adolescents. In R. E. Ames & C. Ames (Eds.), *Research on motivation in education* (Vol. 3, pp. 139-186). San Diego: Academic Press.

Feldman, S. S., & Elliott, G. R. (Eds.). (1990). *At the threshold: The developing adolescent.* Cambridge, MA: Harvard University Press.

Felner, R. D., & Adan, A. M. (1988). The school transitional environment project: An ecological intervention and evaluation. In R. H. Price, E. L. Cowen, R. P. Lorion, I. Serrano-Garcia, & R. J. Ramos-McKay (Eds.), *Fourteen ounces of prevention: A casebook for practitioners* (pp. 111-122). Washington, DC: American Psychological Association.

Fine, M. (Ed.). (1994). *Chartering urban reform.* New York: Teachers College Press.

Oxley, R. (in press). Educational systems intervention. In J. Rappaport & E. Seidman (Eds.), *Handbook of community psychology.* New York: Plenum.

Reyes, O., & Jason, L. A. (1991). An evaluation of a high school dropout prevention program. *Journal of Community Psychology, 19,* 221-230.

Roderick, M. (1995). School transitions and school dropout. In K. Wong (Ed.), *Advances in educational policy.* Greenwich, CT: JAI.

Ruble, D., & Seidman, E. (1996). Social transitions: Windows into social psychological processes. In T. Higgins & A. Kruglanski (Eds.), *Social psychology: Handbook of basic principles.* New York: Guilford.

Rutter, M. (1987). Psychosocial resilience and protective mechanisms. *American Journal of Orthopsychiatry, 37*(3), 317-331.

Sarason, S. (1971). *The culture of schools and the problem of change.* Needham Heights, MA: Allyn & Bacon.

Seidman, E. (1987). Toward a framework for primary prevention research. In J. Steinberg & M. Silverman (Eds.), *Preventing mental disorders: A research perspective.* Washington, DC: Government Printing Office.

Seidman, E. (1991). Growing up the hard way: Pathways of urban adolescents. *American Journal of Community Psychology, 19,* 169-205.

Seidman, E., Aber, J. L., Allen, L., & French, S. (1996). The impact of the transition to high school on the self-system and perceived social context of poor urban youth. *American Journal of Community Psychology, 24,* 489-515.

Seidman, E., Allen, L., Aber, J. L., Mitchell, C., & Feinman, J. (1994). The impact of school transitions in early adolescence on the self-system and social context of poor urban youth. *Child Development, 65,* 507-522.

Simmons, R. G., & Blyth, D. A. (1987). *Moving into adolescence: The impact of pubertal change and school context.* Hawthorne, NY: Aldine.

Weissberg, R. P., Caplan, M. Z., & Sivo, P. J. (1989). A new conceptual framework for establishing school-based social competence promotion programs. In L. A. Bond & B. E. Compas (Eds.), *Primary prevention and promotion in the schools* (pp. 255-296). Newbury Park, CA: Sage.

Whelage, G. G., Rutter, R. R., Smith, G. A., Lesko, N., & Fernandez, R. R. (1989). *Reducing the risk: Schools as communities of support.* London: Falmer.

• CHAPTER 9 •

Understanding the School Performance of Urban Blacks: Some Essential Background Knowledge

JOHN U. OGBU

The Problem and Its Explanations

Why do Black children in urban schools not perform well academically? Many competing explanations have been proposed for the relatively low school performance of Blacks and similar minority groups. These explanations either focus on *school structures, school resources, and transactions inside the school* and *inside the family*, or they focus on factors in *the biography/biology of the individual child*. They rarely examine how the social history of the minority groups and their present structural situation may affect directly or indirectly the ideas and behaviors their children bring to school. In addition, these theories do not account for the differences in school adjustment and academic performance among minority groups; these minority groups are comparable in their distance from mainstream Whites in terms of socioeconomic status and culture, but some groups have higher school performance than others.

AUTHOR'S NOTE: The preparation of this chapter was supported by the University of California faculty research funds and by grants from the California Policy Seminar, Carnegie Corporation of New York, W. T. Grant Foundation, Russell Sage Foundation, and Spencer Foundation.

Some explanations are phrased within a framework that has been called *production function analysis* of schooling (Hanushek, 1977). This framework dates back to the Coleman Report (Coleman et al., 1966) and assumes that school achievement or output, at least at the precollege level, is a function of the amount of resources (input) available to schools. Its critics call it a factory model of schooling; its proponents think it is a good model for educational policy purposes, which it probably is. The production function analysis, however, tends to ignore both the macroeconomic and sociological events that also affect school achievement.

Other theorists say the problem is not necessarily that inner-city schools have changed or are lacking resources, but rather that *the quality of their students has changed* and has resulted in some adverse effects on the output of the schools (Peterson & Wong, 1990). More specifically, the theorists say that even though inner-city schools have about the same or even more resources as the schools outside the central city, their Black students do not test as well as Black students attending suburban and rural schools, because of the characteristics of the inner-city students themselves.

Other explanations of minority educational problems include resistance and reproduction theories that focus on working-class and minority adolescents. These explanations are limited because of an overemphasis on school curriculum and other school requirements categorized as "contested terrains" over which working-class, minority, and female students tend to fight with the schools. These theories fail to explain the fact that, in situations with no detectable conflicts, students' academic efforts are derailed by other factors (Holland & Eisenhart, 1990). One thing not generally acknowledged in the reproduction and resistance theories is that some working-class students and some minority groups (Gibson, 1988; Ogbu, 1983) actually actively seek to learn the curriculum and to meet other requirements of the school, including language requirements, all of which are within the culture of the dominant group, *no questions asked.*

Educational anthropologists generally attribute the lower school performance of minority students to cultural and language differences (Jacob & Jordan, 1993). In cross-cultural comparison, however, this turns out not to be the case. For example, in my study in Oakland, California, 90% of Chinese Americans and 89% of Mexican Americans in Grades 7 to 12 were in bilingual education programs in the 1989-1990 school year; about 58% of Chinese Americans and 63% of Mexican Americans also were in limited-English-proficiency programs. But the two minority groups had different attitudes toward schooling and performed differently: The grade point average (GPA) of the Chinese Americans was 2.95, whereas it was 1.75 for the Mexican Americans. The differences in school performance cannot be attributed to degrees of cultural distance from mainstream White Americans; consider the relationship between cultural distance and school performance in one junior high school in Oakland. The GPA of the ethnic minorities, in descending order, was Vietnamese Americans: 3.2; Chinese Americans: 3.0; the Mien Americans: 2.5; Cambodian Americans: 2.2; Mexican Americans: 2.0; Black Americans: 1.66 (see also Gibson & Ogbu, 1991). Certainly, one would not make the argument that Chinese Americans are closer culturally to Whites than are Mexican Americans and therefore have a higher GPA.

All the explanations reviewed above share many limitations, one of which is that they fail to recognize some unique features of the school performance problems of "traditional minorities"—Black Americans, Mexican Americans, Native Hawaiians, Native Americans, and Puerto Ricans. These unique features include, but are not limited to, the following: (a) The problem is historical and more or less enduring or persistent, and (b) the problem is not limited by geographic residence or social class membership. Although I use Black Americans to illustrate these unique features, this chapter is really about minority school performance in general. Its objective is threefold: (a) to present a general theoretical framework for explaining the gap in school performance between White Americans and some minorities, (b) to explain the gap in school performance between Blacks and Whites in particular, and (c) to explain the differences in school performance among minority groups themselves. But before doing so, I discuss the historical and persistent nature of the problem of the lower school performance of Black Americans.

Historical and Persistent Nature of Black Low School Performance

The historical and persistent nature of low school performance of Blacks is well reflected in two school movements: school desegregation and compensatory education. One goal of desegregation was to improve the school performance of Black children. Note that a few years before *Brown v. Board of Education,* several Southern school districts began to publish test scores of Blacks and Whites, using Black lower test scores to support their opposition to educat ing their children with Blacks in the same schools (Ogbu 1978; *Southern School News,* 1952). Furthermore, in relatively affluent urban Black communities such as Durham, North Carolina (Clement et al., 1978), and in relatively poor ones such as Memphis, Tennessee (Collins & Noblit, 1978), Blacks lagged behind Whites in school performance, and in both cities, desegregation was intended to close the performance gap. It did not necessarily do so (Ogbu, 1978). In Northern states, the situation was not much better.

The use of compensatory education to improve urban Black school performance began in St. Louis, Missouri, as far back as 1956 and spread to New York City by 1959 (Gordon & Wilkerson, 1965). By 1961, this intervention strategy existed in many Northern cities. Evaluations of the twin strategies in the late 1960s and through the 1970s suggested, however, that compensatory education either as a preschool, preventative strategy or as a remedial strategy for children already in the public schools did not close the academic performance gap. This is not to say that compensatory education and desegregation have not benefited many minority and low-income students. The point is that the problem of low school performance persists.

Two points are worth emphasizing about the school performance of urban Black Americans and similar minorities. First, their school performance gap is not a recent development, contrary to the claims made by some people. Second, the problem existed when middle-class Blacks lived together with poor Blacks in segregated urban Black communities.

Beyond Poor Blacks and Beyond the Inner City

The existing school performance gap is not limited to poor Blacks living in the central city, and it never was. It is true that *among Blacks, as among Whites, the middle class as a group does better in school than the lower class.* Note, however, that the correlation between socioeconomic status and academic performance is not as strong among Blacks as it is among Whites. For example, a study of some 4,000 high school graduates in California in 1975 found that, among Blacks and Mexican Americans, children from affluent and well-educated families were not doing as well as expected, but they, too, had trouble getting into college like children from poorer families (Anton, 1980). Furthermore, in a study of statewide testing in 1987 in California, it was found that eighth-grade Black children whose parents had completed 4 or more years of college did not do as well as other Black children whose parents had attended but had not finished college (Haycock & Navarro, 1988). This was also true to some extent for Mexican American eighth-grade students.

More important, *when Blacks and Whites from similar socioeconomic status backgrounds are compared, at every class level Blacks consistently perform lower than their White counterparts.* An example is the comparison of the test scores of Black and White candidates taking the S.A.T. in the 1980-1981 season. According to a report in *The New York Times* (Slade, 1982), Black candidates from homes with an average annual income of $50,000 or more had median verbal scores at about the same level as White candidates from homes with an average annual income of $13,000 to $18,000; and Black candidates from homes with an average annual income of $50,000 or more had about the same median math score as White candidates from homes with an average annual income of $6,000 or less. Who would disagree that Black candidates from homes with an average annual income of $50,000 or more in 1980 were underclass living in the inner city? Clearly, the problem is not simply an issue of class.

Some concern has been expressed over the performance of Blacks in teacher certification examinations throughout the United States (Chernoff et al., 1987; Gorth & Chernoff, 1986). Black teachers who do not do well in the certification examinations are certainly not poor inner-city residents. I once attended a meeting of a Black professional group where a state-mandated licensing test was extensively discussed. Many members in attendance with doctoral degrees reported that they had taken and failed the test several times; they passed it and got their licenses only after the norm was lowered for minorities. Again, these professionals with doctoral degrees did not have difficulties with the tests because they were poor Blacks living in the inner city. It is interesting, however, that often when I discuss with Black teachers and other professionals the school performance problem of minorities, many tell me that the poor Blacks in the inner city or the "underclass Blacks" are the ones doing poorly in school. Apparently, the teachers do not perceive their own difficulties with teacher certification tests, professional licensing, or civil service tests as related to the students' performance problem.

That the problem of poor school performance is not confined to inner-city children is also evident when one turns to Black students living in suburban school districts inhabited by middle-class Blacks who may have fled from the "underclass" in the central city. Let me start with my own research in Oakland, California, a place one might call a central or inner city. Three high schools in my study represented different levels of socioeconomic status. One served very low income Black Americans, Chinese Americans, Mexican Americans, and White Americans; another served students from working-class neighborhoods; and a third served students from the most affluent neighborhoods in the city. *In none of the three high schools did Black students achieve a GPA of 2 points both in the regular school courses and in the courses required for admission to the University of California system.* So, in Oakland, whether Black Americans lived and attended school in the inner city or lived and attended school in the most affluent neighborhoods, they still performed less well than the Chinese and White students.

For several years, I have looked into the performance of Black students in affluent communities throughout the United States, particularly on the East Coast. These communities include Arlington County, Virginia; Fairfax County, Virginia; Montgomery County, Maryland; and Prince Georges County, Maryland. In every one of these communities and in every measure of school achievement, Black students lag behind both their White peers and some other minorities. And they lag behind despite the fact that these communities often had special programs or extra resources meant to increase their school performance.

One study in a Southeastern suburban elementary school illustrates the gravity of this problem. In this community, Black households had higher educational attainment, better job status, and higher income than White households; yet the school performance of Black children lagged behind that of White children. In fact, in this specific suburban community, about twice as many Black adults as White adults had college degrees, and about one and one-half times as many Blacks as Whites held managerial and professional jobs; Black unemployment was almost the same as White unemployment. The average annual income of a Black household was about 39.1% higher than the average annual income of a White household, a difference of about $10,000 per household in favor of Blacks. In terms of class status, most Black parents were of higher socioeconomic status than White parents. And yet Black children still lagged behind their White peers in the school district in academic achievement. Thus, in 1980-1981, the third-grade students at the elementary school (80% Black) scored at the 2.6 grade equivalent level, or about the 10th percentile nationally, and the county or school district average was 3.1 grade-level-equivalent score. In the same year, fifth-grade students at the elementary school scored at 4.7 grade-equivalent-level, or about the 38th percentile nationally, whereas the school district average was 5.2 (Stern, 1986).

Three features of Black school performance, both in the central city schools and in the suburban schools, are worrisome. First, although all minorities may start lower than their White peers in the early grades, some minorities improve as they progress through higher grades and eventually catch up with or even surpass their White peers. For Blacks, however, the progression is in the opposite direction: The gap between them and Whites increases over the years. Second, of all subgroups of minorities, Black males fare the worst. In a personal communication, one school official in a suburban school system told me that the average GPA of Black males in his school system was 1.8. Third, Black students are highly underrepresented in courses that would enhance their chances of pursuing higher education. In the inner city and in the suburbs, few Black students take advanced placement courses. A 1990 report by Prince Georges County Public Schools sums up the situation as I have heard it from many parts of the country and what is also true in Oakland, California:

While African Americans are more likely than ever before to complete 12 years of schooling, they are more likely than their White counterparts to spend this time in curriculum programs emphasizing basic remedial, as opposed to acquisition of advanced knowledge and skills that would help them in higher education. (Prince Georges County Public Schools, 1990, p. 65)

I conclude that the phenomenon of low academic performance of Black students is not a product of mere poverty, inner-city residence, or "underclass status" for the following reasons: (a) It is found both among poor Blacks in central cities as well as among affluent suburban Blacks, (b) it existed when poor and affluent Blacks lived together in segregated urban communities, and (c) it has continued to exist among both poor and middle-class Blacks even after the latter left the inner city. From a comparative perspective, low academic performance appears to be a problem faced by Black Americans as a minority group. Some other minorities do relatively better while attending the same schools as Blacks and perhaps living under the same material circumstances. Blacks experience this problem because of their particular type of minority status. In the remainder of this chapter, I clarify their minority status and explain why Blacks perform less well than both Whites and some other minorities in school. The theoretical framework that I use to accomplish this is described below.

A Cultural-Ecological Perspective

In the early 1980s, I developed what is now called a cultural-ecological perspective or framework to explain both the differences in school performance between minorities and mainstream Whites and among the minorities themselves. The initial argument was that minorities, primarily Black Americans, and Whites occupied different effective environments in U.S. society with unequal economic and social opportunities; schooling for the two groups was different and prepared them for different adult positions in their respective ecological environments. And the two groups responded to schooling in ways that reinforced their participation in different and unequal ecological niches. My emphasis initially was on the effects of labor market barriers. But when I began to wrestle with differences in school performance among the minorities themselves, I also began to study non-labor market factors that I call *community forces*. Community forces include language, culture, identity, social relations, and other factors within the minority communities, along with their interactions with school factors. In short, I began to study minority groups as distinct populations in the United States, a research approach to be discussed more fully later.

Cultural-Ecological Adaptation
in Modern Societies

In the United States and other modern urban industrial societies, the effective environment to which people adapt consists of (a) the society's economic, political, and other institutional resources (the exploitable resources); (b) *qualifications* or strategies for subsistence, survival, and status; and (c) possession of the repertoire of appropriate instrumental skills, personal attributes, and behaviors (Inkeles, 1966). Members of modern societies adapt to their environment (gain livelihood, status, and self-respect) by obtaining wage labor, other forms of employment, and social positions "by achievement" or *qualification*. The latter takes the form of school credentials.

Two Sides of the Credentialing Problem

The qualification problem has two sides. Credentials have to be granted by the schools, a societal institution; and people have to be willing to meet the criteria required to obtain the credentials. Let me describe how the two sides work to accomplish the task of qualification.

The School as a Delegate Agency
in the Adaptation

The preparation of children for adaptation in the United States and other urban industrial societies is not done by the family, but instead has been *delegated* to the school. Families do not teach children even rudimentary practical skills associated with specific wage labor or professional employment, partly because families do not know the specific jobs their children will perform as adults. During infancy and early childhood, however, families prepare children so that the latter will be able and willing to learn what schools will teach them.

The school is the agency to which society has delegated the role of preparing children for various *cultural tasks* they will perform as adults. These cultural tasks are found in the economic, political, health, and other domains. In consideration of schooling, the most important are in the economic sphere. Schools not only teach young people knowledge and practical skills (e.g., reading, writing) but also credential them to enter the labor market. The importance of school credentials is illustrated by my research finding in Stockton, California, where I interviewed two groups of informants. One group consisted of U.S. citizens who claimed to know boat repair and carpentry but could not practice these trades as professionals because they did not have the "papers to show for it"; that is, they had not been *credentialed or licensed* by some educational agency in the United States. The other group was made up of immigrant professionals, mostly dentists from the Philippines. Although these immigrants had been trained in the best institutions in their countries of origin and had practiced there, they could not practice in Stockton without first receiving credentials from California educational institutions.

From a societal point of view, schools are structured to prepare citizens to both believe in and support the economic system as producers, workers, and consumers. Through credentialing them, schools allocate people into the labor force.

Community Forces: Why People Go to School,
Folk Theory of "Making It,"
and the Status Mobility System

The acts of going to school and of learning what schools teach are shared or collective cultural norms, values, and behaviors; the decisions underlying these behaviors are also cultural. Neither the economic nor the political interests of society, not the changing labor force requirements, and not even the efforts of the schools can guarantee that schools will succeed in "educating" a client population. *Whether schools succeed or not depends, in part, on the place of schooling in people's own folk theory of success.* For some groups or parts of a society, schooling may be the main route to success; for another group, schooling may be only one of several factors shaping their folk theory of getting ahead. This is particularly true in a stratified society in which other factors are also important, including the overall status of members of a client population, their economic niche, their historical experience in the opportunity structure or labor market, and their cultural values. The extent to

which and how people pursue education depends on their perceptions and interpretations of their labor market experiences or how
much comparative value they assign to school credentials.

A concept that enables one to better understand people's educational attitudes and efforts is *status mobility system,* or *folk theory
of getting ahead* (Figure 9.1). Every population (e.g., mainstream
White Americans, Black Americans, Chinese Americans) has its own
theory of getting ahead or notion of how one gets ahead as a
member of his or her group. Each folk theory tends to generate its
own ideal behaviors and its own ideal successful persons or *role
models*—the kinds of people who are widely perceived by members
of the population as successful people or as people who can get
ahead because of their personal attributes and behaviors. Parents
usually try to raise their children to be like such people, and as
children grow older, they, too, strive to be like such people (LeVine,
1967; Ogbu, 1978).

In a population in which a significant number of people of
varying backgrounds are known to have become successful or to
have "made it" through wage labor (broadly defined) because of
their school success or school credentials, people will tend to
believe strongly that the way to get ahead is by acquiring good
school credentials. In such a population, people will also develop
appropriate norms and behaviors that enhance school success. In
general, if members of a population perceive school success *over a
reasonable period of time* to result in desirable jobs, wages, promotions on the job, and other forms of self-betterment, they will
incorporate the pursuit of education into their status mobility
system or folk theory of success. The strong connection between
school success and later success in adult life will generate positive
images of schooling; people will value going to school, and they
will learn to work hard, persevere, and do well in school. What
makes people succeed academically (strategies used by successful
students) will become common knowledge and may eventually
become a part of the people's folklore. Members of the population
will develop shared beliefs, values, attitudes, and behaviors that
support both desiring school credentials and working hard and
persevering in pursuit of the credentials. The perceptions, beliefs,
values, and practices that enhance academic success will eventually
become institutionalized in the culture and be manifested at appro-

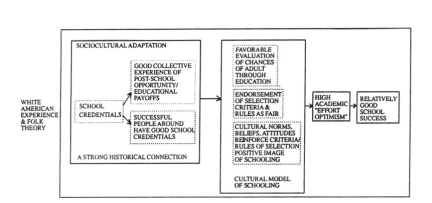

Figure 9.1. Opportunity Structure, White Folk Theory of Success, and Schooling

priate times and places as categorical and instrumental values, qualities, and behaviors by individuals.

When this situation develops in a population, parents and other child-rearing agents will teach children consciously and unconsciously and convey expectations, the categorical beliefs, values, attitudes, and behaviors that promote academic success; they will also guide and supervise children in ways that ensure that the latter actually conform to expectations of school success and accept their own academic responsibility. For their part, children will tend to respond positively to schooling. By positive response, I mean that children accept and internalize the community beliefs, values, or norms and expectations that support striving for school success, including those supporting the economic system and other societal institutions; children will make concerted efforts to learn what schools teach; and as they get older, they will even take the initiative to search out those qualities essential for future competition in the labor market. It is not sufficient, however, for parents and schools to encourage children to respond positively to schooling. *Children themselves must also observe* that, among adult members of their family and community, there is *a believable connection between school success on the one hand and success in getting jobs, wages, and other societal benefits on the other.* Or, *the children must believe that such a connection can be reasonably expected when they finish school.* To reiterate, children's positive responses are reinforced when the shared cultural knowledge and "folklore" of their community about the relationship between school success and success in adult life, based on collective experience and collective expectations, are not too discrepant with the verbal encouragement of parents and other adults.

From what children learn in the community and from the direct and indirect teachings of the schools themselves, children acquire the "facts" and "beliefs" that enable them to form appropriate "cognitive maps" or mental pictures of their community's status mobility system and how schooling fits into it. That is, children eventually develop cultural or community ideas of how to get ahead or how to "make it" and what role schooling plays in getting ahead. Where schooling so facilitates getting ahead, children are taught and/or learn to believe consciously or unconsciously that school success requires a reasonable degree of conformity to schools' rules of behavior and practices for academic achievement (children learn to conform to schools' requirements and expectations). *The children learn how to go to school and how to succeed. In this kind of community, children usually have some tacit understanding of their academic responsibility even without explicit teaching by parents or other adults. They know what is expected of them and what to do.*

But, as you will later see, both children of immigrant minorities and children in non-Western traditional societies participating in Western-type schooling can also learn how to go to school (to conform to schools' requirements and expectations), and they do succeed academically even though they have not been brought up in communities where schooling has served as a cultural route to success in adult life. These children, along with their parents and communities, usually believe that school credentials will, in the future, lead to success in adult life. In contrast, children of non-immigrant minorities in modern industrial societies do not learn quite so successfully or easily how to go to school, nor do they do well academically. What accounts for this is discussed later.

Explaining the Gap in School
Performance Between Mainstream
White Americans and Minorities

Mainstream White American Status
Mobility System and School Performance

The adaptive function of schooling described above is more applicable to mainstream White Americans than to U.S. minority groups. *School success is central in the status mobility system of mainstream White Americans* (see Figure 9.1).

Historically, a large proportion of White Americans have found jobs, earned wages and salaries, and advanced on the job through promotions commensurate with their school credentials. Furthermore, Whites have usually attained social positions commensurate with their educational credentials. This situation accounts for the high correlation between jobs and schooling in one study of White populations (Duncan & Blau, 1967). These educational payoffs, which also constitute a recognition of and reward for individual accomplishments, encourage White Americans to pursue school credentials or academic success through hard work and perseverance and teach their children to do the same.

In addition to receiving early training that prepares them to be positively disposed toward school rules of behavior for academic achievement or school requirements, *mainstream White American children acquire the utilitarian view of schooling held by their parents,* which is that people go to school to obtain credentials for good jobs and wages. They are willing to follow their parents' guidance in school matters, at least in their early years, because they can see from their parents' experience and/or from the experience of other adults in their community that getting good jobs, wages, and advancement are a result of school success or good school credentials. Children's beliefs and knowledge are also reinforced by their observations of the experiences of their older siblings, friends, and teachers (Figure 9.1), along with what they see in textbooks and the mass media. Their own experiences as they get older and begin to look for part-time or summer jobs further reinforce their beliefs and knowledge. As a result, White middle-class children increasingly come to share their parents' image that the person who gets ahead in society is one who succeeded in obtaining a good school credential. This image and its associated beliefs shape White children's attitudes toward school and encourage them to persevere and maximize their school performance.

Lower School Performance of Subordinate Minorities

Historically, the experience of non-White minority groups has been different from that of mainstream White Americans. I use Black Americans as an example.

After Black emancipation from slavery, White Americans used a job ceiling and other barriers to exclude Blacks from the more richly endowed sections of the U.S. environment. In fact, before the 1960s, Black Americans were not permitted to compete freely as individuals for any jobs they wanted and for which they had the school credentials and ability. The history and extent of this job ceiling against Blacks is well documented (see Myrdal, 1944; Norgren & Hill, 1964; Ogbu, 1978; Ross & Hill, 1967).

A major ecological consequence of the job ceiling is that Blacks have historically occupied portions of the U.S. environment characterized by scarcity of jobs, low wages, few chances for advancement on the job, and little social credit as measured by the values of the larger society. Even today, some Black Americans occupy parts of the U.S. environment or an ecological niche almost devoid of wage labor, although they contain social resources that include other residents and caretaker institutions (Harrison, 1972). Of equal importance is the fact that the ecological niche of Blacks includes a sub-economy or street economy. The *street economy* is a market for the distribution of goods and services in demand that is officially outlawed for social and moral reasons (Bullock, 1973).

School as a Delegate Agency in Black Ecological Adaptation

The school serves also as a delegate agency in Black ecological adaptation in the United States; that is, schooling prepares Black children for their place in the adult opportunity structure assigned to them by the dominant society. The ecological niche of Blacks before 1960, as noted above, was characterized by a scarcity of high-status jobs and by menial jobs, low wages, few chances of advancement on the job, little social credit, caretaker institutions, and a street economy. It was also characterized by high rates of unemployment and underemployment. The rate of unemployment was highest among the most highly educated, a situation in contrast with that of mainstream White Americans (Killingsworth, 1967). Most jobs available to Blacks did not require mainstream White school credentials, nor did they reward such credentials. Thus, the school, serving as a delegate agency, did not prepare Blacks for the same adult positions that White children were destined to occupy when they grew up, but rather prepared Blacks for a life below the job ceiling.

In three ways, schooling performed its delegate function for U.S. society and ensured that Blacks were prepared for their inferior positions below the job ceiling. First, as discussed above, U.S. society relegated Blacks to jobs and other positions below the job ceiling, which did not require White, middle-class school success. Furthermore, even when Blacks had the qualifications, they were not fully rewarded for them. By denying Blacks the opportunity to enter the labor force and to advance according to their educational qualifications and individual abilities, and by denying them adequate wage rewards for their educational effort, U.S. society discouraged them from investing time, effort, hard work, and perseverance into the pursuit of education; that is, U.S. society discouraged the pursuit of school success by giving Blacks jobs and positions that did not require school credentials and by not rewarding them adequately when they managed to obtain school credentials.

Second, schools channeled Blacks into inferior education that prepared them mainly for inferior jobs and positions below the job ceiling. For example, before 1960, Blacks were subjected to inferior education by formal statutes in the South and informal practices in the North. Black schools were staffed with inadequately trained, overworked, and underpaid teachers; the schools had different and inferior curricula; and they received inadequate funding, facilities, and services. In the South, Black children had shorter school terms than White children. Formal aspects of unequal educational opportunity have been abolished by law, but vestiges of past discrimination remain (Pierce et al., 1955).

Third, schooling performed its delegate function through the treatment of Blacks within the school and within the classroom. These treatments included lowered teacher expectations and the labeling of Black students as "educationally handicapped," which has resulted in the disproportionate number of Blacks channeled into special education (which, some believe, is inferior education). School personnel often do not understand the culturally based behaviors of Black children, and this shortcoming results in conflicts, poor relations with teachers, and poor school performance.

Black American Status Mobility System and School Performance

The Black status mobility system represented schematically in Figure 9.2 differs in many ways from the status mobility system of mainstream White Americans. Generations of Blacks have experienced, to a greater degree than Whites, a discrepancy between educational accomplishments or credentials and societal rewards; that is, proportionately, more Blacks have usually been educationally overqualified for their jobs, underpaid for their educational achievement, and denied advancement on the job (Newman, Amidei, Carter, Kruvant, & Russell, 1978; Norgren & Hill, 1964; U.S. Commission on Civil Rights, 1978). In all parts of the United States, Blacks' gradual access to more desirable jobs, even in post-civil rights legislation years, has been accomplished largely through collective or civil rights struggles, rather than through individual competition.

The job ceiling and other discriminatory practices against Black Americans have shaped their perceptions of their chances to succeed as adults in the opportunity structure and have influenced the evolution of their status mobility system. In their folk theory, Black Americans think that school success is important and necessary *but not sufficient* for them to make it. They "wish" it were so. They are generally bitter, frustrated, and resentful that (a) they do not have equal access to "quality education" and that (b) the job ceiling and other barriers prevent them from getting the full benefits of the education they do manage to get. The extent of this bitterness, frustration, and resentment can be seen in the amount of time,

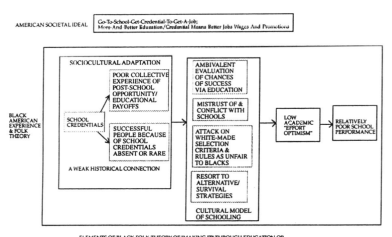

Figure 9.2. Opportunity Structure, Black Folk Theory of Success, and Schooling

resources, and effort they expend trying (a) to desegregate schools and achieve equal educational opportunity and (b) to break down, raise, or circumvent the job ceiling. These "collective struggles" have been documented for various periods and regions (see Benjamin, 1992; Drake & Cayton, 1970; Matusow, 1989; Newman et al., 1978; Ogbu, 1974; U.S. Commission on Civil Rights, 1977).

The Black American status mobility system has many features that differentiate it from the White status mobility system. I speculate that these differential features do not necessarily encourage and may even detract from the pursuit of school credentials. Among them are the following:

1. *Rejecting and changing the rules.* Because Blacks do not really believe that societal rules for self-advancement that work for White Americans work for them (e.g., having good test scores and/or good school credentials), they try to change the rules. One example of this is the argument that civil service tests should be abolished

because it is alleged that the tests are designed to favor Whites and to discriminate against Blacks (Huff, 1974; Ogbu, 1977).

2. *Collective struggle.* This strategy includes both what White Americans approve of and legitimate as civil rights activities and such nonlegitimated activities as rioting and other forms of collective action that promise to increase opportunities or to pool resources available to the Black communities (Newman et al., 1978).

3. *Clientship or "Uncle Tomming."* Black Americans have long known that one way to enhance survival and self-betterment is through favoritism, not merit. They have also learned that favoritism can be solicited by being dependent, compliant, and manipulative; as a result, Blacks may seek White Americans, both as individuals and as organizations, to serve as patrons to individual Blacks and to Black groups and organizations. The federal government in particular has tended to assume the patron's role, serving as an employer, a sponsor of educational and other training programs, an adviser and protector of civil rights, and a distributor of subsistence assistance or "welfare."

4. *Entertainment and sports.* The strategy of entertainment includes the activities of a wide variety of performers, such as singers, musicians, preachers, comedians, disc jockeys, and writers (Keil, 1977). In addition to providing meaningful adult roles and subsistence means, entertainment and sports also satisfy Black people's need for entertainment and serves as a therapy that enables them to cope with the problem of subordination. In recent decades, entertainment and sports have become increasingly important in exploiting mainstream resources.

5. *Hustling and pimping and passing.* These traditional strategies are used for exploiting nonconventional resources, or the street economy. Selling drugs is one kind of "hustle" (McCord, Howard, Friedberg, & Harwood, 1969; Valentine, 1978). In the past, "passing for White" was a strategy open to a limited number (Burma, 1947).

In the course of many generations, these alternative and survival strategies became institutionalized and integrated into the Black status mobility system. Note that changes in the opportunity structure through civil rights legislation and programs since the 1960s have modified the Black status mobility system. The changes, however, have gone neither far enough nor long enough to undo the effects of generations of subordination and unequal access to decent jobs and wages.

Conflict and Mistrust
and School Performance

Another factor contributing to the lower school performance of Black students is the historical conflict and mistrust between Blacks and the schools controlled by White Americans. The history of Black-White relations contains many episodes that have left Blacks with the feeling that they cannot trust either White Americans or the societal institutions the White Americans control to treat and reward Blacks with fairness and equity (Poussaint & Atkinson, 1973, p. 176). There appears to be a general feeling among Blacks that the public school cannot be trusted to provide Black children with the "right education." Current mistrust of schools arises partly from perceptions of past and continuing discriminatory treatment by the public schools, a treatment fully documented by several investigators (Bullock, 1970; Ogbu, 1995; Pierce et al., 1955).

Blacks' mistrust of schools works against the ability of Black parents to successfully teach their children to accept the goals, standards, and instructional approaches of the schools and to follow school rules of behavior for achievement. It is probably for the same reason that Black parents' discussions of schooling with their children tend to focus on handling interpersonal relations, rather than on subject matter. I suspect that Black parents are ambivalent about what they teach their children about schooling, and this situation may work against the children's ability to accept and internalize such teachings.

How the Job Ceiling, Other Barriers,
and Black Responses Affect Black Children's
Perceptions of and Responses to Schooling

The historical experience of Black Americans in the labor market and their own responses in the forms of collective struggle, Uncle Tomming, and the like described above have had an impact on the attitudes and behaviors of Blacks toward schooling. Blacks' historical and continuing experience of discrimination in the labor market and their responses to this discrimination have generated shared knowledge, folklore, and folk consciousness among them. Because Black children live and grow up in the Black community where these things are perceived as a social reality, they form a part of what Black children learn.

Quite early in life, Black children learn about the job ceiling and other types of discrimination, as well as about conflicts with and mistrust of White people and White-controlled institutions. They learn about these things from the experiences of their own parents, older siblings, relatives, and other adults around them (Ogbu, 1974, p. 100). They also learn about them from observing public demonstrations for more jobs and better wages, from demonstrations and public hearings for school desegregation/integration, and from reports in the mass media. From such observations, Black children begin to realize that, among Blacks, the connection between school success and ability to get ahead in adult life is dismal or not as good as the connection is for their White peers. As the children get older and experience personal frustrations in looking for part-time or summer jobs, their unfavorable perceptions and interpretations of their future opportunities relative to their White peers become even more crystallized and discouraging. Although Blacks' perceptions and interpretations may be incorrect (e.g., that employment opportunities for their White peers are unlimited), they nonetheless result in increasing disillusionment about the future and to doubts about the value of schooling (Ogbu, 1974, 1995; see also Fordham, 1995; Frazier, 1940). Black children are aware of the various features of the Black status mobility system described earlier. As I suggested earlier, Blacks "wish" that their status mobility system were like the White status mobility system and that they could get ahead through school credentials without racial barriers, *but they know they cannot. The result is that although Blacks may verbally express high educational aspirations, they do not necessarily match these with sufficient effort and perseverance.* This failing gives rise to a paradox of high aspiration coupled with low performance.

I have used Black Americans as an example, but I could just as well have used Mexican Americans, Native Americans, Native Hawaiians, or Puerto Ricans. Of course, in that case, I would have noted some differences with respect to certain issues.

Understanding Why Minorities
Differ in School Performance

Evidence of Differences
in School Performance

As previously noted, by 1982, more information became available on the school performance of both U.S. "traditional minorities" (Black Americans, Mexican Americans, Native Americans, Native Hawaiians, and Puerto Rican Americans) and on other minorities (e.g., Afro-Caribbean Americans, Chinese Americans, Cuban Americans, East Indian Americans, Latinos, Japanese Americans). The new information served as strong evidence that the minority groups differed in social adjustment and academic performance even when they faced similar barriers in opportunity structure, as well as in culture, language, and other areas in school and society. Evidence of the variability existed in the United States within the same school districts and within the same schools (Gibson, 1988; Matute-Bianchi, 1986; Ogbu, 1974, 1978; Suarez-Orozco, 1989; Valverde, 1987), and it existed at the national level as well. There were also reports of such differences in other countries. In Britain, for example, East Asian students do considerably better than West Indian students even though the former are less fluent in English than the latter (Ogbu, 1978; Tomlinson, 1982). In New Zealand, the native Maori language minority does less well in school than immigrant Polynesians who share similar language and culture (Penfold, personal communication, 1981).

For me, a new research task emerged: *Why are some minority groups relatively more academically successful, whereas other minorities are not, even though all the minority groups face cultural and language barriers in school and even though they all face limited employment opportunities after finishing school?*

Variability in Minority Responses and the Reasons

In a comparison of the school performance of minority children from different cultural backgrounds, it is evident that, at least initially, all minority groups encounter social adjustment and academic learning problems. For some groups, these tend to diminish over time, so they eventually learn more or less successfully. For others, however, the problems tend to persist and may increase over time.

To answer this new question, I decided to study selected minority groups themselves—Black Americans, Chinese Americans, Mexican Americans, and so on—as distinct populations in the United States, rather than just study their school experience; that is, I would study Black Americans, Chinese Americans, Mexican Americans, and so on as anthropologists would study the Ibos of Nigeria, the Nayar of India, the Ainu of Japan, and so on. I thought that, by acquiring an anthropological knowledge of these minorities as distinct populations and as cultural groups, I would better understand which students' attitudes and behaviors are community based and which are a result of school encounters; I would also have a better grasp of the similarities and differences among the minorities in their school experience (Ogbu, 1984).

The information provided by this kind of research has been very useful in comparing the groups. From a comparative perspective, it appears that the main reason for the differential academic performance does not lie in the mere fact that the children speak a different language or dialect or have a different communication style; nor do differences in school performance occur because the children have different cognitive styles, different styles of social interaction, or different styles of learning; it is not even because their children face different barriers in the future adult opportunity structure that minorities differ in their school performance. *Although cultural, language, and opportunity structure barriers are very important for all minorities, my research suggests that the main factor differentiating the more academically successful from the less successful minorities appears to be the nature of the minority group's history, subordination, and exploitation, as well as the nature of their own interpretations of and responses to their treatment by the Whites that enter into the process of their schooling.* In other words, school performance is not determined only by what schools and society do or do not do to and for the minorities when they arrive at school; school performance is *also* affected by how the minority communities and their children perceive, interpret, and respond to what they encounter in school and society; and their interpretations and responses are dependent on their social history. These interpretations and responses make the minorities accomplices to their own school success or failure.

Thus, school success or school failure of minority students has three sources: (a) treatment by society, (b) treatment by the school, and (c) the minority communities' responses to this treatment, or "community forces." The societal and school sources are similar to those already described for Black Americans. I focus here on community forces because therein lies the clue to the differences in the school performance among the minority groups.

Different Kinds of Minorities

My study of minority populations suggests two kinds of minorities in the context of the variability of school performance: immigrants and non-immigrants. Furthermore, the two kinds of minorities differ in how they perceive, interpret, and respond to the economic, social, cultural, and language barriers they encounter in the United States at large and in the schools *because of their different social histories.*

Immigrant or voluntary minorities are people who chose to come to the United States voluntarily because they believed that this move would lead to greater economic, political, or social well-being. Members of a voluntary minority group do not usually believe that their presence in the United States was forced on them by the actions of the U.S. government or White Americans. Although immigrants experience subordination once they are in the United States, the positive expectations they bring with them influence their perceptions of U.S. society and the public schools. Voluntary minorities are relatively successful in school even though they may face labor market barriers, as well as cultural and language barriers. Chinese Americans in Stockton, California (Ogbu, 1974) and Punjabi Indians in Valleyside (Gibson, 1988) are examples of voluntary minorities. *Refugees and migrant workers* are not immigrant minorities and are not a part of this classification.

Involuntary or non-immigrant minorities are people who are a part of the U.S. society because of slavery, conquest, or colonization, rather than because they chose to belong with expectations of a better future. Members of an involuntary minority group usually believe that their presence in the United States was forced on them by the U.S. government or by White Americans. They have no other homeland to which to return if their situation in the United States becomes unbearable. Examples of involuntary minorities in the United States are Black Americans who were brought to America as slaves; Mexican Americans or Chicanos who were conquered in the 19th century in the Southwestern United States; Native Americans who were the original owners of the land and who were conquered and confined into "reservations"; Native Hawaiians who were colonized; and Puerto Ricans who consider themselves a colonized people. It is the involuntary minorities both in the United States and elsewhere (e.g., Buraku outcasts in Japan, Maoris in New Zealand, Malays in Singapore) who do not do well in school.

Differential Community Forces
and School Performance

Having studied minority populations and their education from historical and comparative perspectives, I now think that (a) an essential key to understanding the differences in minority school performance is to understand their cultural models and the educational strategies that result from these cultural models and that (b) the operative cultural model and educational strategies are dependent, in part, on the group's interpretations of its history, present situation, and future expectations (their sociocultural or cultural-ecological adaptation). What I mean by *cultural model* is the people's understandings of their world that guide their interpretations of events in that world and their own actions in that same world. *Folk model* is a comparative term (Bohannan, 1957; Holland & Quinn, 1987; Ogbu, 1974). *Educational strategies* are the attitudes, plans, and actions that minorities use or do not use in their pursuit of school credentials. In cultural-ecological theory of schooling, cultural models and educational strategies are combined into the broader concept of *community forces* (see Figure 9.3).

Community forces are different for immigrant and non-immigrant minorities, and this difference is the source of the differences in school performance between immigrant and non-immigrant minorities. The immigrants have cultural models of U.S. society and of schooling and educational strategies (community forces) that are more conducive to school success. Specifically, immigrant minorities who came to the United States because they believed that this

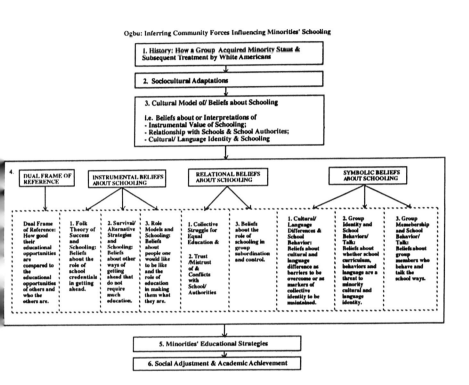

Figure 9.3. Inferring Community Forces Influencing Minorities' Schooling

move would lead to greater economic, political, or social well-being tend to do the following:

- See good school credentials as both necessary and sufficient to achieve upward social mobility.
- Interpret cultural and language differences as barriers to be overcome to achieve the goals of their emigration. They do not interpret cultural and language differences as detrimental to their collective identity;

rather, the immigrants think their cultural and language problems are a result of a lack of know-how: that they do not yet know how to talk or behave like mainstream White Americans in school and the workplace.

• Trust or at least be acquiescent in their relationship with public schools and school personnel.

As a consequence of these beliefs and attitudes, immigrant minorities adopt strategies, including working hard, that help them do relatively well in school.

Involuntary minorities who were incorporated into the U.S. society against their will, have experienced a long history of a job ceiling and other forms of discrimination, and have no "homeland" situation to which they can compare their situation in the United States tend to do the following:

• Believe that their poor situation is primarily a result of their minority status.

• Believe that school credentials and hard work are necessary but not sufficient criteria for them *as minorities* to get good jobs and to achieve upward social mobility. They usually have many examples of members of their group who have good educations but not the jobs or social positions comparable to those of their White peers.

• Interpret cultural and language differences they encounter more or less as markers of collective identity, rather than as barriers to be overcome. They do not think their problem is that they do not yet know how to talk or behave like White Americans. They have examples of members of their community who talk or behave like White people but are not employed in comparable jobs or treated like their White peers.

• Believe that school personnel often expect non-immigrant minority children to give up their way of talking or behaving in order to learn to talk and behave in the school (or "White") way, a demand the children consciously or unconsciously resist. The children might also consciously believe and fear that they will have to give up the way they talk before they can learn to "talk properly" in school. Under this circumstance, the non-immigrants appear, consciously or unconsciously, to perceive crossing cultural and language boundaries as threatening to their minority identity.

• Mistrust the public schools and those who control them. As a consequence of these beliefs and attitudes, non-immigrant or involuntary minorities are ambivalent toward school, work less hard, and adopt other strategies that result in their lower school performance (Ogbu, 1993).

In summary, immigrant and non-immigrant minorities differ in school performance because they differ in community forces. Because of their different histories, they perceive, interpret, and respond to treatment in the labor market and other areas (e.g., cultural, language) differently. Consequently, they also perceive and interpret schooling in different ways that produce differences in behavior with different outcomes.

How Community Forces Get Into Minority Children and Their Schooling

How do community forces get into the minority child so that he or she comes to behave at school in the manner described above? In brief, the initial terms of incorporation into U.S. society (voluntary immigration or involuntary incorporation), together with subsequent subordination and adaptation, shape each minority group's cultural models of (a) its minority status and (b) U.S. society; that is, these events and experiences influence the understanding of members of given minority groups in the United States. These understandings, in turn, affect their sociocultural adaptation that generates their cultural models. The latter consists of beliefs and attitudes about schooling and the strategies for getting an education (see Figure 9.3).

A minority group's sociocultural adaptations to minority status, its cultural model of schooling, educational orientations, and educational strategies form an integral part of the minority culture. The latter, minority culture, is the cultural curriculum that the minority child learns in the course of growing up in the minority community. This curriculum—minority sociocultural adaptation, cultural model of schooling, educational orientations, and strategies of a given minority group—is taught to the child consciously and unconsciously through culturally appropriate processes or techniques by agents responsible for the child's upbringing, which includes the family, peer groups, religious organizations, the mass media, and role models. As the minority child grows older, he or she may actively seek to acquire the sociocultural adaptations, cultural models, educational orientations, and strategies of his or her community. Thus, when the minority child comes to school, he or she comes with an emerging knowledge, set of attitudes, and strategies that can promote or discourage good social adjustment and academic performance, depending on what the child encounters at school; that is, the minority child comes to school with a culturally based or community-based set of attitudes, knowledge, or understandings (cultural models) that predisposes him or her toward doing well or poorly, depending on what he or she encounters in school. What the immigrant minority child and the non-immigrant minority child bring to school—community forces—differ in many respects. Consequently, the two groups of children have different experiences at school that affect their social adjustment and academic performance.

Implications

Understanding why minority children do not perform in school like mainstream White children is a step toward determining what can be done to improve minority children's performance. Similarly, understanding why some minorities do well and others do not under similar circumstances is also a step toward finding some solution for the lower academic performance of some minorities. In explaining why minorities perform less well than Whites, I pointed to opportunity barriers in the wider society and to discriminatory treatment in school. These barriers and discriminatory treatments must end to enhance minority school performance. But I also noted that the perceptions and responses of the minorities themselves are an important part of the problem; such perceptions and responses may even exist where societal and school barriers have been eliminated. So far, I have found no policies or programs addressing this side of the matter seriously, although there should be.

The comparative study of immigrant and non-immigrant minorities provides some important clues about helping all minorities, as well as the specific needs of non-immigrant minorities. The most obvious need of immigrant minorities in school is a transitional, bilingual education program to help them learn the English they need to participate more fully in the public schools. Non-immigrant minorities, such as Black Americans, also need bilingual education; treating Black English vernacular as a distinct language like Cantonese will (a) discourage teachers from forcing Black children to give up "their language" in order to learn the standard English and (b) make Black students realize that they do not have to give up their language in order to learn the standard English that would serve as a tool for educational and other purposes; this will reduce the psychological burden on the children.

One problem faced by involuntary minority students is the difficulty of separating their collective identity from their academic identity. The latter is sometimes equated with "White identity" and is understood as oppositional to the minority identity. Some programs are needed to help students develop ways to manage their academic identity while affirming their collective or minority identity (see Mehan, Hubbard, & Villanueva, 1994).

References

Anton, K. P. (1980). *Eligibility and enrollment in California public higher education.* Unpublished doctoral dissertation, University of California, Graduate School of Education, Berkeley.

Benjamin, L. (1992). *The Black elite: Facing the color line in the twilight of the 20th century.* Chicago: Nelson-Hall.

Bohannan, P. (1957). *Justice and judgment among the Tiv.* London: Oxford University Press.

Bourdieu, P., & Passeron, J.-C. (1977). *Reproduction in education, society, and culture.* Beverly Hills, CA: Sage.

Bullock, H. A. (1970). *A history of Negro education in the South: From 1619 to the present.* New York: Praeger.

Bullock, P. (1973). *Aspiration v. opportunity: "Careers" in the inner city.* Ann Arbor: University of Michigan Press.

Burma, J. H. (1947). The measurement of Negro passing. *American Journal of Sociology, 52,* 18-22.

Chernoff, M. L., Nassif, P. M., & Gorth, W. P. (Eds.). (1987). *The validity issue: What should teacher certification tests measure?* Hillsdale, NJ: Lawrence Erlbaum.

Clement, D. C., et al. (1978). *Moving closer: An ethnography of a Southern desegregated school.* Final report, unpublished manuscript. Washington, DC: National Institute of Education.

Coleman, J. S., Campbell, E. Q., Hobson, C. J., McPartland, J., Mood, A. M., Weinfeld, F. D., & York, R. L. (1966). *Equality of educational opportunity.* Washington, DC: Government Printing Office.

Collins, T. W., & Noblit, G. W. (1978). *Stratification and resegregation: The case of Crossover High School.* Final report, unpublished manuscript. Washington, DC: National Institute of Education.

Drake, S. C., & Cayton, H. R. (1970). *Black metropolis: A study of Negro life in a Northern city* (Vols. 1 & 2). Orlando, FL: Harcourt Brace.

Duncan, O. D., & Blau, P. (1967). *The American occupational structure.* New York: John Wiley.

Fordham, S. (1995). *Black out.* Chicago: University of Chicago Press.

Frazier, E. F. (1940). *Negro youth at the crossways: Their personality development in the middle states.* Washington, DC: American Council on Education.

Gibson, M. A. (1988). *Accommodation without assimilation: Punjabi Sikhs in an American high school and community.* Ithaca, NY: Cornell University Press.

Gibson, M. A., & Ogbu, J. U. (1991). *Minority status and schooling: A comparative study of immigrant and involuntary minorities.* New York: Garland.

Gordon, E. W., & Wilkerson, D. A. (1965). *Compensatory education for the disadvantaged: Programs and practices: Preschool to college.* New York: College Entrance Examination Board.

Gorth, W. P., & Chernoff, M. L. (Eds.). (1986). *Testing for teacher certification.* Hillsdale, NJ: Lawrence Erlbaum.

Hanushek, E. A. (1977). *A reader's guide to educational production function.* Unpublished manuscript.

Harrison, B. (1972). *Education, training, and the urban ghetto.* Baltimore, MD: Johns Hopkins University Press.

Haycock, K., & Navarro, S. (1988). *Unfinished business: Report from the Achievement Council.* Unpublished manuscript, Achievement Council of California, Oakland, CA.

Holland, D., & Eisenhart, M. (1990). *Educated for romance.* Chicago: University of Chicago Press.

Holland, D. C., & Quinn, N. (Eds.). (1987). *Cultural models in language and thought.* San Diego, CA: Academic Press.

Huff, S. (1974). Credentialing by tests or by degrees: Title VII of the Civil Rights Act and *Criggs v. Duke Power Company. Harvard Educational Review, 44,* 246-269.

Inkeles, A. (1966). Social structure and socialization of competence. In the Editors, *Harvard Educational Review: Socialization and schools.* Cambridge, MA: Harvard University Press.

Jacob, E., & Jordan, C. (Eds.). (1993). *Minority education: Anthropological perspectives.* Norwood, NJ: Ablex.

Keil, C. (1977). The expressive Black male role: The bluesman. In D. Y. Wilkinson & R. L. Taylor (Eds.), *The Black male in America today: Perspectives on his status in contemporary society.* Chicago: Nelson-Hall.

Killingsworth, C. C. (1967). Negroes in a changing labor market. In A. M. Ross & H. Hill (Eds.), *Employment, race, and poverty: A critical study of the disadvantaged status of Negro workers from 1865 to 1965* (pp. 49-75). Orlando, FL: Harcourt Brace.

LeVine, R. A. (1967). *Dreams and deeds: Achievement motivation in Nigeria.* Chicago: University of Chicago Press.

Matusow, B. (1989, November). Alone together: What do you do when the dream hasn't come true, when you're Black and middle-class and still shut out of White Washington, when it seems quite trying. *Washingtonian,* pp. 153-159, 282-290.

Matute-Bianchi, M. E. (1986). Ethnic identities and patterns of school success and failure among Mexican-descent and Japanese-American students in a California high school: An ethnographic analysis. *American Journal of Education, 95*(1), 235-255.

McCord, W., Howard, J., Friedberg, B., & Harwood, E. (1969). *Lifestyles in the Black ghetto.* New York: Norton.

Mehan, H., Hubbard, L., & Villanueva, I. (1994). Forming academic identities: Accommodation without assimilation among involuntary minorities. *Anthropology and Education Quarterly, 25*(2), 91-117.

Myrdal, G. (1944). *An American dilemma: The Negro problem and modern democracy.* New York: Harper & Row.

Newman, D. K., Amidei, B. K., Carter, D. D., Kruvant, W. J., & Russell, J. S. (1978). *Protest, politics, and prosperity: Black Americans and White institutions, 1940-1975.* New York: Pantheon.

Norgren, P. H., & Hill, S. E. (1964). *Toward fair employment.* New York: Columbia University Press.

Ogbu, J. U. (1974). *The next generation: An ethnography of education in an urban neighborhood.* San Diego, CA: Academic Press.

Ogbu, J. U. (1977). Racial stratification and education: The case of Stockton, California. *IRCD Bulletin, 12*(3), 1-26.

Ogbu, J. U. (1978). *Minority education and caste: The American system in cross-cultural perspective.* San Diego, CA: Academic Press.

Ogbu, J. U. (1979). Desegregation in racially stratified communities; A problem of congruence. *Anthropology and Education Quarterly, 9*(4), 290-294.

Ogbu, J. U. (1983). Minority status and schooling in plural societies. *Comparative Education Review, 27*(2), 168-190.

Ogbu, J. U. (1984). *Understanding community forces affecting minority students' academic effort.* Unpublished report prepared for the Achievement Council of California, Oakland.

Ogbu, J. U. (1993). Minority school performance: A problem in search of an explanation. In E. Jacob & C. Jordan (Eds.), *Minority education: Anthropological perspectives* (pp. 83-111). Norwood, NJ: Ablex.

Ogbu, J. U. (1995). *Community forces and minority educational strategy: Final report #1.* Unpublished manuscript, University of California, Department of Anthropology, Berkeley.

Peterson, P. E., & Wong, K. (1990). *The changing urban school system.* Unpublished manuscript, Social Science Research Council.

Pierce, T. M., et al. (1955). *White and Negro schools in the South: An analysis of biracial education.* Englewood Cliffs, NJ: Prentice Hall.

Poussaint, A., & Atkinson, C. (1973). Black youth and motivation. In E. G. Epps (Ed.), *Race relations: Current perspectives* (pp. 167-177). Cambridge, MA: Winthrop.

Prince Georges County Public Schools. (1990). *Black male achievement: From peril to promise. Report of the Superintendent's Advisory Committee on Black Male Achievement.* Unpublished manuscript, Prince Georges County Public Schools, Upper Marlboro, MD.

Ross, A. M., & Hill, H. (Eds.). (1967). *Employment, race, and poverty.* Orlando, FL: Harcourt Brace.

Slade, M. (1982, October 24). Aptitude, intelligence, or what? *New York Times.*

Southern School News. (1952). Under survey. 3(1), 2.

Stern, S. P. (1986, December). *School-imposed limits on Black family participation: A view from within and below.* Paper presented at the Eighty-Fifth Annual Meeting of the American Anthropological Association, Philadelphia.

Suarez-Orozco, M. M. (1989). *Central American refugees and U.S. high school: A psychosocial study of motivation and achievement.* Stanford, CA: Stanford University Press.

Tomlinson, S. (1982). *Sociology of special education.* London: Routledge and Kegan Paul.

U.S. Commission on Civil Rights. (1977). *The unfinished business.* Washington, DC: Government Printing Office.

U.S. Commission on Civil Rights. (1978). *Social indicators of equality for minorities and women.* Washington, DC: Government Printing Office.

Valentine, B. A. (1978). *Hustling and other hard works: Lifestyles in the ghetto.* New York: Free Press.

Valverde, S. A. (1987). A comparative study of Hispanic high school dropouts and graduates: Why do some leave school early and some finish? *Education and Urban Society, 19*(3), 320-329.

• CHAPTER 10 •

Extended Day Programs for Urban Children and Youth: From Theory to Practice

DONALD R. HELLISON

NICHOLAS J. CUTFORTH

Much has been spoken and written about the plight of "inner-city" children and youth—the poverty and racism they experience, the war zones they live in, the paucity of functional male adults, the number of dysfunctional families and pregnant teens, and the influence of gangs and drug trafficking. The list goes on and on. Unfair stereotypes have emerged from this barrage of media coverage—for example, the notion that all poor families are dysfunctional or that all inner-city youth engage in violence or that nothing positive happens in these communities. It is fair to say, however, that children and youth in the typical inner-city neighborhood are exposed to a wide range of negative influences beyond those experienced by their suburban and rural counterparts (though the gap may be closing):

Thousands of young children in America's cities are growing up amidst a worsening problem of community violence: shootings and stabbings on the street, domestic violence that spills out of house-holds into public view, widespread awareness of murders and serious assaults within a community, evident gang activity. In Chicago the rate of serious assault increased 400 percent from 1974 to 1991. More than half the murders and aggravated assaults in the city take place in a few high-crime "war zones"—neighborhoods that are poor, socially isolated, and often dominated by gangs. (Garbarino, Dubrow, Kostelny, & Pardo, 1992, p. xi)

It is also fair to say that most of these young people do not receive enough help with their cognitive, emotional, and social development. They are, in a word, underserved. Organizations that do serve inner-city children and youth, such as schools, social agencies, and churches, are overburdened and underfunded, and they may need to be reformed as well. Lois Weiner (1993) persuasively argued that urban schools and urban teacher education programs need to change in fundamental ways if they are to truly meet these children's needs; as James Comer put it, "The sources of risk are in the schools, as well as in societal and family conditions outside the school" (1987, p. 14). This argument can be extended to other youth services as well. One longitudinal study includes this observation: "A major risk for the future is the abdication of responsibility by conventional institutions that borders on anarchy in some . . . communities" (Cairns & Cairns, 1994, p. 264).

If the negative influences are greater and the services fewer and less effective, it is no wonder that many young people feel outrage and frustration. Listen to a few of their voices:

"You can't trust nobody but yourself."

"The future be dead."

"All of us want to be somebody. Nobody wants to be out there [on the street] doin' that shit." (McLaughlin, Irby, & Langman, 1994, pp. 207, 208, 215)

In our view, these young people are not the problem; in fact, they do incredibly well, given the negative influences they have to navigate through and the minimal institutional support available to them. They just need some help in becoming "somebody," in envisioning possible futures, in their struggle to develop cognitively, emotionally, and socially. They need programs that work.

Focusing on programs, however, ignores fundamental issues of poverty, racism, and other social, economic, and political ills of our society that underlie the problems of growing up in the inner city. These forces will not be altered by offering "programs that work." But, as Joy Dryfoos (1991) pointed out, such programs can help:

Child advocates are admittedly hanging on the incremental edge, chipping away at those situations that are amenable to change, with insufficient force to alter the social environment that generates many of these problems. Even so, there is much incremental work that can and must be done. (p. 634)

Such programs work better if they are integrated. Sufficient evidence now exists to show the overlaps and gaps in education, health, and social services when programs for children and youth operate in isolation from one another, as well as to suggest guidelines for providing integrated services (Hooper-Briar & Lawson, 1994). A review of 100 successful prevention programs demonstrated "the importance of broad communitywide, multiagency, multicomponent interventions" (Dryfoos, 1991, p. 631). Ianni (1989) called for a "youth charter" in each community so that all service providers share the same goals for youth. Examples of integrated services are the Suder School Partnership in Chicago, which includes a variety of prevention-oriented social service programs; the collaboration of more than 40 agencies in Durham, North Carolina, to provide comprehensive services to decrease juvenile delinquency (Brown, 1995); and the California State University, Fullerton, collaborative services seminar, which is designed to "train" future teachers, nurses, and youth workers in integrated services (Zuniga-Hill & George, 1995).

Extended Day Programs

Extended day programs serve children and youth before and after school and on weekends. They are sponsored by social agencies such as the YMCA and the Boys and Girls Club, by churches and park districts, by schools, and by other individuals or groups trying to make a contribution to the lives of young people. These programs have become increasingly important, with the rise of unsupervised (discretionary) time in recent years, which now averages about 5 hours per day for public school students. In the inner city, the need for safe places to go during free time, as well as the emerging concept of integrated services, has also intensified the interest in extended day programs. For example, the Suder School Partnership in Chicago includes extended day programs as an integral part of its plan to serve the students of Suder School. Inner-city extended day programs have even been a topic of political debates—for example, the recent furor over funding of such programs as Midnight Basketball in federal crime legislation.

This chapter focuses on the state of the art and the state of practice of inner-city extended day programs. We define *state of the art* as what is known to work and *state of practice* as what typically goes on in extended day programs. One problem with this framework is that, according to Milbrey McLaughlin, who is perhaps the leading investigator of inner-city extended day programs, "Little is known about what makes a program work" (McLaughlin et al., 1994, p. 5). Studies and scholarly opinions, however, including those of McLaughlin, do suggest criteria for programs that work, as well as the reasons why programs fail.

State of Practice

Available attendance figures for inner-city extended day programs suggest an immediate problem: Extended day programs fail to attract very many participants over age 12. This information can be interpreted in different ways. Some, perhaps many, think it is evidence that inner-city adolescents are a "lost cause," that they prefer gangs, drugs, and criminal activity. Attendance and waiting list data, however, show that a few programs have high demand; for example, one program cannot meet the demand of gang members who want to join (McLaughlin et al., 1994). McLaughlin and her associates recognize that some inner-city youth are sociopaths (or "cranks") but estimate that 75% of the youths want to participate in programs that address their needs.

Most extended day programs, however, do not address the needs of inner-city youth. A primary reason for the lack of interest is the very nature of the majority of these programs. Potential participants are not interested in programs that (a) "blame the victim" by attributing inner-city problems to the youth themselves, rather than to the current system (e.g., ineffective schools and social services, meager economic opportunities, unresponsive government); (b) focus on fixing participants' deficiencies instead of building on their strengths; (c) attempt to control deviant behavior, for example, by such program goals as keeping youth off the streets; or (d) promote white, middle-class nuclear family values. Luis Rodriguez

(1994) explained that programs need to "address the burning issue of adolescent rage" by nurturing the "warrior energy" of youth:

> The warrior needs to be nurtured, directed, and guided—not smothered, crushed, or corralled. This energy needs to be taken to the next highest level of development, where one matures into self-control, self-study, self-actualization. Most anti-gang measures have nothing to do with any of this. A serious effort would address . . . a basic need for food, shelter, and clothing, but also needs for expressive creativity and community. . . . You want to stop the body count? Empower the youth. (pp. 58-59)

Another important reason for the failure of extended day programs is the nature of funding provided by the federal government and often by foundations as well. McLaughlin and Heath (1993) pointed out the difficulty in getting support for programs based on state-of-the-art criteria described below:

> The demand from public and private funders for "accountability" tops youth workers list as an impediment to the flexible, responsive programming associated with effective youth programs. Complaints [focus on] the types of evidence demanded. Requirements to specify "treatments" and outcomes in advance constrain program staff to identify "outputs" that can be easily measured, counted, and demonstrated. The "softer" outcomes, such as improved self-concept, an expanded sense of possible futures, a connection with a coherent system of values and beliefs, and a sense of personal and emotional safety, elude typical evaluation instruments and so do not "count." Yet these are the outcomes that matter most to youth and to their productive futures. (p. 230)

State of the Art

The following list of the key criteria (summarized in Table 10.1) for state-of-the-art extended day programs was drawn primarily from McLaughlin's several-year investigation of more than 60 programs with 24,000 members in three major cities (McLaughlin et al., 1994), as well as the work of other scholars and policy experts (Cappel, 1995; Carnegie Council on Adolescent Development, 1992; Heath & McLaughlin, 1993; Ianni, 1993; Villarruel & Lerner, 1994; "Youth Employment," 1994):

TABLE 10.1 Key Criteria for State-of-the-Art Extended Day Programs

---

 1. Treat youth as resources to be developed. Build on the strengths they already possess and emphasize their competence and mastery.
 2. Focus on the whole person.
 3. Respect their individuality, including cultural differences and developmental needs.
 4. Empower them.
 5. Give them clear, demanding (but not unreasonable) expectations based on a strong, explicit set of values.
 6. Help youth envision possible futures for themselves.
 7. Provide both a physically and psychologically safe environment.
 8. Keep program numbers small and encourage participation over a long period of time; emphasize belonging and membership.
 9. Maintain a local connection.
10. Provide courageous and persistent leadership in the face of systemic obstacles.
11. Provide significant contact with an adult who cares about them.

---

1. Treat youth as resources to be developed, rather than as problems to be managed. Work from their strengths, rather than from their weaknesses, and emphasize their competence and mastery, thereby building their self-confidence, self-worth, and ability to contribute. Don't label them as at-risk, but rather as "at promise" (Swadener & Lubeck, 1995).

2. Focus on their emotional, social, educational, and economic needs—in other words, on the whole person, rather than on a single issue such as reading skills or basketball. (A single issue can provide an organizational focus for the program, but to be effective the whole person must be addressed. Programs that are just recreational or fun are not effective!)

3. Respect their individuality, including cultural differences and developmental needs. Be aware of rapid behavioral fluctuations as a result of intense pressures encountered in their daily lives. Although cultural differences are important, there is no substitute for being sensitive and responsive to the ideas, issues, and attitudes that individuals bring to the program. Both Weiner (1993) and Heath and McLaughlin (1993) argue that there is much more to young people than their race or ethnicity (or gender, for that matter). Not only do ethnic labels mask subtle ethnic differences, but "students who are demographically identical may be psychologically quite different"

(Weiner, 1993, p. 111). Moreover, "in the end, everyone's culture is different, because everyone's experience is different" (Kennedy, 1989, p. 21).

4. Empower them; encourage a perception of independence and control over their own lives through active participation, a voice in the program, and leadership responsibilities. Help them learn to control themselves and each other. Despite the recent popularity of authoritarian boot camps for juvenile offenders, this approach is "demeaning and punitive" (McLaughlin et al., 1994, p. 8).

5. Build clear expectations into the program. Make these expectations demanding but reachable by those who are unexceptional. Expectations should challenge but not defeat. "Discipline lies centrally in the expectations" (McLaughlin & Heath, 1993, p. 218). Expectations should be based on a strong, explicit set of values. Unlike the battle being waged in public education over the teaching of specific values, state-of-the-art inner-city extended day programs must teach values to offset the values of "the street." As John Gardner put it,

> Absence of instruction in values is the least of our problems. What is a problem is that the values taught may be destructive. The young person is bombarded by value instruction, for good or evil, every waking hour. . . . No one escapes. (cited in McLaughlin et al., 1994, p. x)

6. Help them envision possible futures for themselves, especially future vocational and avocational activities they may not see as relevant to their lives, and ways to get there. According to two psychologists, the "possible selves" of youth play a pivotal role in their future activities (Oyserman & Markus, 1990).

7. Provide a psychologically as well as physically safe environment. It is one thing to ensure freedom from physical harm; it is quite another to detect and control emotional abuse and ridicule, which are often disguised as humor or gesture or innuendo.

8. Keep program numbers small and encourage participation over several years to create a sense of belonging and membership, encourage the development of close personal relationships, and reduce the need for management so that program goals can be addressed.

9. Maintain a local (e.g., community) connection. Forge linkages with people in the neighborhood—parents, teachers, youth workers, ministers, and business leaders. Seek to enrich the community, rather than disparage it.

10. Provide the kind of courageous and persistent leadership that makes the program work despite systemic obstacles. Haberman (1995) argued that effective urban teachers "learn how to gain the widest

discretion for themselves and their students without incurring the wrath of the system" (p. 780).

11. Provide significant contact with an adult who cares and offers support. This is perhaps the most significant finding in the resiliency literature (Gordon & Song, 1994; Ianni, 1993). As inner-city Oakland physician Barbara Staggers observed:

> With all the kids I know who make it, there's one thing in common: an individual contact with an adult who cared and who kept hanging in with the teen through his hardest moments. . . . People talk programs and that's important. But when it comes down to it, individual person-to-person connections make the difference. . . . Every kid I know who made it through the teenage years had at least one adult in his life who made that effort. (quoted in Foster, 1994, pp. 53-54)

These criteria for state-of-the-art extended day programs are strikingly similar to some of the criteria for state-of-the-art alternative schools for so-called at-risk youth (Raywid, 1994):

- Build on strengths. *[Criterion 1]*
- Empower students (and faculty). *[Criterion 4]*
- Keep the school and classes small. Small class size (15 students per teacher) is also specified in an urban education reform plan in Wisconsin (Cohen, 1995). *[Criterion 8]*
- Develop a local connection. *[Criterion 9]*
- Operate separate from the system. *[Criterion 10]*
- Be first and foremost student-centered rather than subject matter specialists. *[Criterion 11]*

Studies of the resiliency of inner-city children and youth, which focus on those who succeed despite their environment, also support some criteria for state-of-the-art extended day programs (Norman Garmezy, cited in "Resilience in Action," 1994; Wang, Haertel, & Walberg, 1994):

- Provide training and experiences in self-motivation and autonomy. Emphasize a personal sense of purpose. *[Criteria 1 & 4]*
- Provide opportunities for success, task mastery, and problem solving. *[Criterion 1]*

- Build on prior cultural knowledge rather than exploit weaknesses. *[Criteria 1 & 3]*
- Create an atmosphere of belonging and involvement. Emphasize positive social interactions and teach peer support. *[Criterion 10]*

From Theory to Practice:
A Field-Based Model

Although support for these criteria is considerable, specific examples of state-of-the-art programs in practice are not so plentiful. McLaughlin and her associates described six such programs, most of which are multipurpose (McLaughlin et al., 1994), and Villarruel and Lerner (1994) described several exemplary programs, including those with mathematics, science, and computer themes. We have chosen two inner-city extended day programs to describe in some detail, not from this literature, but from our own experiences in dual roles as both instructors and investigators. These examples will, we hope, demonstrate that these ideas can be put into practice and suggest some specific ways of doing so.

Both of these programs are based on a model that emerged experientially as the result of fieldwork over the past 25 years (Hellison, 1978, 1985, 1995), well before much of the state-of-the-art data and professional opinion cited above was published. The model uses *taking responsibility for one's own well-being and for being sensitive and responsive to the well-being of others* as the overriding purpose for extended day clubs organized around specific physical activities—for example, basketball, martial arts, and fitness (though the model has been used in classroom activities as well [Hellison, 1995]). Three broad goals that go well beyond the purposes of traditional sport and exercise programs provide direction for all these responsibility-based programs: (a) *self-responsibility* for one's motivation and self-direction, (b) *social responsibility* for respecting the rights and feelings of others and for being sensitive and responsive to the needs of others, and (c) *group responsibility* for cooperation and group betterment. To make clear what participants are to take responsibility for, the goals of the model are presented to program participants as five specific responsibilities:

1. Respect the rights and feelings of others (including self-control, team-work and cooperation, and peaceful conflict resolution)
2. Be self-motivated (explore one's motivation, try new things, define success for oneself)
3. Have self-direction (develop, carry out, and evaluate personal goals)
4. Help others and work together for the group's welfare
5. Implement responsibilities outside the gym (trying out the responsibilities in school, at home, and on the street)

Several strategies are employed to help participants become aware of these five responsibilities, experience them, and make decisions in relation to them:

Awareness talks
Responsibilities-in-action
Individual decision making for each responsibility
Group meetings
Reflection time
Instructor-student interaction

Awareness talks introduce club members to the five responsibilities at the beginning of the program and remind them of their responsibilities throughout the program. *Responsibilities-in-action* build the responsibilities into the day's session so that participants can experience and get a "feel" for them. For example, requiring all teammates to touch the ball before shooting (e.g., in soccer, basketball, or floor hockey) helps them experience cooperation, and requesting that they compare their current performance to their own past performances rather than to those of other club members helps them be self-motivated.

Individual decision making, group meetings, and *reflection time* shift responsibility to club members. Individual decision-making strategies are used at each level of responsibility. Someone who shows disrespect for others negotiates the consequences of this action, and if several are involved in a conflict, a time-out is called (by a club member or, if necessary, the instructor) so that the involved individuals can problem solve and reach a decision. The instructor negotiates personal plans with individuals who struggle with the respect issue or any of the other four responsibilities. To facilitate self-motivation, participants are encouraged to define success for themselves and can choose from a range of less competitive to more competitive game options. Club members learn to become more self-directed by choosing and carrying out their own goals and activities at a specified time during the session. Club members are routinely offered opportunities to volunteer as coaches, teachers, and in other helping roles.

In *group meetings,* club members evaluate the program, the instructor, and each other and problem-solve issues that arise and suggest ways to improve the program. *Reflection time* at the end of each lesson gives participants the opportunity to self-evaluate the extent to which they were responsible (e.g., respectful, self-motivated) during the session. By self-evaluating their attitudes and behaviors in a journal entry, on a checklist, or in a meeting with the instructor, they can begin to judge not only how they are doing but also whether such responsibilities matter to them.

Instructor-student interaction is not so much a separate strategy as a prerequisite to the other strategies. Although 11 instructor qualities in addition to competence in teaching the content contribute to effectively putting the five responsibilities into practice (Hellison, 1995), it is perhaps most important for the instructor to "live the levels" insofar as possible—that is, to treat participants with respect, include everyone, solve problems peacefully, be self-motivated, engage in self-improvement, care about them, do these things outside the gym, and so on. Although this guideline is not an implementation strategy in the usual sense, such qualities are very influential in making the model work. As Bill Ayers (1989) wrote, "There is no clear line delineating the person and the teacher. Rather, there is a seamless web between teaching and being, between teacher and person. Teaching is not simply what one does, it is who one is" (p. 130).

A strategy for emphasizing instructor-student interaction is *counseling time,* which means conducting brief, informal, one-to-one meetings with all club members, not just those in trouble or those who stand out, to check in and co-evaluate what has been (or not been) going on. For example, a few words can be exchanged when participants come into the gym or when someone is not directly involved in an activity.

Qualitative program evaluations designed to investigate the model's impact on program participants were conducted well after most of these criteria were discovered experientially. These studies have been, for the most part, supportive of the model (DeBusk & Hellison, 1989; Hellison, 1978; Kallusky, 1991; Lifka, 1989; Mulaudzi, 1995; Puckett & Cutforth, 1996; Williamson & Georgiadis, 1992), as was one quantitative study (Keramidas, 1991), although other quantitative data were not so positive (Hellison, 1978). Despite the experiential nature of this approach and the reflective, interpretive character of much of the writing about it, scholars have continued to cite it as an exemplary curriculum model (Bain, 1988; Steinhardt, 1992), an exemplary model for curriculum inquiry (Georgiadis, 1992; Kirk, 1993), an alternative approach to discipline problems (Graham, Holt/Hale, & Parker, 1993; Rink, 1993), and an exemplary approach for special populations (Searle, Winther, & Reed, 1994; Siedentop, Mand, & Taggart, 1986; Winnick, 1990). Rovegno and Kirk (1995) made this point about its contribution to social problems: "[It offers] genuinely alternative forms of social organization . . . in an attempt to constructively redress the social conditions placing some young people's well-being at risk" (p. 451). Doubts about its effectiveness have been expressed by the instructor-investigator (Hellison, 1990), however, and Shields and Bredemeier (1995) found both the inquiry process and the model's structure to be problematic to some extent.

Federal, foundation, private industry, and school district grants have partially supported the development and field testing of this model for more than two decades, but because funding agencies are not as interested in goals and outcomes that are "softer" and not easily measured (see the previous extract by McLaughlin & Heath, 1993), models such as this one have more difficulty attracting funding support.

The background, rationale, and detailed description of this model, as well as sample applications in specific settings, are contained in *Teaching Responsibility Through Physical Activity* (Hellison, 1995).

From Theory to Practice:
Visiting Two Program Sites

The primary purpose of this chapter is not to share in detail the theoretical-philosophical underpinnings of this model or the program evaluation data, but rather to provide specific inner-city examples of the state-of-the-art extended day program criteria in practice. Both of the following examples are presented in experiential narrative to bring the reader as close as possible to the state-of-the-art criteria in practice. Italicized references to the state-of-the-art criteria listed in Table 10.1 are included throughout both examples.

The Coaching Club

To visit this before-school program, it is necessary to travel to a school on the south side of Chicago. The neighborhood is Englewood, one of the most well-known "war zones" in the city. A recent ethnography described the neighborhood this way:

> Graffiti-covered walls [are] scrawled by gang members who fight for control of the sale of crack cocaine in the neighborhood. During one month in 1992, there were 74 homicides within three miles of the school, a record for the city. . . . Parents believe that the neighborhood has deteriorated in recent years with more drive-by shootings and drug use. Some of the parents . . . are known drug users and dealers. . . . [P]osters which appeal for the killing to stop hang in the school and in the neighborhood. (Cutforth, 1994, pp. 32-33)

We need to be at the kindergarten-to-eighth-grade all-African-American school by 8 a.m., an hour before school starts. We drive up about 10 minutes early, and two or three students are waiting for us. One of them grabs the bag of basketballs out of the open trunk and trudges into the school's cramped, dimly lit, overheated gym. "Is this a basketball club?" the visitor inquires. One boy, who has grabbed a ball and is headed for one of the two baskets, stops in stride and says, "Can't you see the sign? It's called the Coaching Club," as if this explains everything *[Criterion 2]*. The club, with 15 or so current members, has met once a week for an hour before school for 3 years *[Criterion 8]*. Most will graduate from eighth grade this year, although two have already flunked a grade and another two or so may not graduate on time.

More youngsters straggle in, get balls, and participate in a shoot-around. Both girls and boys show up, although in this neighborhood basketball is supposed to be a boys' sport. One of the staff, a university student who grew up in this neighborhood, circulates, showing a clipboard to some of the youngsters. They look briefly, nod, and change what they are doing. "It's their personal goals," he explains to the visitor *[Criteria 4 & 5]*, as he tosses the clipboard onto a pile of coats and goes over to give someone a few shooting cues *[Criterion 11]*.

Club members are still coming through the door when everyone assembles in a circle on the floor for an awareness talk. A quick reminder is given about the five responsibilities *[Criteria 2 & 5]*, a quick check-in to see whether anyone has anything to offer (someone asks about taking a trip to the university, someone else wants to coach, someone else tells another club member to pay attention), and coaching volunteers are requested *[Criteria 4 & 5]*. All of this takes less than 5 minutes, and they are on their feet, separated into teams.

Meanwhile, a few youth have gathered at the door, asking, some for the 100th time, whether they can be members of the club. It took about 2 years to achieve such a reputation. Current club members are now considered to be an elite group even though the club includes a very representative sample of the backgrounds, problems, and achievements of all the students in the school. A second club, Coaching Club II, has just been started at the request of the principal (who selected students having trouble in school) *[Criterion 9]*; it is led by one of the senior authors' graduate students with help from three members of the first Coaching Club *[Criteria 1, 4, & 6]*.

Coaches take over *[Criteria 1, 4, & 6]*, with some nudging from staff members, and lay out the offense and defense for their teams. Then they conduct a brief (maybe 10 minutes) practice. At the end of practice, coaches are called together and are reminded of their duties during the game. A coin flip determines who gets the ball, and the games get underway. (The number of games depends on how many club members show up.)

The first thing the visitor notices is that the skill level of the players varies enormously. One looks like NBA material; another is close; two others look suspiciously like beginners; another takes five steps for every dribble. But the ball is passed all around before anyone shoots (even though this places an eventual shot in some jeopardy!). The visitor learns that this is a rule *[Criteria 3 & 5]*, although the youth have modified this rule in group meetings *[Criterion 4]*. It also appears that the better players are giving those with less developed skills on the opposing team a bit of a break when guarding them *[Criterion 3]*. One player even calls a foul on himself. Eventually, one team falls behind; this team's zone defense has some gaping holes. Apparently, the coach notices this too because she calls a time-out. Both coaches talk to their teams, and others chime in. An argument breaks out on one team, and a staff member goes over to help but not take over for the coach *[Criteria 1, 4, & 11]*.

Time flies by. At 8:50 a.m., everyone circles up again. Hands shoot up to volunteer evaluations of the game *[Criteria 1 & 4]*. One player is implicated twice as being selfish. He defends himself. Staff members talk last. Then it is journal time, and the youngsters pick up their journals, fish for a pencil in a gym bag, and lie here and there on the floor or write standing up against the wall. The visitor looks over one shoulder as a club member writes about the extent of his respect for others, self-motivation, self-direction, and leadership during the session *[Criteria 1, 2, 3, 4, & 5]*. (Staff members write responses to these comments later in the day.) After they straggle out, some of them reluctantly ("Ronald, go to class!" a staff member shouts *[Criterion 5 but not 4!]*), the visitor reads their anonymous evaluations of the club that are conducted periodically:

"The club helped me to understand people more" *[Criteria 2 & 3]*.

"I learned that girls can play basketball" *[Criteria 1 & 5]*.

"It is helping me because before I was in the club I had a very bad attitude" *[Criteria 3, 5, & 7]*.

"I learned that I have responsibility, and you all helped me find it" *[Criterion 4]*.

"The club helped my self-control in school with the teachers" *[Criteria 5, 7, & 9]*.

From Brenda,[1] who shoved this program evaluation into the senior author's face to read even though it was supposed to be anonymous: "The club made me put my attitude behind *[Criterion 5]* and gave me enough skills to make the school basketball team. I'm the only girl that made it and I am very proud thanks to the club" *[Criteria 1 & 9]*. (From the school basketball coach: "I've got five of your kids on the team, and I can tell they are in your club. Thanks for helping me out" *[Criterion 9]*.)

From Trenise, who signed her evaluation and whose basketball skills are not very well developed: "When we played the teachers in basket-

ball I thought that we was going to lose, but we didn't *[Criterion 9]*. So I think that this club improved my skills in a great way. It also helps me to look at things in a new way" *[Criterion 5]*.
"It help me improve my conduct in school" *[Criterion 9]*.
In response to how the club could be improved: "It don't have to be improved, because it's improved enough!"

Of course, every day does not run this smoothly, although in this, the third year, most days do. In the first 2 years of the club, disruption and conflict were common occurrences. They are still a bit erratic, with an angry outburst or sullen nonresponse here and there, but this is to be expected, given the students' life experiences. For example, Brenda came in late one day because her brother had just been shot in the head (he survived). She has been a problem for the first author throughout the club's existence, sometimes to the point of exasperation and often leading to direct confrontation. Her perspective, however, was a bit different. She told her counselor and other girls in her counseling group that he was one of the very few adults who had continued to be positive with her, to "hang in" with her, even though she did a lot of "wrong things." That's one of the club's goals *[Criteria 1 & 11]*, but it was nice to get some confirmation from someone who should know!

At the end of the school year, the whole Coaching Club was invited to become "apprentice teachers" in a summer basketball program for younger children; it was to be held at the university and sponsored by Nike. This program is explicitly designed to help club members think about their "possible futures" as service providers either vocationally or as volunteers *[Criterion 6]*. The plan is to stay in touch with club members for the next 4 years through this summer program *[Criterion 8]* and to encourage graduation from high school *[Criteria 6 & 9]*.

All the criteria for state-of-the-art extended day programs except two have been cited several times in this description of the Coaching Club. Criterion 10, providing courageous and persistent leadership in the face of systemic obstacles, has not really been much of an issue. The principal, security guard, basketball coach, PE teacher, and some parents have been very supportive, especially in the third year of the program, and the principal, Penny Kerr, has been a wonderful colleague and advocate and has even put some funds and her own after-school time into the program *[Criterion*

9]. The University of Illinois at Chicago's Great Cities initiative has provided support for such outreach activities, and the development of a leadership course for university students who want to partici- pate in this or other inner-city outreach programs based on the responsibility model has further supported the program.

Significant contact with an adult who cares *[Criterion 11]* is, we hope, provided by the first author, who has been with these young- sters for all 3 years, and by African American university students who have spent 1 semester, 1 year, or more with club members. Some of the above club member quotes support the idea that the staff does care about them and has supported them. This year, two of the university students were from the same Englewood neighbor- hood *[Criterion 9]*, and they did some straight talking about the influences in the neighborhood and what the youngsters needed to do to combat these influences *[Criterion 6]*. In addition, an African graduate student, who was a staff member for 2 years, made the school's Afro-centric curriculum more relevant for Coaching Club members *[Criterion 9]*.

The Energizers: An After-School Club

From the south side of Chicago, we travel west to Colorado to visit a gym in an elementary school on Denver's depressed north- west side. We arrive at the end of the school day and hurry to the school gym to meet he after-school program's instructor, a second- year assistant professor from a local university (and the second author) who has been directing this program for more than a year. As we observe from the sidelines, 16 fourth- and fifth-grade Mexi- can American boys and girls drift into the gym, put their bags and coats against one wall, and sign their names on a pad by the gym door. It is mid-February, and the program has been in existence since September.

At warm-up, the instructor tells the children to practice the volleyball skills learned in previous lessons. As the children scatter to different areas of the gym and begin the activity, he observes how they are responding to the challenge of practicing the skills without direct teacher supervision. For several children in the program, the opportunity to shoot the volleyball at one of the basketball hoops or to engage in criticisms of other students' efforts or to kick someone else's volleyball are sufficiently enticing to distract them from the assigned task. Today, he notices that some of the 16 club members are playing volleyball against the wall, others are practicing the volley pass in pairs, and others are playing a game of "keep the ball up" in threes. He is pleased because only one student is having difficulty focusing on the task. Noticing a boy kicking a stray ball belonging to another pair, the instructor approaches him and asks him quietly whether his actions were appropriate and whether he could have returned the ball in a different way. Realizing his error, the boy quickly apologizes to his two peers and adds that he should have passed the ball back instead of kicking it away. Satisfied, the instructor reverts to his observer role and the boy returns to the original activity.

Five minutes later, the instructor calls the players into a circle for an awareness talk and, after welcoming them, congratulates them on their self-direction during the opening activity despite the presence of more attractive options. He then reminds them of their five responsibilities in the club (his version: self-control, trying, self-direction, caring, and outside the gym), adding that these are their responsibilities, that they are expected to take responsibility for their own behavior and learning, and that they will have many opportunities in the ensuing weeks and months to work on their own without direct supervision.

The instructor's comments serve as a bridge for the next activity, a fitness circuit, which the students perform once each week. He asks them whether they can remember their specific circuit responsibilities. "To try your best," one boy volunteers. "To beat your own score," says a girl. Then, after a few seconds of silence, another girl offers, "To be a good partner by encouraging them, counting their scores, and being honest."

The students divide into pairs or fours and scatter to one of the five stations that comprise the circuit. At each station, they take turns performing the assigned task and spurring their partners toward increased effort while counting their repetitions. Then they record their scores on cards that also contains results of their previous weeks' efforts. At the end of the circuit, many of the students lie exhausted on the gym floor. Consulting his card, one boy says enthusiastically, "I beat my score at the chest pass and jump rope stations!"

The instructor calls them into a circle for a quick reflection time and asks who carried out the circuit responsibilities. Without hesitation, most say they managed to do all of them. On reflection, however, a few admit they could have tried harder, and one boy confesses that he didn't encourage his partner as much as he should have. The instructor reinforces their comments, adding specific examples, and praises them for the seriousness with which they approached both their responsibilities and the exercises themselves.

The final activity of the session is jump rope. As the instructor turns a long rope with one student, he explains that the challenge is for every club member to reach the other side of the rope by running through it without making any contact. He adds that if anyone touches the rope, then the whole group has to begin the challenge again.

After asking a few questions, the children form a line and stand apprehensively watching the turning rope. Eventually, a boy plucks up courage and sprints through the rope to the applause of his classmates. Next, a girl bolts through the rope and is greeted by high fives from the boy on the other side. Others run through until one boy catches his heel on the turning rope. His efforts are met with a groan from the others as they realize that they will have to begin the challenge again. They walk around the rope to the other side and re-form the line. This time, however, several students suggest that the previously unsuccessful boy should go first while others instruct him how to time his entry into the turning rope and direct him to run faster. Nervously, he approaches the turning rope, but his anxiety is quickly replaced by relief and satisfaction when he is successful on his first attempt. The others run through the rope, and more high fives and even hugs greet them on the other side. As the final individual dashes through the rope, her classmates cheer as they realize that they have achieved their goal.

As the cheers subside, the instructor calls the students into a circle for a group meeting. The boy who touched the rope says that he felt bad when he heard the other students groan but that he was grateful for the encouragement he received from them before and after his second attempt. Several others admit to feeling nervous as they waited for their turn, and all admit to feeling pleased at accomplishing the challenge. The instructor asks them what they thought was the purpose of the activity. Their responses include, "To work together," "Not to blame each other," and "Not to give up." After a brief discussion about how these issues relate to the children's lives in the classroom and outside school, the instructor concludes the session by asking the children to make a reflection time journal entry describing the extent to which they carried out their responsibilities during the past hour.

These events occurred during the second year of an after-school program taught by the second author in an inner-city Denver elementary school. Initially, the school faculty were skeptical about a university professor's motivation for teaching the program and his ability to control the students: Several teachers asked him how often he would come to the school, whether this was just another research project, and why he didn't stay in his office and write articles like most other university professors! Their skepticism, however, was not shared by the 80 fourth- and fifth-grade students who returned the permission forms that were necessary for consideration for the program. This high response, which is indicative of the dearth of extended day programs in this urban neighborhood, meant that the instructor had to ask the teachers to nominate the most needy students so that the participant group was held to a manageable size *[Criterion 8]*. As the principal said, "All the kids are needy here, but the kids in your program are extra needy because of their behavior, attitude toward school, and lack of social skills."

Whereas the Coaching Club in Chicago has been operating for several years, the Denver program is only in its second year. Still, we see indications that several of the criteria for state-of-the-art extended day programs (see Table 10.1) are present in the Denver program:

Early during the program's first year, the students selected the name "Energizers" to describe their club, and the name has endured into the second year *[Criterion 8]*. Although several students' attitudes and behaviors present huge management challenges, the instructor does not treat them as remedial, but rather as "resources to be developed" *[Criterion 1]*. The antics of the boy who kicked the volleyball during the warm-up are representative of the challenges these students present, and their varied needs and fluctuations in behavior require that the instructor take an "I'm going to hang in there" attitude with certain individuals *[Criterion 3]*. For added insight into the needs of club members, the instructor maintains contact with the children's teachers by visiting them in their classrooms before the school day ends *[Criterion 9]*.

Clear expectations for the program and a set of five explicit values, called responsibilities, are infused into all activities and experiences *[Criterion 5]*, resulting not only in a clear purpose but a psychologically and physically safe environment as well *[Criterion 7]*. As the above vignette illustrates, the program focuses on competence and self-worth through individual- and group-oriented activities, instead of highly competitive ones *[Criterion 1]*. Traditional sports such as volleyball, soccer, and basketball are introduced, but they are played within a cooperative value system that downplays winning and losing and encourages the inclusion of all, regardless of ability *[Criterion 7]*. Although the medium is physical activity, the message is that "this is not just another sports program"; instead, the focus is on the whole child *[Criterion 2]*. Children are empowered to take greater control of their lives in several ways *[Criterion 4]*: (a) They become involved in their own development by setting goals as they participate in individual warm-ups, fitness activities, and group games; (b) they contribute to the development of others by coaching and refereeing; and (c) they contribute to the development of the program by giving their reactions to what they have experienced and by providing suggestions for what they would like to do in future weeks.

Students' and teachers' comments contained in an end-of-year evaluation further elaborate on progress toward meeting the criteria. Here are some of the students' comments:

"The program teaches us self-control and respect for other people" *[Criterion 5]*.

"In the program, people learned to like everybody" *[Criteria 2, 5, & 7]*.

"When we were playing, we would get together and forget about our problems" *[Criterion 7]*.

"I learned to have faith in myself" *[Criterion 1]*.

"The program taught me to control my temper, and now I don't lose it so fast" *[Criteria 2, 5, & 7]*.

"I learned that we can do lots of things if we really put our minds to it" *[Criteria 1 & 4]*.

"When I achieved my goal, I felt great" *[Criteria 1 & 4]*.

"After I leave this school, I want to come back and help you teach in your program" *[Criterion 6]*.

"It was great how you kept coming every week" *[Criterion 10]*.

The teachers also evaluated the program. Here is a sample of their comments:

"I liked the attitude you had toward the kids" *[Criteria 1 & 11]*.

"I have noticed a big difference in Luis. He used to be very shy in the classroom, but now he is more confident. I think this change has a lot to do with your program" *[Criteria 1 & 3]*.

"I think it's really nice and important to have the university-school connection. It helps make it more like there are real people that are teachers at college too!" *[Criterion 9]*.

Although this feedback confirms the presence of several of the criteria for state-of-the-art extended day programs, one feature of the Denver program has limited the degree to which these criteria have been met. This limitation has its origins in the relatively large number of students being served by the program and the resulting management problems that often occur. As was described above, the large number of students who expressed initial interest in the program meant the instructor had to compromise his wishes regarding student numbers and to allow more students into the program than he would have liked *[Criterion 8]*. Although on most occasions he has been able to deal successfully with the challenges presented by individual students, there have been several instances of failure. For example, according to his own reflective journal entries, he does not always view troublesome students in a positive light *[Criterion 1]*. Also, his inability to deal effectively with some of the more difficult students means that, on occasions, they verbally abuse other students. Therefore, some club members do not always experience a psychologically safe environment *[Criterion 7]* and as a result do not always attend the club meetings *[Criterion 8]*. His journal contains many references to the management issues that have hindered the effectiveness of the program in its first year. For example:

"I couldn't focus on both soccer games because I was too concerned about management issues."

"The kids knew I was getting angry, and that only made things worse."

"Several students told me that it wasn't good today."

"Ricardo had been in trouble in school and never really settled down in class today. How can I deal with all his problems when I have 15 other kids to watch and teach?"

"I am frustrated about not being able to reach some of the kids."

These sentiments are indicative of the instructor's desire to increase the effectiveness of the program in meeting all students' needs and prompted him to explore ways to reduce the management challenges. The acquisition of a grant from a local foundation will enable him to obtain some release time from university teaching duties, thus ensuring the continuity and long-term stability of the program *[Criterion 8]*. Plans include recruiting and training community members as assistant teachers and coaches *[Criterion 9]*, thus increasing the contact time with students.

Conclusion

Inner-city children and youth feel outrage and frustration from their daily experiences with negative influences, as well as the failure of institutions to provide enough educational, economic, emotional, and social help. Better programs cannot meet all the needs of inner-city young people, such as freedom from the poverty characteristic of inner-city neighborhoods, but they can help. Such programs exist, but more are needed, as well as more collaboration among service providers.

Extended day programs in particular can make a difference in the lives of inner-city children and youth. Adolescents are at greater risk for a number of reasons, one of them being the failure of most extended day programs to attract them. These programs fail because they don't treat youth with the dignity and worth they deserve; instead, they treat the youth as a problem to be controlled. Who wants to be treated that way? As the youngsters' awareness grows, so does the dropout rate.

Fortunately, scraps of evidence from here and there, when pieced together, provide a mosaic of criteria for state-of-the-art extended day programs that not only attract youth but also contribute to their personal and social well-being. We have identified 11 such criteria, briefly described a model that reflects these criteria, and visited two specific extended day program sites to, in a sense, experientially observe state-of-the-art programs.

Scholars always seem to call for more research, whereas service providers need to take action now. Both are right, at least in the instance of inner-city extended day programs. We know enough to

offer adolescents better programs than are now generally available
to them. We especially know what attracts young people and what
does not, and we have access to case studies that demonstrate the
positive impact of such programs. Eleven state-of-the-art criteria
identified by a survey of systematic studies and professional opinion
and validated by our experiences as instructors and investigators of
inner-city extended day programs provide guidance for changing
current programs and developing new ones.

Yet there is more to do. This information needs to be made
available to youth workers and policymakers, and more research
needs to be conducted to validate and extend the findings reported
here. In particular, given the importance attached to "hard" data
by funding agencies and others, more quantitative studies need to
be carried out to explore the impact of state-of-the-art programs
on rates of school dropout, teen pregnancy, drug abuse, gang
membership, and other at-risk factors. If, in the process, however,
the "softer" outcomes lauded by McLaughlin and Heath (1993) are
eclipsed by such findings, whether these findings are positive or
not, inner-city youth will be the losers, and the rest of us will suffer
the consequences as well.

Note

1. All student names are pseudonyms.

References

Ayers, W. (1989). *The good preschool teacher: Six teachers reflect on their lives.* New
    York: Teachers College Press.
Bain, L. L. (1988). Curriculum for critical reflection in physical education. In R. S.
    Brandt (Ed.), *Content of the curriculum: 1988 ASCD yearbook* (pp. 133-147).
    Washington, DC: Association for Supervision and Curriculum Development.
Brown, K. H. (1995). Alternatives through intragency collaboration. *Journal of
    Physical Education, Recreation, and Dance, 66,* 35-37.
Cairns, R. B., & Cairns, B. D. (1994). *Lifelines and risks: Pathways of youth in our
    time.* New York: Cambridge University Press.
Cappel, M. L. (1995). Sista-2-sista: A self-improvement program. *Journal of Physical
    Education, Recreation, and Dance, 66,* 43-45.

Carnegie Council on Adolescent Development. (1992). *A matter of time: Risk and opportunity in the nonschool hours* (Report of the Task Force on Youth Development and Community Programs). New York: Carnegie Corporation of New York.

Cohen, P. (1995, May). Urban education needs resources. *Education Update, 37,* 5.

Comer, J. P. (1987). New Haven's school community connection. *Educational Leadership, 44,* 13-16.

Cutforth, N. J. (1994). *The place of physical education in schooling: An ethnographic study of an urban elementary school.* Unpublished doctoral dissertation, University of Illinois at Chicago.

DeBusk, M., & Hellison, D. (1989). Implementing a physical education self-responsibility model for delinquency-prone youth. *Journal of Teaching in Physical Education, 8,* 104-112.

Dryfoos, J. G. (1991). Adolescents at risk: A summation of work in the field—programs and policies. *Journal of Adolescent Health, 12,* 630-637.

Foster, D. (1994). The disease is adolescence. *Utne Reader, 94,* 50-56.

Garbarino, J., Dubrow, N., Kostelny, K., & Pardo, C. (1992). *Children in danger: Coping with the consequences of community violence.* San Francisco: Jossey-Bass.

Georgiadis, N. (1992). *Practical inquiry in physical education: The case of Hellison's personal and social responsibility model.* Unpublished doctoral dissertation, University of Illinois at Chicago.

Gordon, E. W., & Song, L. D. (1994). Variations in the experience of resilience. In M. C. Wang & E. W. Gordon (Eds.), *Educational resilience in inner-city America: Challenges and prospects* (pp. 27-43). Hillsdale, NJ: Lawrence Erlbaum.

Graham, G., Holt/Hale, S., & Parker, M. (1993). *Children moving: A reflective approach to teaching physical education* (3rd ed.). Palo Alto, CA: Mayfield.

Haberman, M. (1995). Selecting "star" teachers for children and youth in urban poverty. *Phi Delta Kappan, 76,* 777-781.

Heath, S. B., & McLaughlin, M. W. (Eds.). (1993). *Identity and inner-city youth: Beyond ethnicity and gender.* New York: Teachers College Press.

Hellison, D. (1978). *Beyond balls and bats: Alienated (and other) youth in the gym.* Washington, DC: AAHPER.

Hellison, D. (1985). *Goals and strategies for teaching physical education.* Champaign, IL: Human Kinetics.

Hellison, D. (1990). Making a difference: Reflections on teaching urban at-risk youth. *Journal of Physical Education, Recreation, and Dance, 61,* 44-45.

Hellison, D. (1995). *Teaching personal and social responsibility through physical activity.* Champaign, IL: Human Kinetics.

Hooper-Briar, K., & Lawson, H. A. (1994). *Serving children, youth, and families through intraprofessional collaboration and service integration: A framework for action.* Oxford, OH: Danforth Foundation & the Institute for Educational Renewal at Miami University.

Ianni, F. A. J. (1989). *The search for structure: A report on American youth today.* New York: Free Press.

Ianni, F. A. J. (1993). *Joining youth needs and program services* (Urban Diversity Series No. 104, ERIC Clearinghouse on Urban Education, Institute for Urban and Minority Education).

Kallusky, J. P. (1991). *A qualitative evaluation of a physical education mentoring program for at-risk children.* Unpublished master's thesis, California State University, Chico.

Kennedy, M. M. (1989). Kenneth Zeichner reflecting on reflection. *National Center for Research on Teacher Education Colloquy, 2,* 15-21.

Keramidas, K. (1991). *Strategies to increase the individual motivation and cohesiveness of a junior male basketball team.* Unpublished master's thesis, University of Illinois at Chicago.

Kirk, D. (1993). Curriculum work in physical education: Beyond the objectives approach? *Journal of Teaching in Physical Education, 12,* 244-265.

Lifka, R. (1989). *Implementing an after-school alternative wellness/activities program for at-risk Hispanic youth.* Unpublished master's thesis, University of Illinois at Chicago.

McLaughlin, M. W., & Heath, S. B. (1993). Casting the self: Frames for identity and dilemmas for policy. In S. B. Heath & M. W. McLaughlin (Eds.), *Identity and inner-city youth: Beyond ethnicity and gender* (pp. 210-239). New York: Teachers College Press.

McLaughlin, M. W., Irby, M. A., & Langman, J. (1994). *Urban sanctuaries: Neighborhood organizations in the lives and futures of inner-city youth.* San Francisco: Jossey-Bass.

Mulaudzi, L. (1995). *A program evaluation of an implementation of a responsibility model for inner-city youth.* Unpublished master's thesis, University of Illinois at Chicago.

Oyserman, D., & Markus, H. (1990). Possible selves in balance: Implications for delinquency. *Journal of Social Issues, 46,* 141-157.

Puckett, K., & Cutforth, N. J. (1996). *A qualitative evaluation of an urban cross-age teaching program.* Paper presented at the Annual Allied Health Forum, College of Associated Health Professions, University of Illinois, Chicago.

Raywid, M. A. (1994). Alternative schools: The state of the art. *Educational Leadership, 52,* 26-31.

Resilience in action at Hiawatha School. (1994). *Cityschools, 1,* 16-18.

Rink, J. (1993). *Teaching physical education for learning* (2nd ed.). St. Louis, MO: Times Mirror/Mosby.

Rodriguez, L. (1994). Rekindling the warrior. *Utne Reader, 94,* 58-59.

Rovegno, I., & Kirk, D. (1995). Articulations and silences in socially critical research on physical education: Toward a broader agenda. *Quest, 47,* 447-474.

Searle, M. S., Winther, N. R., & Reed, M. (1994). *An assessment of the daily life experiences of Native youth: Implications for Northern Fly-In Sports Camps, Inc.* Winnipeg, Manitoba: University of Manitoba, Health, Leisure, and Human Performance Research Institute.

Shields, D. L. L., & Bredemeier, B. J. L. (1995). *Moral development and action in physical activity contexts.* Champaign, IL: Human Kinetics.

Siedentop, D., Mand, C., & Taggart, A. (1986). *Physical education: Teaching and curriculum strategies for grades 5-12.* Palo Alto, CA: Mayfield.

Steinhardt, M. (1992). Physical education. In P. W. Jackson (Ed.), *Handbook of research on curriculum* (pp. 964-1001). New York: Macmillan.

Swadener, B. B., & Lubeck, S. (Eds.). (1995). *Children and families "at promise": Deconstructing the discourse of risk.* Albany: State University of New York Press.

Villarruel, R. M., & Lerner, R. M. (Eds.). (1994). *Promoting community-based programs for socialization and learning.* San Francisco: Jossey-Bass.

Wang, M. C., Haertel, G. D., & Walberg, H. J. (1994). Educational resilience in inner cities. In M. C. Wang & E. W. Gordon (Eds.), *Educational resilience in inner-city America: Challenges and prospects* (pp. 45-72). Hillsdale, NJ: Lawrence Erlbaum.

Weiner, L. (1993). *Preparing teachers for urban schools: Lessons from 30 years of school reform.* New York: Teachers College Press.

Williamson, K. M., & Georgiadis, N. (1992). Teaching an inner-city after-school program. *Journal of Physical Education, Recreation, and Dance, 63,* 14-18.

Winnick, J. (1990). *Adapted physical education and sport.* Champaign, IL: Human Kinetics.

Youth employment. (1994, Summer). *Home front.* Washington, DC: U.S. Department of Housing and Urban Development, Drug-Free Neighborhoods Division.

Zuniga-Hill, C., & George, J. B. (1995). Developing integrated services for children and families: A cross-disciplinary approach. *Journal of Teacher Education, 46,* 101-108.

PART IV

Health

• CHAPTER 11 •

A Public Health Perspective on Urban Adolescents

KELLI A. KOMRO

FRANK BINGCHANG HU

BRIAN R. FLAY

The goal of this chapter is to provide a broad overview of urban adolescent health issues and promising approaches to promote their health. This chapter includes four sections. The first section briefly defines public health and the rationale for a population approach to prevent disease and promote health. The second section presents the leading causes of death and the prevalence of health-related behaviors among a representative sample of U.S. adolescents, comparing youth who live in urban areas with suburban and rural youth. The third section provides a comprehensive overview of risk factors for health-compromising behaviors prevalent among urban adolescents. Finally, the fourth section reviews promising approaches to prevent health compromising and promote health-enhancing behaviors among adolescents.

AUTHORS' NOTE: Kelli A. Komro was a Postdoctoral Fellow at the Prevention Research Center, University of Illinois at Chicago, when this chapter was prepared. Work on this chapter was supported by Training Grant #07293 and Research Grant #DA06307, both from the National Institute on Drug Abuse, and Grant #HD30078 from the National Institute of Child Health and Human Development.

A Public Health Perspective

The mission of public health is to protect and promote health and to prevent disease and injury. Public health is population focused, unlike the field of medicine, which is individually focused. One rationale for a population-based approach to prevent disease and promote health is that the distribution of health-related characteristics moves up and down as a whole. Two examples are that (a) the average amount of alcohol consumed by a population determines the prevalence of heavy drinking in a population and (b) the average blood pressure of a population predicts the number of hypertensive people (Rose & Day, 1990). The frequency of those at risk in a population can be understood only in the context of a population's characteristics. Therefore, as the population mean for a health characteristic shifts toward the "healthy" side, it lowers the level of risk and health-related problems in the population. Another rationale for a population approach is that it is not the most deviant or high-risk individuals who account for most cases of diseases; rather, "a large number of people at a small risk may give rise to more cases of disease than the small number who are at high risk" (Rose, 1985, p. 37). Therefore, targeting only the highest-risk individuals may not have the greatest impact on the prevention of disease.

Individual-level prevention seeks to identify high-risk suspectible individuals and to offer them some individual protection or early treatment, whereas a population strategy seeks to control the determinants of incidence in the population as a whole (Rose, 1985). The social and physical environments have a large influence on health. Individual-level approaches do not affect environmental influences, but rather try to influence the individual and how the individual interacts with the environment. The population strategy is an attempt to control ultimate determinants of incidence, to lower the mean level of risk factors, and to shift the whole distribution of exposure in a favorable direction (Rose, 1985). The population strategy in its traditional public health form has involved mass environmental control methods (e.g., water treatment, inoculation); in its modern form, it is attempting to alter some of society's norms of behavior (Rose, 1985). The advantages of a population strategy are powerful:

The first is that it is radical. It attempts to remove the underlying causes that make the disease common. It has a large potential, often larger than one would have expected, for the population as a whole. From Framingham data one can compute that a 10 mm Hg lowering of the blood pressure distribution as a whole would correspond to about a 30% reduction in the total attributable mortality. The approach is behaviorally appropriate. If nonsmoking eventually becomes "normal," then it will be much less necessary to keep on persuading individuals. Once a social norm of behavior has become accepted and (as the case of diet) once the supply industries have adapted themselves to the new pattern, then the maintenance of that situation no longer requires effort from individuals. The health education phase aimed at changing individuals is, we hope, a temporary necessity, pending changes in the norms of what is socially acceptable. (Rose, 1985, p. 37)

Individual-level strategies tend to emphasize education, whereas a population-level approach may include education but emphasize environmental change. Individual-level strategies for health-related behavior change are not adequate for population-level change. "Both approaches are probably necessary to some extent for effective long-term public health solutions. Population-level support is needed to sustain educational programs, and popular support in terms of cumulative individual opinion is needed to sustain population-level action" (Jeffery, 1989, p. 1200).

Public health combines classical epidemiological observations of health and disease, investigation into the causes and prevention of major diseases, developing and testing methods of modifying disease risk in whole populations, application and evaluation of programs to prevent disease and promote health in whole populations, and the syntheses of evidence on which rational public policy can be based. This chapter includes an overview of (a) the epidemiology and etiology of adolescent health behaviors and (b) promising approaches for adolescent health promotion.

Leading Causes of Death and Health-Related Behaviors

We sought to describe health status differences and similarities between children living in urban areas and those living in suburban and rural areas. Very little has been published on adolescent health status by urbanicity or metropolitan status. Therefore, we obtained two national data sets that include urbanicity variables and analyzed them for this chapter: the 1992 mortality statistics and the 1992 Youth Risk Behavior Survey.

Leading Causes of Death

A 1994 publication by the National Center for Health Statistics (NCHS) reported comparisons based on urbanicity for all age-groups combined. Residents of large, core metropolitan areas had the highest age-adjusted death rate, followed by residents in rural areas. This pattern was consistent for 1980-1991 for whites and blacks. The death rate for black 1- to 24-year-olds has been consistently higher than for white youth for 1950-1991. Death rates for white 1- to 14-year-olds, white 15- to 24-year-olds, black 1- to 14-year-olds, and black 15- to 24-year-old females has decreased from 1950. This is not the case for black 15- to 24-year-old males, whose death rate has not declined. More recent data were available for Hispanic youth (1990-1991), whose death rate falls between those for white and black youth.

To look specifically at urbanicity differences for youth, we obtained the 1992 mortality statistics on tape from the NCHS, which is the primary source of vital and health statistics for the United States (U.S. Department of Health and Human Services [USDHHS], 1994a). Mortality data by underlying cause of death included all deaths occurring within the United States. Deaths of U.S. citizens and deaths of members of the armed forces occurring outside the United States are not included. Data were obtained from certificates filed for deaths occurring in each state. Causes of death for 1992 were coded according to the International Classification of Diseases, 9th Revision, Clinical Modification. Variables used for the present analysis included metropolitan status, age, race, gender, and underlying cause of death. Unfortunately, a measure of economic status is not available in this data set. Adolescents aged 12 to 17 were included in the present analysis. Underlying causes of death were recoded to 72 cause-of-death groups.

The five leading causes of death for metropolitan status by racial groups are presented in Table 11.1. Motor vehicle crash, homicide, and suicide are among the five leading causes of death for all six metropolitan and racial groups for those aged 12 to 17 years. This means that almost all deaths among 12- to 17-year-olds are preventable and related to specific behaviors (e.g., drinking and driving, involvement in physical fights). There are substantial ethnic and regional differences, however.

Motor vehicle crash is the leading cause of death among all nonmetropolitan youth (42%, white; 26%, black; 33%, Hispanic) and metropolitan white youth (36%). The rate is lower for metropolitan Hispanic youth (20%), for whom motor vehicle crash is the second leading cause of death, and much lower for metropolitan black youth (11%).

Homicide is the leading cause of death for black (47%) and Hispanic (39%) youth in metropolitan areas and the second leading cause of death among black youth in nonmetropolitan areas (21%). Homicide rates are much lower among white youth in both metropolitan areas (7%) and nonmetropolitan areas (4%) and among nonmetropolitan Hispanics (5%).

Suicide is the third leading cause of death among whites (15%, metropolitan; 13%, nonmetropolitan) and Hispanics (9%, metropolitan; 14%, nonmetropolitan). It is the fourth or fifth leading cause of death for black youth (6% for both metropolitan and nonmetropolitan).

Leading Risk Factors for Youth

Among adults in the United States, the five leading causes of death, in order, are (a) diseases of the heart, (b) malignant neoplasms, (c) cerebrovascular diseases, (d) chronic obstructive pulmonary diseases, and (e) unintentional injuries (NCHS, 1994). These leading causes of death are closely linked with health-related behaviors (U.S. Public Health Service, 1988). Cigarette smoking is recognized as the most important single preventable cause of death in the United States. Cigarette smoking is responsible for more neoplasms and more neoplasm deaths than any other known agent. Smoking is also a prime risk factor for heart and cerebrovascular disease, chronic bronchitis, and emphysema. Alcohol and other drugs play causal or contributing roles in deaths due to unintentional injuries, homicide, and suicide, as well as such diseases as cirrhosis and neoplasms. Diet is associated with cardiovascular disease, neoplasms, and diabetes. Established benefits of regular

TABLE 11.1 Five Leading Causes of Death (Number of Deaths and
Percentage of Deaths Due to Cause) Among 12- to
17-Year-Old Youth by Metropolitan Status and Race

METROPOLITAN					
Race	*n*		*n*		*n*
	%		*%*		*%*
White		*Black*		*Hispanic*	
Motor vehicle	1,459	Homicide	908	Homicide	434
crash	(36)		(47)		(39)
Suicide	602	All other	216	Motor vehicle	231
	(15)	accidents	(11)	crash	(20)
All other	453	Motor vehicle	214	Suicide	99
accidents	(11)	crash	(11)		(9)
All other	324	Suicide	112	All other	73
diseases	(8)		(6)	accidents	(7)
Homicide	267	All other	102	All other	62
	(7)	diseases	(5)	diseases	(6)
Other listed	945		390		228
causes	(23)		(20)		(20)
Total	4,050		1,942		1,127
	(100)		(100)		(100)

physical activity include reduced risk of coronary heart disease, improved ability to maintain desired weight, reduced symptoms associated with temporary anxiety states, and relief from feelings and other symptoms associated with mild to moderate depression. Early sexual activity is a risk factor for sexually transmitted disease and unplanned pregnancy. Clearly, health-related behaviors are significant risk factors for the primary causes of mortality in the United States.

Adolescence is a critical period when health-related behaviors are tried and established. Health-related behaviors begun in early adolescence have been shown to track into young adulthood (Kelder, Perry, Klepp, & Lytle, 1994). Therefore, adolescence is an important time for the development and support of healthy behavior patterns, with implications for health not only during adolescence but through-

TABLE 11.1 *Continued*

NONMETROPOLITAN					
Race	*n*		*n*		*n*
	%		%		%
White		*Black*		*Hispanic*	
Motor vehicle crash	934 (42)	Motor vehicle crash	97 (26)	Motor vehicle crash	43 (33)
All other accidents	341 (15)	Homicide	78 (21)	All other accidents	21 (16)
Suicide	289 (13)	All other accidents	67 (18)	Suicide	18 (14)
All other diseases	144 (7)	All other diseases	26 (7)	All other diseases	12 (9)
Homicide	86 (4)	Suicide	21 (6)	Homicide	7 (5)
Other listed causes	419 (19)		80 (22)		28 (22)
Total	2,213 (100)		369 (100)		129 (100)

NOTE: "All other diseases (accidents)" are those not listed in the 72 causes of death.

out the life span. The following discussion reviews national data on health-related behaviors among adolescents by residence.

The Youth Risk Behavior Survey (YRBS) is a component of the Centers for Disease Control and Prevention's Youth Risk Surveillance System, which periodically measures the prevalence of priority health-risk behaviors among adolescents (Kolbe, Kann, & Collins, 1993). In 1992, the YRBS was conducted as a follow-back survey to the National Health Interview Survey (NHIS) (USDHHS, 1994b). The 1992 NHIS was conducted among a representative sample of the civilian noninstitutionalized U.S. population by using a multistage cluster-area probability design of approximately 120,000 persons representing 49,000 households. The YRBS included a representative sample of persons aged 12 to 21 years in the sampled households. Adolescents who did not attend school were oversam-

pled. From April 1992 to March 1993, respondents listened to a
tape recording of the questionnaire and recorded their responses
on a standardized answer sheet. Questionnaires were completed by
10,645 (77.2%) eligible respondents.

For this chapter, youth aged 12 to 17 years were selected for
analysis ($n = 6{,}321$). The SUDAAN software (Shah, Barnwell,
Hunt, & LaVange, 1991) was used to compute all standard errors
for the estimated prevalence rates by residence, race, and poverty.
The CATAN procedure was used to estimate loglinear models for
the contingency table analyses. The log-linear model was run for
each behavior separately, with residence, race, poverty, and interactions among them as independent effects. If the interaction terms
were not significant, they were eliminated from the model and the
model was reestimated with main effects only. Wald chi-squares
were used to test the significance of the parameters in the models.
The NHIS poverty index is based on family size, number of children
less then 18 years old, and family income, using 1991 poverty levels
derived from the August 1992 Current Population Survey. For this
data set, we were able to break residence into three categories:
Metropolitan Statistical Area (MSA) central city, MSA not central
city (suburb), and non-MSA (rural).

The majority of black and Hispanic youth live in central cities
(52.7% and 51%, respectively), followed by living within suburbs
(26.4% and 40.9%, respectively), with a minority living in rural areas
(20.9% and 8.1%, respectively). The majority of white youth reside
within suburbs (55.1%), followed by rural areas (27.5%) and central
cities (17.3%).

Among youth who live in central cities, 9% of white youth, 43%
of black youth, and 40% of Hispanic youth live below the poverty
threshold. Among youth who live in suburbs, 5% of white youth,
29% of black youth, and 27% of Hispanic youth live below the
poverty threshold. In rural areas, 14% of white youth, 57% of black
youth, and 55% of Hispanic youth live below the poverty threshold.

Figures 11.1 through 11.6 display the prevalence of the following
health behaviors by residence, race, and poverty: (a) participated
in a physical fight at least once during the 12 months preceding the
survey, (b) ever had sexual intercourse (14- to 17-year-olds), (c)
smoked cigarettes on 1 or more of the 30 days preceding the survey,
(d) ever drank alcohol, (e) lifetime marijuana use, and (f) engaged
in moderate physical activity at least 30 minutes at a time during 5

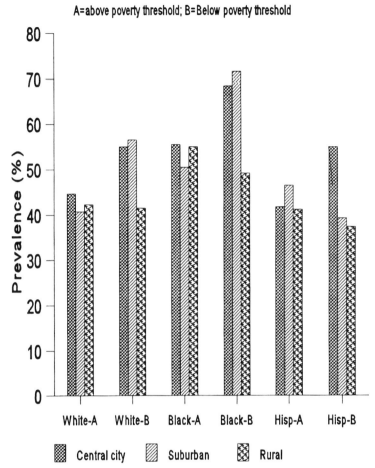

Figure 11.1. Prevalence of Physical Fight by Race, Residence, and Poverty

or more of the 7 days preceding the survey. (The appendix at the end of this chapter provides the parameter estimates and standard errors for each independent variable by behavior.)

Figure 11.1 displays the prevalence of having participated in a physical fight at least once during the 12 months preceding the survey by race, residence, and poverty. Rates range from around 40% for all Hispanic groups except those below the poverty level living in central cities (55%), to around 70% for blacks below the poverty level living in cities or suburbs. Poverty appears to be associated with an increase in the number of youth who have participated in physical fights among all races, especially among blacks (interaction between blacks and poverty: $\chi^2 = 4.45, p = .03$). After controlling for race and poverty, place of residence is not statistically associated with participation in physical fights in the past year among 12- to 17-year-olds.

Figure 11.2 displays the prevalence of ever having had sexual intercourse among 14- to 17-year-olds by race, residence, and poverty. Rates range from a low of 31% for rural Hispanic youth above the poverty level to 65% to 70% for most black youth, especially those below the poverty level. After controlling for race and poverty, youth aged 14 to 17 living in central cities are more likely to have engaged in sexual intercourse than youth living in suburbs ($\chi^2 = 18.4, p < .01$) (true for all groups except whites living in poverty) or youth living in rural areas ($\chi^2 = 4.5, p = .03$) (true for all groups except rural Hispanics living in poverty). Youth living in poverty are also more likely to have engaged in sexual intercourse than youth living at or above the poverty threshold ($\chi^2 = 10.5, p < .01$) (true for all groups except blacks). Black youth are more likely to have engaged in sexual intercourse than other youth, although this is statistically significant only for the comparison with white youth ($\chi^2 = 63.1, p < .01$).

Figure 11.3 displays the prevalence of current cigarette use (smoked cigarettes on 1 or more of the 30 days preceding the survey) by race, residence, and poverty. Rates vary from a low of 6% to 7% for black youth above the poverty level to highs above 30% for poor white youth. It is immediately apparent that white youth smoke the most and that black youth smoke the least. White youth are more likely to be current cigarette smokers than Hispanic youth ($\chi^2 = 8.7, p < .01$) and much more likely than black youth ($\chi^2 = 131.5, p < .01$). Youth living below the poverty threshold are more likely to be current smokers than youth at or above the poverty threshold ($\chi^2 = 4.4, p = .04$) (not true for Hispanics). After controlling for race and poverty, residence is not statistically associated with current cigarette use.

Figure 11.4 displays the prevalence of lifetime alcohol use by race, residence, and poverty. Rates are fairly invariant, being in the 50% to 60% range except for poor black youth (42%, city; 37%, suburb; 29%, rural). Youth living below the poverty index, how-

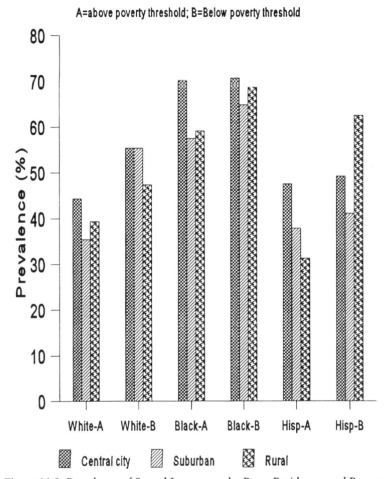

Figure 11.2. Prevalence of Sexual Intercourse by Race, Residence, and Poverty

ever, were less likely to ever have drunk alcohol than youth at or above the poverty threshold ($\chi^2 = 11.8, p < .01$). White youth were more likely to report lifetime alcohol use than black youth ($\chi^2 = 18.1, p < .01$), and no significant differences were found in lifetime alcohol use between whites and Hispanics ($\chi^2 = .2, p > .05$). After controlling for race and poverty, place of residence is not associated with the prevalence of lifetime alcohol use.

Figure 11.5 displays the prevalence of lifetime marijuana use by race, residence, and poverty. Poor whites living in cities are most

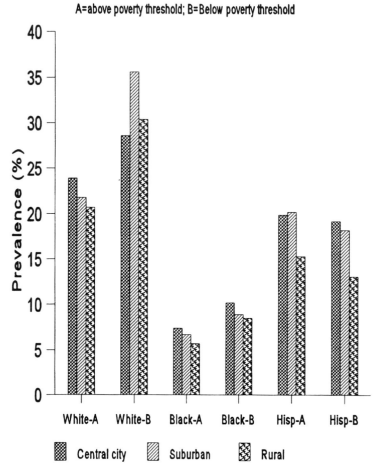

Figure 11.3. Prevalence of Current Cigarette Smoking by Race, Residence, and Poverty

likely to have used marijuana (30%), and rural blacks are least likely (5%). Black youth were significantly less likely to report lifetime marijuana use than white youth overall ($\chi^2 = 30.6$, $p < .01$). After controlling for race and place of residence, poverty is not significantly associated with marijuana use. After controlling for race and poverty, youth living in central cities were more likely to report lifetime marijuana use than youth living in suburbs ($\chi^2 = 14.5$, $p < .01$) or youth living in rural areas ($\chi^2 = 27.4$, $p < .01$).

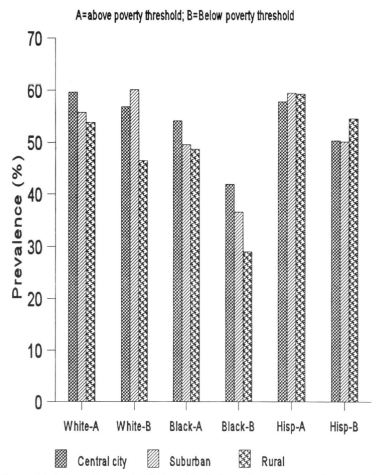

Figure 11.4. Prevalence of Lifetime Alcohol Use by Race, Residence, and Poverty

Figure 11.6 displays the percentage of youth who engaged in moderate physical activity at least 30 minutes at a time during 5 or more of the 7 days preceding the survey by race, residence, and poverty. Rates for most groups are in the 55% to 65% range, with poor city whites being on the low side (47%) and rural Hispanics above the poverty threshold appearing to have the most active lifestyle (81%). In addition, youth in poverty were less likely to report involvement in moderate physical activity than youth living

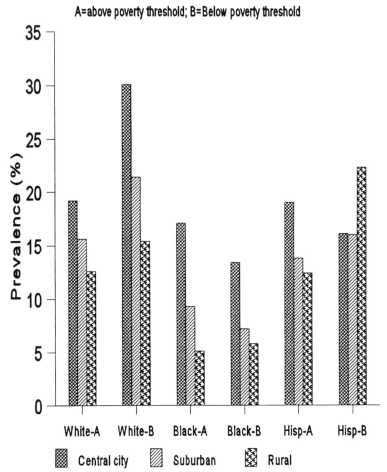

Figure 11.5. Prevalence of Marijuana Use by Race, Residence, and Poverty

at or above the poverty threshold ($\chi^2 = 5.6$, $p = .02$). Race is not significantly associated with involvement in physical activity. After controlling for race, youth living in central cities were less likely to report involvement in moderate physical activity than youth living in suburbs ($\chi^2 = 20.3$, $p < .01$) or youth living in rural areas ($\chi^2 = 14.5$, $p < .01$).

In summary, the majority of black and Hispanic youth live in central cities, and a high proportion of these youth live in poverty.

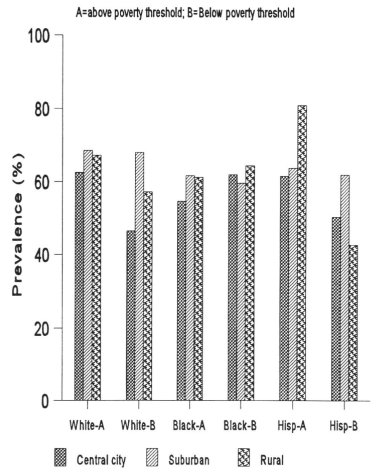

Figure 11.6. Prevalence of Subjects Who Engage in Regular Physical Activities by Race, Residence, and Poverty

There are high levels of engaging in health-compromising behaviors. After adjusting for race and poverty level, residing in central cities significantly increases the risk of health-compromising behaviors among youth. In particular, residing in central cities appears to be associated with a higher prevalence of ever having had sexual intercourse, lifetime marijuana use, and less physical activity among 12- to 17-year-old youth when compared with those residing in suburbs and rural areas. In addition, poor black youth are at increased risk of being involved with physical fights, and because the majority of black youth live in central cities and many of them live below the poverty level, violence is a priority concern for urban youth. These behavior patterns have critical implications for both short- and long-term health and well-being.

Etiology of Health-Related Behaviors Among Adolescents

Given the mortality and health behavior statistics presented above, priority areas for youth living in urban areas include efforts to prevent violence, precocious and unsafe sexual activity, and drug use and to promote such health-enhancing behaviors as physical activity. Successfully developing effective programs to prevent health-compromising behaviors and promote health-enhancing behaviors among urban adolescents depends on identifying priority health-related behaviors and the causes of those behaviors. Moreover, identifying those causes depends on a combination of theory and research. Theory can tell us where to search for causes of health-related behaviors and suggest the means of prevention, whereas research can tell us whether our search has been successful and whether our prevention efforts have been effective (Flay & Petraitis, 1991). Given the importance of both theory and research, in this section we review both (a) a comprehensive theory of health-related behaviors and (b) empirical reviews of the research on predictors of health-related behaviors among adolescents.

Flay and Petraitis (1994) proposed a new comprehensive, macro-level theory that integrates constructs from numerous microtheories into one coherent framework, the theory of triadic influence (TTI). (See Petraitis, Flay, & Miller, 1995, for a review of many of the theories that are integrated in the TTI.) According to the TTI, behaviors have roots in a person's current social situation, general cultural environment, and personal characteristics. Health-related behaviors are most immediately controlled by decisions or intentions, and decisions are a function of one's (a) social normative pressures to perform health-related behaviors, (b) attitudes toward performing health-related behaviors, and (c) perceptions of self-efficacy in performing health-related behaviors. Behavioral influences can, therefore, be categorized into three streams of influence. First, social influences are thought to originate in one's current social situation or immediate microenvironment and to flow through factors that affect social normative beliefs regarding health-related behaviors. Second, attitudinal influences are thought to originate in the broad culture or macroenvironment and to flow through factors that affect health-related values, knowledge, expectations, and evaluations regarding the personal, financial, and social consequences of health-related behaviors. Third, intrapersonal influences are thought to originate in inherited dispositions and personality characteristics of the actor and to flow through sense of self, social competence, and health-related skills and self-efficacy.

In addition to the three streams of influence, one basic assumption of the TTI is that causes of health-related behaviors exist on varying levels of influence: (a) ultimate, (b) distal, and (c) proximal. Table 11.2 provides definitions and constructs within the three streams and levels of influence. *Ultimate* causes of behavior, factors in one's background and environment, are believed to be deep-seated, root causes of behavior. They include social situations and contexts in which the behavior takes place, one's sociocultural heritage and the macroenvironment in which one is raised and lives, and inherited traits and personality dispositions. At the *distal* level, the ultimate causes interact to provide social bonding and role models, general knowledge and values, and sense of self and social competence. On the more *proximal* level, properties of the distal level become more specific to the particular behavior one wishes to predict. For example, general knowledge influences beliefs about the particular consequences of a particular behavior. In addition, proximal influences include social normative beliefs, attitudes, and self-efficacy. The social cognitions determine the final single predictor of any one behavioral action, the decision/intention to act in a certain way in a particular situation.

According to this distinction, proximal variables (e.g., positive attitudes toward behavior) are highly predictive but focus only on the most immediate precursors of a behavior and do little to explain the deeper roots of behaviors. Distal variables help explain less immediate causes of behaviors (e.g., general life values). Finally, ultimate causes are exogenous causes beyond the immediate control

TABLE 11.2 Types and Levels of Influence on Adolescent Health-Related Behaviors (adapted from Petraitis, Flay, & Miller, 1995).

Type of Influence:	Social	Attitudinal	Intrapersonal
Level of Influence:			
Ultimate	*Definition:* Characteristics of people who make up adolescents' most intimate social support system. These characteristics are not specific to a particular behavior and are beyond the personal control of adolescents but nonetheless put them at risk for succumbing to social pressure to perform a particular behavior.	*Definition:* Aspects of adolescents' surroundings, neighborhoods, social institutions, and culture that, though beyond the personal control of adolescents, put them at risk for developing positive attitudes toward behavior.	*Definition:* Personality traits and intrapersonal characteristics that, though beyond the easy control of adolescents, might promote some internal motivation to perform a particular behavior.
	Constructs: Infrequent opportunities for rewards from family members; Lack of parental warmth, support, or supervision; Negative evaluations from parents; Home strain; Parental divorce or separation; Unconventional values of parents; Unconventional values among peers.	*Constructs:* Local crime and unemployment rates; Inadequate schools; Poor career and academic options; Infrequent opportunities for rewards at school; Media depictions of behavior; Availability; Public policies.	*Constructs:* Lack of impulse control; External locus of control; Aggressiveness; Extraversion; Sociability; Risk taking; Emotional instability; Intelligence.

Distal	*Definition:* Emotional attachments of adolescents and the behavior-specific attitudes and behaviors of influential role models who encourage behavior. *Constructs:* Weak attachments to and weak desire to please family members; Strong attachment to and strong desires to please peers; Greater influence by peers than parents; Behavior-specific attitudes and behaviors of role models.	*Definition:* General values and behaviors of adolescents that contribute to their attitudes toward a behavior. *Constructs:* Weak commitment to conventional values, school, and religion; Social alienation and criticism; Weak desire for success and achievement; Rebelliousness; Desire for independence from parents; Tolerance of deviance.	*Definition:* Affective states and general behavioral skills of adolescents that promote some internal motivation to perform a particular behavior and that undermine their refusal skills. *Constructs:* Low self-esteem; Temporary anxiety, stress, or depressed mood; Poor coping skills; Inadequate social skills; Weak academic skills.
Proximal	*Definition:* Beliefs about the normative nature of behavior and pressure to perform behavior. *Constructs:* Prevalence estimates; Beliefs that important others encourage behavior.	*Definition:* Beliefs and evaluations about the costs and benefits of a behavior. *Constructs:* Expected costs and benefits of behavior; Attitudes toward behavior by others; Attitudes toward behavior by self.	*Definition:* Beliefs about one's ability to perform a particular behavior and one's ability to avoid performing a behavior. *Constructs:* Refusal skills; Determination to perform behavior; Behavior self-efficacy; Refusal self-efficacy.
Immediate Predictors	Decisions/Intentions Trial Behavior Related Behaviors		

SOURCE: Copyright © 1995 by the American Psychological Association. Adapted with permission.

of individuals but clearly are major determinants of their behavior (e.g., neighborhood characteristics). When compared with more proximal causes, ultimate causes probably are more deeply rooted but less predictive for any one individual or group. This is because they might have little variance in most studies, they might change little over time for whole populations, and they are not easily changed or manipulated experimentally.

Although the TTI depicts three primary streams of influence on health-related behaviors (social situation/context, sociocultural environment, genetic traits and personality dispositions), it does not assume that all influences flow neatly down one stream or another. On the contrary, it recognizes that factors that primarily affect one stream might also, to a lesser extent, contribute to other streams. Interstream pathways demonstrate the overpowering importance of the most distal or "ultimate" causes of health-related behaviors. Because the effects of more immediate social settings, the sociocultural environment, and fundamental personality characteristics flow both within and between streams, they contribute to health-related behaviors in innumerable ways. Consequently, prevention programs that can address these ultimate causes will have the greatest impact over the long term. Therefore, it is suggested that altering the ultimate causes of health-compromising behavior and disease will lead to the greatest public health impact. Unfortunately, however, the most distal causes of behavior are often the most difficult to influence.

The significance and relevance of factors that influence behavior outlined in the TTI has been supported by etiological research of various health-related behaviors. Several recent research reviews on the causes of adolescent health-related behaviors were reviewed for this chapter, and a summary of findings is presented in Tables 11.3 through 11.6, using the framework of the TTI. Behaviors reviewed include health-compromising behaviors that are prevalent among urban adolescents, put them at risk of detrimental social and physical consequences, and have been adequately studied. These health-compromising behaviors include precocious sexual activity (Brooks-Gunn & Paikoff, 1993; Dryfoos, 1990; Office of Technology Assessment [OTA], 1991), pregnancy (Dryfoos, 1990; OTA, 1991), delinquency (Dryfoos, 1990; Tolan & Guerra, 1994; OTA, 1991), illicit substance use (Hawkins, Catalano, & Miller, 1992;

Petraitis et al., 1995), alcohol use (Komro, 1994), and tobacco use (Conrad, Flay, & Hill, 1992; USDHHS, 1994c).

Social Predictors

As Table 11.3 suggests, *ultimate social influences* are significant predictors for cigarette, alcohol, and illicit substance use; delinquency; early sexual activity; and pregnancy. Ultimate social influences include family characteristics and parenting styles. In particular, low socioeconomic status (SES) of parents is predictive of cigarette and alcohol use, delinquency, early sexual activity, and pregnancy. High SES of parents is associated with illicit substance use. Low educational attainment of parents and living in a single-parent household is associated with cigarette use, early sexual activity, and pregnancy. Having a large immediate family is associated with delinquency and early sexual activity. Home strain is associated with illicit substance use and pregnancy. Family disruption and conflict is associated with alcohol and illicit substance use and delinquency. Lack of parental support is associated with cigarette and illicit substance use, delinquency, early sexual activity, and pregnancy. Low parental supervision or restriction is associated with cigarette and alcohol use, delinquency, and early sexual activity. Repressive and abusive parenting styles and inadequate family problem solving are associated with delinquency. Low parental expectations are associated with cigarette use.

Distal social influences include emotional attachments and significant others' behaviors. Weak family bonds are associated with cigarette, alcohol, and illicit substance use and with delinquency. Strong peer bonds are associated with cigarette and illicit substance use, delinquency, and early sexual intercourse; bonds to deviant peers are associated with illicit substance use and delinquency. Adult and peer substance use is predictive of substance use among adolescents. Having a mother who had been a teen mother and having unmarried sisters who are teen mothers are predictive of adolescent pregnancy.

Proximal social influences include an adolescent's estimates of others' behaviors and perceived approval of behaviors by significant others. High estimates of cigarette use by adults, peers, and friends are associated with cigarette use among adolescents. Perceived adult,

TABLE 11.3 Social Predictors of Health-Compromising Behaviors Organized by Level of Influence

Level of Influence	Predictors	Cigarette Use	Alcohol Use	Illicit Substance Use	Delinquency	Early Sexual Activity	Pregnancy
Ultimate Influences	FAMILY CHARACTERISTICS						
	Parents' education	* (low)	* (low)	* (high)	* (low)	* (low)	* (low)
	Parents' SES	* (low)				* (low)	* (low)
	Single-parent household	*				*	*
	Large family			*	*		*
	Home strain		*	*	*		
	Family disruptions and conflict						
	PARENTING STYLE						
	Lack of parental support	*		*	*	*	*
	Low parental supervision or restrictions	*	*		*	*	
	Inadequate family problem-solving and coping skills	*			*		
	Low parental expectations						
	Repressive parents				*		
	Abusive parents				*		

274

Distal Influences					
EMOTIONAL ATTACHMENTS					
Weak family bonds	*		*		
Importance of peers vs. family		*	*		
Strong peer bonds		*	*	*	
Bonds to deviant peers		*	*		
Number of friends					
Poor peer relation skills			*		
OTHERS' BEHAVIORS					
Adult cigarette use	*	*	*		
Adult alcohol use	*	*	*		
Family history of alcoholism	*				*
Peer cigarette use		*			*
Peer alcohol use		*			
Peer marijuana use		*	*		
Peer narcotic use		*			
Peer offers of drugs		*			
Older sibling cigarette use					
Mother was teen mom					
Unmarried sisters are teen moms					
Family history of criminality, violence, mental illness					

TABLE 11.3 Continued

Level of Influence	Predictors	Cigarette Use	Alcohol Use	Illicit Substance Use	Delinquency	Early Sexual Activity	Pregnancy
Proximal Influences	BEHAVIOR ESTIMATES						
	Estimates of adult's behavior	*					
	Estimates of peer's behavior	*					
	Estimates of friend's behavior	*					
	PERCEIVED APPROVAL						
	Perceived adult approval	*	*				
	Perceived peer approval	*	*	*			
	Perceived sibling approval	*		*			*

peer, and sibling approval has been consistently associated with substance use.

Cultural/Attitudinal Predictors

As Table 11.4 suggests, attitudinal influences were also found to be significant predictors of health-compromising behaviors among adolescents. *Ultimate cultural/attitudinal influences* include availability of substances and school and community characteristics. Availability of cigarettes, alcohol, and illicit substances is predictive of use of the respective substance. School strain is predictive of cigarette and illicit substance use. A repressive school environment, tracking, and poor school management are predictive of delinquent behaviors among students. Segregated schools—that is, schools with a primarily black student body—are predictive of higher rates of early sexual activity and pregnancy. Significant neighborhood characteristics include urban areas and areas with a high rate of poverty, unemployment, crime, and mobility. Poverty and high unemployment areas are associated with higher rates of delinquency, early sexual activity, and pregnancy among adolescents. Urban areas and areas with high crime and mobility are associated with higher rates of delinquency.

Distal attitudinal influences include general values and behaviors. A high value on independence and nonconformance, low religious commitment, low school commitment, and low educational aspirations are predictive of five of the six health-compromising behaviors reviewed. Rebelliousness is associated with cigarette, alcohol, and illicit substance use. Social alienation is predictive of cigarette and illicit substance use. Tolerance of deviance is predictive of tobacco and alcohol use. Perception of poor life options is associated with early sexual activity and pregnancy among adolescents. School absenteeism is predictive of alcohol and illicit substance use, delinquency, and early sexual activity.

Proximal attitudinal influences include positive beliefs and attitudes toward behavior, and knowledge regarding the consequences of performing a particular behavior. The research reviews suggest the positive beliefs are predictive of cigarette and alcohol use; that positive attitudes are predictive of cigarette, alcohol, and illicit substance use; and that lack of knowledge regarding consequences of behavior is predictive of tobacco use and early sexual activity.

TABLE 11.4 Attitudinal Predictors of Health-Compromising Behaviors Organized by Level of Influence

Level of Influence	Predictors	Cigarette Use	Alcohol Use	Illicit Substance Use	Delinquency	Early Sexual Activity	Pregnancy
Ultimate Influences	AVAILABILITY	*	*	*			
	SCHOOL CHARACTERISTICS						
	School strain	*		*			
	Repressive						
	Tracking				*		
	Poor management				*		
	Segregated				*	*	*
	NEIGHBORHOOD CHARACTERISTICS						
	Poverty area				*	*	*
	High unemployment					*	*
	Urban				*		
	High crime				*		
	High mobility				*		

Distal Influences						
VALUES						
Socially alienated, critical	*					
Independent, nonconforming	*	*	*	*	*	
Rebellious	*	*	*	*	*	
Tolerant of deviance	*	*	*	*	*	
Low religious commitment	*			*	*	*
Perception of poor life options				*		*
Low school commitment	*	*	*	*	*	
Low education aspirations	*	*	*	*	*	
BEHAVIORS						
School absenteeism		*	*	*	*	*
Prior deviant behaviors		*	*	*	*	
Proximal Influences						
Positive beliefs toward behavior	*	*	*	*		
Positive attitudes toward behavior	*	*	*	*		*
Knowledge about physical consequences	*					

279

Intrapersonal Predictors

Intrapersonal influences are presented in Table 11.5. *Ultimate intrapersonal influences* include individual characteristics and personality traits. Males are more likely to be involved with episodic heavy drinking, delinquency, and early sexual activity. White adolescents are more likely to use illicit substances. Black adolescents are more likely to be involved in violence, early sexual activity, and pregnancy. Adolescents who experience early pubertal development are more likely to be involved in early sexual activity and pregnancy. Low behavioral control is associated with cigarette and illicit substance use and delinquency. Low emotional stability and extraversion are associated with illicit substance use. Introversion, external locus of control, and intelligence are associated with cigarette use.

Distal intrapersonal influences include affective states and behavioral skills. Low self-esteem and high levels of curiosity are associated with tobacco use. Anxiety is associated with delinquency. Learning problems and low school grades are predictive of alcohol use, illicit substance use, delinquency, early sexual activity, and pregnancy among adolescents.

Proximal intrapersonal influences include self-efficacy to resist influences to engage in a particular behavior. Refusal self-efficacy is associated with cigarette, alcohol, and illicit substance use and delinquency.

Immediate Precursors

Immediate precursors of health-compromising behaviors are presented in Table 11.6 and include intentions and prior or related behaviors. Intentions to perform a particular behavior are predictive of cigarette and illicit substance use. Prior substance use is predictive of all six of the health-compromising behaviors reviewed. Antisocial behaviors or delinquency are associated with cigarette and alcohol use, delinquency, early sexual activity, and pregnancy. Early sexual activity is predictive of alcohol use, delinquency, and pregnancy. Unprotected sexual activity is predictive of pregnancy. Low involvement in extracurricular activities is associated with delinquency.

TABLE 11.5 Intrapersonal Predictors of Health-Compromising Behaviors Organized by Level of Influence

Level of Influence	Predictors	Cigarette Use	Alcohol Use	Illicit Substance Use	Delinquency	Early Sexual Activity	Pregnancy
Ultimate Influences	INTRAPERSONAL CHARACTERISTICS						
	Sex		* (males)		* (males)	* (males)	
	Race			*(whites)	* (blacks)	* (blacks)	* (blacks)
	Early pubertal development						
	PERSONALITY TRAITS						
	Low emotional stability			*			
	Extraversion/Introversion	* (Intro)		* (Extra)			
	Low behavioral control	*		*			
	External locus of control	*					
	Intelligence	*			*		
Distal Influences	AFFECTIVE STATES						
	Low self-esteem	*					
	High levels of curiosity	*			*		
	Anxiety						
	BEHAVIORAL SKILLS						
	Learning problems/ Low school grades		*	*	*	*	*
Proximal Influences	Refusal self-efficacy	*	*	*	*		

TABLE 11.6 Immediate Precursors of Health-Compromising Behaviors Organized by Level of Influence

Level of Influence	Predictors	Cigarette Use	Alcohol Use	Illicit Substance Use	Delinquency	Early Sexual Activity	Pregnancy
Immediate predictors	INTENTIONS	*		*			
	PRIOR/RELATED BEHAVIORS						
	Prior substance use	*	*	*	*	*	*
	Antisocial behaviors/Delinquency	*	*		*	*	*
	Early sexual activity		*		*		*
	Unprotected sexual activity						
	Extracurricular activities						

Summary

Predictors of health-compromising behaviors among adolescents can be categorized into social, attitudinal, and intrapersonal influences. In addition, the level of influence can be specified and is important to consider for prevention. We believe that the TTI, supported by research, provides a fairly comprehensive understanding of how health-related behaviors are caused and offers practical guidance on how they can be changed. In the next section, we describe ultimate-, distal-, and proximal-level strategies aimed at preventing health-compromising behaviors and promoting health-enhancing behaviors among urban adolescents.

Promising Approaches for the Promotion of Health Among Adolescents

Priority health risks are determined by epidemiological research; risk and protective factors are determined through etiological theory and research. Epidemiology and etiological knowledge form the foundation for the development of prevention strategies (Holder et al., 1995). Research is critical to tell us whether specific prevention strategies are effective; this knowledge, in turn, aids in making policy decisions and resource allocation.

In the following section, we review prevention strategies that have support in the literature for being effective in the promotion of adolescent health. Again, the framework of the TTI is used to present promising and effective health-promotion and disease-prevention strategies for priority health-related behaviors among urban youth. Interventions based on any one stream are likely to have limited effects on health-related behaviors. Similarly, it is important to consider the multiple levels of influence because focus on only one or two levels of influence is also unlikely to have much effect. The TTI emphasizes the importance of the ultimate-level prevention strategies, although often strategies at this level are more difficult to influence and evaluate.

In the following section, we highlight successful and feasible strategies at the ultimate, distal, and proximal levels. Several recent reviews of adolescent health promotion and disease prevention were used in the preparation of this section (DeJong, 1994; Dryfoos,

1990; Mrazek & Haggerty, 1994; Millstein, Petersen, & Nightingale, 1993; OTA, 1991; Tolan & Guerra, 1994; Toomey, Jones-Webb, & Wagenaar, 1993; USDHHS, 1994c). Because health-compromising behaviors are interrelated, as discussed above, the section that follows is not categorized by specific health-related behavior. Rather, we present the strategies all together to emphasize overall health promotion for urban adolescents, with an emphasis on the priority areas of violence, precocious and unsafe sexual activity, drug use, and the promotion of health-enhancing behaviors.

Social Context Prevention Strategies

The goals of strategies in the social contextual area are to influence, in a positive direction, characteristics of people who make up adolescents' most intimate social support system, enhance emotional attachments between adolescents and healthy role models, encourage adults and peers to model and support healthy behaviors, influence beliefs that unhealthy behaviors are not normative, and aid understanding about the pressures to perform unhealthy behaviors (see Table 11.7). Successful ultimate-level strategies include family support services, parent skills training, and recruitment and mainstreaming of high-risk children.

Distal-level prevention strategies include increasing exposure to healthy adult and peer role models and having those role models reinforce healthy behaviors. Social influences and peer-led curricula are effective classroom programs (USDHHS, 1994c). Increasing social support for youth is also a promising approach; examples are (a) pairing high-risk children with adult volunteers (Dryfoos, 1990), (b) encouraging stable peer support by assigning a small group of students in a large junior high or high school to attend academic classes together (Compas, 1993; OTA, 1991), and (c) enhancing the role of the homeroom teacher in that she or he acts as an administrative link between the school, parents, and child, providing counseling and support as necessary (Compas, 1993; OTA, 1991).

Proximal level strategies include such classroom activities as exploring inaccurate normative expectations and exploring factors that influence health-related behaviors (Hansen & Graham, 1991).

TABLE 11.7 Social Context Prevention Strategies for Healthy
Development of Urban Adolescents

Level of Influence	Prevention Strategies
Ultimate	Access to family support services
	Provide parent skills training:
	increase guidance and support from parents
	improve parent behavior management
	improve family problem-solving skills
	improve skills to promote emotional cohesion within the family
	Recruit and mainstream high-risk children
Distal	Adults and peers model healthy behaviors
	Adults and peers reinforce healthy behaviors
	Train peer leaders to model and promote healthy behaviors
	Social skills training
	Pair high-risk children with adult volunteers
	Encourage stable peer support (e.g., assign a small group of students within a large middle or high school to attend all the same academic classes)
	Enhance social support at school (e.g., homeroom teacher serves as a link between school, child, and parents)
Proximal	Explore inaccurate normative expectations
	Explore factors that influence health-related behaviors

Cultural/Environmental Prevention Strategies

The goals of cultural/environmental prevention strategies are to
(a) effect changes in or enhance positive, health-enhancing environments (e.g., school, community, media, nation); (b) create opportunities for youth to participate in healthy behaviors; and (c)
enhance the development of healthy values, beliefs, and attitudes
(see Table 11.8). Ultimate-level strategies are aimed at improving
the environment and are as diverse as educational and community
improvements, specific laws restricting particular behaviors, and
providing opportunities to engage in healthy activities. Important
general ultimate-level strategies include upgrading of the quality of
education, particularly for disadvantaged children, and community
improvement efforts to decrease unemployment, poverty, drug
trafficking, and violence. Examples of more specific activities in-

TABLE 11.8 Cultural/Environmental Prevention Strategies for Healthy
Development of Urban Adolescents

Level of Influence	Prevention Strategies
Ultimate	Upgrade quality of education
	Begin community improvement efforts
	Begin community watch organizations
	Provide youth recreation
	Have mass media campaigns to promote healthy behaviors and to counter advertisements
	Limit advertisements
	Distribute health-promoting print materials
	Restrict tobacco and alcohol use in public places
	Restrict minors' access to tobacco and alcoholic products
	Enact gun control laws
	Maintain higher real prices for detrimental products through excise taxes: tobacco, alcohol, guns, and ammunition
	Require license/increase license fees for selling tobacco, alcohol, guns, and ammunition
	Enforce age-of-sale laws
	Reduce density of alcohol outlets
	Provide school-based clinics
	Provide access to free and confidential health care (minors consent without parental approval)
	Actively distribute condoms
	Provide contraceptives, pregnancy testing, counseling, abortion
	Enact motorcycle helmet and safety belt laws
	Increase minimum driving age
	Facilitate use of public transportation
	Have automatic protection (e.g., automatic safety belts)
	Produce environmental improvements (e.g., better street design, improved lighting)
	Increase access to fitness-promoting activities/public facilities and community programs
	Deliver regular vigorous exercise programs in physical education classes
	Modify food preparation in schools to reduce fat and salt
	Require fast-food restaurants to provide nutrition information at point of sale

clude providing safe, chaperoned recreational activities for youth
after school and on weekends and block watch programs that link
residents and police to work proactively to reduce crime in neigh-

TABLE 11.8 *Continued*

Level of Influence	Prevention Strategies
Distal	Provide youth employment programs
	Teach job preparation
	Provide community service/volunteer programs
	Have older adolescents serve as helpers to younger adolescents/children
	Encourage peer leadership
	Provide opportunities for involvement in healthy activities
	Conduct classroom discussions on issues related to self-awareness and social awareness
	Educate about cultural awareness
	Provide values education
Proximal	Convey short-term negative consequences of behavior
	Examine reasons for performing behavior and discuss healthy alternatives
	Teach decision-making skills
	Teach problem-solving skills

borhoods. Mass media campaigns can be designed to promote health behaviors and have been found to have direct effects on youth smoking (USDHHS, 1994c). In addition, limits on advertisements can be established. For example, communities can ban billboard advertisements of tobacco and alcohol near schools.

Restricting minors' access to detrimental products is a critical prevention strategy and includes such tactics as age-of-sale laws, restricting use in public places, and reducing density of outlets. Restricting minors' access to tobacco and alcohol deters young people who are unwilling to break the law, adds to the perceived social unacceptableness of use, emphasizes the dangerous nature of the product, and reinforces and supports messages that young people hear in school and other settings (USDHHS, 1994c). Despite age-of-sale laws, tobacco (USDHHS, 1994c) and alcohol (Forster et al., 1994) continue to be easily accessible to minors. Enforcement is crucial if these laws are to prevent minors' access and use. A reduction in the availability of tobacco and alcohol to minors can be expected only if retailers are licensed and if random unannounced inspections are conducted frequently (Toomey et al., 1993; USDHHS, 1994c).

Increased excise taxes are a successful prevention strategy, especially among adolescents, who are sensitive to price increases. Studies have found an association between increased price and lower use of tobacco (USDHHS, 1994c) and alcohol (Toomey et al., 1993). Excise taxes could also be used to effect increases in the cost of firearms and ammunition.

In addition to limiting access to tobacco and alcohol, evidence points to an immediate need to limit access of firearms to adolescents and to foster attitudes that would make use of weapons seem cowardly or otherwise unacceptable. As presented above, homicide is the leading cause of death for black and Hispanic urban adolescents. The firearm homicide rate for 15- to 19-year-olds increased 61% from 1979 through 1989, and the rate of homicide by all other methods remained stable or declined (Carter Center, 1994). The existing patchwork of laws leaves firearms and ammunition supplies largely unregulated, and the vast numbers of guns on the street ensure that they will be readily available to virtually anyone who wants them (Carter Center, 1994). Examples of approaches to reduce children's and adolescents' access to firearms are (a) make cracking down on illegal gun trafficking a priority for local law enforcement; (b) establish a significant annual fee for a gun dealer license; (c) establish strict licensing and storage standards for gun manufacturers, sellers, and owners; (d) establish criminal penalties for adult gun owners for whom unsafe firearms storage methods result in death, injury, or firearms being taken to school; (e) delay driving privileges for juveniles convicted of possessing a handgun; (f) ban any person from obtaining handgun ammunition without a handgun license; (g) mandate gun safety features such as trigger locks and loading indicators; (h) ban particularly hazardous and nonsporting forms of ammunition; (i) ban the manufacture and sale of assault weapons; and (j) establish confidential hotlines to report students carrying guns at school (Youth Alive, 1994).

Motor vehicle crashes also account for a large percentage of deaths among adolescents (number-one cause for metropolitan white youth, second cause for metropolitan Hispanic youth, and third cause for metropolitan black youth). Research has not supported the use of driver education as it is currently delivered as an effective strategy to reduce motor vehicle crashes (OTA, 1991). Examples of effective legislative measures are motorcycle helmet and safety belt laws. Other examples are nighttime driving curfews for adolescents and changes in the minimum driving age, which has been shown to be effective in reducing adolescent vehicle crashes (OTA, 1991). States with nighttime curfews for 16-year-old drivers have reduced the fatalities in this age group by as much as 69% (OTA, 1991).

Access to free and confidential health care services is critical, especially as a strategy to reduce sexually transmitted diseases (STDs) and unwanted pregnancies, a priority for urban adolescents.

> Although the most effective method for preventing the transmission of HIV and STDs is to abstain from sexual intercourse, many U.S. adolescents do not abstain from sexual intercourse. For adolescents who cannot be persuaded to refrain from sexual intercourse, the use of latex condoms lubricated with nonoxynol-9 is the most effective method to lower the risk of HIV and STD infection. (OTA, 1991, p. 289)

Health care services should include STD testing, provision of contraceptives, pregnancy testing, counseling, and abortion services (Dryfoos, 1990; OTA, 1991). The most effective school clinics are those that are opened beyond school hours, highlight contraceptive services, have specially trained staff to provide contraceptive services, include outreach activities, and have community support (Brooks-Gunn & Paikoff, 1993). Adolescents must be educated regarding the fact that parental notification and permission are not required for STD treatment. Almost all states have enacted legislation specifically authorizing minors to consent without parental approval to health services related to STDs (OTA, 1991). A successful program that showed reduced rate of adolescent pregnancy included intensive school- and communitywide education, along with the provision of contraceptives and one-on-one contraceptive counseling (OTA, 1991). Evaluations of condom distribution programs suggest that active efforts to distribute condoms is more likely to get adolescents to use condoms than is a more passive effort such as offering condoms through the mail (OTA, 1991).

As reported earlier, the rate of involvement in physical activities was significantly lower among youth living in central cities. Successful strategies that alter the school environment for the promotion of healthful diet and physical activity include cafeterias serving healthful foods and physical education offering and teaching vigorous physical activities. Food service personnel can be trained to alter their food procurement and preparation practices to lower sodium and fat content of meals. These interventions alone produced 15% to 20% decreases in sodium and saturated fats intake, and blood pressures decreased significantly (Sallis, 1993). "Regular vigorous exercise programs delivered in physical education classes produce increases in cardiovascular fitness and decreases in body fat in children, so changes in school policy toward physical education have the potential to promote physical activity effectively for both the poor and the affluent" (Sallis, 1993, p. 226). Examples of community strategies include providing access to fitness-promoting activities and public facilities and requiring fast-food restaurants to provide nutrition information at point of sale.

Distal-level environmental strategies include providing healthy activities for youth such as youth employment programs, job preparation, community service or volunteer programs, peer leadership activities, and helper programs. Youth employment programs seem to delay out-of-wedlock childbearing (OTA, 1991). Students involved with volunteer opportunities are less likely to have behavior problems, especially among older adolescents (Compas, 1993). Helper programs can include adolescents serving as interns, assistants, and helpers two or three times per week in early childhood and after-school child care programs, senior centers, community agencies, and other appropriate settings. Programs that can increase the motivation of high-risk youth to attend and perform in school and to engage in prosocial community activities are important strategies (Tolan & Guerra, 1994).

Proximal-level strategies can take place in the classroom or through the media to convey short-term negative consequences of behavior, examine reasons for performing health-compromising behaviors, and discuss healthy alternatives.

Intrapersonal Prevention Strategies

The goals of strategies in the intrapersonal realm attempt to enhance a child's or adolescent's sense of self, social competence, self-determination, social skills, and self-efficacy to resist negative influence and to perform positive, healthy behaviors (see Table 11.9). Ultimate-level strategies include access to quality prenatal care so that a child can begin life healthy. Access to quality pre-

TABLE 11.9 Intrapersonal Prevention Strategies for Healthy
Development of Adolescent Urban Residents

Level of Influence	Prevention Strategies
Ultimate	Access to quality preschool programs Coordination of social services Early interventions

Distal	General life skills development:
	  life skills training
	  consumer skills training
	  personal and social skills training
	  critical media consumer training
	Social competence curricula

Proximal	Resistance skills training Health behaviors skills training (e.g., aerobic exercise, how to read food labels, conflict resolution skills)

school programs for social and intellectual development is important, especially for the prevention of delinquency (Dryfoos, 1990; OTA, 1991). Additional ultimate-level strategies include coordinated social services and early interventions.

Distal-level intrapersonal strategies include general skill development in personal and social skills, social competence, critical media viewing, and consumer skills. These strategies are usually implemented in the classroom. Curricula focus on the development of a set of attitudes and behaviors that foster positive feelings toward the self, mutually adaptive relations with others, and skills to solve life problems and stressors (Compas, 1993). Results of social competence curricula have shown improved ability to solve social problems effectively; increased peer involvement; increased impulse control; improved sociability with peers; improved academic performance rated by teachers; and decreased self-reports of misbehavior, including fighting, stealing, and being sent out of the classroom (Compas, 1993).

Proximal prevention strategies focus more on specific health-related behaviors. Strategies include teaching how to resist influences to participate in risky or health-compromising behaviors and skill training for specific health behaviors, such as conflict resolution skills, aerobic exercise, and reading food labels.

Summary

Interventions based on any one stream are likely to have limited effects on health-related behaviors. Similarly, it is important to consider the multiple levels of influence; the TTI suggests that focus on one or two levels of influence is also unlikely to have much effect. Proximal-level strategies have been successful; however, usually only short-term effects have been found. Distal- and ultimate-level strategies need to support changes at the proximal level for population and long-term effects. For instance, the effect of a curriculum that primarily targets health-related decisions and/or refusal skills is likely to be short-lived unless attempts to affect more distal factors that influence health-enhancing decisions and support for refusal skills are made. Teaching conflict resolution skills might be a necessary final step in decreasing violence among peers, but it needs to be supported by interventions that begin further "up-stream." Laws and the cultural image of violence need to be changed. Availability of handguns, alcohol, and illicit substances needs tighter controls. Social conditions that promote violence need to be rectified. Sense of self and social competence need developing so that adolescents have the will and skill to control their own behaviors.

Summary and Discussion

We analyzed national mortality data for youth aged 12 to 17 years and found that motor vehicle crash, homicide, and suicide are among the five leading causes of death for all six metropolitan and racial groups. Motor vehicle crash is the leading cause of death among metropolitan white youth and all nonmetropolitan youth. Homicide is the leading cause of death for black and Hispanic youth in metropolitan areas. Suicide is the third leading cause of death among whites and Hispanics. The pervasiveness of death due to alcohol-involved crashes and interpersonal violence, particularly among urban youth, suggests a need for increased attention to the problems of (a) alcohol and other substance use by youth and (b) interpersonal violence among youth.

We also analyzed national behavioral risk data for youth aged 12 to 17 years. The majority of black and Hispanic youth live in central cities, and a high proportion of these youth live in poverty. After adjusting for race and poverty level, residing in central cities significantly increases the risk of health-compromising behaviors among youth. In particular, residing in central cities appears to be associated with a higher prevalence of ever having had sexual intercourse, lifetime marijuana use, and less physical activity among 12- to 17-year-old youth when compared with those residing in suburbs and rural areas. Also, poor black youth are at increased risk for involvement in physical fights. Each of the leading causes of death among 12- to 17-year-olds has environmental and behavioral determinants. Each of the leading causes of death among adults also has numerous social and behavioral determinants, many of which start during childhood or adolescence. Given that the causes of premature deaths among both youth and adults have social/environmental and behavioral determinants, almost all premature deaths are preventable.

According to many theories of behavior integrated by the theory of triadic influence, health-related behaviors are determined by three streams of influence that occur at three levels. According to the TTI, behaviors have roots in a person's current social situation, general cultural environment, and personal characteristics. These ultimate influences are the most pervasive, and their effects flow through distal and proximal levels of influence. The significance and relevance of the many factors that influence behavior outlined in the TTI has been supported by etiological research of various health-related behaviors (summarized in Table 11.2). We categorized findings on the predictors of health-compromising behaviors among adolescents into social, attitudinal, and intrapersonal influences and specified the level of influence. We believe that the TTI, supported by research, provides a fairly comprehensive understanding of how health-related behaviors are caused and offers practical guidance on how they can be changed.

In the final section, we described ultimate-, distal-, and proximal-level strategies aimed at preventing health-compromising behaviors and promoting health-enhancing behaviors among urban adolescents. Because ultimate influences are the most pervasive, preventive efforts that successfully alter them will have the greatest effects on behavior. Unfortunately, ultimate influences are also often the most difficult to change, so interventions at the other levels are also almost always necessary.

Our recommendations for future public health efforts for disease prevention and promotion of healthy behaviors among adolescents living in urban areas are in line with the theoretical framework outlined above. The framework can be applied to either drug use or violence-prevention programs. It can be applied to both urban and rural adolescents. First, comprehensive preventive intervention programs are needed to address multiple influences of risky behaviors. Although schools are the major context for prevention programs, it is essential to involve families, communities, and mass media in the programs. This involvement is more important for promoting nonviolence and no-drug programs in urban areas because such prevention efforts are highly likely to fail if the community and family climates do not change accordingly. Second, the prevention programs need to be sensitive to cultural differences (Mrazek & Haggerty, 1994) because different cultural groups may have different attitudes, values, beliefs, and practices. Finally, intervention programs should be guided by theories. We believe that theory-based prevention research is important not only for enhancing adolescent health but also for better understanding of the causal processes of the risky behaviors.

References

Brooks-Gunn, J., & Paikoff, R. L. (1993). "Sex is a gamble, kissing is a game": Adolescent sexuality and health promotion. In S. G. Millstein, A. C. Peterson, & E. O. Nightingale (Eds.), Promoting the health of adolescents: New directions for the twenty-first century (pp. 180-208). New York: Oxford University Press.

Carter Center. (1994). Not even one: A report on the crisis on children and firearms. Atlanta, GA: Interfaith Health Program of the Carter Center.

Compas, B. E. (1993). Promoting positive mental health during adolescence. In S. G. Millstein, A. C. Petersen, & E. O. Nightingale (Eds.), Promoting the health of adolescents: New directions for the twenty-first century (pp. 159-179). New York: Oxford University Press.

Conrad, K. M., Flay, B. R., & Hill, D. (1992). Why children start smoking cigarettes: Predictors of onset. British Journal of Addiction, 87, 1711-1724.

DeJong, W. (1994). Preventing interpersonal violence among youth: An introduction to school, community, and mass media strategies. Washington, DC: U.S. Department of Justice, Office of Justice Programs, National Institute of Justice.

Dryfoos, J. G. (1990). Adolescents at risk: Prevalence and prevention. New York: Oxford University Press.

Flay, B. R., & Petraitis, J. M. (1991). Methodological issues in drug use prevention research: Theoretical foundations. In C. G. Leukefeld & W. J. Bukoski (Eds.),

Drug abuse prevention intervention research: Methodological issues (Monograph 107, pp. 81-109). Washington, DC: National Institute on Drug Abuse Research.

Flay, B. R., & Petraitis, J. (1994). The theory of triadic influence: A new theory of health behavior with implications for preventive interventions. In G. S. Albrecht (Ed.), *Advances in medical sociology: Vol 4. Reconsideration of models of health behavior change* (pp. 19-44). Greenwich, CT: JAI.

Forster, J. L., McGovern, P. G., Wagenaar, A. C., Wolfson, M., Perry, C. L., & Anstine, P. S. (1994). The ability of young people to purchase alcohol without age identification in northeastern Minnesota, USA. *Addiction, 89,* 699-705.

Hansen, W. B., & Graham, J. W. (1991). Preventing alcohol, marijuana, and cigarette use among adolescents: Peer pressure resistance training versus establishing conservative norms. *Preventive Medicine, 20,* 414-430.

Hawkins, J. D., Catalano, R. F., & Miller, J. T. (1992). Risk and protective factors for alcohol and other drug problems in adolescence and early adulthood: Implications for substance abuse prevention. *Psychological Bulletin, 112*(1), 64-105.

Holder, H., Boyd, G., Howard, J., Flay, B., Voas, R., & Grossman, M. (1995). Alcohol problem prevention research policy: The need for a phases model. *Journal of Public Health Policy, 16*(3), 324-346.

Jeffery, R. W. (1989). Risk behaviors and health: Contrasting individual and population perspectives. *American Psychologist, 44,* 1194-1202.

Kelder, S. H., Perry, C. L., Klepp, K. I., & Lytle, L. L. (1994). Longitudinal tracking of adolescent smoking, physical activity, and food choice behaviors. *American Journal of Public Health, 84,* 1121-1126.

Kolbe, L. J., Kann, L., & Collins, J. (1993). Overview of the Youth Risk Behavior Surveillance System. *Public Health Reports, 108*(Suppl.), 2-10.

Komro, K. A. (1994). *Feasibility and effectiveness of peer-planned, alcohol-free activities for the prevention of alcohol use among young adolescents: The Project Northland Peer Participation Program.* Unpublished doctoral dissertation, University of Minnesota, Minneapolis.

Millstein, S. G., Petersen, A. C., & Nightingale, E. O. (Eds.). (1993). *Promoting the health of adolescents: New directions for the twenty-first century.* New York: Oxford University Press.

Mrazek, P. J., & Haggerty, R. J. (Eds.). (1994). *Reducing risks for mental disorders: Frontiers for preventive intervention research.* Washington, DC: National Academy Press.

National Center for Health Statistics. (1994). *Health, United States, 1993* (DHHS Pub. No. PHS 94-1232). Washington, DC: Government Printing Office.

Office of Technology Assessment (OTA). (1991). *Adolescent health: Vol. 2. Background and the effectiveness of selected prevention and treatment services* (OTA-H-466). Washington, DC: Government Printing Office.

Petraitis, J., Flay, B. R., & Miller, T. Q. (1995). Reviewing theories of adolescent substance use: Organizing pieces in the puzzle. *Psychological Bulletin, 117,* 67-86.

Rose, G. (1985). Sick individuals and sick populations. *International Journal of Epidemiology, 14,* 32-38.

Rose, G., & Day, S. (1990). The population mean predicts the number of deviant individuals. *British Medical Journal, 301,* 1031-1034.

Sallis, J. F. (1993). Promoting healthful diet and physical activity. In S. G. Millstein, A. C. Petersen, & E. O. Nightingale (Eds.), *Promoting the health of adolescents: New directions for the twenty-first century* (pp. 209-241). New York: Oxford University Press.

Shah, B. V., Barnwell, B. G., Hunt, P. N., & LaVange, L. M. (1991). *SUDAAN user's manual, release 5.50.* Research Triangle Park, NC: Research Triangle Institute.

Tolan, P., & Guerra, N. (1994). *What works in reducing adolescent violence: An empirical review of the field.* Boulder: University of Colorado, Institute for Behavioral Sciences, Center for the Study and Prevention of Violence.

Toomey, T. L., Jones-Webb, R. J., & Wagenaar, A. C. (1993). Policy: Alcohol. *Annual Review of Addictions Research and Treatment, 3,* 279-292.

U.S. Department of Health and Human Services (USDHHS), National Center for Health Statistics. (1994a). *Catalog of electronic data products* (DHHS Pub. No. PHS 94-1213). Washington, DC: Government Printing Office.

U.S. Department of Health and Human Services (USDHHS). (1994b). Health-risk behaviors among persons aged 12-21 years: United States, 1992. *Morbidity and Mortality Weekly Report, 43,* 231-235.

U.S. Department of Health and Human Services (USDHHS). (1994c). *Preventing tobacco use among young people: A report of the Surgeon General.* Atlanta, GA: U.S. Department of Health and Human Services, Public Health Service, Centers for Disease Control and Prevention, National Center for Chronic Disease Prevention and Health Promotion, Office on Smoking and Health.

U.S. Public Health Service, Office of Disease Prevention and Health Promotion. (1988). *Disease prevention/health promotion: The facts.* Palo Alto, CA: Bull.

Youth Alive. (1994). *Firearm facts.* Washington, DC: U.S. Department of Health and Human Services, Public Health Service, Health Resources and Services Administration, Maternal and Child Health Bureau, National Center for Education in Maternal and Child Health.

Appendix:
Parameter Estimates and
Standard Errors by Behavior

The reference group is white youth who live in a central city and above the poverty threshold.

Behavior Independent Variable	Parameter Estimate	Standard Error	p-Value
Involvement in a Physical Fight During Previous Year			
Black*Poverty	−.09	.04	.04
Black	.18	.04	< .01
Hispanic	.01	.02	.80
Suburb	−.03	.02	.06
Rural	−.04	.02	.10
Poverty	.12	.03	<.01
Ever Had Sexual Intercourse			
Black	.22	.03	< .01
Hispanic	−.00	.03	.97
Suburb	−.09	.02	< .01
Rural	−.06	.03	.03
Poverty	.08	.02	<.01
Cigarette Smoking During Previous Month			
Black	−.16	.01	<.01
Hispanic	−.05	.02	<.01
Suburb	−.01	.01	.42
Rural	−.03	.02	.13
Poverty	.03	.02	.04
Ever Drank Alcohol			
Black	−.09	.02	<.01
Hispanic	.01	.02	.64
Suburb	−.02	.02	.18
Rural	−.04	.02	.06
Poverty	−.08	.02	< .01
Ever Used Marijuana			
Black	−.07	.01	<.01
Hispanic	−.03	.01	.08
Suburb	−.05	.01	<.01
Rural	−.08	.01	<.01
Poverty	.01	.01	.37

continued

Behavior *Independent Variable*	*Parameter* *Estimate*	*Standard Error*	*p-Value*
Engaged in Moderate Physical Activity at Least 30 Minutes at a Time 5 or More of the 7 Days Preceding the Survey			
Black	−.03	.02	.11
Hispanic	.00	.02	.91
Suburb	.07	.02	< .01
Rural	.08	.02	< .01
Poverty	−.04	.02	.02

• *CHAPTER 12* •

Health Perspectives on Urban Children and Youth

ROBERT L. JOHNSON

The urban American child, especially the minority urban child, has a poorer health status than his or her nonminority counterpart. A number of commonly cited health status parameters readily demonstrate this disparity:

- The United States has the highest infant mortality rate among the world's 21 leading industrialized nations. Although this rate has declined during the past 35 years, the African American infant mortality rate remains twice as high as the rate for nonminorities (U.S. Department of Health and Human Services [USDHHS], 1990).
- Urban children experience excessive mortality and disability caused by controllable illnesses such as asthma.
- These stark differences in health status are dramatically demonstrated in the differential penetration of preventive measures such as immunization and the prevalence of severe infectious illnesses such as HIV disease. In the 1991-1992 reporting year, the Centers for Disease Control and Prevention identified 871 cases of pediatric acquired immunodeficiency syndrome (AIDS) in white children under the age of 13. In the same year, it identified 2,300 cases among African American children and 1,027 cases among Hispanic children of the same age group. Most of these children lived in America's urban environments.

- Violence is the leading cause of death in all American adolescent population groups. In nonminority population groups, this mortality is overwhelmingly related to automobile accidents. In minority populations, especially urban minority populations, this preventable mortality is overwhelmingly related to handguns and knives. Indeed, homicide is the leading cause of death among African American adolescent males aged 15 to 24 (National Center for Education in Maternal and Child Health, 1991).
- Teenage pregnancy, which poses a risk to both infant and mother, is three times higher among urban minority groups than in nonminorities. Premature parenthood is central to a continuation of a syndrome of undereducation, unemployment, and poverty, which adds to and perpetuates the maladies complicating the lives of urban children.

The New Morbidity

Although most adverse outcomes are directly related to behaviors, they are measured as biological phenomena that are expressed as adverse health statistics. Invariably, these adverse outcomes are related to a series of behaviors that becomes part of the lives of children (infants, children, adolescents, and young adults). They are exposed to and experiment with many maladaptive behaviors as they develop their adult identities. Often, these behaviors contribute to the development of biological and psychosocial problems that impede their healthy growth and maturation and compromise their health status. "Healthiness" is further compromised for many urban children and youth by factors related to race and ethnicity. Several indicators found among the children in our clinical population in Newark, New Jersey, emphasize the significance of this relationship.

Violence

Among New Jersey adolescents, homicide accounts for 28.5% of African American male and 12.7% of African American female deaths. Among their Caucasian counterparts, however, homicide accounts for only 4.2% of male deaths and 6.3% of female deaths. The death rate for African American males is 150 per 100,000 versus 85 per 100,000 for Caucasian males. Sixty percent (60%) of minority male adolescents in New Jersey report that their lives are significantly affected by violence. In Newark, the teen death rate is 120% worse than the state average (Association for Children of New Jersey, 1993).

Substance Abuse

The use of drugs and alcohol begins early among adolescents in our community. In one of our community programs, 45.9% of the 12- to 14-year-old minority males regularly consume alcoholic beverages, 27.3% smoke cigarettes, and 5.4% smoke marijuana. Not only is the use of these substances associated with their own well-recognized negative health consequences, but they also increase the probability that one of these young men will "regress" to the use of more dangerous substances in the future.

Sexual Activity

In Newark, which has a population that is 71.4% minority, the birth rate to teens in 1990 was 185% higher than the average birth rate to teens for the entire state of New Jersey (National Center for Education in Maternal and Child Health, 1991). In 1991, more than one third of females receiving prenatal care at University Hospital were under 18 years of age.

The consequence of the type of risky sexual behavior that produces these high teenage fertility rates is not restricted to adolescent pregnancy only. It also contributes to high rates of sexually transmitted diseases. In New Jersey, urban minority teens aged 15 to 19 have the highest rates of gonorrhea, syphilis, chlamydia, and hospitalization for pelvic inflammatory disease. A 1990 seroprevalence study reported that 1.5% to 2.0% of the adolescents in our community are infected with HIV (Keller et al., 1991).

Nutrition

Minority adolescents are more likely to have poorer nutritional habits and associated nutritional problems than nonminority adolescents. These behaviors result in a higher incidence of nutritional anemias, obesity, and complaints of chronic fatigue. Additionally, nutritional behaviors associated with the consumption of fat and

TABLE 12.1 Comparative Health Status Indicators for Camden County and Camden City, New Jersey

Indicator	Camden County	Camden City
Percentage Minority	23	81
Percentage Low Birth Weight	7	12
Percentage No Prenatal Care	2	5
Infant Mortality	10.2/1,000	16.6/1,000
Births to Teens	64/1,000	173/1,000
Child Abuse/Neglect	12.3/1,000	42.4/1,000
Child Death Rate	2.7/10,000	5.5/10,000
Teen Death Rate	10.1/10,000	20.9/10,000

salt contribute to the high incidence of hypertension and heart disease that will be found in these minority adolescents as they grow into adulthood.

Health status is one component of a larger picture of economic, social, environmental, and behavioral maladies—a "new morbidity" that complicates the lives of children and youth in U.S. urban communities. Undoubtedly, the realization of excellence in health for all people is closely associated with a host of social and economic issues that are beyond the general scope of health promotion. The continued worsening of these and other indicators of urban children's health, however, demonstrates that traditional therapeutic, health education, and disease-prevention approaches have been inadequate.

Health Status of the Urban Child:
A Case Study

The health status of any region or group of persons is usually measured in terms of a variety of regularly collected statistics. The comparison of data between U.S. urban and non-urban communities presents a stark contrast that attests to the poorer health status of children in urban communities. Table 12.1 presents comparative health status indicators for Camden County and Camden City, both of which are in the southern part of New Jersey neighboring

Philadelphia. Camden County data contain statistics for Camden City, as well as data from the very affluent communities of Camden County. Camden City data contain only reports from Camden City, which is noted for its representation of all the maladies that beset urban America. In each of these parameters, the children in this urban community experience outcomes that are significantly worse than the life experiences of their suburban counterparts.

Although the foregoing observations are useful examples of the qualitative dimensions of the health-related problems of the urban child, they are not sufficiently quantitative to define the dimensions of the whole problem and assist in the development of a credible solution. This consideration requires accurate data on urban child health status.

Several factors that are a function of race and ethnicity, however, compromise the usefulness of the national data collected on minority children. In the light of the concentration of minority children in urban communities, these factors are particularly pertinent to the interpretation of urban health status data. These deficiencies interfere with an accurate definition of health needs and prevent adequate planning for services and assistance. In the report of its AAP Task Force on Minority Children's Access to Pediatric Care, the American Academy of Pediatrics (1994) commented on the extent of this problem in its analysis of six commonly cited health status data sources.

1. *Hispanic Health and Nutrition Examination Survey (HHANES):* This was the first special population survey undertaken by the National Center for Health Statistics (NCHS) and represents the most comprehensive survey of Latino health status in the United States. It was conducted from 1982 to 1984 in the three regions of the United States where Latinos are concentrated. The total population was 9,000, and the NCHS estimated that the survey represented 76% of the 1980 Latino civilian, non-institutionalized population from age 6 months to 74 years living in the United States. The information includes demographics, economic conditions, health insurance coverage, health services use and satisfaction, acculturation, and health assessments. No follow-up has been made.

2. *National Ambulatory Medical Care Survey (NAMCS):* This is an annual survey of discharge abstracts from nonfederal short-stay

hospitals. Although information is available on patient diagnosis and surgical procedure, it lacks socioeconomic status or racial identifiers.

3. *National Health Interview Survey (NHIS):* This is an annual, household-based survey conducted by the NCHS that focuses on health status, use of services, and sociodemographic information. The information about access is derived from medical and dental visits, recent illnesses, health status, and differentials in sites of medical delivery. Supplemental sections are needed to study specific problems. These include the 1981, 1988, and 1991 Child Health Supplement; the 1987 Cancer Control Supplement; and the 1988 AIDS Supplement. The 1988 Child Supplement contains information on a survey of subjects including child care, injuries, exposure to cigarette smoke, school attendance, behavioral problems, health insurance, and sources of medical care. Information is also available regarding racial/ethnic groups. The most recent NHIS, conducted in 1989, oversampled Mexican Americans.

4. *National Maternal and Infant Health Survey (NMIHS):* This survey of mothers and providers is conducted by the NCHS. It was conducted in 1988, with longitudinal follow-up in 1991.

5. *National Medical Expenditure Survey* (NMES): This survey is conducted every 8 to 10 years by the Agency for Health Care Policy and Research. The most recent survey was conducted in 1987, but the information is not yet publicly available. It provides information regarding health services use, expenditures, insurance coverage, and estimates of people with functional disabilities and impairments. It oversamples the Latino population, allowing for national estimates. The database also includes information on Native Americans.

6. *National Survey of Family Growth (NSFG):* This household interview survey of non-institutionalized women 15 through 44 years of age in the continental United States is conducted periodically by the NCHS. It includes information regarding family planning, in addition to other maternal and child health issue. The 1982 survey includes information on the major national origin subgroups of Latinos in the United States.

The standard birth certificate was revised in 1989 in ways that have important implications for understanding the health of minority women and children. Variables documenting behavioral issues that affect pregnancy outcome, such as the use of alcohol and tobacco, were added to the information collected. Perhaps most important, the algorithm for assigning infant race was changed. The NCHS formerly used a complicated algorithm that assigned the nonwhite race of a parent to the infant, with the exception that if both parents were nonwhite, the infant was assigned the race of the father. The revision assigned the race of the mother to the infant, which has increased the number of white births.

Although the AAP Task Force uncovered limited available health statistics for African American, Latino, and Native American children, an extensive review of the biomedical literature failed to uncover any nationally representative sources of information on Asian American children. Investigators are, however, interested in documenting the health status of Asian children from such countries as the United States, the United Kingdom, Canada, and Australia.

The U.S. literature is often descriptive in format and addresses a variety of issues, including provider perceptions of Asian patients and various measures of health status, such as infant mortality and injury death rates. International articles detail the dental status of immigrant Asian children.

The Asian/Pacific Islander subgroup is the fastest growing population in the United States. Three fifths, or 60%, of the Asian American population is of Japanese, Chinese, or Filipino origin, and these groups are of approximately similar size. The remaining 40% of the Asian population in the United States is approximately evenly divided between South Indians, Koreans, and Southeast Asians. Although the AAP Task Force has already noted the relative lack of consistent representative data for other minority groups, Asian Americans should be highlighted as a group about whom even less is known. No nationally representative information is available about Asian Americans (Nickens, 1990).

Despite the lack of national information, however, it has been noted that the refugee populations of Southeast Asia, which migrated to the United States following the Vietnam War, face significant socioeconomic and health problems. Tuberculosis and other diseases of poverty are especially prevalent in this group despite the overall median family income of Asian/Pacific Islanders, which is higher than that of whites.

The Biopsychosocial Dimension

In the remainder of this chapter, I discuss the barriers that contribute to the impaired comparative adverse health outcomes cited above. A full appreciation of the dimensions of the issues, however, requires a discussion of the biological and psychosocial maturational factors that contribute to these barriers or at least make them more complicated. These factors are particularly salient for the adolescent who is experiencing the most profound change in his or her relationship to his or her body and environment. All these children are subject to several generative forces that take them through childhood into adolescence and into adulthood. These forces have both biological and psychosocial parameters.

Biological puberty begins with an endocrinological cascade that starts in the brain in the area of the hypothalamus with the production of releasing hormones. These substances travel to the pituitary gland, where they cause it to release another set of hormones known as *gonadotropins*. These substances stimulate the final stages of development of the testicles in the male and the ovaries in the female, leading to the production of testosterone (the male sexual maturation hormone) and estrogen and progesterone (the female sexual maturation hormones). These hormonal substances are largely responsible for the sexual development of male and female adolescents.

Female Pubertal Development

The first visible signs of female puberty (average age range 9-13 years) are the appearance of breast buds under the nipples and the growth of pubic hair in the genital area. Development during the next 3 years will include increased height and increased weight, in addition to change in the size and contour of the breasts and increased amount and distribution of pubic hair. Puberty for the adolescent female ends 2½ years after the appearance of the breast bud with menarche (the first menstrual period).

This first menstrual period is a good historic marker for development in the adolescent female. Today, most girls experience menarche somewhere between 11½ and 12½ years of age. Anecdotal records suggest that the age of menarche for girls living in the

United States at the time of the American Revolution was approximately 17 years. These same records indicate that, at the time of the American Civil War, the age of menarche had dropped to 15½ years. At the beginning of the 20th century, the average age of menarche had decreased to 13 years. As I indicated above, currently the average age of first menstrual period is 11½ to 12½ years. Indeed, the age of menarche has decreased approximately 2 or 3 months for every decade since the beginning of the 20th century.

Given the veracity of these partially anecdotal observations, this shift toward earlier biological maturity has profound social implications. Pregnancy at ages as early as 11 are more common today than they were in the 1950s partly because of the acceleration of the age of biological maturity. In the 1950s, very few 11-year-old adolescent females could become pregnant! Furthermore, this commentary is irrefutable evidence that children are growing up faster. The 13- or 16-year-old of the 1990s is indeed different from the 13- or 16-year-old of the 1950s!

One of the more difficult problems in adult society's collective relationship with children and youth is our tendency to conceptualize "childhood and teenage normality" in the context of our own experiences, rather than in the context of contemporary children and adolescents. Our context may be 10, 20, 30, or 40 years out of sync with the 1990s. Such dissynchronicity impedes communication and comprehension.

Male Pubertal Development

Puberty in the adolescent male (average age range 11-18 years) begins with enlargement of the testicles. This event is attributable to the opening of the tubules inside the testicles. This phenomenon heralds the increased production of spermatozoa, the growth of pubic hair, and increase in the size of the penis. Throughout this process, the young man's total body size increases, with growth in both height and weight. As in the female, the most rapid portion of growth in height is known as the *growth spurt*.

The total pubertal process in the male adolescent occurs during a 6-year period of time, as compared with 3 years in the adolescent female. In addition, the typical male will initiate pubertal events 1½ years after the typical female.

No event in the male adolescent is exactly comparable to menarche. It has been suggested, however, that the first "wet dream" indicates a time at which the male is producing sperm at a rate and amount great enough to increase significantly the probability that ejaculation during sexual intercourse will cause pregnancy. This event has been called *semenarche,* and it usually occurs at age 13 ± 1 year.

Adolescence

Adolescence is a period of time that a given culture or society sets aside for its children to learn how to be adults. In an earlier time in history, children and youth were directly taught how to be adults. Alex Haley, in his book *Roots* (1976), describes the ancient African adolescence of the young Kunta Kinte:

At about 12 years of age, the boys of the village were separated from their families and taken to a camp in the jungle by the men of the community. Over a period of 6 weeks, the boys were taught all the lessons of adulthood. At the end of the encampment, they were tested to determine whether they had learned these lessons of adulthood. Those boys who successfully passed the test were granted adult status. Accordingly, they were circumcised as a visible sign of their manhood. They left their village as boys, and they returned to the village and to their society as men.

The Task of Adolescence

Young men and women growing up in U.S. urban communities must accomplish the same task of adolescence as Kunta Kinte:

- *Emancipate* themselves within the structure that gave them nurture and support during their childhood (usually the family or some similar surrogate structure)
- Establish their *sexual identity* and make decisions about maleness and femaleness and love-object gender
- Establish their *intellectual identity* and place themselves within the religious, cultural, ethnic, moral, and political constructs of society
- Establish their *functional identity* and decide "what they are going to do with the rest of their lives"—how they will support themselves and contribute to their families and to society

- Complete *cognitive development* and develop the capacity to use abstract thought to consider life options and alternatives

Modern Western culture has no short, concentrated periods of instruction in manhood or womanhood. There are no tests that prove that boys and girls have become men and women. There are no societally recognized ceremonies that mark the transition from childhood into adulthood and no visible signs of that new status. The adolescence of American children is drawn out over a protracted period of as many as 10 to 15 years. They learn how to be men and women, not from lessons that are carefully taught by designated adults, but rather from observations they make of individuals who are significant in their lives. Often, these important adult role models are found in the family; but if the quality and quantity of this observational contact is impaired, limited, or absent, this component of the lessons of manhood or womanhood may be abdicated to the streets or to the media.

School has become another important source of instruction in adulthood in U.S. culture. School is the first environment outside the home within which the lessons learned at home can be tested. Furthermore, the quality of educational exposure will be a major determinant of the scope of possible functional identities. Unfortunately, the poor quality of many urban educational environments often corrupts the beneficial gains that urban children might have received in school.

Finally, in the United States, children and youth learn important lessons about adulthood from the media. The media have effectively established standards and norms of behavior that have crossed regional, color, economic, and educational lines. Popular dress styles—symbols of adolescent status—are equally prevalent among children and youth in every regional, ethnic, racial, and economic group. Indeed, they have become so important that children, especially urban children, are "killing each other to get them." Much of the appeal of this and other contrived symbols is attributable to their association with desirable media images. The effect of the media on an individual adolescent, however, is still a function of the quality and quantity of the lessons presented within the family context.

Stages of Adolescence

Adolescence is divided into three stages: early adolescence, middle adolescence, and late adolescence.

Early Adolescence. The early adolescent (typical age range 12-14 years) is caught in the midst of rapid body changes. Secondary sexual characteristics begin to appear, growth accelerates, and biology becomes a major focus of daily concerns. Cognitively, these young people possess thought patterns that are still relatively concrete; they have difficulty projecting themselves into the future. This difficulty becomes a particular problem when they are asked to modify their behaviors and to delay gratification for some distant future goal. This relative weakness of projective reasoning becomes a particularly important issue when early adolescents are asked to change desired behaviors to attain a specific health-related goal in the distant future (e.g., stop eating enjoyable "fatty foods" as a teen to prevent heart disease as an adult).

Although early adolescents may test adult authority within the family "to see what they can get away with," they will generally acquiesce to parental guidance. In this stage, they also begin to identify their peer group in an effort to find other young people who they sense are similar to themselves. Sexual behaviors are tested, but typically sexual activity is limited. Many urban youth (especially males) who will become sexually active during adolescence will initiate sexual intercourse during this stage (ages 13-14), but they will not become regularly sexually active until they approach biological maturity (16-17 years).

Middle Adolescence. Middle adolescence (typical age range 15-17 years) is the developmental home of the majority of problem behaviors found in all adolescent population groups. The transitions in this stage are so dramatic that they seem to occur overnight. The secondary sexual characteristics become fully established, and the growth rate decelerates. Physically, these young people look more like the adults they will become and less like the children they were.

The psychosocial hallmarks of this stage are the development of abstract thought patterns and the attainment of a set of psychological supports that act as if they were an Armor of Middle Adolescence. This important protective gear consists of the Helmet of

Omniscience, which makes them all-knowing; the Breast Plate of Omnipotence, which makes them all-powerful; and the Shield of Invincibility, which gives them the ability to defend against and defeat every foe.

This Armor of Middle Adolescence is a dual-functioning, double-edged sword. The armor provides the supportive structure that allows these young people to emancipate themselves and move outside the structure that had nurtured and sustained them for most of their lives. But it also allows them to participate in dangerous and destructive risk-taking behaviors and believe that they cannot be harmed (e.g., "I can pass a test without studying," "I can drive a car even though I have never taken a driving lesson," "I can steal a car and not get caught," "I can stop a bullet and not die," "I can have unprotected sexual intercourse and not get pregnant").

In this stage, most youth begin the process of emancipation from the limitations of the structures that supported their childhood. In some families, the struggle for emancipation is played out through major conflicts over parental control and authority. Often, these battles move outside the home environment to encompass a challenging of authorities in other arenas (e.g., school, police).

As adolescents participate in this process of separation from the family, they cleave more tightly to the peer group they defined for themselves in early adolescence. Within this context, the peer group begins to define the rules of behavior. Additionally, the peer group acts to affirm and reaffirm the adolescent's self-image. The peer group is often cited as the source of many problem behaviors because of the pressure it brings to the adolescent to conform to its norms and codes of behavior. Because these young people define their own peer group according to their self-identity, however, and because they participate in the definition of the peer norms and behavioral codes, they thus share responsibility for their own actions within the group, as well as outside the group.

Sex and sexual expression are a major focus of the lives of middle adolescents. Both the young men and the young women suddenly seem to become sexual in all aspects of their being. The health and social risks associated with unprotected sexual intercourse become issues of paramount importance during this stage.

Late Adolescence. Late adolescents (typical age 18+ years) have attained full physical maturity. Cognitively, they achieve formal operations and become fully aware of their limitations and how their past will affect their future. They make a major transition from the fantasies of middle adolescence into the realities of adulthood. They realize that all things are not possible. More important, they become fully aware of their natural limitations, as well as the limitations that are a result of the earlier "life mistakes" they may have made as middle adolescents. Most late adolescents negotiate this bit of the adult transition with little difficulty. At the other extreme, others become depressed and incapacitated because of the loss of their dreams.

Within the family, late adolescents move to a more adult-to-adult relationship with their parents and begin to realistically consider the process of establishing their own homes. The peer group recedes in importance as a determinant of behavior, and sexuality becomes closely tied to commitment and planning for the future.

In the previous section, I briefly described the dynamic context within which all adolescents experience their lives. Within that context, most urban children and youth pass from childhood into adulthood with few problems. Some of these young people, however, become involved with one of a variety of encumbrances—drugs, alcohol, premature parenthood, violence, suicide, school failure/dropout, delinquency, and so on—that impedes their orderly transition and further compromises their health status.

Barriers to Health Care Access

The factors that compromise the health status of urban children can be understood in terms of barriers to access to care. This paradigm assumes that the central issue in adverse outcomes is access. Furthermore, this paradigm assumes that, given complete access, the urban child will have health status outcomes similar to those of children who do not suffer from health care restrictions.

Although this paradigm is generally credible, social issues (see above) add to the prevalence of adverse health status outcomes. For example, the higher rates of violence-related mortality and morbidity among urban youth are not a function of barriers to care as much as they are a function of the social pathologies that contribute to the development of the conditions that facilitate the occurrence of this type of violence. Nevertheless, within the specific domain of health care, the central contributor to equalizing these rates is a function of access.

Financial Barriers

Financial barriers disproportionately affect populations in urban settings, especially minorities, because of the tendency of adverse shifts in the national economy to affect them disproportionately. For the past 50 years, unemployment among minority group members has been approximately twice that of nonminorities. Almost one third of minority families live below the poverty level. Nearly half (49%) of minority-group children younger than 6 years of age, compared with 18% of white children in the same age group, live in a poverty-level household (Nickens, 1990).

The public assistance programs (e.g., Medicaid, Medicare) that have sought to reduce the impact of this barrier have been tied to the economy and have thus suffered from recession, inflation, and increased costs of health care. A "two-class" system of health care has emerged as program cutbacks, health care costs, and inflation marginalize the poor and the near-poor. In many areas of the United States, health care for poor urban children is provided in public clinics, emergency rooms, and those hospitals remaining in the inner cities as private practitioners have moved to the suburbs.

These financial barriers have four predominant expressions:

1. The effect that money has on the ability of an individual to purchase health care
2. The adequacy of the care that a family can purchase (e.g., the benefits)
3. The effect of financial factors on the prioritization that health care receives within the family's needs structure
4. The environmental factors imposed by one's financial status (e.g., environmental hazards, safety)

Effect That Money Has on the Ability of an Individual to Purchase Health Care

No greater barrier affects the access of urban children to health care than the lack of financial resources to obtain it. This problem is further exacerbated by the fact that more than half of the population living in poverty (20.6% of all children in the United States live at or below the poverty level) are not eligible for federal health care assistance.

Commonly, health care is purchased through membership in one of a variety of health insurance plans. The lack of family membership in such a plan is a function of family income. Health care insurance has been demonstrated to have a direct impact on health services use. Uninsured persons visit doctors less often and have fewer hospitalizations than those who have insurance. This difference persists even when controlled for acuity of illness.

Eighty-seven million people in the United States have a significant problem with the adequacy of their ability to purchase insurance. Approximately 37 million are without any form of public or private health insurance. Two million of these are children under the age of 21. Another 50 million are underinsured; they have inadequate insurance protection for major hospital and medical expenses (Cleveland, 1991).

Lack of adequate health insurance results in an absence of a usual source of care and produces fragmented care that contains fewer preventive services. Routine counseling, anticipatory guidance, and early screening for developmental disabilities are health care and preventive modalities rarely used when a child's usual source of care is a different health care provider in a different health care facility at each visit. The AAP has stressed the importance of the availability of a "medical home" for every child to ensure that every child receives the best care (AAP Ad Hoc Task Force on the Definition of the Medical Home, 1992). This fragmentation has especially serious effects in urban environments because disadvantaged minority families are disproportionately burdened with excess disease, have fewer skills to negotiate a complicated health care bureaucracy, and face continual pressures to meet the needs of daily survival.

Adequacy of the Care
That a Family Can Purchase

Since 1966, Medicare for the elderly and Medicaid for those of low income have become major sources of health care reimbursement for many persons in poverty who live in urban U.S. communities. Since the 1970s and 1980s, however, fluctuating eligibility and benefits and declining provider reimbursement have made these programs less effective; this has been particularly true of Medicaid reimbursement for pediatric services. Medicaid expenditures increased from approximately $3.5 billion in 1968 to approximately $20 billion in 1979, and the number of Medicaid recipients more than doubled from 11.5 million in 1968 to 23.5 million in 1976. In the late 1970s and early 1980s, however, the eligibility restrictions reduced the population that those programs were designed to serve, whereas the number of persons in need of these services continued to increase.

Compounding the problem are additional restrictions to access to services caused by the refusal of many physicians to provide care for children eligible for Medicaid and other preventive programs (e.g., early periodic screening diagnosis and treatment). In discussing the scope of this problem with reference to minority children, the AAP cites the following contributory factors: (a) low reimbursement rates, (b) payment delays and administrative red tape, (c) bureaucratic obstacles (e.g., forms returned, clarifications, additional information), (d) lack of awareness of a population at need in the area, and (e) misperceptions of increased risk of medical liability (AAP, 1994).

An additional reimbursement issue is produced by fluctuations in eligibility. In its report, the AAP described the impact of these variations:

> Medicaid eligibility fluctuates at a rate health care providers may not be able to track. Physicians often render care to a patient only to learn that Medicaid eligibility status has only changed, thus denying reimbursement. The National Center for Health Services Research has estimated that up to 57% of Medicaid recipients are not covered continuously throughout the year. Since minority group children are four times as likely as all other children to have public insurance, they are disproportionately affected. Consequently, even with some form of insurance, minority group children have limited access to available health care. (AAP, 1994, p. 12)

Increasingly, states are turning to "managed care" as a solution to the inadequacies of this system. Persons who receive public health care insurance are being enrolled into one of several health

maintenance organizations (HMOs). These administrative entities
have contracted to provide a full range of preventive and direct care
benefits. As this trend becomes more prevalent in U.S. urban
centers, it is essential that the provision of care be monitored to
ensure that this solution does not degenerate into an iteration of
an already inadequate solution. In this regard, the managed care
system must be most carefully monitored to ensure that it responds
to the health care complexities created by the social issues that
complicate the lives of many children living in urban America.

Effect of Financial Factors on the
Prioritization That Health Care Receives
Within the Family's Needs Structure

The consequences of poverty create a prioritization of values in
which the need for basic survival supersedes all. Poverty is associated with a range of profound economic and social problems that
mitigates the importance of preventive care and treatment seeking
for minor illness. Indeed, even in families with employed adults,
health care seeking is often intolerably juxtaposed against the
requirements imposed by an employer. In addition, limited education and limited knowledge of health-related issues can lead to
delay in seeking health care, inattention to preventive services, and
poor compliance with medication and medical instructions. As the
urban poor are enrolled into managed care systems, provisions must
be made to mitigate these effects of poverty on the ability of
minority group parents to access the health care system effectively,
to use preventive health services, and to promote and maintain
healthy lifestyles for themselves and their children.

Environmental Factors Imposed
by One's Financial Status

Problems such as violence, environmental hazards (e.g., lead
exposure in substandard housing), accidents (e.g., automobiles in
crowded streets, unguarded windows in tall apartment buildings),
and safety (e.g., guns, knives), or at least the intensity of these
problems, is to a major extent a function of where a person lives.
In the inner city, the greater prevalence of these problems results

in a greater effect on the children in these regions and a greater effect on adverse outcomes.

Geographic Barriers

Health care is geographically barred when a given location lacks health care providers. This issue is particularly pressing in the poorer urban environments where declining Medicaid reimbursement rates and the declining number of physicians willing to serve "Medicaid patients" have contributed to the development of substandard, overcrowded health care facilities. These factors have also contributed to the overuse of emergency facilities as sources of primary care. The ultimate result is fragmented care that minimizes the opportunities for achievement of child health promotional goals (e.g., immunization, anticipatory child guidance). The problem has become critical in many cities. In certain areas of New York, for example, 97% of physicians will not see Medicaid recipients (AAP, 1994). Recently, this barrier has become more acute in the inner city as medical centers and hospitals, the traditional sources of care, have restricted services in response to the financial restraints imposed by managed care systems.

Language Barriers

Urban communities have become the first port of entry for many new inhabitants of the United States. These new inhabitants bring with them a cultural and language background that enriches the fabric of U.S. culture. In a health care setting, however, their relative lack of facility becomes a communicative impediment that significantly affects the quality of care they receive. This is not only an issue for non-English-speaking groups such as Latinos and Asians but also for subgroups of Asian Americans and subgroups of African Americans with different regional accents and dialects.

In the past, many urban medical facilities have responded with the development of a corps of bi- or trilingual translators specially trained to work in health care settings. Although these individuals are a critical adjunct to proper diagnosis, treatment, and health care guidance, their expense was usually not reimbursable. Accordingly, this service has suffered from efforts of urban health care facilities to reduce their cost to become more competitive in a managed care market.

Race and Ethnicity Barriers

The population of minority children is growing significantly faster than the population of nonminority children. By the year 2020, approximately 40% of school-age Americans will be minority-group children (Jones, 1991; Nickens, 1990). These minority children primarily live in urban environments. Race and ethnicity as barriers to health care are intuitively apparent but not easily understood. All people operate with a set of behaviors that is the outcome of multiple experiential, environmental, genetic, and cultural imputes. Consequentially, these patterns vary to some degree between persons of different racial and ethnic groups. Furthermore, these variations are apparent in all life settings. In this regard, they are particularly apparent in the ways people respond to the stress of the health care environment. Although the diversity of the United States produces a multiplicity of such cultural variations, the white or European culture is dominant because it represents the cultural heritage of the overwhelming majority of the people in the United States. This Eurocentric pattern is what is usually observed and, consequentially, is what is usually expected. It becomes the system-wide standard expected in the "normal condition." Consequently, all "normal persons" are expected to have the same health care capacities, resources, and access. If that does not exist, then they are relegated to an abnormal condition for which it is acceptable for them to receive substandard care. Therefore, higher infant mortality rates, lowered immunization rates, poorer nutrition, and increased incidence of environmental illness become acceptable because they exist within this substandard condition. Investigators have commented on the results of these institutional biases:

1. In their evaluation of the impact of budget deficits on health services for children, Blum and Blank (1991, p. 575) concluded, "Racism and classism make it easier to ignore children in poor neighborhoods; indeed, racism and classism may even make it more attractive to care for babies in the highly technological professional neonatal environment than in the communities to which they return."

2. The excess infant mortality and morbidity that exist among African American infants is, to some degree, related to issues that are specific to being "black in America." These issues include the racial discrimination and class distinctions that contribute to the environmental factors that adversely affect infants' and children's health. With specific reference to infant mortality, discrimination so profoundly affects a black woman's chance of being in poverty and of having limited access to care that it becomes a factor that may cause physiological reactions that result in preterm birth. In this regard, discrimination becomes an environmental stressor that influences a woman's susceptibility to having a poor pregnancy outcome in the same way that the physical environment influences susceptibility to disease (Krieger, Rowley, Herman, Avery, & Phillips, 1993).

3. For many years, members of minority groups have consistently (a) received fewer health care services per person, (b) received fewer services in relation to need, (c) received a greater proportion of services from a non-optimal or inappropriate source of care, (d) received services that are more often not corresponding to the type needed, and (e) experienced a greater proportion of unfavorable outcomes attributable to care (Wyszewianski & Donabedian, 1981).

Conclusion

The daily health and well-being of many of America's children can be told in the frequency of the occurrence of several adverse outcomes that have a uniquely higher frequency of occurrence in urban environments. These outcomes are related to environment, social pathologies, economics, race/ethnicity, and a series of other barriers that adversely affects health status. Society in general and the health care professions in particular cannot afford to allow these inequities to exist if we are to fulfill our moral obligations to the health and well-being of all Americans. In addition, managed care, especially Medicaid managed care, has added the preservation of health resources to the responsibilities of the primary health care provider system. The execution of this responsibility can only be achieved if the barriers to health care are removed for all persons. To this end, health care professionals require cultural sensitivity

320 CHILDREN AND YOUTH

and cultural competence training that will allow them to develop a facility with patient interactions within the cultural and ethnic groups found in their community.

Additionally, health policy must be redirected in such a way that multiple standards of care as outcomes of varying access to care are no longer acceptable; all citizens must have a right to the same high standard of care. To this end, the barriers that have differing impacts on differing communities must be ameliorated in each community to establish health access equality. This policy shift may require differing levels of health benefits that vary as a function of social economic status. Ultimately, in the case of the nation's children, it must guarantee that no child is sacrificed.

References

AAP Ad Hoc Task Force on the Definition of the Medical Home. (1992). The medical home. *Pediatrics, 90, 5.*
American Academy of Pediatrics (AAP). (1994). *Report of the AAP Task Force on Minority Children's Access to Pediatric Care.* Elk Grove Village, IL: Author.
Association for Children of New Jersey. (1993). *Report of the Association for Children of New Jersey.* Newark, NJ: Author.
Blum, B., & Blank, S. (1991). Children's services in an era of budget deficits. *American Journal of Diseases of Children, 145,* 575.
Cleveland, W. W. (1991). Redoing the health care quilt: Patches or whole cloth? *American Journal of Diseases of Children, 145,* 499-504.
Haley, A. (1976). *Roots.* Garden City, NY: Doubleday.
Jones, D. A. (1991). *Question of diversity.* Washington, DC: Association for the Care of Children's Health Network.
Keller, S. E., Bartlett, J. A., Schleifer, S. J., Johnson, R. L., Pinner, E., & Delaney, B. (1991). HIV infection and HIV-relevant sexual behaviors among a healthy inner-city heterosexual adolescent population in an endemic area of HIV. *Journal of Adolescent Health, 12,* 44-48.
Krieger, N., Rowley, D. L., Herman, A. A., Avery, B., & Phillips, M. T. (1993). Racism, sexism, and social class implications for studies of health disease and well-being. *American Journal of Preventive Medicine, 9*(Suppl.), 82-122.
National Center for Education in Maternal and Child Health. (1991). *A data book of child and adolescent injury.* Washington, DC: Children's Safety Network.
Nickens, H. W. (1990). Health promotion and disease prevention among minority populations. *Health Affairs,* 133-143.
U.S. Department of Health and Human Services (USDHHS). (1990). *Health status of the disadvantaged chart book.* Washington, DC: Government Printing Office.
Wyszewianski, L., & Donabedian, A. (1981). Equity in the distribution of quality care. *Medical Care, 21*(Suppl.), 28-56.

• *CHAPTER 13* •

Families and Health in the Urban Environment: Implications for Programs, Research, and Policy

SUZANNE FEETHAM

Major changes are being legislated for the health and social resources that affect many of our most vulnerable citizens—including children,[1] pregnant women, the disabled, and the elderly. This legislation also has a direct effect on families, particularly those that are impoverished. Changes in the provision of and access to health services are occurring at a time when it is becoming increasingly evident that morbidity and mortality for many diseases and conditions are directly linked to individual behaviors and that comprehensive, multifaceted interventions may be required to change these risk behaviors.

It is known that the initiation of risk behavior patterns begins in early childhood, and that these patterns are fostered by the environment (family, social, and economic) in which the child resides (National Institute of Nursing Research, 1993; National Institutes of Health, 1991; National Research Council, 1994). More specifically, since the 1960s, the burden of illness for adolescents has shifted from traditional disease etiology to behavior-related

AUTHOR'S NOTE: I would like to thank Mary Wendehack for her reviews and editing recommendations in the development of this chapter.

morbidity and mortality that result from sexually transmitted diseases, motor vehicle accidents, gun-related homicides and accidents, depression leading to suicides, and substance abuse (Carnegie Council on Adolescent Development, 1995; National Center for Health Statistics, 1995).

These trends have multiple implications for intervention programs, research, and policy. Because the family is described as the "primary social agent in the promotion of health and well-being" (World Health Organization, 1976, p. 17), knowledge of the family and its relationship to the health of its members is central to changing these trends. In this chapter, through the analysis of health research on children and families, recommendations are made for future intervention research that will inform health policy and lead to improved health of individual family members through health programs directed at the family unit.

Analysis of health programs for urban children shows that they usually lack three characteristics. First, to achieve the greatest and most lasting effect in changing health behaviors and health outcomes in children, programs must be comprehensive and focus on more than one health or risk behavior. Second, the interventions must be framed in the broader context of the community, which includes social, economic, and political environments. Third, for health programs to be most effective, they must be conducted in the context of the family (Carnegie Council on Adolescent Development, 1995; Doherty & Campbell, 1988; Dryfoos, 1990; Small, 1990). The necessity for including these characteristics stems from the recognition that the functioning of the family and its members is interdependent with broader social, economic, and political systems (Bronfenbrenner, 1986; Burr, Herrin, Day, Beutler, & Leigh, 1988; Feetham, 1984, 1991; Milio, 1970; Small, 1990).

In this chapter, the factors that constitute the family context are identified and the characteristics of effective family-based interventions are presented with descriptions from single research projects and comprehensive programs and integrative reviews of health-related programs for children. The purpose of this chapter is to raise the reader's awareness of the contributions of family-based programs to children's health and of the benefits of these programs for improved health outcomes for all family members. What is known about families and the characteristics of successful programs is summarized, along with recommendations for directions in program development, research, and policy.

Families and Health

The relationship among health, economic, and social conditions has long been known. Poverty and the conditions associated with it are identified as correlates to the 16-fold difference in asthma hospitalizations across the United States, with the highest prevalence in the poorest areas of cities (Gergen, Mullally, & Evans, 1988). During the 1980s, nationwide hospitalization rates increased 4.5% annually for persons with asthma who are younger than 17 years of age. New York City, with less than 3% of the U.S. population, accounted for around 6% of all asthma hospitalizations (American Academy of Pediatrics, 1994).

In the past 20 years, researchers have given increased attention to the influence of the family context on the health and illness of its members (Campbell & Patterson, 1995; Doherty & Campbell, 1988; Litman, 1974; Litman & Venters, 1979; National Institute of Nursing Research, 1993). Publications by Litman (Litman, 1974; Litman & Venters, 1979) are cited as pivotal in the increase of research on families and their role in the health of family members. As evidence of continuing attention to this issue, during the past decade, a significant amount of research has been published in integrated review articles on the relationships between family characteristics and health (Campbell, 1986; Doherty & Campbell, 1988; Feetham, 1984, 1991; Fisher, Terry, & Ransom, 1990; Gilliss, 1983; Turk & Kerns, 1985).

Investigators have observed that research strongly supports the relationship between family structure and functioning, and the health-related outcomes for children (Campbell & Patterson, 1995; Gilliss & Davis, 1993; Kazak, 1989; Patterson & Garwick, 1994; Pokorni, Katz, & Long, 1991). In a recent review of the effectiveness of family interventions in the treatment of physical illness, however, Campbell and Patterson (1995) noted that although researchers demonstrate the family's strong influence on physical health, there is less evidence of the effectiveness of family-based interventions.

Research on health promotion also contributes to the understanding of the role of the family in the health of its members. The relationship between family lifestyles and health behaviors and those adopted by the children in the family has been well documented. Research has shown that health risk factors cluster in families because members often have similar diets, activity patterns, behaviors such as smoking and alcohol abuse, and a common physical environment (Campbell & Patterson, 1995; Carnegie Council on Adolescent Development, 1995; National Institute of Nursing Research, 1993).

Research on the family's impact on health has some common characteristics. For example, although the relationship between families and health is well documented, Doherty and Campbell noted in 1988 (and it is still apparent today) that much of the existing research on family and health is not grounded in theory and that the research does not test the components of these relationships to determine their direct effect on health outcomes. Historically, this research has been derived from a disease model, so the onset of illness has been the independent variable and the consequences to the individual family members or the family the dependent variable. This model suggests a linear causality between the illness or problem within the family and the outcomes or consequences to the family. More recently, research has begun to address the interdependence of multiple variables affecting the family and its members.

Health

There is a consistent concept across many definitions of health—that it is a dynamic state of being in which the developmental and behavioral potential of an individual is realized to the fullest extent possible (Broering, 1993; Irwin & Vaughan, 1988; Office of Technology Assessment [OTA], 1991; Pender, 1990). Health promotion builds on this concept and is interpreted as actualizing the health potential of the individual (Huch, 1991), with the expectation that the individual will perform the actions to fulfill this potential (Igoe, 1991). Effective interventions in health promotion incorporate an understanding of what health means to individual family members, to the family as a unit, and how the environment influences their health actions. These health promotion actions occur at the individual, family, community, and broader social system levels (Carnegie Council on Adolescent Development, 1995; National Institute of Nursing Research, 1993).

Health Promotion

Health promotion is a multidimensional concept that is on a continuum ranging from disease prevention to optimal health and that emphasizes physical capabilities and social and personal resources. Most causes of mortality and morbidity in children and adolescents are a result of behavior and lifestyle and technically could be prevented through behavior change (OTA, 1991). Health-promotion actions are the primary means of achieving this change.

The advantage to focusing on health promotion is that a disease-prevention approach tends to blame the victim and is limited to the reduction or elimination of specific health-compromising behaviors. Health promotion is more inclusive than prevention because, in addition to risk reduction, it focuses on health-enhancing behaviors and views behavior as integrated within the environment (Guthrie, Loveland-Cherry, Frey, & Dielman, 1994). This environmental concept is also consistent with Breslow (1983), who stated that this concept of health promotion will require social action to strengthen individuals and families by changing societal conditions and institutions.

Health-promotion activities occur at the level of the individual, family, community, and larger social institutions. Conducting such activities in schools, work sites, health care agencies, and communities will extend benefits to all persons and is critical to successful health promotion in urban families. Coordination and collaboration among all related systems, including health care, education, and social support systems, are essential to the success of this approach (Daka-Mulwanda, Thornburg, Filbert, & Klein, 1995).

Although progress is being made in understanding how such factors as health attitudes of the family, behaviors, social norms, peer pressure, and the media affect health in children, there is still much to be learned. It is particularly important to learn how knowledge of cognitive, emotional, genetic, and social influences can be transferred to the health practices of children.

The research and programs included in this review are categorized as health promotion to demonstrate the potential of this framework in managing the health of urban families. For example, programs for the care of children with asthma may be more successful if interventions are targeted toward overall health promotion and not limited to the treatment of the condition. In addition, the health-promotion framework provides a broader context for interventions.

Definition of Family

No universal definition of family has been adopted by family scientists and the clinical disciplines that work with or study families. How the family is defined determines the factors that will be examined to evaluate their effects on individual family members and the family unit. When examining health in the context of the family, the family constitutes the group of persons acting together to perform functions required for the survival, growth, and health of family members.

Burr et al. (1988) added to the definition of family through their discussion of the characteristics that differentiate the family from other social institutions. They concluded that knowledge of family has been limited by research and program outcomes that do not distinguish the family from other social institutions, such as governments, religions, and educational systems. They also concluded that when the family is viewed strictly as a social institution, biological, environmental, nutritional, and other phenomena are not addressed. The unique dimensions that make families different from other social institutions are their:

Generational relationships and familial memories
Unique sets of rules, standards, ethics, priorities, and processes
Unique sets of aspirations, feelings, temporal orientations, achievements, and interactions
Cultural influences (Burr et al., 1988, pp. 185-210)

These unique dimensions affect family functions, and for a family-based intervention to be effective, they must be considered in program planning and research.

Definition of Family Functions

It is generally accepted that family functions include the socialization, development, and well-being of its members. Specific functions include providing basic resources and safety, socializing family members to perform in the larger social environment, and serving as a mediator between family members and the broader environment. Safety functions include not only protection from harm but also, as noted by Small (1990), protection of the physical, psychological, spiritual, and cultural integrity of family members from threats by the natural and social environments.

The family functions identified by family scientists have tended to be psychological rather than societal or economic functions. In an analysis of research constructs and measures of successful families, only 1 of 15 groups of family theorists explicitly included a function related to the health of the family or its members (Krysan, Moore, & Zill, 1990). The omission of the health function is one reason for the lack of attention to the family in health-related programs and research.

It is well documented that many factors can deter a family from fulfilling its basic functions and meeting the needs of its members. These deterrents include health problems of family members and inadequate social and economic resources, which are confounded for urban families that also lack safe neighborhoods along with inadequate and unsafe transportation and housing. A primary goal of family-based, health-related interventions is to increase the ability of the family to fulfill its basic functions.

Family Context

Evaluations of health programs frequently result in recommendations for the inclusion of a family context in future work. What constitutes such a family context, however, is not described. The constructs that support a family context from an illness perspective are that (a) the family constitutes perhaps the most important social context within which illness is resolved, (b) interactions within the family system affect the health outcomes of family members, (c) progression of disease and disability can be linked with the family, and (d) patterns of health service use are related to family structure and health beliefs (Wright & Leahey, 1994).

Constructs that underlie health-promotion programs within a family context are that (a) more than one serious health risk behavior tends to occur in the same individual, (b) risk behaviors often have interrelated antecedents in early childhood and can even be intergenerational, (c) there is interdependence among and between circumstances in an individual child's life, (d) behaviors seen in one individual may be evident in other family members of the same and previous generations, and (e) the activities of an individual are interdependent with his or her family and the environment in which they live (National Institute of Nursing Research, 1993; National Institutes of Health, 1991).

To clarify the concept of family context further, Coleman (1988, 1990) suggested that the assessment of family context could be enhanced through the recognition of two constructs: human capital and social capital. *Human capital* is defined as those resources that originate in the skills and knowledge of the family. *Social capital* is defined as those resources that derive from the quality of relationships among family members. Feetham's (1984, 1991) criteria for the research of families can be used to provide direction for distinguishing the context of family-based interventions from other interventions. In family-based interventions, knowledge of family structure and functions is used in the assessment, intervention, and measurement of the outcomes of the intervention.

Although identified as an important component/predictor of the success of health-promotion programs for children and families, the inclusion of family members or the family context in such programs has been limited. For example, in a review of more than 100 programs reported as successful in changing high-risk behaviors of delinquency, substance abuse, teen pregnancy, and school failure in adolescents, Dryfoos (1990) found that 60% were school-based interventions, 30% were community-based or multiagency programs, and only about 10% included a family-based intervention. Although many of the school- and community-based programs did include recognition of the family context, the primary focus of the intervention was not the family system. Although a goal of the Maternal and Child Health Bureau's *Healthy Tomorrows Partnership for Children* program is to assist children and their families to achieve their developmental potential, many of the 54 projects in the program are categorical and focus only on children (National Center for Education in Maternal and Child Health, 1995).

For a program to be classified as having a family context, it must recognize the family environment as a significant variable affecting the outcomes of health-related interventions for the members. Programs meeting this criterion can be conducted in any setting, including the home, and can include either an individual family member or all members of the family (Szapocznik, Kurtines, Foote, Perez-Vidal, & Hervis, 1983; Wright & Leahey, 1994; Wright, Watson, & Bell, 1996).

Many factors are responsible for the paucity of programs conducted in the context of the family. One factor may be the complexity of the methodological and measurement requirements for effective problem assessment. Another factor may be that assessment and intervention tend to occur at the personal health level (individual family member or family), whereas the problem is identified through epidemiological methods at the public health level. The result is a disconnection between the personal and the public health perspectives, and scientists or practitioners from one perspective may not see the merit of another perspective. In addition, program teams may not include expertise in family theory, research, and clinical issues. Finally, the family context may not be recognized as an essential factor in programs directed to the health of children.

When the family context is addressed in program development and research, different theoretical frameworks are used, different questions are asked, and different measures and analyses are required.

Research on Urban Families and Health

A multifaceted process was used and several factors were considered to identify the programs and research discussed in this chapter. Several database searches were conducted by using the terms *family* and *health*. From these searches, abstracts were reviewed for the relevancy of the publications to the health of urban children and their families. References from the selected articles were also used to identify other possible reports of research or programs focusing on the health of urban children and their families. From these searches, more than 200 publications (including refereed journals and fugitive literature) were analyzed for their contribution to knowledge of the health of urban children and their families. Some research or programs that were categorical and did not focus on families were retained if they contributed knowledge to the characteristics of successful interventions and/or included recommendations for family-based programs. These categorical programs include programs directed to one behavior or condition such as drug abuse, teen pregnancy, or improving home safety practices for children (Dryfoos, 1990; Newcomb & Bentler, 1989; Small, 1990).

The results of this process are reported in two ways. First, some programs have been selected as exemplars of health-related interventions conducted in the context of urban families. These programs, or research related to critical health issues for urban children and their families, are presented as exemplars to guide future research and the development of intervention programs. Characteristics of interventions that achieved success in sustaining improved health outcomes are also identified. Second, an analysis across 16 reviews of child health programs is presented to identify the characteristics of family-based interventions. Throughout the chapter, research theory and methods for meeting the challenges in family-based intervention research are described.

Exemplars of Family-Based
Health Interventions

Low-Birth-Weight Infants
and Their Families

The incidence of giving birth to low-birth-weight (LBW) infants is highest in minority women and women living in poverty. Interventions to improve the health and developmental outcomes of these infants serve as one example of family-based health promotion programs and demonstrate the need for the early initiation of these programs.

A transitional care program developed by nurse scientists at the University of Pennsylvania has been documented to improve health outcomes of at-risk populations following discharge from the hospital. The first in a series of studies examined the outcomes for LBW infants who received follow-up care in the home by advanced practice nurses (APN-Master's prepared nurse). Of note is that earlier hospital discharge, along with the support of an APN, can result in enhanced parent-infant interaction, a potential reduction in child abuse and foster care, and increased support of the family unit (Brooten et al., 1988; Brooten et al., 1986; Donahue et al., 1994). This family intervention to support the development of LBW infants is a clear example of a health-promotion activity.

A more comprehensive project with a longer follow-up for mothers of high-risk infants has also shown improved outcomes (Olds, Henderson, Chamberlin, & Tatelbaum, 1986; Olds, Henderson, Tatelbaum, & Chamberlin, 1986, 1988). This project, based on an ecological model, recognizes the multiple factors affecting high-risk, young families. The intervention in this project is based on evidence that parental behaviors have significant influence on the health of high-risk infants. Nurses delivered the comprehensive intervention in the home. The enrollment of 400 women during the prenatal period, a time known to contribute to high retention of subjects following the delivery of the infant, was key to this program. Follow-up continued for one group through the first 2 years after the birth of the infant. Significant differences observed in the experimental group included fewer emergency room visits and lower incidences of child abuse and neglect. Mothers in the intervention group had an 82% better employment history and 43% fewer pregnancies. Adolescent mothers returned to school more quickly than the control group. This study demonstrated a cost-effective program with improved outcomes to the mothers and infants (Olds, Henderson, & Kitzman, 1994; Olds, Henderson, Phelps, Tatelbaum, & Chamberlin, 1993).

Other family-based interventions in urban families with high-risk, low-birth-weight, and full-term infants have demonstrated similar results. To be effective, these programs required that the nurse or other home visitor who was conducting the intervention facilitate the family in responding to crises and survival problems, in addition to focusing on the infant (Hardy & Streett, 1989; Meyer et al., 1994). For example, if the family had no heat or food, an intervention to teach the mother about her infant would be less effective until these survival needs of the family were met. These studies demonstrate the complexity of issues that must be considered with at-risk urban families and show that multidimensional interventions conducted over time are required for positive outcomes for the infants and their families.

Smoking Prevention and Cessation

Cigarette smoking is a leading cause of health problems in the United States. It is estimated that 3,000 teenagers begin smoking each day (Pierce, Fiore, Novotny, Hatziandreu, & Davis, 1989). In their review, Doherty and Allen (1994) reported a high correlation between parental smoking behaviors and the initiation of smoking in adolescence. Parental smoking behaviors were also reported as a significant predictor of attendance for an education program for parents of children with asthma. Fish, Wilson, Latini, and Starr (1996) reported that, in a study of 178 families, non-attendance rates for the educational program were 24%, 42%, and 78% in nonsmoking, one-smoker, and two-or-more-smoker families, respectively. Families with two or more smokers also showed a tendency to deny the child's asthma.

The limited success of smoking-cessation education programs is thought to be due to multiple factors affecting the initiation and cessation of smoking. Programs targeted to children should consider the family and social context to increase the potential for success of the programs (Campbell & Patterson, 1995). Doherty and Allen (1994) urge that family functioning be given a high priority in health research related to the onset of smoking and that family factors be addressed in planning antismoking programs for children. Because of the multiple factors affecting risk behaviors and families, smoking prevention must be combined with other health-related programs, such as those directed at nutrition and physical fitness and exercise.

Families With Children With Asthma

Asthma is a multifactorial condition with interactions among genetic, immune, and environmental factors. African-American children are more likely than Caucasian children to have asthma (4.4% vs. 2.5%). Social and environmental factors are known to exert a measurable influence on the incidence of asthma and account for much of the racial and economic difference in the prevalence rates. Poverty status, maternal cigarette smoking, family size, size of the home, low birth weight, and maternal age are all associated with the occurrence of asthma in urban African-American children (Gergen et al., 1988; Weitzman, Gortmaker, & Sobol, 1990).

The diagnosis and treatment of children with this condition requires consideration of family variables. Traditionally, family interaction has been seen as one antecedent to the incidence of asthma episodes. Recent studies challenge this assumption. Researchers have found that, contrary to studies conducted retrospectively, prospective studies of families at risk for asthma demonstrate that family interactions are affected once the onset of asthma occurs, rather than being an antecedent to respiratory symptoms (Campbell & Patterson, 1995; Gustafsson, Bjorksten, & Kjellman, 1994; Klinnert, Mrazek, & Mrazek, 1994; Wissow, Gittelsohn, Szklo, Starfield, & Mussman, 1988).

Research conducted with urban families of children with asthma demonstrates the interaction of the multiple factors affecting their outcomes (Butz et al., 1994). From a random selection of 42 schools in two Eastern cities, 392 children were identified as having asthma (approximately 10% of the children). Trained lay community health workers (CHWs) were able to reach 88% of the families of these children to obtain baseline health and family data (see Figure 13.1). Although the treatment of asthma usually requires close medical follow-up, 27% of the families reported no primary care provider, and only a few reported specific asthma care—although 87% reported being on medications. Even families reporting primary care providers showed a significant incidence of the misuse and misunderstanding of the medications (Huss et al., 1994; Malveaux & Fletcher-Vincent, 1995). This lack of adequate health care for children with asthma has also been reported by Wissow et al. (1988).

In addition, 43% of the children had been admitted to the hospital, and 84% had been treated in an emergency room, with 56% having been treated in the past 6 months. The average number of school days missed in the past year related to asthma was 9.8 (Malveaux & Fletcher-Vincent, 1995).

Adapting the physical environment of the child to limit exposure to allergens is an important component of care. The ability to change the environment was limited for many of these families: 73% were renting their homes, and 61.5% reported smokers in the household (Huss et al., 1994; Malveaux & Fletcher-Vincent, 1995). As reported by Fish et al. (1996), the number of smokers in the home is predictive of parental participation in asthma education and the degree to which the asthma is recognized in the child.

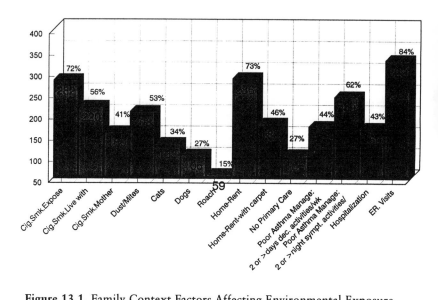

Figure 13.1. Family Context Factors Affecting Environmental Exposure of 392 Urban Minority Children With Asthma

SOURCE: Butz, Malveaux, Eggleston, Thompson, Huss, Kolodner, and Rand (1995); Butz, Malveaux, Eggleston, Thompson, Schneider, Weeks, Huss, Murigande, and Rand (1994); Huss, Rand, Butz, Eggleston, Murigande, Thompson, Schneider, Weeks, and Malveaux (1994); Malveaux and Fletcher-Vincent (1995).

The family factors identified in this study have led to a second study in which the lay CHWs have been augmented with home health nurses and the length of the intervention has been extended from 5 months to 2 years. The nurses respond to the families' questions about the management of the illness and serve as case managers to provide linkages between the families and the multiple agencies such as primary care providers, teachers, and social services (A. M. Butz, personnel communication, May 21, 1996).

The cumulative effect of poor medication management, inadequate access to care, emergency and hospital admissions, school days missed, and effects on family interaction documents the challenges that asthma presents to families. Family-based interventions need to provide opportunities for improving problem-solving capabilities and the ability to determine strategies to respond to situations related to the child's condition. These studies of children with asthma demonstrate that improved health outcomes result from comprehensive, family-based interventions and explain why single-dimension, short-term programs do not achieve sustained improvement in these children. Although single-intervention research can add to the knowledge of particular components/factors affecting health outcomes in families, these programs have significant limitations for urban families with complex social and health needs.

Gergen states that the complex, multifactorial problem of increasing asthma morbidity, especially in minority communities, will not be solved by single-dimensional programs and that multidimensional programs appropriately targeted to the individuals and their families are required (Gergen & Goldstein, 1995). The 10% incidence of asthma in these urban, school-age children is considered representative (Malveaux & Fletcher-Vincent, 1995). It can also be surmised that the problems reported in these families are also representative and reinforce the significance of asthma as a national concern for children and families.

Substance Abuse

Substance abuse is a significant public health problem affecting individuals, families, communities, and society. Substance use is also associated with other problems resulting in increased morbidity and mortality in urban children, including accidents and violence (Millstein, 1988). Although considerable research has demonstrated the connection between family-related factors and substance abuse, little research has been conducted to demonstrate the efficacy of family-based programs. More commonly, interventions are conducted as single-dimensional at the level of primary prevention, with short, time-limited educational programs for groups of children in schools and other community settings (Anderson, 1996; Gloss, 1995).

Although various family-based approaches to reducing or eliminating drug use and abuse have been tested, they represent only 4.1% of published studies related to children and adolescents

(Kazdin, Bass, Ayers, & Rodgers, 1990; Liddle & Dakof, 1995). Although reporting small samples and some measurement problems, the advantages of family-based drug treatment for adolescents over other approaches are evident from the findings of 10 controlled studies reviewed by Liddle and Dakof (1995). The work of Szapocznik and colleagues is considered a landmark in establishing family interventions as an effective treatment for adolescent drug abuse (Liddle & Dakof, 1995). These investigators have conducted a family-based program of research during the past two decades and have made significant contributions to clinical, theoretical, and measurement issues in research with high-risk adolescents and their families. They report a change in abstinence rates from 7% at admission to 80% at termination (Szapocznik et al., 1983; Szapocznik, Kurtines, Foote, Perez-Vidal, & Hervis, 1986; Szapocznik et al., 1988). A basic premise of their program of research is the recognition that therapeutic interventions must be responsive to the constant changes in societal conditions (Szapocznik et al., in press; Szapocznik, Kurtines, Santisteban, & Rio, 1990; Szapocznik et al., 1993).

While addressing the issue of acculturation, these scientists have moved from a single-culture intervention in Hispanic adolescents to a multicultural, intergenerational, conflict-resolution intervention. Family effectiveness training in the form of a 12-lesson psychoeducational modality has been developed to enhance bicultural skills in all family members. A measurement of structural family change has been developed.

Two common problems in clinical work with high-risk families have been (a) difficulties in implementing family therapy techniques and (b) the inability to engage family members. Frequently, only one family member may seek resolution of family issues, and often even the family member who initiates contact with a resource may not continue past the initial consultation. Szapocznik and his colleagues have tested two program arms—a model for one-person family therapy and a model for engaging hard-to-reach families (Santisteban et al., in press; Szapocznik, Hervis, Kurtines, & Spencer, 1984).

The future goals of the team are to (a) test that this program is an effective replicable model; (b) refine the interventions through further testing of the structural ecosystem approach, recognizing that all social contexts are embedded within a complex set of cultural influences; and (c) test the model with other populations, such as families with children who have health problems, HIV-seropositive women, and families with adult children who have disabilities (Szapocznik et al., in press; Szapocznik et al., 1993).

Although health promotion outcomes are difficult to measure, clearly enough evidence has been accumulated to justify greatly increased attention to family-based health promotion programs and the expenditure of human and financial resources for these programs at the community, state, and national level.

Characteristics of Family-Based Programs

Eight categories of characteristics were identified from the analysis of 16 reviews of child health programs. The eight categories were determined by the author following the content analysis of characteristics reported as contributing to the success of health programs for children. The components addressed by the various programs are described for each category as a basis for recommendations for health interventions for urban families and their children (see Table 13.1 for a summary). Although many of the reviews did not include specific family-based interventions, these characteristics of successful programs apply to family-based programs. The eight categories of characteristics are interdependent; for example, to address the broader social systems, the program would be comprehensive (provide many health services) and would need collaboration across multiple agencies and services. A significant component of the program would be to ensure the active inclusion (both what is and what should be) of the family and its members within these systems.

The characteristics of successful programs are not specific to a target group or issue, such as the prevention and reduction of risk behaviors in the cases of smoking, poor nutritional intake, or exposure to HIV. The characteristics are consistent across programs whether they are age related (school-age), behavior related (abstinence), or targeted risk groups (the poor, HIV/AIDS). Substantial data, based on analysis of the reviews, support the idea that these characteristics are critical if sustained change is to occur.

(text continued on page 343)

TABLE 13.1 Characteristics of Health-Related Programs for Children and Adolescents

Program review	Review/ Program Focus	Family Context*	Interventions Appropriate to the Target Groups	Compre-hensive/ Multiple Services	Research and Theory	Broader Social Context	Time Factors	Environ-mental Support	Policy
Schorr, L. B. (1988). *Within our reach: Breaking the cycle of disadvantage.* New York: Anchor.	Disadvantage	F R	X	X		X		X	X
Millstein, S. G. (1988). *The potential of school-linked center to promote adolescent health and development* (Working Paper for Carnegie Council on Adolescent Development). Washington, DC: Carnegie Corporation of New York.	School-based health	F R	X	X	X	X			X
Dryfoos, J. G. (1990). *Adolescents at risk.* New York: Oxford University Press.	100 studies categorical—risk	R	X	X	X	X	X	X	X

338

Reference	Description	F						
Small, S. A. (1990). *Preventive programs that support families with adolescents* (Working Paper for Carnegie Council on Adolescent Development). Washington, DC: Carnegie Corporation of New York.	41 preventive programs—families & adolescents	F	X	X	X	X	X	X
Kirby, D. (1991). School-based clinics: Research results and their implications for future research methods. *Evaluation and Program Planning, 4,* 35-47.	6 studies		X		X			X
Kirby, D., Short, L., Collins, J., Rugg, D., Kolbe, L., Howard, M., Miller, B., Sonenstein, F., & Zabin, L. S. (1994). School-based programs to reduce sexual risk behaviors: A review of effectiveness. *Public Health Reports, 109,* 339-360.	23 studies of school-based clinics & sexual behavior							
Mortimer, A. M. (1993). *Consultation on after-school programs.* Washington, DC: Carnegie Corporation of New York.	After-school programs	F	X	X	X			X

TABLE 13.1 *Continued*

Program review	Review/Program focus	Family context*	Interventions appropriate to the target groups	Comprehensive/Multiple services	Research and theory	Broader social context	Time factors	Environmental support	Policy
Weissberg, R. P., & Elias, M. J. (1993). Enhancing young people's social competence and health behavior: An important challenge for educators, scientists, policymakers, and funders. *Applied and Preventive Psychology, 2,* 179-190.	School-based health programs	I	X	X	X	X	X	X	X
Christopher, F. S. (1995). Adolescent pregnancy prevention. *Family Relations, 44*(4), 384-391.	Pregnancy prevention		X	X	X	X			
Kelly, J. A. (1995). Advances in HIV/AIDS education and prevention. *Family Relations, 44,* 345-352.	HIV prevention	R						X	

340

Reference	Category	Type							
Campbell, T. L., & Patterson, J. M. (1995). The effectiveness of family interventions in the treatment of physical illness. *Journal of Marital and Family Therapy, 21*(4), 545-584.	Families & children with physical illness	F R					X	X	
Liddle, H. W., & Dakof, G. A. (1995). Efficacy of family therapy for drug abuse: Promising but not definitive. *Journal of Marital and Family Therapy, 21*(4), 511-543.	Drug abuse	F R	X			X	X	X	X
National Center for Education in Maternal and Child Health. (1995). *Healthy tomorrows partnership for children: Abstracts of active projects FY 1995.* Arlington, VA: Author.	Child health	F	X				X		X
Nelson, D. W. (1995). *The path of most resistance: Reflection on lessons learned from new futures.* Baltimore: Annie E. Casey Foundation.	Health programs				X		X		X

TABLE 13.1 *Continued*

Program review	Review/ Program focus	Family context*	Interventions appropriate to the target groups	Compre-hensive/ Multiple services	Research and theory	Broader social context	Time factors	Environ-mental support	Policy
Daka-Mulwanda, V., Thornburg, K. R., Filbert, L., & Klein, T. (1995). Collaboration of services for children and families: A synthesis of recent research and recommendations. *Family Relations, 44,* 219-223.	Services for children & families	F	X	X	X	X			X
Bogenschneider, K. (1996). An ecological risk/protective theory for building prevention programs, policies, and community capacity to support youth. *Family Relations, 45,* 127-138.	5 models for youth prevention programs	F R	X	X	X	X	X	X	

F: Family-based intervention; R: Recommended family-based intervention; I: Inferred family-based intervention.

Family Context

Considerable research has shown that the family has a strong influence on lifestyle and that health behaviors are developed, maintained, or changed within the family. Nevertheless, there is a paucity of research on family-based, health-related interventions and service programs that incorporate a family-based context.

Although most of the reviews identified the family as a factor in successful health programs for children, few gave specific examples of inclusion of families in any phase of the program from initial assessment through implementation. Programs that do not address the perspective of the family may have reduced participation and less effect (Millstein, 1988; Small, 1990).

Who constitutes the family is another consideration. Dilworth-Anderson (1989) urged attention to the different family forms. Although family functions remain constant, how they are performed and the resources they require are affected by different family forms. For example, whereas single-parent households may need assistance from external sources to meet the caregiving needs of a child with asthma, the two-parent family may have the flexibility and support to handle the care, and the multigenerational family may be able to reach beyond the immediate family system for support (Campbell & Patterson, 1995; Dilworth-Anderson, 1989).

Frequently, the family is identified as an antecedent of risk behaviors in children. Mortimer (1993) suggested that involving parents at all levels in school-based programs could result in more effective partnerships to reduce risk behaviors. In summarizing 100 successful programs, Dryfoos (1990) was more direct and suggested targeting outreach to parents through home visits and providing them with specifically defined roles such as classroom aides and advisory board members. As was demonstrated in the research of low-birth-weight infants and children with asthma, the most effective programs used health professionals (nurses) who work directly with families in the home and provide intensive interventions for problems that extend beyond the care of the target child.

Interventions conducted in the context of the family can occur in any setting and with one or more family members. For example, applying what is known about the family variables affecting the care of urban children with asthma, any intervention would include obtaining information on the family's history of allergies, living environment, and smoking exposure to the child.

Interventions Appropriate to the Target Groups

Many concepts were described in the reports related to expectations for target groups. Although it may be assumed that programs would be developmentally appropriate and sensitive to the culture and ethnic orientation of the target groups, these concepts are not central to many programs. To design relevant programs, children and their families should be involved in program planning. Family members should serve on program advisory boards and be integral to the evaluation of the programs. The work of Szapocznik and colleagues demonstrates the process for developing culturally and ethnically relevant family-based interventions (Szapocznik et al., 1990; Szapocznik et al., in press; Szapocznik et al., 1993).

Historically, research has focused on pathologies and deficits in the functioning of minority families, rather than on the range of family experiences. As a result, little is known about the strengths and processes that enable families with limited economic and social resources to meet their family functions. Frameworks that are culturally sensitive, recognize varying family structures, and contribute to the knowledge of building family strengths are needed (Bogenschneider, 1996; Dilworth-Anderson, 1989).

Intensive individualized interventions are reported to be more successful than nonspecific group interventions (Butz et al., 1994; Meyer et al., 1994; Olds et al., 1993; Olds et al., 1988). Although these programs may be more costly initially, they may have a better cost-benefit ratio than group interventions that have no sustained effect on health outcomes. Conducting these interventions in the context of the family also increases the potential for sustained change because the behavior would be supported in the "real world" of the child (Anderson, 1996; Dryfoos, 1990; Hardy & Streett, 1989).

When considering the target group, school-based programs appear to be the logical setting for health and family-based interventions. Dryfoos (1990) and Small (1990), however, have noted that some of these programs do not provide developmentally appropriate or individual interventions and that only a few programs address the context of the family. In several programs, contact with the families was limited to parental permission for the child to receive health services. Mortimer (1993) recommended that, for these programs to be appropriate to children and their families, the students and families should be involved in the development and evaluation of the programs.

Comprehensive/Multiple Services

Health programs targeted to one condition or behavior are known to be less effective because risk behaviors often occur in clusters. Comprehensive school-based programs can be designed to integrate health services, health teaching, and community-based outreach. Weissberg and Elias (1993), however, reported that although there is increasing agreement about the need for comprehensive, long-term (K-12) school programs for students and their families, there is little evidence of such programs. What is occurring are multiple categorical programs targeted to specific groups or behaviors with little or no integration among the programs (Dryfoos, 1990; Weissberg & Elias, 1993).

Reviews of categorical programs related to reducing pregnancy in adolescents have similar findings (Christopher, 1995; Kirby, 1991; Kirby et al., 1994). The programs reporting higher levels of success in changing pregnancy-related behaviors in adolescents were multidimensional programs that went beyond limited contact with the targeted youth and made use of community networks. Nevertheless, parents were only included in the outreach efforts of one program (Vincent, Clearie, & Schluchter, 1987).

Research and Theory

One reason for the perpetuation of unsuccessful programs is that empirical evidence from earlier programs and scientific studies is not applied in the development of new programs. Although the research on health in children and families may have methodological problems, considerable knowledge has been generated that can be applied to intervention programs, as well as used to inform policymakers.

The application of intervention theory and a five-stage model for prevention program development can contribute to advancing the science and improving the quality and outcomes of family-based health programs (Christopher, 1995; Coie et al., 1993; Dumka, Roosa, Michaels, & Suh, 1995). The five-stage process of problem analysis, program design, pilot testing, advanced testing, and dissemination has recursive, or feedback, components for each stage. Attention to these components for the development of intervention programs would result in program developers and scientists determining the perspective and needs from members of the target group, planning for the introduction into the community, developing recruitment and retention strategies, and determining outcome measures by using the appropriate theory and research findings (Dumka et al., 1995).

Broader Social Context

A frequent recommendation emanating from the reviews analyzed for this chapter is that programs should address the realities/context of the broader social system. For example, a consistent theme is the difficulty in effecting and sustaining change in the behavior of individuals, let alone families and communities. It is acknowledged that, to have an opportunity for change, programs must be multidimensional and that communities, in and of themselves, cannot alter poor educational, social, and health outcomes (Breslow, 1983). Nelson (1995) reported that change strategies must include social-capital and economic development initiatives that target entire communities. This concept also applies to school-based programs, for which to optimize the students' potential for learning, their social, emotional, and physical well-being must be addressed (Dryfoos, 1990).

The work of Milio (1970) serves as a classic example of a program designed within the broader social context. As a public health nurse in Detroit, she determined that her work with families would be limited unless the families were seen within the broader social, economic, and political context of their lives. From this perspective, she worked with officials from the city, the Visiting Nurses Association, and the Public Health Department to establish the Moms and Tots Center. In contrast with traditional public health services, the center provided comprehensive services so that family members received preventive health care and social services and participated in Head Start programs. The concepts implemented by Milio match recommendations in more recent reviews of health programs (Dryfoos, 1990; Millstein, 1988; Small, 1990), such as incorporation of community groups in the development of the center, inclusion of all family members in the delivery of health services, and collaboration with policymakers to build ongoing funding into the program. Milio also recognized that, to improve outcomes for children and their families, social and economic factors must be addressed concurrently with health concerns.

The success of this program is evident in its protection by the community and survival during the Detroit riots of 1967 and its continuation into the 1980s when the center was closed because of cutbacks in federal funding. At that time, some programs, such as the day care, were discontinued, and others were dispersed among other city programs. Those programs funded through Medicaid continue but not at the community-based setting (N. Milio, personal communication, June 11, 1996). Today, two programs applying the concepts used by Milio are being conducted to serve the same area of Detroit. In contrast with the Moms and Tots Center, however, these two programs—INREACH (Fry-McComish, Lawlor, & Laken, 1996) and Family Road (Lienert, 1995)—are conducted from traditional health care settings.

Time Factors

Program timing has two primary dimensions. First, interventions must be implemented prior to the assumption of risk behaviors. For health behaviors, this must occur in early childhood because many risk behaviors are well established in the early school years. Second, interventions must be administered over an extended period of time to sustain changes in health behaviors. For example, Weissberg and Elias (1993) proposed school-based health programs that are integrated with educational programs from kindergarten through high school. School- and family-based interventions that target the middle and high school years are too late for many behaviors, including smoking, substance abuse, and sexual activity.

Environmental Support

Societal norms and public policy contribute to the environment of children by the kinds of behaviors they reinforce. The activities that children observe in their communities and in the media influence patterns of initiation or abstinence. In describing school-based programs, Small (1990) cautioned that health programs must teach skills applicable to the "real life" of the children. Programs presented in isolation without reinforcement in a child's environment have little chance to be sustained. For example, Anderson (1996) reported in a study of incarcerated female adolescents that although the young women proclaimed commitments for sobriety and the discontinuation of other risk behaviors following their release, they also expressed concern that they would not be able to maintain these behaviors when they encountered the same people and situations that originally led them to substance abuse.

Recommendations for enhancing the environmental support for healthy behaviors are as diverse as the application of intervention theory and the development of collaborative partnerships with the media in order to change societal norms to decrease risk behaviors in children and families.

Policy

Comprehensive policy directed specifically to the health of children and families is not a tradition in the United States. Policy for children and families tends to be directed to specific conditions or circumstances, such as pediatric AIDS or Head Start (Huston, 1994; Langley, 1991). This categorical approach addresses social and health issues with respect to the family and its members apart from their larger environmental context. The United States also has been an adult- rather than a child-oriented society, in which risks perceived to affect adults are more often acknowledged and more apt to receive attention and resources than risks perceived to affect children (Lum & Tinker, 1994).

Several factors contribute to the continued inattention to the issues of children and families, particularly those living in poverty. These families are not active, vocal constituents of policymakers, and their issues are presented categorically rather than through unified coalitions with a common voice seeking coordinated programs (Huston, 1994; Langley, 1991; Meister, 1993). The data from the research of family-based programs can help in changing the perspective of policymakers and ultimately changing the health outcomes of urban children and their families.

A primary source for influencing the formulation of policy that strengthens urban families rests with researchers, who can frame their programs and findings to inform policy. As noted in Table 13.1, policy recommendations are not included in all program reviews, let alone in reports of single studies. Policy-relevant research is of three types: (a) policy analysis, (b) policy research, and (c) discipline research (Huston, 1994; Milio, 1984). As expected, most scientists conduct discipline research. In the discipline research, however, few investigators consider policy implications when planning their studies and disseminating their results. This approach was effective, for example, in the research on low-birth-weight infants. Scientists collected economic data in their studies and conducted cost-benefit analyses. As a result, this research provides data of interest to policymakers—the cost-effectiveness of these interventions (Brooten et al., 1986; Huston, 1994; Olds et al., 1993).

Fortunately, family scientists and others are beginning to frame their research to inform policy, and increasing information is available in professional publications to provide direction for these efforts (Huston, 1994; Langley, 1991; Meister, 1993; Milio, 1984). Several factors must be considered in framing research to inform policy. Two distinct paradigms have emerged in the study of health and illness—the personal health paradigm and the public health paradigm. A critical need is for programs to build upon the complementary strengths of the personal health and public health perspectives. Whereas health programs and research emanate from both paradigms, policy is more apt to be informed by the public health paradigm. Different methodologies tend to be used in each paradigm. Public health researchers use epidemiological approaches with large samples and quantitative methods. In contrast, studies of personal health constructs may have small samples (from 10 to 100s) and use quantitative and qualitative methods. Whereas interventions stemming from public health and personal health studies are often community based, public health programs may use mass media information campaigns, rather than the small-group or individual interventions associated with personal health practice.

To bridge the personal and public health paradigms, scientists whose research focuses at the level of the individual child and family must consider the implications of their work beyond the

individual family system to multiple families, the community, and
society. Research synthesis through meta-analysis and integrative
reviews can be used to aggregate information from these smaller,
convenient, nonrepresentative samples to strengthen the application to the broader social systems. Research from the personal health
perspective can also inform those who conduct research from the
public health view and narrow the gap between the two perspectives.
An exchange of perspectives is critical to the synergistic relationship
required to achieve comprehensive, interactive health programs at
all levels—from the individual child and family to society.

To frame traditional discipline research to inform policy, the
following questions should be asked during the planning stages for
family-based interventions:

Will the research improve health outcomes?
What outcome or effect will the research have on health care services,
    including costs?
Which institutions or agencies of government may be interested in the
    research?
How will the results of the research be shared and disseminated?
How can the results be made a permanent component of services for
    urban children and their families?
                        (Meister, Feetham, Durand, & Girouard, 1991)

To inform policy, reliable outcome data are required. These data
must be accessible, timely, and framed to the policymakers' interests
and understanding. When reporting research results, scientists should
begin with information that personalizes the issue or provides a
tangible example of the critical nature of the problem in relation
to families. Aggregate data can then be presented to describe the
scope of the problem in relation to families and reinforce its
economic significance. The report should conclude with the critical
"so what" question to explain what the research suggests for
individual families and the larger aggregate of urban families. For
example, in the report of the program of research on children with
asthma, the data clearly show the growth of this problem in urban
children. The work by Butz and colleagues (Butz & Alexander,
1993; Butz et al., 1994) can be quantified to the cost of emergency
room (ER) visits, hospitalizations, missed school days, and missed
parent workdays to care for the children. The decrease in ER visits,

hospitalizations, and missed school days that result from their intervention can be quantified as tangible improvement in the health of the children and costs of care.

Policy-relevant research should also provide evidence that the recommendations for future programs and research are based on outcome data from related work (Shelov, 1994). The policy analysis by Weissberg and Elias (1993) does this very well. Their recommendations for coordinated education and health programs for Grades K through 12 are based on a systematic analysis of research on and evaluation of school-based programs. To inform policymakers, however, this comprehensive review should be reframed to a few pages, including endorsements from related groups, scientists, and health professionals to demonstrate broad agency and system support.

The program reviews analyzed in this chapter document the considerable evidence of what constitutes a successful intervention. Nevertheless, many parallel, categorical, single-dimension programs continue to be tested and reported despite evidence that such programs are not effective with children and families, particularly with urban, high-risk families.

Research and Program Recommendations

Using empirical data and integrated reviews, recommendations have been proposed to improve family-based research and programs (Bogenschneider, 1996; Coie et al., 1993; Daka-Mulwanda et al., 1995; Dumka et al., 1995; Farrow, 1991; Feetham, 1984, 1991; Muehrer & Koretz, 1992; Weissberg & Elias, 1993). Many of these recommendations are central to any child health program or research; others are essential for the success and effectiveness of family-based interventions. These recommendations are interdependent and have implications for family theory development, family interventions, and policy formulation.

Several factors have been identified in this chapter regarding the paucity of family-based research and programs. One is the different lens or focus of the disciplines within which the research is conducted and the lack of family expertise of those conducting the studies. Multidisciplinary research is required to bridge these gaps and to develop the most appropriate, comprehensive, policy-relevant, family-based programs to improve the health of urban children.

A second factor is the complexity and cost of conducting family-based programs, particularly community-based programs. Multisite, comprehensive, coordinated programs that demonstrate what is known to work may be more cost-effective than the current single-faceted, categorical programs in the long run. To achieve support for these coordinated, family-based programs, coalitions need to be formed across the various policy and scientific interest groups. For example, clinicians and scientists interested in substance abuse may not obtain the resources necessary to prevent and treat children unless such coalitions are formed. Because of historical neglect of family policy in the United States, coalitions are even more critical if these programs are to be family based (Huston, 1994; Langley, 1991; Shelov, 1994).

Future Directions

- Broaden the concept of prevention to the full continuum of health promotion.
- Apply appropriate family theoretical frameworks to the research.
- Develop multidisciplinary teams with experts at the levels of public health and personal health and those with theoretical and clinical knowledge of family interventions.
- Frame research findings to inform policy.
- Develop programs with a goal to strengthen families.
- Develop empirically based, comprehensive, flexible, multidimensional programs.
- Identify all stakeholders in program outcomes and include children and their families in program planning.
- Assess and build from the strengths of the children, their families, and the community.
- Develop interventions that start in early childhood and continue throughout adolescence.
- Address cultural, ethnic, and family diversity in both research and programs.
- Develop programs that are a win-win across the age continuum to avoid resource competition between vulnerable populations.
- Apply complementary knowledge from the personal health and public health paradigms.
- Develop collaboration across and among agencies and programs.

- Frame the programs within the context of social and health policy.
- Target policy change along a continuum from the inception of programs at the child and family level through community, city, state, and national systems.

Summary

In this chapter, strong evidence of the influence of the family on the health of its members is analyzed to reinforce the potential of family-based intervention programs (Campbell & Patterson, 1995). How definitions of family and health affect research and programs is examined. The characteristics of successful research of families and intervention programs are analyzed. Reports of health programs and research are used to demonstrate the complexity of issues facing urban families and to explicate the process for developing effective family-based intervention programs (Butz et al., 1995; Butz et al., 1994; Huss et al., 1994; Malveaux & Fletcher-Vincent, 1995; Szapocznik et al., in press). The isolation among agencies and disciplines is noted, and the potential benefits of linking the complementary components of the personal health and public health paradigms are discussed. Directions are provided for the formation of policy-relevant, comprehensive, interdisciplinary, family-based programs to improve the health outcomes of urban children and their families.

Note

1. In this chapter, the term *children* refers to infants, youth, and adolescents—persons from birth through adolescence.

References

American Academy of Pediatrics. (1994). *Report of the American Academy of Pediatrics Task Force on Minority Children's Access to Care*. Elk Grove Village, IL: Author.
Anderson, N. L. R. (1996). Decisions about substance abuse among adolescents in juvenile detention. *IMAGE: Journal of Nursing Scholarship, 28*(1), 65-70.

Bogenschneider, K. (1996). An ecological risk/protective theory for building prevention programs, policies, and community capacity to support youth. *Family Relations, 45,* 127-138.

Breslow, L. (1983). The potential of health promotion. In D. Mechanic (Ed.), *Handbook of health, health care, and the health professions* (pp. 50-66). New York: Free Press.

Broering, J. M. (1993). The adolescent, health, and society: Commentary from the perspective of nursing. In S. G. Millstein, A. C. Petersen, & E. O. Nightingale (Eds.), *Promoting the health of adolescents: New directions for the twenty-first century* (pp. 151-157). New York: Oxford University Press.

Bronfenbrenner, U. (1986). Ecology of the family as a context for human development: Research perspectives. *Developmental Psychology, 22*(6), 723-742.

Brooten, D., Brown, L. P., Monroe, B. H., York, R., Cohen, S. M., Rancoli, M., & Hollingsworth, A. (1988). Early discharge and specialist transitional care. *IMAGE: Journal of Nursing Scholarship, 20*(2), 64-68.

Brooten, D., Kumar, S., Brown, L. P., Butts, P., Finkler, S. A., Bakewell-Sachs, S., Gibbons, A., & Delivoria-Papadopoulos, M. (1986). A randomized clinical trial of early hospital discharge and home follow-up of very-low-birth-weight infants. *New England Journal of Medicine, 315*(15), 934-939.

Burr, W. R., Herrin, D. A., Day, R. D., Beutler, I. F., & Leigh, G. K. (1988). Epistemologies that lead to primary explanations in family science. *Family Science Review, 3,* 185-210.

Butz, A. M., & Alexander, C. (1993). Anxiety in children with asthma. *Journal of Asthma, 30*(3), 199-209.

Butz, A. M., Malveaux, F. J., Eggleston, P., Thompson, L., Huss, K., Kolodner, K., & Rand, C. S. (1995). Social factors associated with behavioral problems in children with asthma. *Clinical Pediatrics, 34*(11), 581-590.

Butz, A. M., Malveaux, F. J., Eggleston, P., Thompson, L., Schneider, S., Weeks, K., Huss, K., Murigande, C., & Rand, C. S. (1994). Use of community health workers with inner-city children who have asthma. *Clinical Pediatrics, 33*(3), 135-141.

Campbell, T. L. (1986). Family's impact on health: A critical review. *Family Systems Medicine, 4*(2 & 3), 135-328.

Campbell, T. L., & Patterson, J. M. (1995). The effectiveness of family interventions in the treatment of physical illness. *Journal of Marital and Family Therapy, 21*(4), 545-583.

Carnegie Council on Adolescent Development. (1995). *Turning points preparing American youth for the 21st century: Recommendations for transforming middle grade schools* (Abridged version). Washington, DC: Carnegie Corporation of New York.

Christopher, F. S. (1995). Adolescent pregnancy prevention. *Family Relations, 44*(4), 384-391.

Coie, J. D., Watt, N. F., West, S. G., Hawkins, J. D., Asarnow, J. R., Markman, H. J., Ramey, S. L., Shure, M. B., & Long, B. (1993). The science of prevention: A conceptual framework and some directions for a national research program. *American Psychologist, 48*(10), 1013-1022.

Coleman, J. S. (1988). Social capital in the creation of human capital. *American Journal of Sociology, 94*(Suppl.), S95-S120.

Coleman, J. S. (1990). *Foundations of social theory.* Cambridge, MA: Harvard University Press.

Daka-Mulwanda, V., Thornburg, K. R., Filbert, L., & Klein, T. (1995). Collaboration of services for children and families: A synthesis of recent research and recommendations. *Family Relations, 44,* 219-223.

Dilworth Anderson, P. (1989). Family structure and intervention strategies: Beyond empirical research. *Sickle Cell Disease, Annals of the New York Academy of Science, 565,* 183-188.

Doherty, W. J., & Allen, W. (1994). Family functioning and parental smoking as predictors of adolescent cigarette use: A 6-year prospective study. *Journal of Family Psychology, 8,* 347-353.

Doherty, W. J., & Campbell, T. L. (1988). *Families and health.* Newbury Park, CA: Sage.

Donahue, D., Brooten, D., Roncoli, M., Arnold, L., Knapp, H., Borucki, L., & Cohen, A. (1994). Acute care visits and rehospitalization in women and infants after cesarean birth. *Journal of Perinatology, 14*(1), 36-40.

Dryfoos, J. G. (1990). *Adolescents at risk: Prevalence and prevention.* New York: Oxford University Press.

Dumka, L. E., Roosa, M. W., Michaels, M. L., & Suh, K. W. (1995). Using research and theory to develop prevention programs for high-risk families. *Family Relations, 44,* 78-86.

Farrow, F. (1991). Services to families: The view from the states. *Families in Society: The Journal of Contemporary Human Services, 72,* 268-275.

Feetham, S. L. (1984). Family research: Issues and directions for nursing. In H. H. Werley & J. Fitzpatrick (Eds.), *Annual review of nursing research* (pp. 3-25). New York: Springer-Verlag.

Feetham, S. L. (1991). Conceptual and methodological issues in research of families. In A. Whall & J. Faucett (Eds.), *Family theory development in nursing: State of the science and arts* (pp. 55-68). Philadelphia: F. A. Davis.

Fish, L., Wilson, S. R., Latini, D. M., & Starr, N. J. (1996). An education program for parents of children with asthma: Differences in attendance between smoking and nonsmoking parents. *American Journal of Public Health, 86*(2), 246-248.

Fisher, L., Terry, H. E., & Ransom, D. C. (1990). Advancing a family perspective in health research: Models and methods. *Family Process, 29*(2), 177-189.

Fry-McComish, J., Lawlor, L. A., & Laken, M. (1996). INREACH: Linking walk-ins and their infants to community-based care. *American Journal of Maternal Child Nursing, 21*(3), 132-136.

Gergen, P. J., & Goldstein, R. A. (1995). Does asthma education equal asthma intervention? *International Archives of Allergy and Immunology, 107*(1-3), 166-168.

Gergen, P. J., Mullally, D. I., & Evans, R., III. (1988). National survey of prevalence of asthma among children in the U.S. 1976 to 1980. *Pediatrics, 81*(1), 1-7.

Gilliss, C. L. (1983). The family as a unit of analysis: Strategies for the nurse researcher. *Advances in Nursing Science, 5*(3), 50-59.

Gilliss, C. L., & Davis, L. L. (1993). Does family intervention make a difference? An integrative review and meta-analysis. In S. Feetham, S. Meister, C. Gilliss, & J. Bell (Eds.), *Nursing of families: Theory/research/education/practice* (pp. 259-265). Newbury Park, CA: Sage.

Gloss, E. (1995). Children and drug education: The P.I.E.D. pipers: People Involved in Education about Drugs. *Nursing Outlook, 43*(2), 66-70.

Gustafsson, P. A., Bjorksten, B., & Kjellman, N. I. (1994). Family dysfunction in asthma: A prospective study of illness development. *Journal of Pediatrics, 125*(3), 493-498.

Guthrie, B. J., Loveland-Cherry, C., Frey, M., & Dielman, T. E. (1994). A theoretical approach to studying health behaviors in adolescents: An at-risk population. *Contemporary Issues in Family and Community Health, 17*(3), 35-48.

Hardy, J. B., & Streett, R. (1989). Family support and parenting education in the home: An effective extension of clinic-based preventive health care services for poor children. *Journal of Pediatrics, 115*(6), 927-931.

Huch, M. H. (1991). Perspectives on health. *Nursing Science Quarterly, 4*(1), 33-40.

Huss, K., Rand, C. S., Butz, A. M., Eggleston, P. A., Murigande, C., Thompson, L. C., Schneider, S., Weeks, K., & Malveaux, F. J. (1994). Home environmental risk factors in urban minority asthmatic children. *Annals of Allergy, 72*(2), 173-177.

Huston, A. C. (1994). Children in poverty: Designing research to affect policy. *Social Policy Report: Society for Research in Child Development, 8*(2), 1-12.

Igoe, J. B. (1991). Empowerment of children and youth for consumer self-care. *American Journal of Health Promotion, 6,* 55-65.

Irwin, C. E., Jr., & Vaughan, E. (1988). Psychosocial context of adolescent development: Study group report. *Journal of Adolescent Health Care, 9*(Suppl.), 11S-19S.

Kazak, A. E. (1989). Families of chronically ill children: A systems and social-ecological model of adaptation and challenge. *Journal of Consulting and Clinical Psychology, 57*(1), 25-30.

Kazdin, A. E., Bass, D., Ayers, W. A., & Rodgers, A. (1990). Empirical and clinical focus of child and adolescent psychotherapy research. *Journal of Consulting and Clinical Psychology, 58*(6), 729-740.

Kelly, J. A. (1995). Advances in HIV/AIDS education and prevention. *Family Relations, 44,* 345-352.

Kirby, D. (1991). School-based clinics: Research results and their implications for future research methods. *Evaluation and Program Planning, 4,* 35-47.

Kirby, D., Short, L., Collins, J., Rugg, D., Kolbe, L., Howard, M., Miller, B., Sonenstein, F., & Zabin, L. S. (1994). School-based programs to reduce sexual risk behaviors: A review of effectiveness. *Public Health Reports, 109*(3), 339-360.

Klinnert, M. D., Mrazek, P. J., & Mrazek, D. A. (1994). Early asthma onset: The interaction between family stressors and adaptive parenting. *Psychiatry, 57,* 51-61.

Krysan, M., Moore, K. A., & Zill, N. (1990). *Identifying successful families: An overview of constructs and selected measures.* (Available from Child Trends, Inc., 2100 M Street, NW, Suite 610, Washington, DC 20037)

Langley, P. A. (1991). The coming of age of family policy. *Families in Society: The Journal of Contemporary Human Services, 72*(2), 116-120.

Liddle, H. A., & Dakof, G. A. (1995). Efficacy of family therapy for drug abuse: Promising but not definitive. *Journal of Marital and Family Therapy, 21*(4), 511-543.

Lienert, A. (1995). On the road to success. *Wayne State Magazine, 9*(4), 10-13.

Litman, T. J. (1974). The family as a basic unit in health and medical care: A social-behavioral overview. *Social Science and Medicine, 8,* 495-519.

Litman, T. J., & Venters, M. (1979). Research on health care and the family: A methodologic overview. *Social Science and Medicine, 13A*(4), 379-385.

Lum, M. R., & Tinker, T. L. (1994). *A primer on health risk communication principles and practices.* Washington, DC: U.S. Department of Health and Human Services, Public Health Service, Agency for Toxic Substances and Disease Registry.

Malveaux, F. J., & Fletcher-Vincent, S. A. (1995). Environmental risk factors of childhood asthma in urban centers. *Environmental Health Perspective, 103*(6 Suppl.), 59-62.

Meister, S. B. (1993). The family's agents: Policy and nursing. In S. Feetham, S. Meister, C. Gilliss, & J. Bell (Eds.), *Nursing of families: Theory/research/education/practice* (pp. 3-10). Newbury Park, CA: Sage.

Meister, S. B., Feetham, S. L., Durand, B. A., & Girouard, S. (1991). Creating and extending successful innovations: Practice and policy implications. In E. Groetsman (Ed.), *Differentiating nursing practice into the twenty-first century* (pp. 315-328). Kansas City, MO: American Academy of Nursing.

Meyer, E. C., Coll, C. T., Lester, B. M., Boukydis, C., McDonough, S. M., & Oh, W. (1994). Family-based intervention improves maternal psychological well-being and feeding interaction of preterm infants. *Pediatrics, 93*(2), 241-246.

Milio, N. (1970). *9226 Kercheval: The storefront that did not burn.* Ann Arbor: University of Michigan Press.

Milio, N. (1984). Nursing research and the study of health policy. In H. H. Werley & J. Fitzpatrick (Eds.), *Annual review of nursing research* (pp. 3-25). New York: Springer-Verlag.

Millstein, S. G. (1988). *The potential of school-linked centers to promote adolescent health and development* (Working Paper for Carnegie Council on Adolescent Development). Washington, DC: Carnegie Corporation of New York.

Mortimer, A. M. (1993). *Consultation on after-school programs.* Washington, DC: Carnegie Corporation of New York.

Muehrer, P., & Koretz, D. S. (1992). Issues in preventive intervention research. *Current Directions in Psychological Science—American Psychological Society, 1*(3), 109-112.

National Center for Education in Maternal and Child Health. (1995). *Healthy tomorrows partnership for children: Abstracts of active projects FY 1995.* Arlington, VA: Author.

National Center for Health Statistics. (1995). *Healthy people 2000 review 1994.* Hyattsville, MD: U.S. Public Health Service.

National Institute of Nursing Research. (1993). *Health promotion of older children and adolescents.* Bethesda, MD: Author.

National Institutes of Health. (1991). *Health and behavior research: NIH report to Congress.* Bethesda, MD: Author.

National Research Council. (1994). *Meeting the nation's needs for biomedical and behavioral scientists.* Washington, DC: National Academy Press.

Nelson, D. W. (1995). *The path of most resistance: Reflection on lessons learned from new futures.* Baltimore, MD: Annie E. Casey Foundation.

Newcomb, M. D., & Bentler, P. M. (1989). Substance use and abuse among children and teenagers. *American Psychologist, 44*(2), 242-248.

Office of Technology Assessment (OTA). (1991). *Adolescent health: Summary and policy options* (Vol. 1). Washington, DC: Government Printing Office.

Olds, D. L., Henderson, C. R., Jr., Chamberlin, R., & Tatelbaum, R. (1986). Preventing child abuse and neglect: A randomized trial of nurse home visitation. *Pediatrics, 78*(1), 65-78.

Olds, D. L., Henderson, C. R., Jr., & Kitzman, H. (1994). Does prenatal and infancy nurse home visitation have enduring effects on qualities of parental caregiving and child health at 25 to 50 months of life? *Pediatrics, 93*(1), 89-98.

Olds, D. L., Henderson, C. R., Jr., Phelps, C., Tatelbaum, R., & Chamberlin, R. (1993). Effect of prenatal and infancy nurse home visitation on government spending. *Medical Care, 31*(2), 155-174.

Olds, D. L., Henderson, C. R., Jr., Tatelbaum, R., & Chamberlin, R. (1986). Improving the delivery of prenatal care and outcomes of pregnancy: A randomized trial of nurse home visitation. *Pediatrics, 77*(1), 16-28.

Olds, D. L., Henderson, C. R., Jr., Tatelbaum, R., & Chamberlin, R. (1988). Improving the life-course development of socially disadvantaged mothers: A randomized trial of nurse home visitation. *American Journal of Public Health, 78*, 1436-1445.

Patterson, J., & Garwick, A. W. (1994). The impact of chronic illness on families: A family systems perspective. *Annals of Behavioral Medicine, 16*(2), 131-142.

Pender, N. J. (1990). Expressing health through lifestyle patterns. *Nursing Science Quarterly, 3*(3), 115-122.

Pierce, J. P., Fiore, M. C., Novotny, T. E., Hatziandreu, E. J., & Davis, R. M. (1989). Trends in cigarette smoking in the United States: Projections to the year 2000. *Journal of the American Medical Association, 261*(1), 61-65.

Pokorni, J. L., Katz, K. S., & Long, T. M. (1991). Chronic illness and preterm infants: Family stress and support issues. *Early Education and Development, 2*, 227-239.

Santisteban, D. A., Szapocznik, J., Perez-Vidal, A., Kurtines, W. M., Murray, E. J., & LaPerriere, A. (1996). Efficacy of intervention for engaging youth and families into treatment and some variables that may contribute to differential effectiveness. *Journal of Family Psychology, 10*(1), 35-44.

Schorr, L. B. (1988). *Within our reach: Breaking the cycle of disadvantage.* New York: Anchor.

Shelov, S. P. (1994). Editorial: The children's agenda for the 1990s and beyond. *American Journal of Public Health, 84*(7), 1066-1067.

Small, S. A. (1990). *Preventive programs that support families with adolescents* (Working Paper for Carnegie Council on Adolescent Development). Washington, DC: Carnegie Corporation of New York.

Szapocznik, J., Hervis, O., Kurtines, W. M., & Spencer, F. (1984). One-person family therapy. In B. Lubin & W. A. O'Connor (Eds.), *Ecological approaches to clinical and community psychology* (pp. 335-355). New York: John Wiley.

Szapocznik, J., Kurtines, W. M., Foote, F. H., Perez-Vidal, A., & Hervis, O. (1983). Conjoint versus one-person family therapy: Some evidence for the effectiveness of conducting family therapy through one person. *Journal of Consulting and Clinical Psychology, 51*(6), 889-899.

Szapocznik, J., Kurtines, W. M., Foote, F. H., Perez-Vidal, A., & Hervis, O. (1986). Conjoint versus one-person family therapy: Further evidence for the effectiveness of conducting family therapy through one person with drug-abusing adolescents. *Journal of Consulting and Clinical Psychology, 54*(3), 395-397.

Szapocznik, J., Kurtines, W. M., Santisteban, D. A., Pantin, H., Scopetta, M., Mancilla, Y., Aisenberg, S., Mcintosh, S., Perez-Vidal, A., & Coatsworth, J. D. (1997). The evolution of a structural ecosystems theory for working with Latino families. In J. Garcia & M. C. Zea (Eds.), *Psychological interventions and research with Latino populations.* Needham Heights, MA: Allyn & Bacon.

Szapocznik, J., Kurtines, W. M., Santisteban, D. A., & Rio, A. T. (1990). Interplay of advances between theory, research, and application in treatment interventions aimed at behavior problem children and adolescents. *Journal of Consulting and Clinical Psychology, 58*(6), 696-703.

Szapocznik, J., Perez-Vidal, A., Brickman, A. L., Foote, F. H., Santisteban, D., Hervis, O., & Kurtines, W. (1988). Engaging adolescent drug abusers and their families in treatment: A strategic structural systems approach. *Journal of Consulting and Clinical Psychology, 56*(4), 552-557.

Szapocznik, J., Rio, A. T., Murray, E., Richardson, R., Alonso, M., & Kurtines, W. M. (1993). Assessing change in child psychodynamic functioning in treatment outcome studies: The psychodynamic child ratings. *Revista Interamicana de Psicologia, 27*(2), 147-162.

Turk, D. C., & Kerns, R. D. (1985). *Health, illness, and families: A life-span perspective.* New York: John Wiley.

Vincent, M. L., Clearie, A. F., & Schluchter, M. D. (1987). Reducing adolescent pregnancy through school and community-based education. *Journal of the American Medical Association, 257*(24), 3382-3386.

Weissberg, R. P., & Elias, M. J. (1993). Enhancing young people's social competence and health behavior: An important challenge for educators, scientists, policymakers, and funders. *Applied and Preventive Psychology, 2*(4), 179-190.

Weitzman, M., Gortmaker, S. L., & Sobol, A. M. (1990). Racial, social, and environmental risks for childhood asthma. *American Journal of Diseases of Childhood, 144,* 1189-1194.

Wissow, L. S., Gittelsohn, A. M., Szklo, M., Starfield, B., & Mussman, M. (1988). Poverty, race, and hospitalization for childhood asthma. *American Journal of Public Health, 78*(7), 777-782.

World Health Organization. (1976). *Statistical indices of family health* (Report No. 589). Geneva, Switzerland: Author.

Wright, L. M., & Leahey, M. (1994). *Nurses and families: A guide to family assessment and intervention* (2nd ed.). Philadelphia: F. A. Davis.

Wright, L. M., Watson, W. L., & Bell, J. M. (1996). *Beliefs: The heart of healing in families and illness.* New York: Basic Books.

PART V

Conclusion

• CHAPTER 14 •

Afterword:
Strengthening the Families,
Education, and Health of
Urban Children and Youth

HERBERT J. WALBERG

OLGA REYES

ROGER P. WEISSBERG

CAROL BARTELS KUSTER

Each of the foregoing chapters deserves close reading and reflection. Their authors have reviewed the circumstances of urban children and youth from diverse disciplinary perspectives and have offered constructive recommendations regarding future research, theory, practice, and policy regarding urban families, education, and health. They have provided fertile ground from which readers may wish to derive implications for their own thinking and action. In this last chapter, however, we, the editors, draw together some recommendations for changes in practice and social policy. These were inferred from preceding chapters and other current writing and research on children and youth (e.g., Carnegie Council on Adolescent Development, 1995; Carnegie Task Force on Meeting the Needs of Young Children, 1994; National Commission on Children, 1991; National Commission on the Role of the School and the Community in Improving Adolescent Health, 1990; National Research Council, 1993; Office of Technology Assessment, 1991; Weissberg & Greenberg, 1997). The recommendations represent the editors' views, not necessarily the collective wisdom of the chapter authors.

Academic books often recommend more research, but this does not offer a clear set of directions to those whose obligation is to decide what to do today. Although we do offer recommendations, first we provide a context with several key observations:

- Although often encumbered by limited social and material resources, urban families have many untapped skills and abilities that can be developed, strengthened, and converted into "human capital."
- Some problems of urban children and youth are chronic, and others are acute; but, given the right circumstances and programs, many causal conditions may be addressed and improved.
- Parents and families are primarily responsible for nurturing children's social, emotional, moral, intellectual, and physical development. In addition, community institutions—such as schools, service and charitable organizations, religious institutions, social and health care services, businesses, and governments—play a critical role in creating environments that both support parents in meeting this responsibility and foster positive youth development.
- It is wiser and more economically efficient to prevent rather than to "cure" young people's problems.
- Great promise lies in the collaboration of families, communities, organizations, and academic institutions and the respective resources that each of these can contribute to both the understanding and the amelioration of social ills in the inner city.
- Multidisciplinary teams that combine theoretical and clinical knowledge from diverse perspectives are needed to establish coordinated and comprehensive programs for urban children and families.
- The fact that programs have worked well in one place suggests that they may work elsewhere, provided they are adapted to the circumstances of the children and youth to be served and are implemented with integrity.

Aside from these general observations, we offer selective and abbreviated recommendations. Although they have been organized according to the main parts of the book, it is worth noting that these three areas overlap. We hope they serve as food for thought and action for ourselves and others.

Families

- Communities should develop networks that link families, child care programs, schools, and religious and service organizations that serve children and youth. These networks might include parent peer support groups, cooperative child care arrangements, parent-teacher organizations, and Scout troops.

- Family-based programs should articulate clear goals; establish sound assessment procedures; specifically address presented problems with relevant, appropriate, and effective interventions; and evaluate outcomes.

- Family-based, competence-enhancement, and health-promotion programs that assess and build from the strengths of children, families, schools, and communities are needed.

- Programs that provide culturally sensitive parent education and promote close ties among families and schools have succeeded in fostering positive attitudes toward schools, academic achievement, and social behavior.

- Home-based, parent-education programs to assist families in making homes more academically and socially stimulating can provide critical foundational skills so that children are better able to succeed in school.

- During adolescence, when involvement of parents with both their children and their children's school tends to decrease, junior and senior high schools should make concerted efforts to promote parent involvement in education.

Schools

- Some methods of classroom teaching work far better than others and yet may not be prevalent; we need to disseminate effective programs, systematically train new program implementers, and monitor and evaluate program implementation and outcomes in new sites.

- Urban school systems may better succeed by adopting decentralized decision making and "customer-driven" policies and procedures.

- To accomplish more, urban school systems should require accountability systems to measure achievement progress.

- Other things being equal, smaller schools seem to provide more satisfying environments for students and staff.

- The transitions to junior and senior high schools are stressful for many students; special programs designed to address the developmental needs of students and to make these institutions more welcoming will lead to better academic and social outcomes.

- Programs that reconcile or allow the joint development of minority and academic identities may foster the learning and psychological development of African American and other ethnic groups.

- Extended day programs run by or affiliated with schools and other agencies may promote responsible attitudes and behaviors that make for school and life success.

- Schools must attend to children's social, emotional, and physical problems if they are to accomplish their educational mission.

- School staff can collaborate with those in other neighborhood institutions such as social work agencies, police, hospitals, and businesses to coordinate more efficiently their efforts to improve young people's prospects.

Health

- Parents and family members should foster children's healthy development by protecting their own health; modeling healthful behavior; establishing a safe, health-enhancing home environment; and obtaining essential health services for their children.

- Health care services should be made accessible to all children and youth and be structured to overcome financial, geographic, linguistic, racial, and ethnic barriers.

- Health services for children and youth should be developmentally and culturally appropriate and employ family-based and systems approaches that address behavior-related problems.

- Comprehensive health care services for pregnant women, infants, and preschoolers should be available to all families in order to lay a foundation for healthy development.

- Urban schools must play a central role in enhancing children's health by providing high-quality preschool through high school health education that emphasizes the teaching of responsible decision making, social and emotional competence, and the application of life skills.

- Although schools provide a major setting for mounting prevention programs for young people, it is important to involve families, communities, and the mass media to address such problems as violence and drug use because such programs are likely to fail if family and community climates do not change in supportive ways.

- Preventive interventions should be directed at common risk and protective factors, rather than at categorical problem behaviors (e.g., drug use, violence, teenage pregnancy). With this perspective, it is both feasible and cost-effective to target multiple negative outcomes in the context of a coordinated set of programs.

- Health providers and educators require training in delivering developmentally and culturally appropriate information and services to young people and their families.

- Instilling values, knowledge, tools, and skills necessary to make health-enhancing decisions will require the concerted efforts of many concerned parties such as parents, educators, health care providers, policymakers, urban planners, and the media.

The UIC Series on Children and Youth: Retrospect and Prospect

The primary objective of this book series is to offer an interdisciplinary approach to understanding and improving the conditions of children and youth, particularly those in the most difficult circumstances. We have invited chapters by specialists writing not only for scholars in other fields but also for policymakers and practitioners. This final chapter on general observations and policy and practice implications concludes the first book in the UIC series. The interdisciplinary perspectives represented here anticipate themes we envision for subsequent volumes. The next two volumes, already underway, will focus on statistical trends regarding the social-environmental circumstances and behaviors of children and youth, and model programs that appear to best serve them.

We believe that the chapters presented here offer many insights and implications for scholars, policymakers, and practitioners. We also realize, however, that many research questions remain unanswered and that many policy and practice issues are unresolved. Thus, subsequent volumes will return to many of these research and practical issues, both as chapters and as entire volumes.

The problems and opportunities of children and youth need to be seen comprehensively and from the perspectives of several disciplines and professions. We have attempted to provide this broad view here and hope to achieve a suitable balance of specialized and general books as the series evolves.

References

Carnegie Council on Adolescent Development. (1995). *Great transitions: Preparing adolescents for a new century* (Concluding report of the Carnegie Council on Adolescent Development). New York: Carnegie Corporation of New York.

Carnegie Task Force on Meeting the Needs of Young Children. (1994). *Starting points: Meeting the needs of our youngest children*. New York: Carnegie Corporation of New York.

National Commission on Children. (1991). *Beyond rhetoric: A new American agenda for children and families*. Washington, DC: Government Printing Office.

National Commission on the Role of the School and the Community in Improving Adolescent Health. (1990). *Code blue: Uniting for healthier youth*. Alexandria, VA: National Association of State Boards of Education.

National Research Council, Panel on High-Risk Youth. (1993). *Losing generations: Adolescents in high-risk settings*. Washington, DC: National Academy Press.

Office of Technology Assessment. (1991). *Adolescent health: Vol. 1. Summary and policy options* (OTA-H-468). Washington, DC: Government Printing Office.

Weissberg, R. P., & Greenberg, M. T. (1997). School and community competence-enhancement and prevention programs. In W. Damon (Series Ed.) & I. E. Sigel & K. A. Renninger (Vol. Eds.), *Handbook of child psychology: Vol. 5. Child psychology in practice* (5th ed.). New York: John Wiley.

Index

Academic press, 148-149
Achievement, 47, 52, 56, 60, 83-86,
    106, 113-114, 121-123,
    125-130, 132-135, 137, 142,
    144, 146, 148, 150-153, 156,
    158
Achievement, 160, 161, 190-197,
    203, 204, 206, 209-214, 217,
    218
    education resilience, 119-123,
        127-129, 133-134, 137
    external incentives, 150-152, 159,
        161
    link to parent behaviors, 113, 114,
        121-122, 127, 133, 137
    males, 196
    related to school structure, 144,
        148, 150-151, 153, 156, 158
Adolescence, 308-312
Adolescent development, 167,
    173-175, 182, 184-187
Adolescent pregnancy, 46, 50, 55,
    300
Adult responsibilities, 167, 174, 176
African-American academic
    performance, 190-197, 204,
    206, 209
African-Americans, 46-60
AIDS, 299
Alcohol, 257, 301
Anti-social behavior/delinquency, 172,
    175, 178, 180-181, 183, 186
Asthma, 299, 332

Benefits, 132, 135

Black English vernacular, 218

Carnegie Council, adolescent
    development recommendations,
    186
Characteristics of schools, 120, 123,
    128-129, 133, 137-138
Characteristics of the learner,
    120-121, 127-128, 137
Chicago, 97, 106, 108, 110, 223, 225,
    125
Child development, 13, 23, 30, 45,
    54, 61, 72, 76, 80, 83
    normative and alternative models,
        51, 53
    outcome, 47, 52, 55, 59, 63
    pathways, 51, 54, 56, 70, 79
    role of family, 51, 54, 76
    role of neighborhood, 51
Chronic environmental stress, 80-82
Churches, 101, 107, 108, 111, 112
Clientship ("Uncle Tomming"),
    208-209
Coaching Club, 235
Coleman Report, 142-145, 191
Collective struggle, 207-209
Comer Project, 156-158
Communality, 148-149
Community bridging, 55
Community forces, 197, 213-214,
    217-218
Community-university partnerships,
    13, 23, 30-42
    benefits, 41
    risks, 21, 41

369

About the Editors

Herbert J. Walberg, Research Professor of Education and Psychology at The University of Illinois at Chicago (UIC), was awarded a Ph.D. in educational psychology by the University of Chicago and was formerly Assistant Professor at Harvard University. He recently completed a term as Founding Member of the National Assessment Governing Board, sometimes referred to as "the national school board" because it has been given the mission to set subject matter standards for U.S. students. He has written and edited more than 50 books and contributed more than 380 articles to educational and psychological research journals on such topics as educational effectiveness and productivity, school reform, and exceptional human accomplishments. He frequently writes for widely circulated practitioner journals and national newspapers. He serves as an advisor on educational research and improvement to public and private agencies in the United States and other countries and testifies before state and federal courts and U.S. Congressional committees. A fellow of four academic organizations, he has won awards and prizes for his scholarship and is one of three U.S. members of the International Academy of Education. He holds appointments in the UIC Center for Urban Educational Research and Development and the Mid-Atlantic Laboratory for Student Success sponsored by the U.S. Department of Education.

Olga Reyes is Associate Professor of Psychology at The University of Illinois at Chicago. She received her Ph.D. in clinical-community psychology from DePaul University and her B.A. with Distinction in psychology from The University of Illinois at Chicago. She has devoted her research career to the study of issues that affect the educational attainment of Latino youth. Specifically, her research focuses on resilience and protective factors and the prevention of high-risk behaviors in children and adolescents from urban, minority backgrounds. Her work is concerned with the promotion of academic achievement and high school completion in youngsters from high-risk, urban backgrounds. As an outgrowth of this work, she has served on numerous committees and panels of the Chicago Public Schools, including the Advisory Committee on Curriculum, the Dropout Prevention Committee, and the Hispanic Educational Policy Network. She is also the recipient of the William T. Grant Foundation's 5-year Faculty Scholars Award in Children's Mental Health and serves on several editorial boards of scholarly journals.

Roger P. Weissberg is Professor of Psychology at The University of Illinois at Chicago. At UIC, he is the Director of Graduate Studies in Psychology and directs a NIMH-funded Predoctoral and Postdoctoral Prevention Research Training Program in Urban Children's Mental Health and AIDS Prevention. He also holds an appointment with the Mid-Atlantic Laboratory for Student Success funded by the Office of Educational Research and Improvement of the U.S. Department of Education. The author of more than 100 articles and chapters focusing on preventive interventions with children and adolescents, he has also coauthored nine curricula on school-based social-competence promotion programs to prevent drug use, high-risk sexual behaviors, and aggression. His research interests include school and community preventive interventions, urban children's mental health, and parental involvement in children's education. He received his Ph.D. in clinical psychology from the University of Rochester in 1980 and from 1980 to 1982 was Research Director for the Primary Mental Health Project, a program for the early detection and prevention of school maladjustment. He was a Professor in Yale University's Psychology Department between 1982 and 1992 and also directed its NIMH-funded Prevention Research Training Program. A Past President of the American Psychological Association's Society for Community Research and Action, he is a recipient of the William T. Grant Foundation's 5-year Faculty Scholars Award in Children's Mental Health, the Connecticut Psychological Association's 1992 Award for Distinguished Psychological Contribution in the Public Interest, and the National Mental Health Association's 1992 Lela Rowland Prevention Award.

About the Contributors

William Lowe Boyd is Distinguished Professor of Education at Pennsylvania State University, University Park. A specialist in education policy and politics, he has published more than 100 articles and has coedited nine books. He has served as President of the Politics of Education Association and has been a Visiting Fulbright Scholar in Australia and England and a Visiting Scholar at Gothenburg University, the University of British Columbia, and the University of Wales at Cardiff. He has researched education reform efforts in Australia, Britain, Canada, and Sweden, as well as the United States. As a researcher for the National Center on School Leadership, the National Center on Education in the Inner Cities, and the Laboratory for Student Success, he has studied school effectiveness and efforts to achieve coordinated, school-linked services for at-risk children and their families.

Geraldine K. Brookins holds the Gamble-Skogmo Land Grant Professorship for Child Welfare and Youth Policy at the University of Minnesota and is the first person of color to hold an endowed chair at the University of Minnesota. Her faculty appointments are in the School of Social Work and the Humphrey Institute for Public Affairs. She is also an Adjunct Professor of Child Psychology in the Institute of Child Development. After earning her Ph.D. in clinical psychology and public practice at Harvard University in 1977, she was a Professor of Psychology at Jackson State University in Jackson, Mississippi. Her research focuses on aspects of development among African American children, youth, and families, with a particular interest in assessing strengths. The author of several articles and book chapters, she coedited two books—*Ethnicity and Diversity: Minorities No More* and *Beginnings: The Social and*

Affective Development of Black Children. She chairs the American Psychological Association "Task Force on Poverty, Family Processes, and Child Development Outcomes: Recommendations for Intervention" and has been appointed to the advisory committee for the APA Task Force on Adolescent Girls. She sits on several national boards focused on children and families, and her involvement with federal and state governmental agencies and local community efforts and agencies facilitates a grounded perspective and an integration of research, policy, and practice.

Lisa M. Brooks is a former student in the Hubert H. Humphrey Institute of Public Affairs, where she served as a Research Assistant on urban youth projects. She received her B.A. in sociology from the University of California, Berkeley, in 1994. She is a researcher in Washington, D.C., on energy and environmental policy issues.

Nicholas J. Cutforth is Assistant Professor in the College of Education at the University of Denver. He has taught in a residential facility for delinquent youth near London, England, and has developed, taught in, and evaluated inner-city in-school and extended day programs in Chicago and Denver. He received his Ph.D. in education from The University of Illinois at Chicago in 1994. His articles have been published in *Teaching Education; Journal of Physical Education, Recreation, and Dance;* and *British Journal of Physical Education.* He is a Consultant for the Moral Courage Project in Denver and is directing plans for a Center of Applied Urban Studies at the University of Denver. His research and teaching interests include physical education for urban children and youth; the social, moral, and cultural dimensions of teaching; and ethnographic research.

Suzanne Feetham is Professor and occupies the Harriet Werley Research Chair in the College of Nursing at The University of Illinois at Chicago. She has held joint positions at the National Institute of Nursing Research, National Institutes of Health, and the School of Nursing, University of Pennsylvania. She conducts a program of research on families of children with health problems, focusing on conceptual and measurement issues. She developed the Feetham Family Functioning Survey (FFFS), which is used across disciplines and has been translated into three languages, and she is known for her landmark publications in these areas. She received her basic and graduate education in nursing and her Ph.D. in family sciences. She has received numerous awards for her practice and research, including the 1996 Eastern Nursing Research Society— Distinguished Contributions to Research Award.

Brian R. Flay holds a D.Phil. from the University of Waikato, New Zealand. He was a Fulbright/Hays Postdoctoral Fellow in social psychology and evaluation research at Northwestern University, Evanston, Illinois. He is Professor of Community Health Sciences, School of Public Health; Professor of Psychology; and Director of the Prevention Research Center, The University of Illinois at Chicago. He was previously Associate Professor of Preventive Medicine and Deputy Director of the Health Behavior Research Institute, University of Southern California, and Assistant Professor of Health Studies, University of Waterloo, Ontario, Canada. His research interests include the etiology of adolescent substance use (tobacco, alcohol, and illicit substances); violence and unsafe sex; and abuse prevention through school-, media- and community-based programs.

Sabine E. French is a doctoral student in community psychology at New York University. She received a B.A. in psychology from Yale University, where she was a Fellow at the Bush Center for Child Development and Social Policy. A Senior Research Assistant on the Adolescent Pathways Project, her research interests include school transitions, ethnic identity development, and evaluation research. She is designing an evaluation protocol for a long-term primary prevention program.

Deborah Gorman-Smith is Assistant Professor in the Department of Psychiatry and holds an appointment at the Institute for Juvenile Research at The University of Illinois at Chicago. She received her Ph.D. in clinical and developmental psychology from The University of Illinois at Chicago in 1991. She is collaborating with Patrick H. Tolan on the Chicago Youth Development Study, a longitudinal study of development and risk of inner-city male adolescents and their families. Her major research interest is on the development of urban children, with a particular focus on the effects of community characteristics and exposure to violence.

Geneva D. Haertel is Senior Research Associate at the Temple University Center for Research in Human Development and Education, where she conducts research syntheses on programs and practices that influence the academic achievement of children at risk of school failure. She has published more than 40 articles and chapters in educational and psychological journals and books, and in 1990 she coedited (with Herbert J. Walberg) *The International Encyclopedia of Educational Evaluation.* Her recent publications include the research synthesis "Toward a Knowledge Base for School Learning" and a book chapter on educational resilience in inner cities, both coauthored with Margaret C. Wang and Herbert J. Walberg.

Donald R. Hellison is Professor in the School of Kinesiology at The University of Illinois at Chicago. He is best known for his work with inner-city youth and for the development of affective and humanistic approaches to teaching physical activities in schools and social agencies. He has received the International Olympic Committee President's Prize (1995), The University of Illinois at Chicago Excellence in Teaching Award (1995), and the American Alliance of Health and Physical Education C. D. Henry Award for service to minorities (1994). The author of five books, including *Teaching Responsibility Through Physical Activity* (Human Kinetics, 1995), he is Editor of *Quest,* the journal of the National Association of Physical Education in Higher Education.

Frank Bingchang Hu is a doctoral candidate in The University of Illinois School of Public Health Epidemiology and Biostatistics program. The holder of an M.D. degree from Tongji Medical University, China, he is a research specialist and statistician at the Prevention Research Center, The University of Illinois at Chicago. His research interests include behavioral epidemiology and quantitative methods in epidemiologic studies, especially longitudinal and missing data modeling.

Robert L. Johnson is Professor of Pediatrics and Clinical Psychiatry and Director of Adolescent and Young Adult Medicine at the University of Medicine and Dentistry of New Jersey, New Jersey Medical School. He received his bachelor's degree from Alfred University in 1968 and his medical degree from the College of

Medicine and Dentistry of New Jersey in 1972. He completed an internship and residency in Pediatrics at the Harrison Martland Medical Center in 1974 and then entered a 2-year fellowship in adolescent medicine at New York University Medical Center. He returned to the New Jersey Medical School in 1976, where he founded the Division of Adolescent Medicine. A well-recognized spokesperson for the adolescent and adolescent issues, he has published widely and conducts an active schedule of teaching, research, and clinical practice at the New Jersey Medical School.

Kelli A. Komro holds advanced degrees in behavioral epidemiology and psychology. At the University of Minnesota, School of Public Health, Division of Epidemiology, she is Evaluation Director for Project Northland, a randomized community trial funded by the National Institute of Alcohol Abuse and Alcoholism. The goal of the project is to develop and evaluate strategies at the community, family, and peer level to reduce alcohol use and alcohol-related problems among a cohort of adolescents. Previously, she was a NIDA Postdoctoral Fellow at the Prevention Research Center, School of Public Health, The University of Illinois at Chicago.

Carol Bartels Kuster is Research Associate in Psychology at The University of Illinois at Chicago. She received her Ph.D. in clinical/community psychology from the University of Maryland at College Park. She is collaborating with Roger P. Weissberg on prevention research and intervention programs for inner-city youth. Her major research interests are family violence, parent training and education programs, and prevention of child abuse and neglect.

John U. Ogbu is Alumni Distinguished Professor of Anthropology at the University of California, Berkeley, where he received his B.A., M.A., and Ph.D. in anthropology. He is a member of the National Academy of Education and a former member of the Social Science Research Council Committee on Research on the Urban Underclass and the Governing Council for the Society for Research on Child Development. His principal fields include education and culture, minority education in cross-cultural perspective, and ethnographic research methods. He is the author of several books and more than 90 articles and book chapters.

Anne C. Petersen is Senior Vice President for Programs at the W. K. Kellogg Foundation. She is a former Deputy Director of the National Science Foundation (NSF), where she provided overall organizational management to improve performance in implementing NSF's mission and coordinated activities in interdisciplinary research and education areas, as well as topics that span NSF. Prior to her NSF appointment, she was Vice President for Research and Dean of the Graduate School at the University of Minnesota from 1992 to 1994 and was Professor of Adolescent Development and Pediatrics. For 10 years prior to her arrival at Minnesota, she was Dean of the College of Health and Human Development from 1987 to 1992 and Head of the Department of Individual and Family Studies at Penn State University from 1982 to 1987. A founding member of the Society for Research on Adolescence, she also served as President and as a member of its council, is Past President of the Developmental Psychology Division of the American Psychological Association, and is a Fellow of the American Association for the Advancement of Science, American Psychological Association, and the American Psychological Society. She has authored or coauthored 13 books and more than 140 articles and chapters on adolescent development.

Craig T. Ramey is Professor of Psychology, Pediatrics, and Maternal and Child Health and, along with his wife, Sharon, is Director of the Civitan International Research Center, a multidisciplinary center dedicated to the study of human development at the University of Alabama at Birmingham. He is a life-span developmental psychologist with a specialty in theory-guided interventions designed to improve functional capacity and quality of life for children and families at risk for developmental outcomes. He is the Founding Director of the Abecedarian Project (1972) and Project CARE (1977) and was the Founding Director of the Infant Health and Development Program (1984). The author of more than 175 scientific and educational articles and the editor of two books on high-risk children and children with disabilities, he has also written reviews of the scientific literature on risk factors in early development and their implications for educational, health, and welfare policy. He is directing the research and evaluation of a 32-site, randomized field trial of education reform for approximately 12,000 participants sponsored by the Administration on Children, Youth and Families and known as the Head Start/Public School Transition Demonstration Project.

Sharon Landesman Ramey is Professor of Psychiatry, Psychology, Pediatrics, Sociology, and Maternal and Child Health and, along with her husband, Craig, is Director of the Civitan International Research Center at the University of Alabama at Birmingham. A developmental psychologist, her interests include effects of early experience, human ethology, measurement of family environments and family functioning, prenatal exposure to alcohol and other potential teratogens, mental retardation, and cultural diversity. She is codirecting a national study of more than 12,000 Head Start children and families participating in a 32-site, randomized field trial of extending Head Start-like services through third grade (the National Head Start Public School Early Childhood Transition Demonstration Program) and is engaged in research on the prevention of low birth weight and prematurity and therapeutic interventions for children in orphanages and American Indian families. She is the author of more than 80 chapters, books, and articles and has made more than 50 presentations at local, state, regional, national, and international conferences. A Fellow in the American Association on Mental Retardation and the American Psychological Association, she has received numerous honors for her research contributions. She is a Past-Chair of the Committee on Children, Public Policy, and Public Information of the Society for Research in Child Development.

Sam Redding is Executive Director of the Academic Development Institute in Lincoln, Illinois, and editor of *School Community Journal*. He holds a Ed.D. in education from Illinois State University and is a graduate of Harvard's Institute for Educational Management. He is also a recipient of the Illinois State Board of Education's Award of Excellence for service to public education and of the Ben Hubbard Leadership Award from Illinois State University. He is also a Project Director with the Mid-Atlantic Laboratory for Student Success, a federal education laboratory based at Temple University.

Edward Seidman is Professor of Psychology at New York University. Previously, he was Vice President and Dean of Research, Development, and Policy at Bank Street College of Education, and a Professor of Psychology at The University of Illinois at Urbana-Champaign and the University of Manitoba. He has served as a Senior Fulbright-Hays Research Scholar at the University of Athens, Greece. His earlier intervention research on the diversion of adolescents in legal jeopardy from the juvenile justice system received national awards. He is also the recipient of the award for Distinguished Contributions to Theory and Research in Community Psychology. The foci of his current research and scholarship include the social development of adolescents in the urban context—and in particular, in public schools—primary prevention, and social policy.

Roger C. Shouse is Assistant Professor of Education Policy Studies at Pennsylvania State University College of Education. A former secondary school teacher with more than 10 years of experience in both suburban and urban settings, his research focuses on how school social and normative contexts (e.g., level of affluence, sense of community, academic press) shape the impact of reform practices and influence student academic performance. He is a 1995 recipient of the Spencer Foundation Post-Doctoral Fellowship.

Patrick H. Tolan is Director of Research at the Institute for Juvenile Research, Associate Professor in the Departments of Psychology and Psychiatry, and a Faculty Scholar at the Great Cities Institute at The University of Illinois at Chicago. In 1983, he received his Ph.D. in psychology from the University of Tennessee and then completed a postdoctoral fellowship at the University of Chicago. His major research focus is on the development of inner-city children and their families, with particular focus on prediction and prevention of antisocial behavior. He is collaborating with Deborah Gorman-Smith on a study of longitudinal risk in inner-city adolescent males and with Nancy Guerra and others on a field-trial prevention study to reduce aggression and promote successful development of inner-city children.

Margaret C. Wang is Professor of Educational Psychology and the Founder and Director of the Temple University Center for Research in Human Development and Education, a broad-based interdisciplinary research and development center. She also serves as Executive Director of the Mid-Atlantic Laboratory for Student Success, one of 10 regional educational laboratories funded by the Office of Educational Research and Improvement of the U.S. Department of Education. She is recognized nationally and internationally for her research on classroom learning, student motivation, and implementation and evaluation of innovative school programs that are responsive to student diversity. She is the author or editor of 12 books and has written more than 100 articles published in a variety of research and practitioner-oriented journals and books.